W9-BGB-541

# Behavior Management
## Principles and Practices of
## Positive Behavior Supports

**John J. Wheeler**
*Tennessee Technological University*

**David Dean Richey**
*Tennessee Technological University*

PEARSON

Merrill
Prentice Hall

Upper Saddle River, New Jersey
Columbus, Ohio

**Library of Congress Cataloging-in-Publication Data**

Wheeler, John J.
  Behavior management : principles and practices of positive behavior supports / John J.
Wheeler, David Dean Richey.
      p.  cm.
  Includes bibliographical references and index.
  ISBN 0-13-093989-7
  1. Classroom management. 2. Behavior modification. I. Richey, David Dean. II. Title.

LB3013.W465 2005
371.39'3—dc22

2004011040

**Vice President and**
  **Executive Publisher:** Jeffery W. Johnston
**Acquisitions Editor:** Allyson P. Sharp
**Editorial Assistant:** Kathleen S. Burk
**Production Editor:** Linda Hillis Bayma
**Production Coordination:** Susan Free,
  *The GTS Companies*/York, PA Campus
**Design Coordinator:** Diane C. Lorenzo

**Photo Coordinator:** Sandy Schaefer
**Cover Designer:** Bryan Huber
**Cover image:** Superstock
**Production Manager:** Laura Messerly
**Director of Marketing:** Ann Castel Davis
**Marketing Manager:** Autumn Purdy
**Marketing Coordinator:** Tyra Poole

This book was set in Garamond by *The GTS Companies*/York, PA Campus. It was printed and bound by
Phoenix Color Book Group. The cover was printed by Phoenix Color Corp.

**Photo Credits:** Bachrach Photographers, p. 16 (top left); courtesy of Albert Bandura, p. 16 (bottom);
Corbis/Bettmann, p. 6; Scott Cunningham/Merrill, pp. xx, 320; Laimute Druskis/PH College, p. 72; Kevin
Fitzsimons/Merrill, p. 296; Library of Congress, p. 9; Anthony Magnacca/Merrill, pp. 34, 112, 146, 172; Felicia
Martinez/PhotoEdit, courtesy of Robert Solso, p. 10; Barbara Schwartz/Merrill, pp. 198, 234, 266; B. F. Skinner
Foundation, p. 16 (top right); copyright WHO, p. 8; Shirley Zeiberg/PH College, p. 350.

**Copyright © 2005 by Pearson Education, Inc., Upper Saddle River, New Jersey 07458.**
Pearson Prentice Hall. All rights reserved. Printed in the United States of America.
This publication is protected by Copyright and permission should be obtained from the
publisher prior to any prohibited reproduction, storage in a retrieval system, or transmission in any form or by
any means, electronic, mechanical, photocopying, recording, or likewise. For information regarding permission(s), write to: Rights and Permissions Department.

**Pearson Prentice Hall**™ is a trademark of Pearson Education, Inc.
**Pearson**® is a registered trademark of Pearson plc
**Prentice Hall**® is a registered trademark of Pearson Education, Inc.
**Merrill**® is a registered trademark of Pearson Education, Inc.

Pearson Education Ltd.
Pearson Education Singapore Pte. Ltd.
Pearson Education Canada, Ltd.
Pearson Education—Japan

Pearson Education Australia Pty. Limited
Pearson Education North Asia Ltd.
Pearson Educación de Mexico, S.A. de C.V.
Pearson Education Malaysia Pte. Ltd.

10 9 8 7 6 5 4 3 2 1
ISBN: 0-13-093989-7

*To my mother, Kathleen Bryan Wheeler, my first teacher, who modeled for me the importance of valuing children through her love and tireless devotion. And in memory of my father, William S. Wheeler, who always inspired me with his diligent work ethic, his quiet optimism, and his love and support.*

**J.J.W.**


*To my grandmother, Bethel Robinson Morgan, who served during my formative years as a model of decency, kindness, and caring toward children, and who listened. And to my parents, Claude Henry and Mary Jane Richey, who have shown me what can be accomplished through hard work, commitment, honesty, and faith.*

**D.D.R.**

# Preface

*Behavior Management: Principles and Practices of Positive Behavior Supports* is a text designed to prepare undergraduate and graduate students in the design, delivery, and evaluation of positive behavior supports (PBS) across learning environments. PBS represents a philosophy and practice that extends the application of applied behavior analysis in a user-friendly format aimed at the development of meaningful behaviors in the lives of children and youth and their families.

A central focus of this text is the understanding and design of optimal learning environments and the use of teaching procedures aimed at a goodness of fit based on a learner's developmental strengths and challenges. PBS employs the use of functional behavior assessment to identify those factors that occasion challenging behaviors, the function or purpose served by these behaviors, the development of positive replacement behaviors through planned instruction, and the arrangement of consequences designed to reinforce skill approximations.

The systematic use of PBS also enhances the successful inclusion of students with disabilities in activities and settings with typical same-age peers. Because the focus is on the individual, the developmental appropriateness of behavior, and the naturally occurring and logical consequences that follow, PBS offers efficacious and practical strategies to address challenging behavior and also to prevent undesirable behavior.

In preparing this text, we have sought the input of a number of undergraduate and graduate students in the fields of general and special education who expressed a desire for a text that examines and demonstrates the use of PBS across the range of learning environments. Given the inclusion of functional assessment and behavior support plans within the reauthorization of IDEA in 1997, we believe that this text will enhance the efforts to train educators to use these methodologies in a manner that promotes best and effective practice and meaningful lifestyle outcomes for the students they teach. In fact, we have developed this text from our cumulative experiences of 25 and 30-plus years, respectively, in the delivery of clinical and applied services and supports to children, their families, and their teachers.

Unfortunately, many educators still continue to rely on rapid suppression methods that are punitive to control and suppress the behavior of their students. Although these methods may offer some temporary relief, they are by no means illustrative of best and effective practice. They do not examine the individual and the behavior of concern across the broader context, subsequently resulting in a failure to obtain desired outcomes and leading to frustration on the part of both teacher and learner. Therefore, it is apparent that a new model is needed to prepare future teachers to understand and respond to behavior in children and youth. We believe that this text offers such an alternative, given the documented success of PBS procedures.

A final note about the authors' intentions in the preparation of this text: We wanted to add several dimensions to what we have perceived as either missing or insufficiently addressed in many of the textbooks on this topic. Those dimensions include a focus on families as partners in the process, the importance of understanding and applying ethical standards, the central role of self-determination and quality of life in PBS, and the relevance of PBS at all levels and for all children and youth, whether or not they have a disability, and whether or not they are currently exhibiting challenging behavior.

It is our hope that this text will be one that remains with you throughout your service to children and youth and that it will enrich your life as a teacher and, in turn, the lives of the students in your care.

## ACKNOWLEDGMENTS

We would like to take this opportunity to thank all the people who have assisted us in the development of this text. Among them are the team at Merrill/Prentice Hall, who believed in the project and supported us through the entire process. We would like to especially thank Ann Davis for facilitating this opportunity for us and our very capable editor, Allyson Sharp, who served as our leader from start to finish. Her ability to reinforce our successive approximations toward completion were unmatched, as was her technical expertise in the design of the final product. Thanks also to Kathy Burk for her communications with us concerning manuscript reviews and completion of the final draft. The talented copy editor for this book, Karen Slaght, was both patient and persistent as we worked together to complete the final edits. Thanks must also go to Amanda Richey, who served as a field-based copy editor and who helped make the final product a reality with her care and precision. We are also indebted to the reviewers, who offered their timely and instructive feedback on each of the drafts. These include Karenlee C. Alexander, Bemidji State University; David W. Anderson, Bethel College; Brent A. Askvig, Minot State University; Roger Bass, Carthage College; Greg Conderman, University of Wisconsin–Eau Claire; Dan Ezell, University of Central Florida; Ruth A. Falco, Portland State University; Dan Fennerty, Central Washington University; Kristine Jolivette, University of Kentucky; Joseph E. Justen III, Arkansas State University; Colleen Klein, University of Central Florida; Thomas McFarland, Lewis and Clark State College; Ronald B. Straub, Mansfield University; and Philip Swicegood, Sam Houston State University. We would also like to thank some of our students and colleagues who offered their assistance to us along the way. These persons include Michael Mayton of Western Kentucky University; Rebekah Thomas, Dolly Gerragano, Kim O'Kelley, Elizabeth Brosseau, John Justice, and Bob Baggett of Tennessee Technological University; and Linda Hall Richey of Middle Tennessee State University.

Finally, thanks to our families for the love and support through the years that have enabled us to be who we are.

# Discover the Companion Website Accompanying This Book

## THE PRENTICE HALL COMPANION WEBSITE: A VIRTUAL LEARNING ENVIRONMENT

Technology is a constantly growing and changing aspect of our field that is creating a need for content and resources. To address this emerging need, Prentice Hall has developed an online learning environment for students and professors alike—Companion Websites—to support our textbooks.

In creating a Companion Website, our goal is to build on and enhance what the textbook already offers. For this reason, the content for each user-friendly website is organized by topic and provides the professor and student with a variety of meaningful resources. Common features of a Companion Website include:

### For the Professor—

Every Companion Website integrates **Syllabus Manager**™, an online syllabus creation and management utility.

- **Syllabus Manager**™ provides you, the instructor, with an easy, step-by-step process to create and revise syllabi, with direct links into Companion Website and other online content without having to learn HTML.
- Students may logon to your syllabus during any study session. All they need to know is the web address for the Companion Website and the password you've assigned to your syllabus.
- After you have created a syllabus using **Syllabus Manager**™, students may enter the syllabus for their course section from any point in the Companion Website.
- Clicking on a date, the student is shown the list of activities for the assignment. The activities for each assignment are linked directly to actual content, saving time for students.
- Adding assignments consists of clicking on the desired due date, then filling in the details of the assignment—name of the assignment, instructions, and whether it is a one-time or repeating assignment.
- In addition, links to other activities can be created easily. If the activity is online, a URL can be entered in the space provided, and it will be linked automatically in the final syllabus.

- Your completed syllabus is hosted on our server, allowing convenient updates from any computer on the Internet. Changes you make to your syllabus are immediately available to your students at their next logon.

## For the Student—

- **Overview and General Information**—General information about the topic and how it will be covered in the website.
- **Web Links**—A variety of websites related to topic areas.
- **Content Methods and Strategies**—Resources that help to put theories into practice in the special education classroom.
- **Reflective Questions and Case-Based Activities**—Put concepts into action, participate in activities, examine strategies, and more.
- **National and State Laws**—An online guide to how federal and state laws affect your special education classroom.
- **Behavior Management**—An online guide to help you manage behaviors in the special education classroom.
- **Message Board**—Virtual bulletin board to post and respond to questions and comments from a national audience.

To take advantage of these and other resources, please visit the *Behavior Management: Principles and Practices of Positive Behavior Supports* Companion Website at

**www.prenhall.com/wheeler**

# Educator Learning Center: An Invaluable Online Resource

Merrill Education and the Association for Supervision and Curriculum Development (ASCD) invite you to take advantage of a new online resource, one that provides access to the top research and proven strategies associated with ASCD and Merrill—the Educator Learning Center. At **www.EducatorLearningCenter.com** you will find resources that will enhance your student's understanding of course topics and of current educational issues, in addition to being invaluable for further research.

## HOW THE EDUCATOR LEARNING CENTER WILL HELP YOUR STUDENTS BECOME BETTER TEACHERS

With the combined resources of Merrill Education and ASCD, you and your students will find a wealth of tools and materials to better prepare them for the classroom.

### Research

- More than 600 articles from the ASCD journal *Educational Leadership* discuss everyday issues faced by practicing teachers.
- A direct link on the site to Research Navigator™ gives students access to many of the leading education journals, as well as extensive content detailing the research process.
- Excerpts from Merrill Education texts give your students insights on important topics of instructional methods, diverse populations, assessment, classroom management, technology, and refining classroom practice.

### Classroom Practice

- Hundreds of lesson plans and teaching strategies are categorized by content area and age range.
- Case studies and classroom video footage provide virtual field experience for student reflection.
- Computer simulations and other electronic tools keep your students abreast of today's classrooms and current technologies.

### Look into the Value of Educator Learning Center Yourself

A four-month subscription to Educator Learning Center is $25 but is **FREE** when ordered in conjunction with this text. To obtain free passcodes for your students, simply contact your local Merrill/Prentice Hall sales representative, and your representative will give you a special ISBN to give your bookstore when ordering your textbooks. To preview the value of this website to you and your students, please go to **www.EducatorLearningCenter.com** and click on "Demo."

# Brief Contents

# Contents

*Chapter* **3** **Ensuring Ethical Practices in the Delivery of
Positive Behavior Supports    73**

## Chapter 6    Understanding Functional Behavior Assessment        173

## Chapter 7    Planning Behavior Supports        199

**Chapter 8    Evaluating Positive Behavior Supports    235**

**Chapter 9    Teaching Positive Alternative Behaviors    267**

NOTE: Every effort has been made to provide accurate and current Internet information in this book. However, the Internet and information posted on it are constantly changing, and it is inevitable that some of the Internet addresses listed in this textbook will change.

# Chapter 1

# Understanding Behavior in Children and Youth

## CONCEPTS TO UNDERSTAND

*After reading this chapter, you should be able to:*

- Describe varied perspectives on understanding behavior in children and youth, including biological, developmental, psychodynamic, ecological, behavior, and social learning models

- Describe and discuss the foundations and applications of applied behavior analysis

- Describe the defining characteristics of positive behavior supports (PBS) and the application of PBS across learners and learning environments

## KEY TERMS

Applied behavior analysis

Behavior model

Biological model

Developmental model

Ecological model

Positive behavior supports

Psychodynamic model

Social learning

As a professional educator, your ability to understand teaching and learning is important in facilitating meaningful instructional outcomes for students. One critical prerequisite skill that teachers need is a fluent understanding of behavior and its relationship to learning. This is most important when one considers the potential impact of teachers and related educational professionals as agents of behavior change among students in various learning environments. This chapter will provide you with a comparative overview of the common conceptual models used in understanding human behavior. Information will also be provided on the historical development of positive behavior supports (PBS) as an outgrowth of applied behavior analysis (ABA) and the utility of ABA and PBS across educational environments.

## THEORETICAL MODELS FOR UNDERSTANDING BEHAVIOR

The focus of this text will be on the use of PBS to practically and positively address the behavior needs of students across educational environments. However, numerous theories are used to explain human behavior, each of which offers its own unique perspective and the methodology that it employs toward understanding human behavior and learning.

The purpose behind understanding such contrasting viewpoints is to provide a contextual overview on the topic as you formulate your own philosophy of practice and to better equip you in terms of understanding the efficacy and limitations of each model. Table 1–1 provides a comparison of these varied viewpoints for reference as you read the chapter.

### Biological Model

The **biological model** examines the presence of atypical development and subsequent behavior differences from an organic standpoint. This is most evident in the medical profession, which addresses changes in physiological functioning (optimal health) within the context of presenting symptoms. These physical symptoms are often present as the result of pathogens in the body or other organic causes. Pathogens alter the body's equilibrium and are defined as any causative agent of disease. Within the field of special education, we frequently witness the biological model used to explain the presence of specific disabilities that affect cognitive and behavior functioning in children and youth. Many of these conditions stem from organic causes that alter typical development in children, thus producing disabilities. Early studies, for example, identified brain dysfunction in children with autism and subsequently moved theorists from viewing autism as a psychogenic disorder (a disorder with no known organic basis and likely caused by emotional stress) to viewing it as a condition stemming from organic causes (Golden, 1987). For example, advances in medical science have contributed to our understanding of the causal factors associated with autism, including the neurological and neurochemical aspects of

**TABLE 1–1**
*Theoretical Models for Understanding Human Behavior*

| Theoretical Model | Key Concepts Relating to Behavior |
| --- | --- |
| Biological Model | • Looks at behavior from organic standpoint<br>• Emphasis on pathogens as explanation for disease<br>• Important for medical/health implications |
| Developmental Model | • Pioneered by Piaget<br>• Stresses child's adaptation to environment is genetically programmed<br>• Application of model seen through widespread use of developmentally appropriate practice (DAP) by educators |
| Psychodynamic Model | • Pioneered by Freud, Erikson<br>• Emphasis on unconscious processes, underlying motives of behavior<br>• Development of personality is key to understanding abnormalities |
| Ecological Model | • Pioneered by Bronfenbrenner<br>• Focus on relationships between and within levels of ecosystems<br>• Known for application of Hobbs's Re-Ed program |
| Behavior Model | • Pioneered by Pavlov, Skinner, Watson<br>• Behavior viewed from functional perspective— measured or observed<br>• Early foundation for applied behavior analysis (ABA) |
| Social Learning Model | • Emphasis on modeling—imitation of models most important element in learning<br>• Merges cognitive and behavior models |
| Applied Behavior Analysis | • Emphasis on applied study of socially relevant behaviors<br>• Focus on measurable and observable behaviors with precise measurement |
| Positive Behavior Supports | • Reliance on person-centered planning and interventions<br>• Stresses positive approaches and seeks to enhance quality of life for the learner<br>• A refinement and extension of ABA |

this disorder. Examples include the difficulty of children with autism to modulate sensory input, an atypical neurological response in children (Ornitz, 1983), and neurochemical differences such as deficits in serotinin levels in the brain (i.e., the neurotransmitter found in the brain that controls important system functions such as sleep, appetite, mood, body temperature, and hormone release) (Iverson & Iverson, 1981). These findings are important because they assist us in accurately diagnosing these conditions and hopefully lead to designing appropriate treatment programs, including positive behavior supports as a means of maximizing the learning potential of children and youth affected by conditions such as autism.

There are many other examples of how the biological model has contributed to the knowledge base in the diagnosis and treatment of other forms of cognitive, behavior, and learning disabilities. These include the organic factors associated with mental retardation that encompass chromosomal abnormalities in such conditions as Down syndrome, multiple congenital abnormalities, prenatal difficulties, gene defects, and postnatal brain damage. As special educators, we now have a fuller understanding of the etiology and origins of these disorders and their impact on fetal development. The earlier the genetic problem arises in the developmental sequence, generally the more severe the consequence in terms of level of developmental delay (Batshaw, 1997). This is especially true in the case of children born with severe developmental disabilities, such as chromosomal abnormalities and hereditary multiple anomaly syndromes that affect early embryogenesis, resulting in severe mental retardation (Batshaw, 1997).

The biological model has also assisted in the identification of the neurobiological origins of Attention Deficit Hyperactivity Disorder (ADHD), a prevalent condition found among many school-age children today. Through the use of Magnetic Resonance Imaging (MRI), medical researchers have identified structural differences between the brains of persons affected with ADHD and persons not diagnosed with the condition, and they have observed diminished neuronal activity among persons found to have ADHD (Guyer, 2000; Naugle, Cullum, & Bigler, 1997). Again, earlier research had pointed to psychopathological origins rather than organic causal factors.

As we have also learned, many children diagnosed with ADHD have co-occurring learning disabilities (Dykman & Ackerman, 1991). These conditions have been classified as related neurological disorders that interact with one another and result in learning and behavior challenges for the children affected by them. Subsequent pharmacological research and medical treatment have demonstrated that stimulant medication used in the treatment of children diagnosed with ADHD is effective in improving attention and cognitive functioning (Goldman, Genel, Bezman, & Slanetz, 1998). As a result of these findings, the use of medications to treat children suspected of having ADHD has been reported to be as high as 3% of the school-age population (Frankenberger, Lozar, & Dallas, 1990; Safer & Krager, 1994).

The prevalent use of pharmacological treatment as the treatment of choice for children with ADHD has raised questions about the widespread use of these medications without giving consideration to compiling functional behavior assessment data as a means of differential diagnosis. The limitations of medication as the primary form of treatment for children diagnosed with ADHD have also been questioned in the literature. These limitations include side effects, the lack of maintenance and generalization of behavior change when the medication was withdrawn, issues of medication compliance, and finally, the fact that approximately 25% to 30% of children diagnosed with ADHD do not respond successfully to medication (Horn, Ialongo, Greenberg, Packard, & Smith-Winberry, 1990).

Lastly, another major concern offered within the literature has been that medication has appeared to be the standard response for many when treating ADHD without first systematically examining the presenting behaviors and contextual variables that contribute to their occurrence (Kirk, 1999). It is clearly evident that a functional assessment would be most conducive to ascertaining the relationship between the presence of these behaviors and the contextual variables that may be influencing them before a child is given the diagnosis of ADHD and medical treatment. It has also been advocated in the literature that the use of multimodal interventions that combine medication and positive behavior supports are most effective for the treatment of children with ADHD (Kirk, 1999). This trend continues to gain support among professionals and families. Despite the progress medical science has made in the diagnosis and treatment of conditions such as ADHD, we see that the outcomes from the merger of medical and behavior forms of intervention are more effective than medication alone in successfully treating the condition on a long-term basis.

### Consider This

- What are your thoughts on the treatment of ADHD?
- Should medication be used, and when and how should such a decision be reached?

It is apparent that the biological model has been very helpful in furthering our understanding of the origins of developmental disorders in children and in the diagnosis and medical treatment of these conditions. However, the functional utility of this model in the design and delivery of positive behavior supports within educational environments is minimal. Too often, medical diagnoses and labels impose greater limitations and barriers to effective educational and behavior interventions in that many view them as infallible. The biological model alone cannot provide all the information needed by educational personnel in the delivery of PBS. However, it does contribute to our understanding of conditions relative to their physiological origins and medical/health implications, thus providing a more complete picture when used in conjunction with multiple theoretical perspectives.

## Developmental Model

The developmental perspective has traditionally been associated with the Swiss-born biologist Jean Piaget (1896–1980).

***Jean Piaget***

Piaget's contributions are noteworthy in the field of human development and have served as a cornerstone among developmental theorists. His theory was built on the premise that children's adaptation to their environment was contingent on two processes, namely assimilation and accommodation. Assimilation is the process by which children fit new stimuli into their "comfort zone," or current ability to understand this new information. Accommodation, on the other hand, refers to how children modify their cognitive processing to fit these new or novel stimuli.

The **developmental model** has evolved over time but has essentially maintained that children develop in predictable, genetically programmed processes that are active and internally organized (Cobb, 2001). Developmental theorists also contend that as children age, they proceed through several stages of development, each with its own unique set of characteristics.

The developmental model has been most prominent in the education of young children. Contemporary early childhood educators and early childhood special educators rely on the principle of developmentally appropriate practice (DAP) as the philosophical foundation for the provision of education and related services to young children.

The book, *Developmentally Appropriate Practice in Early Childhood Programs* (Bredekamp & Copple, 1997), outlines a synthesized list of research-based principles that undergird DAP. These principles include the following: (a) recognizing that physical, cognitive, social, and emotional domains associated with child development are related, and that development in each of these areas is interdependent among them; (b) development is an orderly sequence whereby skills are developed in a stepwise fashion with new knowledge and skills building on existing strengths and previous learning; (c) development among individual children is unique and variation for every child is important (i.e., no two children are alike); (d) learning experiences for children have a cumulative effect and long-term implications in terms of the child's growth and development in later years; (e) cognitive development advances from concrete to abstract in terms of the child's ability to acquire and transfer knowledge and skills; (f) child development is influenced by environmental factors; (g) children learn through their active engagement in environments and the events that surround them; (h) development and learning results from a combination of physical maturation and the environments that encompass the child; (i) play is an essential avenue for promoting development and learning in every child; and (j) optimal development is promoted when children are presented with new and enriching experiences that take into account present skill levels and also those skills deemed to be emerging.

Bredekamp and Copple (1997) have provided a comprehensive perspective on theory to practice concerning DAP and its delivery to young children in educational environments.

## Psychodynamic Model

The **psychodynamic model** is an example of a stage theory used to explain human development and behavior. This theory emphasizes the critical importance of unconscious processes (i.e., psychodynamic) as the determinants for abnormal behavior. Although the psychodynamic model represents a cognitive perspective, it does acknowledge how environment contributes to development through internal processes and the battle between internal processes and these external events (Cobb, 2001). One viewpoint for understanding cognitive theories such as the psychodynamic model is offered by Pear (2001), who likened cognitive processing approaches in human beings to that of computers. In short, the view held by psychodynamic theorists is that all people have internal states or thought processes operating as they attempt to process the environmental events that influence the development of these thought processes and, subsequently, their personalities.

The most noted psychodynamic theorist, of course, was Sigmund Freud (1859–1939), the well-known Austrian-born psychoanalyst. He is best known for his theory of personality development and the terms *id, ego,* and *superego,* which are associated with the formation of personality. Each of these components of Freud's structural model serves a unique function, yet they must ultimately balance one another to accommodate the development of the personality. The id is described as the area of the personality that demands immediate gratification of biological impulses, thus operating on the "pleasure principle" (Freud, 1961). The ego, on the other hand, attempts to satisfy these impulses in a more socially acceptable manner. Lastly, the

***Sigmund Freud***

superego is the area of the personality that serves as the moral conscience as the child attempts to internalize moral standards. Freud acknowledged the interaction between biological and environmental forces in the development of the id and superego in the development of personality (Cobb, 2001). In Freud's view, development occurs as a result of the conflicts between the child's internal drives and his social environment. As a result, a psychological balance must be obtained that channels, represses, and/or redirects these drives and thus lays the foundation for the development of the child's personality (Tharinger & Lambert, 1990).

Erik Erikson (1902–1994) expanded Freud's theory on personality through his own theory of psychosocial development. Erikson's theory maintained the importance of ego identity and the healthy personality. This perspective asserts the importance of the ego and emphasizes the process of adaptation and the resolution of opposing forces. Erikson is best known for his eight stages of moral development, each of which is critical for subsequent development and involves a conflict involving maturational and social expectations on which the child progresses before moving to the next stage of development (Erikson, 1950). His stages extend from birth through the senior years, and each of these life stages brings with it a psychosocial crisis that serves as a developmental milestone. Erikson contended that each of these stages of development is consistent for all people, and that at critical periods within each stage the developing personality is most sensitive to the influence of others. He referred to this as the epigenetic principle.

One prominent characteristic of the psychodynamic model is its focus on the underlying motives that govern behavior. The psychodynamic model assumes that the developmental stages previously described are consistent across individuals and that they rely on internal processes to explain subsequent development and learning. This characteristic has become one of the

*Erik Erikson*

major areas of criticism concerning the application of this model. Given the focus of the psychodynamic theory on the development of personality with regard to the internal processing of environmental influences, it is difficult to empirically validate the role these forces play in individual human development. In short, it is impossible to observe and measure the internal thoughts and feelings of individuals. Thus the application of this model in educational environments serving children has been limited in terms of its applied efficacy.

## Ecological Model

The ecological perspective on behavior and learning is a very important viewpoint, especially given the focus of this text, that is, positive behavior supports, and the importance of understanding behavior within the relevant environments (home, school, community) in which the learner lives and functions. Environments and the persons found within them comprise one form of an ecological system. What occurs within this system affects not only one individual but also all who function within it. Thus the **ecological model** is focused on the interactions that occur within these environments and how they influence behavior and learning in each of us.

One of the early theorists who has received much notoriety in recent times from his work in the area of young children and learning is the Russian psychologist Lev Vygotsky (1896–1934). His theory ascertained that children learn by engaging and participating in activities that they enjoy, and that learning is enhanced when children are in social contexts, working with other children who have the same aims (Vygotsky, 1978). Thus environment and social context are important aspects in Vygotsky's theory. Vygotsky emphasized the development of cognitive processes and behaviors in the child

*Lev Vygotsky*

through interactions within the social context. His theory pointed out how children who approximate a certain skill level can learn from other children who are more skilled at a particular task. He termed these phenomena the zone of proximal development, or the distance separating a person's current performance level from that of optimal performance levels. Although not exclusively an ecological theorist, Vygotsky reminds us of the importance of social interaction in meaningful environmental contexts and how such interactions foster cognitive development in children.

Uri Bronfenbrenner (1917–present) is widely known for his application of the ecological model in reference to families. Bronfenbrenner (1994) asserted that a child's development is inseparable from the environments in which he functions, thus comprising his ecology. Bronfenbrenner's theory is composed of a concentric circle, which has the child at its center, and the five systems emerging from the core of the circle. These five systems are the microsystem, the mesosystem, the exosystem, the macrosystem, and the chromosystem. The microsystem is basically the child's immediate environment, such as home and family or peer group association for an adolescent child. The mesosystem is composed of the interactions among contexts in the microsystem, such as school, home, and community. The exosystem refers to settings that influence the child with which she does not have a direct interface, such as school administrators or the employer of her parents. The macrosystem is illustrative of a set of philosophical or ideological patterns of a culture or subculture, such as what the effect is on a child's development within a school culture that practices corporal punishment. Finally, the chromosystem refers to those changes that occur over time to a child within her environment. Examples of this could include the birth of a sibling, divorce, or effects of relocating to a new home and school system (Richey & Wheeler, 2000). Certainly it is easy to ascertain from Bronfenbrenner's theory how interactions across these systems can ripple and affect the child (our point of concern is at the center of this model). It supports what we have learned thus far, that is, the importance of the interactions between environment and individual and the cumulative effect that alterations within these ecologies can have on the optimal learning and development of children and youth. Vignette 1.1 provides more insight into the ecological model applied to children and families affected by poverty.

## Vignette 1.1

### The Ecological Model Applied to Children and Families in Poverty

An elementary teacher working in an Appalachian community beset by poverty, high unemployment, and reliance on subsidized programs commented to a state politician that people do not really understand the complexities of poverty and its effect on children and families as far as development and learning are concerned.

In this example, the community once was a thriving coal mining community in which people were gainfully employed; however, when the demand for coal diminished, the mines closed, and subsequently the community's economy was destroyed. As a result, stores closed, people were left jobless, and some families left the region in search of new opportunities, whereas those families who remained behind worked at less-fruitful jobs paying minimum wage with no insurance or benefits for themselves or their families. The impact began to be felt within all facets of the community, including the local schools. Evidence of this was seen as greater numbers of children began to receive free breakfasts and lunches through subsidy programs. Increasing numbers of children began coming to school without their basic needs met. Local teachers began to feel the impact on their classrooms with individual children. This was evident as, over time, increased numbers of children were identified with developmental delays and as at risk. Other changes were noted within the community, such as increased alcohol and drug abuse, family problems, and criminal activity.

### Reflective Moment

Respond to the problems posed in the vignette by examining the following questions.

- How can we use Bronfenbrenner's model to help us understand this scenario across the various systems?

- What strengths does the ecological model provide as we attempt to identify the contributing factors and ripple effects of these causal factors?

- What are the limitations of this model in assisting us as teachers in facilitating optimal learning outcomes for children affected by such conditions?

One of the most prominent leaders to provide educational and behavior supports to children with emotional and behavior disabilities through the ecological model was Nicholas Hobbs. Best known for his theory on the reeducation of troubled children and youth, Hobbs had many formative experiences that led to the design of the Re-ED program. These included studying how Western European countries provided educational supports to children with disabilities. He became most impressed with the model that he had witnessed in France and the role of child care workers known as psychoeducateurs, a title for which there was no equivalent in the United States (Hobbs, 1974). The psychoeducateur was essentially a child care specialist who had been cross trained in the disciplines of child development, psychology, education, and child care and was responsible for working with children both during school hours and after school hours (Juul, 1977). Hobbs borrowed from this idea and framed the role of teacher–counselor, emphasizing teacher disposition as being the most important attribute for professionals who worked with troubled children.

The defining role of the teacher–counselor emerged, and these professionals were taught to develop trusting relationships with the children and youth in their care and to teach and model positive affirming behaviors that were offered within a context of support and inclusiveness, rather than one of failure and exclusion. Hobbs believed strongly in the development of interpersonal skills in the teacher–counselor and the importance of understanding feelings and expressions of anger and hurt in children and adolescents. He believed in promoting the idea that each child had a bright future and abilities from which to draw and to build from (Hobbs, 1974).

The Re-ED model fortunately came about largely from Hobbs's mounting frustration that psychotherapy, as a form of treatment, was ineffective in dealing with the life problems of troubled children and youth. Hobbs believed that Re-ED offered a positive and more holistic alternative to treatment models at that time and recognized the importance of working not only with the child but also with the child's significant others in natural settings such as the home, community, school, and other relevant settings. An example of the Ecological Model used in the Re-Ed program is illustrated in Figure 1–1.

**FIGURE 1–1**
*Ecological Model*

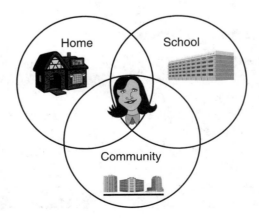

The supporting theory behind Re-ED was that the child is inseparable from his social system or ecological unit. The child and the child's family, school, and neighborhood or community composes this ecological unit. The ultimate goal of treatment was to be able to move each component of the child's life, including those significant others, above threshold (Hobbs, 1974). In the Re-ED model, the parents and family, teachers, and significant others in the life of the child are collaborators in promoting the desired outcomes. The Re-ED model attempted to maintain the child in her home and supported residential placement options for those children and youth who demonstrated a need for intensive reeducation or whose family was incapable of proving in-home supports (Hobbs, 1974).

Re-ED was responsible for demonstrating model practices in the education of children and youth who were challenged by emotional and behavior disorders. Many replication programs were developed from the original schools developed by Hobbs. In reflection, Re-ED represented a new and innovative philosophy and practice in educating children with some significant emotional and behavior challenges. It was a model of practice built on the delivery of child-centered and holistic educational services and supports and was inclusive of natural environments and significant others in the delivery of these behavior supports.

In contemporary practice we see much of the early Re-ED work modeled in the delivery of wraparound services within special education and mental health settings serving children with emotional and behavior disorders (Duckworth et al., 2001). These wraparound services mirror the ecological model in that they involve child, family, school, community, mental health professionals, and others in the design and delivery of supports to children and their families. The ecological model is important in promoting the implementation of educational and behavior supports across multiple environments with persons who are significant in the life of the learner. This approach views the persons within these settings as agents for change and, indeed, targets for change.

### Consider This

- How can you as teacher have influence in the life of a child?
- Does your influence play a part in the child's ability to deal with stressors beyond their educational environment?

## Behavior Model

One defining characteristic of the **behavior model** is that it views behavior from a functional perspective in terms that are both measurable and observable. The behavior model recognizes that all behavior serves a function and has evolved as a direct result of the individual's learning history coupled with interactions within their environment (Sulzer-Azaroff & Mayer, 1991). The historical development of the behavior model provides the foundation for the development of applied behavior analysis and the later evolution toward PBS. Given the importance of understanding this model to the current text, we want to examine it in a way that illuminates the critical points in the evolution of this very important perspective.

The origins of the behavior model were steeped in the research of many prominent theorists, who empirically derived the scientific principles that served as the cornerstone of behavior modification. These include Ivan Pavlov (1849–1936), a Russian psychologist who we credit with discovering the principles of respondent conditioning. In Pavlov's famous experiment, he demonstrated that a dog would salivate when presented with meat (a reflex response). He then paired the presentation of the meat to the dog with the ringing of a bell (a neutral stimulus), and later after repeated trials, Pavlov would ring the bell alone, and the dog would salivate (Pavlov, 1927). This illustrates what is referred to as respondent conditioning. Miltenberger (2001) defines respondent conditioning as "a process in which a neutral stimulus is paired with an unconditioned stimulus (US). The US elicits an unconditioned response (UR). As a result of pairing the neutral stimulus with the US, the neutral stimulus becomes a conditioned stimulus (CS) that will elicit a response similar to the UR, called a conditioned response (CR)" (p. 497).

Later research began to explore the effects of consequences on behavior through the research of Edward Thorndike (1874–1949), who is credited with the discovery of the Law of Effect. The Law of Effect (Thorndike, 1911) basically states that if a behavior produces a favorable outcome on the environment, it is more likely to be repeated in the future. Thorndike established this principle through his research with animals, primarily cats. He trained cats to open their cage doors by pressing a lever to access their food, and on learning of the positive outcome (obtaining their food), the cats not only repeated the process but also did it faster.

As the field of behavior research continued to evolve, John Watson (1878–1958) coined the term *behaviorism,* which served to emphasize the relationship between environmental events and the responses they produced (Watson, 1924). The most prominent force in the development of behavior modification and the application of these principles to human conditions was, of course, B. F. Skinner (1904–1991), known for his work in the area of operant conditioning. Skinner furthered the earlier theories of Watson and Pavlov to more complex behaviors in humans, which he termed operants (Skinner, 1953). Operants are behaviors that are to a considerable degree controlled by their consequences (Sulzer-Azaroff & Mayer, 1991). Operant conditioning occurs when a behavior is followed by a reinforcing consequence that results in the behavior being more likely to occur in a similar context in the future.

Skinner's work on operant conditioning began to be applied in nonlaboratory settings by other researchers and was most evident in the field of developmental disabilities, thus earning the clinical label of behavior modification (Scheerenberger, 1987). Researchers such as Sidney Bijou explored the application of Skinner's theories in working with children and adults with mental retardation. Bijou (1963) advocated the use of applied behavior analysis procedures such as functional analysis in understanding the variables that influence learning and performance in persons with mental retardation and the involvement of systematic instruction and support for parents. Until this time, many persons with developmental disabilities had been warehoused in state institutions with little or no active treatment aimed at learning new skills. Most professionals thought the conditions of these individuals were beyond intervention and that people with mental retardation lacked any potential for learning; consequently, many persons were reduced to custodial care in these facilities. Behavior modification represented an avenue for hope in the design and delivery of interventions aimed at maximizing the human potential of these previously discarded persons.

Numerous skill acquisition studies using behavior approaches began to emerge in the literature. Much of the early literature was directed toward understanding the value of reinforcement in teaching functional skills to persons with developmental disabilities (Reid, Phillips, & Green, 1991). As the research began to provide more evidence in support of behavior modification to enhance the learning potential of persons with developmental disabilities, active programming became more prevalent within state institutions (Anderson & Freeman, 2000).

The application of behavior research to the field of education was strongly encouraged by Skinner (1968) in his book entitled *The Technology of Teaching*. Bijou (1970) advocated that the principles of applied behavior analysis be used within the field of education. These include (a) the importance of understanding the interaction between behavior and environmental events from a scientific perspective that placed emphasis on studying these relationships in terms that were observable, measurable, and reproducible; (b) the interactions between the behavior of an individual and environmental events as lawful and as a function of an individual's instructional history and the context in which the behavior occurs; (c) the importance of understanding the variables that influence complex behavior such as setting conditions, stimulus control, and reinforcement schedules; and (d) that emerging theories should adhere to stringent criteria such as being tied to observable events, having functional utility, and not overlapping existing principles previously identified from research. Bijou (1970) supported the perspective held by Skinner that the teacher was a facilitator of learning by arranging the contingencies within the environment to promote the desired outcome in the child and the use of systematic instruction procedures to promote acquisition of desired skills.

*Ivan Pavlov*

*B. F. Skinner*

*Albert Bandura*

In summary, the behavior model has evolved from basic scientific research aimed at understanding reflexive behaviors in animals to examining complex human behavior, learning, and human development. The behavior model attempts to understand human behavior from a scientific perspective in terms that are observable and measurable. It places emphasis on the relationship between environmental events and behavior, it de-emphasizes past events as being directly related to the occurrence of problematic behavior, and it attempts to identify cause and effect relationships, or what is termed a functional relationship, to explain behavior. The behavior model has undergone significant advancements over the years in the application of these procedures in educational environments and other applied settings. If there has been any limitation of this model toward the development of research-based practices for the treatment of challenging behavior and the application of behavior principles to learning, it has been in its lack of widespread acceptance among teachers and educational administrators. There continues to be resistance to the behavior model by many who believe it to be nonhumanistic or non-functional within school settings. In reality, the progress of applied behavior analysis and the emergence of PBS dispel this belief through its application of positive, person-centered interventions across multiple environments.

## Social Learning Model

The **social learning** perspective (Bandura, 1977) advanced the understanding of learning and behavior to become more inclusive of multiple influences on human development (Kazdin, 1989). Bandura advocated that people learn within a social context and that the environment and models within the environment influence learning in children. Modeling is central to the social learning theory, which believes that the imitation of models is the most important element in learning for children in the areas of language, social behavior, and gender-appropriate behaviors (Papalia, Olds, & Feldman, 1999). The selection of models that children choose to identify is influenced by the characteristics and accessibility of the model, the child's preferences, and the environment to which the child is exposed. The social learning model's perspective on understanding behavior acknowledges the cognitive influences on behavior and the role of models within the child's environment as being very important to subsequent learning in the child (Papalia et al., 1999). The social learning model attempts to merge the cognitive and behavior models and expands the view of each toward a more comprehensive understanding of behavior.

## Applied Behavior Analysis

**Applied behavior analysis** (ABA) represents the study of socially relevant human behavior in applied settings. As Sulzer-Azaroff and Mayer (1991) stated, "ABA is designed to permit people to understand, prevent, and remedy behavioral problems and to promote learning . . . it is performance-based, analytical, technological, socially important, contextual, and accountable" (p. 4). ABA emphasizes the applied study of socially relevant behaviors within naturally occurring contexts. The focus is on overt behaviors that are measurable and observable, the influence of environmental variables on the occurrence/nonoccurrence of the behaviors in question, and precise measurement of these responses. ABA studies behavior over time in relevant environments and employs research-validated teaching procedures that are replicable and specific to the individual needs of the learner and are socially acceptable, implemented by people in everyday life such as teachers and caregivers, and designed to promote increased lifestyle outcomes for the learner.

## Applications of ABA

Applications of ABA are evident across many areas such as special education, in which applied behavior analysis research has resulted in the development of instructional inroads for children and youth with disabilities. These interventions have been refined over time from the early research conducted in the 1960s and 1970s within residential facilities serving individuals with severe disabilities. The research and applications of ABA have been evident in areas such as systematic instruction (Snell & Gast, 1981; Wolery, Ault, & Doyle, 1992), that is, the use of behavior teaching approaches designed to facilitate the acquisition of new skills in learners.

An early leader in the use of systematic instruction to teach meaningful vocational skills to young adults with mental retardation was Marc Gold (1939–1982), an applied researcher from the University of Illinois. Gold tirelessly advocated that persons with developmental disabilities should be provided with meaningful opportunities for learning and gainful skills that would promote employability. Gold (1980) was a proponent of the effectiveness of behavior teaching procedures and stated, "A lack of learning in any particular situation should first be interpreted as a result of the inappropriate or insufficient use of teaching strategy rather than an inability on the part of the learner" (p. 15). Gold's research demonstrated that persons with severe developmental disabilities could be taught complex vocational skills. To illustrate this, Gold taught individuals with varying degrees of mental retardation how to perform complex assembly skills (i.e., bicycle brake assembly) by using task analyses and instructional prompts.

The use of behavior teaching approaches has been most recently acclaimed in the area of autism, largely through the research of Ivar Lovaas. Lovaas demonstrated through his research that the use of discrete trial teaching with young children less than 2½ years of age resulted in dramatic performance increases in these children, which were maintained over time (Lovaas, 1993; McEachin, Smith, & Lovaas, 1993). No other form of treatment has resulted in such significant treatment outcomes in the education of young children with autism (Martin & Pear, 1999).

ABA has also been evident in developing educational programs for children with a range of challenging behavior and learning needs, including the areas of attention deficit disorder (ADD) and attention deficit hyperactivity disorder (ADHD) (Ervin et al., 2000), anger management in adolescents with behavior disorders (Presley & Hughes, 2000), and self-management skills in adolescents and young adults with behavior disorders and mental retardation (Miller, Miller, Wheeler, & Selinger, 1989; Wheeler, Bates, Marshall, & Miller, 1988). These are a few of the numerous research studies supporting the use of ABA procedures in educational environments serving children and adolescents with learning and behavior challenges.

As we have read, ABA has offered an inroad in the delivery of instructional programming within educational environments, but it has also been applied in a variety of other human service and medical settings. As one example, the use of behavior approaches within medical settings has resulted in the formation of the field of behavior medicine, which is interdisciplinary in nature and is aimed at understanding the connections among illness, wellness, and behavior (Martin & Pear, 1999; Poppen, 1988). As Martin and Pear (1999) indicated, the application of behavior medicine, particularly in health psychology, has resulted in enhancements across areas such as treatment of health conditions, treatment compliance, wellness, management of caregivers, and stress reduction. ABA has also been active in working with geriatric populations for conditions such as chronic pain (Wisocki & Powers, 1997) and dementia (Engleman, Altus, & Mathews, 1999; Heard & Watson, 1999) associated with Alzheimer's disease.

ABA is becoming more evident within business and industry in the areas of performance management, worker safety, efficiency, and management–employee relations (Martin & Pear, 1999). Sports psychology has been another area of widespread application of ABA. ABA procedures have been applied to coaching sport-specific skills such as football, gymnastics, and tennis (Allison & Ayllon, 1980); swimming (Koop & Martin, 1983); football (Komaki & Barnett, 1977); soccer skills (Ziegler, 1994); and evaluation of basketball shooting behaviors (Vollmer & Bourret, 2000).

### Consider This

- What do you feel are the strengths and limitations of each of the theories described?
- Which theory do you prefer and why?

## POSITIVE BEHAVIOR SUPPORTS

The evolution of ABA as a method of promoting behavior change has resulted in the widespread application of behavior procedures as evidenced. This trend has continued with the refinement and application of these procedures within new and challenging circumstances. Most noteworthy has been the emergence of **positive behavior supports** (PBS). PBS represents an extension of applied behavior analysis relying on the use of person-centered interventions that depend on the use of positive approaches to engineer environments, teach alternative behaviors, and employ meaningful consequences to enhance the quality of life for the individual.

Horner et al. (1990) advocated for the use of nonaversive behavior supports for persons with severe disabilities. The movement was an outgrowth of the community integration of persons with severe disabilities in community-based residential and employment settings. Changes in service delivery resulted from the increased community-integration initiatives as interventions became more functional and nonaversive (Anderson &

Freeman, 2000). This movement served as fertile ground for the refinement of PBS for individuals with challenging behavior.

Many within the field of ABA have argued that PBS is no different from ABA, yet others view it as an outgrowth and enhancement of ABA (Koegel, Koegel, & Dunlap, 1996). PBS has primarily been directed toward the development of positive behavior interventions for persons with severe and challenging behavior, yet the application of PBS continues to grow and expand and in our view offers an advance in the design and delivery of behavior and instructional supports to learners of all ages and across educational environments.

PBS operates from a values base that highly regards the quality of life of the individual. PBS is composed of intervention methods that are behaviorally based, empirically validated, and congruent with the value of nonaversive intervention embedded within this values-based philosophy. PBS is characterized by three prominent characteristics recognized by Anderson and Freeman (2000). These include (a) PBS operates from a person-centered values base and is designed and delivered specific to the needs and preferences of the individual, thus representing socially valid goals; (b) PBS recognizes the individuality of each person in the delivery of services and supports and therefore takes into consideration the need for flexibility to accommodate the individual's needs as necessary, given life demands in the delivery of behavior supports; and (c) PBS works toward meaningful outcomes that enhance the overall quality of life for the individual, including participation in inclusive educational and community environments (Anderson & Freeman, 2000).

## Components of PBS

The delivery of PBS depends on the use of assessment and intervention practices designed to identify and understand the variables that correspond with the occurrence of challenging behavior and the delivery of interventions designed to teach positive replacement behaviors. The use of functional behavior assessment is an essential component of PBS and is intended to assist in the identification of variables that precipitate and/or maintain challenging behavior, including the setting events/antecedent variables that trigger these behaviors in an individual and the consequences that maintain these responses. It is important that the data gathered from the functional assessment process lead to the development of meaningful instructional interventions (Reichle & Wacker, 1993).

Specific methods associated with functional behavior assessment include the structured interview with key stakeholders such as teachers, family members, and often the learner as a means of identifying the target behavior and those variables of concern that influence this behavior. Other components include the collection of observational data on the learner within relevant environments and, on occasion, actual manipulations of instructional and/or environmental variables. Hypothesis statements are generated concerning the behavior, such as: "What setting events or antecedents appear to trigger the problem behavior?" and "What function(s) does the problem behavior serve for the individual?"

Sugai, Horner, and Sprague (1999) identified five outcomes associated with functional assessment process. These outcomes include (a) operational definitions of target behaviors, (b) identification of conditions that predict when challenging behavior will and will not occur, (c) identification of consequences that maintain challenging behavior, (d) hypothesis statements that state when and where the target behavior will occur and the associated antecedents and consequences, and (e) direct observational data that confirm the accuracy of the hypothesis statements.

Functional analysis (a term you will learn more about later in the text) differs from functional assessment but represents one form of functional assessment. Functional analysis involves the experimental manipulation of antecedents and consequences to demonstrate a cause and effect relationship between specific antecedent and/or consequence variables and the occurrence or nonoccurrence of the behavior in question. Functional analyses are conducted under controlled conditions rather than in applied settings such as educational environments (Sugai, Horner, & Sprague, 1999). Functional assessment is more widely used within learning environments such as classroom settings, given its practicality, whereas functional analysis has been confined more to experimental research settings.

Functional assessment offers the classroom teacher a more user-friendly method for understanding challenging behavior. An applied illustration of how functional assessment can be utilized in the classroom is contained in Vignette 1.2.

## Vignette 1.2

### Functional Behavior Assessment within a Classroom Setting

The behavior specialist, Ms. Thomas, a young and energetic teacher with a master's degree in special education and applied experience in the delivery of positive behavior supports, was asked to lend her assistance within her school district recently. She received a request to serve as a consultant in reference to a 12-year-old boy named Stefan, who was receiving services in a self-contained classroom for children with moderate and severe disabilities. He was displaying some chronic episodes of challenging behavior, and his team needed assistance in the application of functional assessment procedures as a means of understanding his behavior and providing intervention.

Given Ms. Thomas's expertise and strengths in the areas of positive behavior supports and consultation, she was deemed an appropriate liaison for the team to consult. She began the process by meeting with the child's team and discussing the details prior to initiating the formal assessment process.

During this phase, Ms. Thomas assembled relevant information that included the child's age, information on the child's family and his disability, current IEP, learning strengths, and greatest areas of challenge. She then proceeded to ask each member of the child's immediate team, including Stefan's mother, to complete a functional assessment interview (i.e., structured interview questionnaire) related to the behaviors of concern. The functional assessment interview consisted of a series of questions that probed the specifics of the behavior in question, setting events and antecedents that consistently coincided with high occurrences of the behavior, consequences that were likely to be maintaining the behavior, and conversely the environmental events that were present during periods when the behavior did not occur at all. Other relevant questions pertaining to changes in medical and physical health, family and living circumstances, changes in the routine at school and home, and other information as deemed important by the team were then posed.

Upon obtaining the completed interviews, Ms. Thomas compiled the information. She began to sort and collate the information contained in each of the completed interviews. In all, four total questionnaires were completed. These included one from Stefan's teacher, one from the classroom assistant, one from the speech and language therapist, and one from his mother. After reviewing the results, Ms. Thomas ascertained that the target behavior of concern was task avoidance. Stefan was identified with severe mental retardation and had limited communication abilities. It appeared from reading the interview responses that the behavior would frequently escalate if Stefan were not redirected early in the cycle.

Ms. Thomas collaborated with Stefan's team in sharing these immediate hypotheses and then began the next phase of the functional assessment. With the team's assistance, she operationally defined each of the target behaviors in question. The definitions were in terms that were observable and measurable. Once the behaviors were defined, she asked Stefan's teacher and mother to record occurrences of these behaviors across 15-minute time blocks using a scatter-plot data sheet. After 5 days of collecting the scatter-plot information, she could see patterns of behavior emerging. Stefan had virtually no occurrences of the target behaviors at home, high frequencies of the behaviors during specific points of the day while at school, and periods of time while in school when the behaviors were minimal, if present at all.

In conducting subsequent observations during both the peak times and times when the behaviors were not present, the hypotheses became clearer. Stefan was not given opportunities for choice, and when in need of help in performing the task, he would seek to escape rather than seek assistance. A functional communication method was developed for Stefan that included a laminated index card. One side of the card displayed a red circle with the word *help* written beneath it. Stefan was instructed to turn his card over to seek help when he needed the teacher's assistance. This small intervention was responsive to his needs and the need of his teacher in preventing problematic behavior from occurring.

### Reflective Moment

1. After reading the vignette, do you feel that you have a better understanding of the importance of systematic data collection as part of the functional assessment process?

2. What skills would be important to facilitate the completion of such a process while serving as a consulting teacher?

3. What strategies would you use to initiate collaboration among your fellow team members in such a role?

## REAUTHORIZATION OF IDEA

The use of functional behavior assessment in schools has dramatically risen, given the 1997 reauthorization of IDEA (Individuals with Disabilities Education Act). This legislation mandated the use of functional behavior assessment and the design of behavior intervention plans (BIP) to address the needs of learners with problem behaviors. The BIP component of IDEA states that the BIP must be developed based on a functional assessment and developed with the intent of ameliorating the problem behavior (Public Law 105-17, IDEA Amendments of 1997). The reauthorization of IDEA fails to precisely define the components of a functional behavior assessment and behavior support plan, thus uniformity and compliance with the legislation across state and local educational agencies is sketchy at best.

The mandate has served as a catalyst for examining these issues, yet the implications from research with respect to the use of these methods in educational environments continues to emerge without widespread support in terms of uniform policies and implementation on the part of educational systems. Other concerns include the professional preparation of educators in the use of these practices and also the integrity with which functional behavior assessment is implemented. Some have argued in the literature that public policy has exceeded the ability of educators to implement such policies based on these concerns (Howell & Nelson, 1999).

## THE APPLICATION OF PBS ACROSS LEARNERS AND LEARNING ENVIRONMENTS

The past decade has witnessed an increase in the number of applied research studies using PBS; however, the value of this methodology has yet to reach full acceptance within school settings. The use of PBS has been demonstrated to be effective for persons with developmental disabilities (Horner & Carr, 1997) as well as for children and youth with emotional and behavior disorders and learning disabilities (Dunlap, Kern, et al., 1993; Dunlap, Kern-Dunlap et al., 1991; Dunlap, White, Vera, Wilson, & Panacek, 1996; Kern, Childs, Dunlap, Clarke, & Falk, 1994; Umbreit, 1995). Given that PBS has demonstrated efficacy in the research literature across multiple environments and learners, some authors proposed that Congress identify PBS as the intervention of choice in the 1997 reauthorization of IDEA (Turnbull, Wilcox, Stowe, Raper, & Hodges, 2000).

The application of PBS across learning environments illustrates a behavior-based systems approach to enhance the capacity of schools, families, and communities in designing effective environments. Focusing attention on creating and sustaining school environments that improve lifestyle results for all children and youth by making problem behavior less effective, efficient, and relevant and desired behavior more functional, PBS is the integration of (a) behavior science, (b) practical interventions, (c) social values, and (d) a systems perspective (Sugai, Horner, Dunlap, et al., 1999).

## SCHOOLWIDE APPLICATIONS OF PBS

The application of PBS to systemswide problems has slowly drawn increasing interest as experts now recognize the utility of these principles of instruction and support as a prevention tool for promoting safe learning environments for children. Horner and Sugai (2000) pointed out that the consistent features of schools that are actively using schoolwide behavior supports include

- The use of school-based support teams in the design and delivery of PBS
- Administrative buy in and support for schoolwide behavior supports
- School culture defined by a limited number of behavior expectations
- Behavior expectations taught to all students
- Students given recognition through an ongoing system designed to acknowledge student performance
- Students who engaged in disruptive and dangerous behavior corrected and not ignored nor rewarded
- Evaluation of student performance collected in an ongoing manner by school-based teams and used for decision making.

Schoolwide use of PBS has been successful in minimizing problem behavior and school violence and reducing discipline referrals through prevention (Sadler, 2000; Taylor-Greene & Kartub, 2000). Historically, many school systems have relied on rapid suppression procedures for managing problematic behavior. Students who engaged in problematic behavior were usually administered punitive consequences such as expulsion, in-school suspension, and even corporal punishment. These procedures were after-the-fact interventions that were directed at suppressing or controlling the problem behavior. The merits and disadvantages of such approaches have been the source of constant debate over time among professionals, parents, and child advocates. In short, the use of rapid suppression approaches does nothing to promote positive behavior, nor do they promote prevention through the active teaching and reinforcement of prosocial behaviors. They do not enrich the culture or climate within the learning environment, and finally, they are not sensitive to the environmental factors that influence challenging behavior. The data from applied research in the field of PBS points to the merits of such intervention practices at the level of the individual learner and classroom environment and also at the schoolwide level.

# FACTORS INFLUENCING THE DEVELOPMENT OF PBS

One of the most important elements promoting the use of PBS for learners and learning environments is training educational professionals at the in-service and preservice levels. Such training includes preservice teachers who are in the initial stages of professional preparation and professionals who are on the job working as teachers. At present, most teacher training programs allot one course within the curriculum devoted to behavior management or classroom management issues. For preservice teacher training in the field of special education, students typically receive training in one or more courses devoted to ABA or behavior management. Given the outgrowth of PBS, partially as a result of the 1997 reauthorization of IDEA, teacher-training programs must begin to expand to become more inclusive of competencies in PBS. The need for increased training is apparent as the demand for professionals with skills, such as functional assessment and behavior support plan development, is critical in the implementation of the mandate. Effective training practices of preservice and in-service educational professionals will hopefully lead to improved practices in the provision of behavior supports within learning environments and result in greater quality assurance.

Another issue that is most important to the success of PBS with children and youth is the partnership between professionals and families. Families are key players in the process of functional assessment and in the development and success of behavior intervention plans. Parents and families contribute a perspective on the child that is unique and exclusive to them and their role as the child's parents. They provide meaningful information about their children and serve as active team members in the promotion of meaningful behavior and lifestyle outcomes (Stichter & Caldicott, 1999). The importance of a shared vision by the team, including a collaborative partnership between professionals and families, is most important to the success of the team. The use of PBS within the context of a school-based team is important for achieving durable and lasting systemwide impact, and the partnership with families is a major factor that influences such success. More on the importance of professional and family partnerships will be discussed in Chapter 2. Vignette 1.3 provides an illustration of the use of school-based teams in the provision of behavior supports.

## Vignette 1.3

### School-Based Behavior Support Teams and the Provision of PBS

Adams Elementary School and the regional state university have entered into a unique partnership involving the development of school-based teams in the delivery of behavior supports within their school. The partnership is part of a pilot grant project that facilitates the development of systemwide behavior support teams within schools. Adams Elementary School was selected to participate in the project based on several factors. The student body at Adams Elementary is composed of children primarily from lower socioeconomic conditions, and the patterns of problematic behavior that have emerged within the district as the children transition to middle school and junior high school have pointed to the need for early intervention and prevention at the preschool and elementary levels. Thus school officials and university project personnel have developed an innovative project aimed at the development of school-based teams in the area of behavior supports.

To initiate the newly formed partnership, the university project personnel and school-based team from Adams Elementary formulated an agreement to establish goals and objectives for the program and benchmarks for team progress. This agreement also detailed roles and responsibilities of each team member and the appointed role of the university technical assistance team. A special education teacher trained in behavior supports, a school psychologist, a school counselor, an assistant principal, and a general education teacher participated as team members. The university-based technical assistance project consisted of one doctoral-level behavior analyst and two graduate students that worked as partners with the local school-based team.

The next phase of the project implementation was to provide extensive in-service training in the use of PBS for members from the school-based team. The purpose of the in-service preparation phase was to ensure that all members of the team from Adams Elementary and team members from the university-based behavior support project were well versed in a common knowledge base. This knowledge base included the principles of PBS, functional behavior assessment, behavior support plan development, collaboration and consultation, and working in unison with families. The purpose was to build a sense of community within Adams Elementary among all relevant parties, including administrators, teachers, teaching assistants, cafeteria workers, bus drivers, and administrative personnel.

Once the team at Adams Elementary and other school personnel received training and were aware of the purpose of the project, the university-based technical assistance team served as on-site consultants at the school. They began working with the local school-based team in the delivery of PBS practices with children referred to the project. They worked in tandem with classroom teachers and related education personnel with identified children who were experiencing problematic behavior. Applications of PBS practices such as functional behavior assessment and development of behavior support plans were implemented for children identified with such conditions as autism, developmental disabilities, emotional/behavior disorders, attention deficit disorder, and learning disabilities. The purpose of this phase was to model the implementation of these practices for the school-based team and assist in problem solving as they began to implement best and most effective behavior support practices for children within classroom settings. As the team began to sharpen their skills and positive outcomes began to be realized, teachers and administrators became more enthusiastic and supportive. As the first year of the program concluded, school officials were pleasantly surprised with the evaluation outcomes from the project, which included a reduction in office referrals and incident reports and measures of teacher and family satisfaction. During the second year of the program, the team began to generalize these practices throughout the general school population and began involving students in the process by establishing school policies that promoted a sense of community for the students with the intent of improving school climate, such as schoolwide incentives for appropriate conduct and behavior.

The project has resulted in improvements at all levels (individual student, classroom, and schoolwide) and continues with intermittent involvement of the university-based technical assistance team. Adams Elementary has become a model school in the district with its innovative approach to promoting positive student behavior through the use behavior supports. This has resulted in the district using the team from Adams Elementary as districtwide consultants to establish school-based teams at other schools throughout the district.

## Reflective Moment

1. How can such programs be developed within schools without the aid of technical assistance teams?

2. What are some indicators of positive school climate based on your observations within schools?

3. Identify some methods you could use to develop effective behavior support teams within a school.

Vignette 1.3 illustrates the principles of PBS applied within a school-based team context. It is based on an actual project that resulted in the systemic change described within the vignette. The project continues to progress and refine its development based on the projected trends and needs of children and youth within the district. There will undoubtedly be more and more projects such as the one described unfolding as state and local education agencies realize the efficacy of PBS. It is anticipated that widespread implementation of these policies and practices will occur as research findings relative to the efficacy of PBS for learners and learning environments continue to be disseminated.

### Consider This

- How does PBS fit or not fit with your theoretical orientation?

- What, in your view, are the strengths and limitations of PBS?

## SUMMARY

In this chapter the common theories used to understand behavior and development in children and youth were described and include the biological, psychodynamic, developmental, ecological, behavior, and social learning theories. The origins and distinguishing features for each of the theories were described, and examples of each theory applied to practice were presented. The major theorists were introduced, as were their contributions to their respective fields, and the strengths and limitations of each of the theoretical frameworks were also discussed.

Given the focus of this text, much attention was given to the development of the behavior viewpoint and the evolution and development of the field as it is today. Related to the behavior model were the ecological and social learning perspectives, given their close association with the behavior theory. The work of theorists such as Uri Bronfenbrenner and Nicholas Hobbs (ecological theory) and Albert Bandura (social learning theory) were highlighted. The application of their perspectives to the understanding of human development and learning are most relevant toward understanding how to apply behavior supports to children and youth.

The early history of the behavior model applied to animal learning and the later applications to complex human behaviors, pioneered by the work of Skinner and advanced by such leaders as Bijou and others, were elaborated on. This included the development of applied behavior analysis and the outgrowth of positive behavior supports and the application of these methodologies to learners and learning environments.

Applied vignettes provided throughout the chapter described how to generalize the various theoretical frameworks discussed toward solving applied problems involving children, families, and educational systems relative to the delivery of PBS. Finally, the chapter closed with a section devoted to understanding the application of PBS across learners and learning environments. A rationale for the use of PBS with various types of learners and multiple learning environments was provided based on the literature. The utility of these procedures was discussed relative to individual and systemwide applications with children and within learning environments such as classrooms and schools. The barriers to full-scale acceptance and implementation of PBS, such as enhanced preservice and in-service training of teachers and related professionals, systemwide implementation at the local and statewide educational agency levels, and future trends in the development of the field, were examined.

## ACTIVITIES TO EXTEND YOUR LEARNING

1. Develop a matrix for comparing and contrasting the various theoretical viewpoints described in Chapter 1. Identify and list major components of each theory and their applicability to understanding the behavior of children and youth. Use the completed table to initiate a discussion on the merits and limitations of each theory applied to the provision of behavior supports to learners.

2. Discuss the theoretical viewpoints presented in the chapter and select the theory that you most identify with and explain why.

3. Identify and list the merits associated with PBS from Vignette 1.2. Would you have followed the same procedures as Ms. Thomas, and do you

agree with her conclusions following the functional assessment? What would you have done differently?

4. Which of the theoretical viewpoints presented in Chapter 1 do you feel has the most practical application with children and youth in learning environments? Explain why.

5. Evaluate how the philosophy of PBS compliments or contradicts your professional perspective in response to learners with challenging behavior.

## FURTHER READING AND EXPLORATION

1. Visit the OSEP Technical Assistance Center on Positive Behavioral Interventions and Supports at http://www.pbis.org.

2. View the videotape *Autism: The Child Who Couldn't Play,* about the use of behavior approaches to working with children with autism. The video is available from Films for the Humanities & Sciences, P.O. Box 2053, Princeton, NJ 08543-2053, (800) 257-5126 or visit them on the Web at http://www.films.com.

## REFERENCES

Allison, M. G., & Ayllon, T. (1980). Behavioral coaching in the development of skills in football, gymnastics, and tennis. *Journal of Applied Behavior Analysis, 13,* 297–314.

Anderson, C. M, & Freeman, K. A. (2000). Positive behavior support: Expanding the application of applied behavior analysis. *The Behavior Analyst, 23,* 85–94.

Bandura, A. (1977). *Social learning theory.* Upper Saddle River, NJ: Prentice Hall.

Batshaw, M. L., (1997). *Children with disabilities* (4th ed.). Baltimore: Paul H. Brookes.

Bijou, S. W. (1963). Theory and research in mental (developmental) retardation. *The Psychological Record, 13,* 95–110.

Bijou, S. W. (1970). What psychology has to offer education now. *Journal of Applied Behavior Analysis, 3,* 65–71.

Bredekamp, S., & Copple, S. (1997). *Developmentally appropriate practice in early childhood programs.* Washington, DC: NAEYC.

Bronfenbrenner, U. (1994). Ecological models of human development. In T. Husen & T. N. Postlethwaite (Eds.), *International encyclopedia of education* (2nd ed., Vol. 3, pp. 1643–1647). Oxford: Pergamon Press/Elsevier Science.

Cobb, N. J. (2001). *The child: Infants and children.* Mountain View, CA: Mayfield Publishing Company.

Duckworth, S., Smith-Rex, S., Okie, S., Brookshire, M. A., Rawlinson, D., Rawlinson, R., Castillo, S., & Little, J. (2001). Wraparound services for young schoolchildren with emotional and behavioral disorders. *Teaching Exceptional Children, 33,* 54–60.

Dunlap, G., Kern, L., DePerczel, M., Clarke, S., Wilson, D., Childs, K. E., White, R., & Falk, G. D. (1993). Functional analysis of classroom variables for students with emotional and behavioral disorders. *Behavioral Disorders, 18,* 275–291.

Dunlap, G., Kern-Dunlap, L., Clarke, S., & Robbins, F. R. (1991). Functional assessment, curricular revision, and severe behavior problems. *Journal of Applied Behavior Analysis, 24,* 387–397.

Dunlap, G., White, R., Vera, A., Wilson, D., & Panacek, L. (1996). The effects of multi-component, assessment-based curricular modifications on the classroom behavior of children and behavioral disorders. *Journal of Behavioral Education, 6,* 481–500.

Dykman, R. A., & Ackerman, P. T. (1991). Attention deficit disorder and specific learning disability: Separate but often overlapping disorders. *Journal of Learning Disabilities, 24,* 96–103.

Engelman, K. K., Altus, D. E., & Mathews, R. M. (1999). Increasing engagement in daily activities by older adults with dementia. *Journal of Applied Behavior Analysis, 32,* 107–110.

Erikson, E. (1950). *Childhood and society.* New York: W. W. Norton.

Ervin, R. A., Kern, L., Clarke, S., DuPaul, G. J., Dunlap, G., & Friman, P. C. (2000). Evaluating assessment-based intervention strategies for students with ADHD and comorbid disorders within the natural classroom context. *Behavioral Disorders, 25,* 344–358.

Frankenberger, W., Lozar, B., & Dallas, P. (1990). The use of stimulant medication to treat attention deficit hyperactivity disorder (ADHD) in elementary school children. *Developmental Disabilities Bulletin, 18,* 1–13.

Freud, S. (1961). *Collected works, standard edition.* London: Hogarth Press.

Gold, M. (1980). *"Did I say that?"* Champaign, IL: Research Press.

Golden, G. S. (1987). Neurological functioning. In D. J. Chen & A. M. Donnelan (Eds.), *Handbook of autism and pervasive developmental disorders.* Silver Spring, MD: V. H. Winston & Sons.

Goldman, L. S., Genel, M., Bezman, R., & Slanetz, P. (1998). Diagnosis and treatment of attention deficit/hyperactivity disorder in children and adolescents. *Journal of the American Medical Association, 279,* 1100–1107.

Guyer, B. P. (2000). *ADHD: Achieving success in school and life.* Boston: Allyn & Bacon.

Heard, K., & Watson, T. S. (1999). Reducing wandering by persons with dementia using differential reinforcement. *Journal of Applied Behavior Analysis, 32,* 381–384.

Hobbs, N. (1974). A natural history of an idea: Project Re-ED. In J. M. Kauffman & C. D. Lewis (Eds.), *Teaching children with behavior disorders: Personal perspectives.* Columbus, OH: Merrill.

Horn, W. F., Ialongo, N., Greenberg, G., Packard, T., & Smith-Winberry, C. (1990). Additive effects of behavioral parent training and self-control therapy with attention deficit hyperactivity disordered children. *Journal of Clinical Child Psychology, 19,* 98–110.

Horner, R. H., & Carr, E. G. (1997). Behavioral support for students with severe disabilities: Functional assessment and comprehensive intervention. *Journal of Special Education, 31,* 84–104.

Horner, R. H. Dunlap, G., Koegal, R. I., Carr, E. G., Sailor, W., Anderson, J., Allsin, R. W., & O'Neill, R. E. (1990). Toward a technology of "nonaversive" behavioral support. *Journal of the Association for Persons with Severe Handicaps, 15,* 125–132.

Horner, R. H., & Sugai, G. (2000). School-wide behavior support: An emerging initiative. *Journal of Positive Behavior Interventions, 2,* 231–232.

Howell, K. W., & Nelson, K. L. (1999). Has public policy exceeded our knowledge base? This is a two-part question. *Behavioral Disorders, 24,* 331–334.

IDEA Amendments of 1997, Public Law 105-17. ERIC Document Reproduction Service.

Iverson, S. D., & Iverson, L. L. (1981). *Behavioral pharmacology* (2nd ed.). New York: Oxford University Press.

Juul, K. D. (1977). Models of remediation for behavior disordered children. *Educational and psychological interactions* (Rep. No. 62). Malmo, Sweden: School of Education.

Kazdin, A. E. (1989). *Behavior modification in applied settings.* Pacific Grove, CA: Brooks/Cole.

Kern, L., Childs, K. E., Dunlap, G., Clarke, S., & Falk, G. D. (1994). Using assessment-based curricular intervention to improve the classroom behavior of a student with emotional and behavioral challenges. *Journal of Applied Behavior Analysis, 27,* 7–19.

Kirk, K. S. (1999). Functional analysis and selection of intervention strategies for people with attention deficit hyperactivity disorder. In J. R. Scotti & L. H. Meyer (Eds.), *Behavioral intervention: Principles, models and practices,* Baltimore: Paul H. Brookes.

Koegel, L. K., Koegel, R. L., & Dunlap, G. (1996). *Positive behavioral support: Including people with difficult behavior in the community.* Baltimore: Paul H. Brookes.

Komaki, J., & Barnett, F. T. (1977). A behavioral approach to coaching football: Improving the play execution of the offensive backfield on a youth football team. *Journal of Applied Behavior Analysis, 10,* 657–664.

Koop, S., & Martin, G. L. (1983). Evaluation of a coaching strategy to reduce swimming stroke errors with beginning age-group swimmers. *Journal of Applied Behavior Analysis, 16,* 447–460.

Lovaas, I. (1993). The development of a treatment-research project for developmentally disabled and autistic children. *Journal of Applied Behavior Analysis, 26,* 617–630.

Martin, G., & Pear, J. (1999). *Behavior modification—What it is and how to do it* (6th ed.). Upper Saddle River, NJ: Merrill/Prentice Hall.

McEachin, J. J., Smith, T., & Lovaas, I. (1993). Long-term outcome for children with autism who received early intensive behavioral treatment. *American Journal on Mental Retardation, 97,* 359–372.

Miller, M., Miller, S. R., Wheeler, J. J., & Selinger, J. (1989). Can a single-classroom treatment approach change academic performance and behavioral characteristics in severely behaviorally disordered adolescents: An experimental inquiry. *Behavioral Disorders, 14,* 215–225.

Miltenberger, R. G. (2001). *Behavior modification: Principles and procedures* (2nd ed.). Belmont, CA: Wadsworth/Thomson Learning.

Naugle, R., Cullum, C. M., & Bigler, E. D. (1997). *Introduction to clinical neuropsychology.* Austin, TX: PRO-ED.

Ornitz, E. M. (1983). The functional neuroanatomy of infantile autism. *International Journal of Neuroscience, 19,* 85–124.

Papalia, D. E., Olds, S. W., & Feldman, R. D. (1999). *A child's world: Infancy through adolescence.* Boston: McGraw-Hill.

Pavlov, I. P. (1927). *Conditioned reflexes: An investigation of the physiological activity of the cerebral cortex* (W. H. Grant, Trans.). London: Oxford University Press.

Pear, J. J. (2001). *The science of learning.* Philadelphia: Psychology Press.

Poppen, R. (1988). *Behavioral relaxation training and assessment.* New York: Pergamon Press.

Presley, J. A., & Hughes, C. (2000). Peers as teachers of anger management to high school students with behavioral disorders. *Behavioral Disorders, 25,* 114–130.

Reichle, J., & Wacker, D. P. (1993). *Communicative alternatives to challenging behavior: Integrating functional assessment and intervention strategies.* Baltimore: Paul H. Brookes.

Reid, D. H., Phillips, J. F., & Green, C. W. (1991). Teaching persons with profound multiple handicaps: A review of the effects of behavioral research. *Journal of Applied Behavior Analysis, 24,* 319–336.

Richey, D. D., & Wheeler, J. J. (2000). *Inclusive early childhood education: Merging positive behavioral supports, activity-based intervention, and developmentally appropriate practice.* Albany, NY: Delmar.

Sadler, C. (2000). Effective behavior support: Implementation at the district level. *Journal of Positive Behavior Interventions, 2,* 241–243.

Safer, D. J., & Krager, J. M. (1994). The increased rate of stimulant treatment for hyperactive/inattentive students in secondary schools. *Pediatrics, 94,* 462–464.

Scheerenberger, R. C. (1987). *A history of mental retardation: A quarter century of promise.* Baltimore: Paul H. Brookes.

Skinner, B. F. (1953). *Science and human behavior.* New York: Macmillan.

Skinner, B. F. (1968). *The technology of teaching.* New York: Appleton-Century-Crofts.

Snell, M. E., & Gast, D. L. (1981). Applying time delay procedure to the instruction of the severely handicapped. *Journal of the Association for the Severely Handicapped, 6* (3), 3–14.

Stichter, J. P., & Caldicott, J. M. (1999). Families, school collaboration, and shared vision in the context of IDEA. *Journal of Positive Behavior Interventions, 1,* 252–255.

Sugai, G., Horner, R. H., Dunlap, G., Heineman, M., Lewis, T. J., Nelson, C. M., Scott, T., Liaupsin, C., Sailor, W., Turnbull, A. P., Turnbull, H. R., Wickham, D., Ruef, M., & Wilcox, B. L. (1999). *Positive behavioral interventions and supports under the Individuals with Disabilities Education Act.* Lawrence: University of Kansas, Beach Center on Families and Disability, OSEP Center on Positive Behavioral Interventions and Supports.

Sugai, G., Horner, R. H., & Sprague, J. (1999). Functional-assessment-based behavior support planning: Research to practice research. *Behavioral Disorders, 24,* 253–257.

Sulzer-Azaroff, B., & Mayer, G. R. (1991). *Behavior analysis for lasting change.* Fort Worth, TX: Harcourt Brace College Publishers.

Taylor-Greene, S. J., & Kartub, D. T. (2000). Durable implementation of school-wide behavior support. *Journal of Positive Behavior Interventions, 2,* 233–234.

Tharinger, D. J., & Lambert, N. M. (1990). The contributions of developmental psychology to school psychology. In T. B. Gutkin & C. R. Reynolds (Eds.), *The handbook of school psychology* (2nd ed.). New York: John Wiley & Sons.

Thorndike, E. L. (1911). *Animal intelligence: Experimental studies.* New York: Macmillan.

Turnbull, H. R., Wilcox, B. L., Stowe, M., Raper, C., & Hodges, L. P. (2000). Public policy foundations for positive behavioral interventions, strategies, and supports. *Journal of Positive Behavior Interventions, 2,* 218–230.

Umbreit, J. (1995). Functional assessment and intervention in a regular classroom setting for the disruptive behavior of a student with attention deficit hyperactivity disorder. *Behavioral Disorders, 20,* 267–278.

Vollmer, T. R., & Bourret, J. (2000). An application of the matching law to evaluate the allocation of two- and three-point shots by college basketball players. *Journal of Applied Behavior Analysis, 33,* 137–150.

Vygotsky, L. S. (1978). *Mind and society: The development of higher psychological processes.* Cambridge, MA: Harvard University Press.

Watson, J. B. (1924). *Behaviorism.* New York: Norton.

Wheeler, J. J., Bates, P., Marshall, K. J., & Miller, S. R. (1988). Teaching appropriate social behaviors to a young man with moderate mental retardation in a supported competitive employment setting. *Education and Training in Mental Retardation, 23,* 105–116.

Wisocki, P. A., & Powers C. B. (1997). Behavioral treatments for pain experienced by order adults. In D. I. Mostovsky & J. Lomranz (Eds.), *Handbook of pain and aging.* New York: Plenum.

Wolery, M., Ault, M. J., & Doyle, P. M. (1992). *Teaching students with moderate and severe disabilities: Use of response prompting strategies.* New York: Longman.

Ziegler, S. G. (1994). The effects of attentional shift training on the execution of soccer skills: A preliminary investigation. *Journal of Applied Behavior Analysis, 27,* 545–552.

# Chapter 2

## Partnering with Families

## CONCEPTS TO UNDERSTAND

*After reading this chapter, you should be able to:*

- Describe how general education reform and special education reform have impacted the partnerships between families and professionals
- List and describe the six types of involvement from the Epstein model of family–professional partnerships
- Discuss the historical and current roles of families in special education
- Delineate the legislative mandate for partnerships and parent involvement
- Define and differentiate among the terms *partnership, empowerment, collaboration, parent involvement,* and *family-centered supports and services*
- Describe and provide examples of the desired roles of families in the development, implementation, and evaluation of positive behavior supports

## KEY TERMS

Alliance

Behavior support

Collaboration

Empowerment

Family-centered support

Intervention

Parent involvement and participation

Partnership

Reform

Special education principles

# THE NATURE OF FAMILIES AND PARTNERSHIPS IN EDUCATION

What is a partner? As you think about this question, you might respond by providing any number of examples from your experience. There are many forms of partnership, and they may be either formal or informal. What, in general, characterizes a partnership between two or more persons is a sense of sharing and common purpose; a close, cooperative working relationship; and a reasonable balance of rights and responsibilities between the two parties. Some partnerships are successful, some are successful for a period of time but not lasting, others are tenuous and on shaky ground, and still others are failures. What are the factors that contribute to the building and maintaining of a successful partnership?

Of particular interest in this chapter is how this question relates to the partnership between educators and family members. Professionals should seek to understand, establish, and take advantage of this partnership to improve and enrich the lives and self-determination of children and youth with challenging behavior, through application of positive behavior supports (PBS).

A common assumption in education is that parent and family involvement is critically important and is the best predictor of academic success for children and youth in school. A body of research evidence and expert opinion support the powerful influence of parent involvement in schooling (Henderson, 1987; Henderson & Berla, 1995). Take a moment to reflect on what the statement "parents should be involved" might mean to different people. Maybe on reading the statement, one might think generally about what "parent involvement" means to them. For some people this might mean that parents passively support and back up the teachers and the school and that they refrain from interfering with teacher and school decisions. For others it translates simply into the idea that parents will do what is asked of them by teachers and schools. For example, they will be sure that their children do their homework, they will respond to notes sent home by the teacher, they will provide refreshments for a special classroom event, or they will serve the school as part of a fund-raising campaign. Still others might think of parent involvement as parents serving as tutors, extra hands, volunteers, and classroom teaching assistants. And those who have an understanding of special education may associate parent involvement with participation in Individual Education Programs (IEPs) or provision of training experiences for parents. Finally, some might see parent involvement as possibly including some of all of the preceding.

Although we will be dealing in some detail with the different forms of parent involvement, it serves us to pose some questions at this point. How do we account for cultural differences and diversity in determining how parents might be involved? What are the relationships between parents' and family's developmental status (ages, maturity levels, education, parenting abilities, economic well-being) and their involvement as individuals? How do we as professionals relate to parents who have different beliefs, values, and goals from us? Can we genuinely make a place in our professional philosophy and practices for parents to be in an alliance with us—to become our partners and collaborators? And do we have, or are we willing to attain, the knowledge and skills necessary to prepare us to be successful in working with the parents and families of the children whom we teach or provide other services?

For us to be successful as educators in developing and maintaining strong partnerships with families, we must have some knowledge of how the characteristics and functions of families have changed over time. It is necessary to understand what families look like today, as compared to what they were like in the past and what they will be like in the future. Professionals will be better prepared as partners and collaborators if they understand and are accepting of the increasing diversity represented in families and the children who are members of those families. Families are becoming increasingly diverse in their structure and in the way they function. You need only look at census data for the United States to see evidence of this fact. The traditional family comprised of a mother, father, and one or more children now only accounts for approximately one fourth of all families in the United States. Our nation is becoming increasingly diverse with regard to race, ethnicity, and religion. One may view these changes as evidence of a decline of the family, for example, children being raised in families without a father (Popenoe, 1996) or simply as the changing demographic of families. The reality is that the families with whom educators work will look and behave increasingly different from their own families.

Consider one example of how families are changing. Bengtson (2001) acknowledged that families are increasingly diverse in structure and function, and he states that "multigenerational bonds" are becoming more important. As a result of several factors, including the increasing importance of grandparents and other kin in fulfilling family functions and our increasing longevity (life span), families are more connected across generations. Think about how this might impact you as a professional. You are an early interventionist, and your work is primarily to provide home-based support in a family-centered manner. Suppose the nuclear family is the grandmother of an infant with disabilities, the great-grandmother, and the infant's great aunt. They are generally there when you arrive at the home, and they are your partners. Suppose that you are their child's fifth-grade teacher and that, as a part of your parent involvement plan for the year, you have sent a letter inviting family members to be a part of your classroom mentoring and volunteer program. Your thinking and planning have mostly been done with the assumption that the responses you get to this invitation will be from the mothers of your students. One of your "takers" may be a grandfather. Or suppose that you are a special education teacher at the high school level responsible for developing and helping others implement positive behavior support plans for adolescents with challenging behavior. At the IEP meeting you may have the student, her stepmother, and paternal grandfather and grandmother, all of whom are members of the student's nuclear family and very important in her life.

The relationships between parents and other family members and various educational environments and professionals have evolved over the years. A cursory discussion is undertaken here to set the stage for consideration of current issues and practices. Many factors, related both to general education and to special education, have influenced the changes that have occurred. Certainly economic growth and change in the United States, population trends, increased levels of education of the citizenry, scientific and technological advances, increased cultural diversity, societal shifts related to the roles of families and parents, educational reform movements and research findings, and other factors have all influenced this relationship. You might think of your own family and extended family and how these factors may have impacted great-grandparents, grandparents, parents, and others regarding their connections with schools and educational professionals. The shifts that have occurred over time have sometimes been challenging for families, given that they have naturally tended to apply personal models and experiences to guide their ways of understanding and interacting with the education of their children. An example would be the parent(s) in a family who are reluctant to participate in determining educational goals, curricula, or learning experiences because they have been acculturated to believe that education is best left exclusively to the professionals. It is important to note here that the difficulties that arise with regard to changing models of family–professional relationships are not exclusively associated with the consumers (e.g., parents and families). General educators, special educators, school psychologists, counselors, therapists, administrators, early interventionists, and other educational personnel frequently are challenged by expectations to apply new and innovative models of the family–professional partnership.

## EDUCATION REFORM AND FAMILIES

Turnbull and Turnbull (2001) provided a description of how, over the past two or three decades, reforms in both general education and special education have impacted the partnerships between families and professionals in education. More recently we have begun to see a merger of these reform movements, or a "unified systems reform" (McLaughlin, 1998).

The term **reform** suggests that actions are taken to improve the form or condition of something, but also to put an end to something that may be viewed as outdated or ineffective. To reform means to change for the better. Although it is not always so, one would hope that efforts to reform (for purposes here primarily with regard to the matter of educational institutions and their views and treatment of parents and families) are driven by empirical evidence and systematic and thoughtful deliberation, as well as by the wishes and needs of consumers, so that the reform will produce a more desirable result.

It is interesting to examine the public's attitude toward public schools, especially as they relate to the need for reform and the role of parents. In the 32nd Annual Phi Delta Kappa/Gallup Poll of the Public's Attitudes

Toward the Public Schools (Rose & Gallup, 2000), 59% of Americans favored reforming the existing system of public schools, whereas 34% believed that we should find an alternative. And when the respondents were given a specific choice, 75% wanted existing schools to be improved and strengthened, and only 22% would opt for vouchers. Presented with the question, In your opinion, who has the greatest effect on a student's level of achievement in school—the student, the student's teachers, or the student's parents? nationally 53% indicated parents and 26% teachers. In response to the question, In your opinion which is a more important factor in determining whether students learn in school—the school or the student's parents? 69% indicated parents and 30% the school. These findings certainly make clear the public's perception about the importance of parent involvement in achieving desired educational outcomes.

## GENERAL EDUCATION REFORM

Reform in general education has included a number of national as well as state and regional-level studies, reports, and related initiatives. The reader may be familiar with some of these initiatives through the study of the foundations, history, and philosophy of education. If so, think about the extent to which the reforms include content related to the partnership between families and educational settings. For a synopsis of the history of parent and school partnerships in general education, refer to the work of Lori J. Connors and Joyce L. Epstein (1995). Perhaps the most influential impetus for general education reform is the report *A Nation at Risk* (National Commission on Excellence in Education, 1983). And over this same time period, the research and demonstration models of Joyce Epstein (1995) have been the most frequently applied with regard to conceptualizing, planning, and implementing family professional partnerships in general education. In the Epstein model, family, school, and community are seen as "overlapping spheres of influence," and balanced roles of these influences represent the opportunity for partnership. Epstein and Sanders (2002) suggest from their overview of theory, research, and practice that "in educational practice, more educators are moving away from isolation behind classroom doors and toward new models of family-school-community partnerships" (p. 431). They describe six types of involvement in which families and professionals both have roles and responsibilities in order to effectively make use of these partnership strategies (Figure 2–1).

Each of these types of involvement may be applied to a variety of educational environments, children, and families, whether the children are infants, toddlers, preschoolers, school-age children or youth and whether or not they have a disability. Obviously the presence of a disability, ethnicity and language diversity, cultural and religious beliefs, as well as factors such as poverty, single-parent family, education level, and personalities of family members influence the types and intensity of involvement chosen and the ways in which schools and families experience involvement. It is also possible to understand the types of involvement as being to some extent

**FIGURE 2–1**
*Epstein's Six Types of Involvement*

*Type 1: Basic obligations of families for parenting.* Parents have the obligation for parenting their children; passing along their beliefs, attitudes, and customs; seeing to their basic needs, including safety, nutrition, health, guidance, and development; and establishing home conditions conducive to learning. Schools may assist families by providing support, information, and parent education. A two-way exchange between families and schools is central to Type 1 involvement, with schools helping parents and families understand child development and environments conducive to learning and families helping schools to understand family life and to value families and children in a broader context than education.

*Type 2: Basic obligations of schools for communicating.* Schools are obligated to communicate frequently, effectively, and constructively to families about the experiences of children and youth in school. Communication should take a variety of forms specific to the intent and with consideration for how it will be received by individual families. Communication is a two-way street, and families may also strive to improve their connections with their children's learning environments through more frequent and effective communication.

*Type 3: Involvement at school through volunteering.* Volunteers, including family members and others, may share their time, talents, occupations, and interests to support and enhance the learning of their children and the children of others. Mentoring and tutoring are helpful forms of volunteering. Volunteering may occur at the school or elsewhere and at various times, not just during the school day. Schools may facilitate and take advantage of volunteers by establishing and supporting a structure that encourages and values volunteerism.

*Type 4: Involvement in learning activities at home.* Families will know more about their children's curricula and the teacher's methods, the skills being taught, the work that their children are doing, homework assignments, and how to prepare for tests. Families will be able to assist their children apply learning in school by making connections between daily life and schoolwork.

*Type 5: Involvement in decision making, governance, and advocacy.* Schools will encourage and support parent groups and committees and participation of parents and families in leadership and decision-making roles. School advisory councils, committees, PTO, PTA, PTSA, and advocacy groups in the community are examples. Parents' initiatives and their roles as shared decision makers are considered positive and are associated with problem solving rather than as sources of conflict.

*Type 6: Collaborations and exchanges with the community.* Both schools and families make connections with the community, including agencies, businesses, religious organizations, and other groups, for the purpose of extending and enhancing the learning and development of children. These connections serve the purpose of both informing children and families about community resources and providing them access to these resources. Implied in Type 6 involvement is awareness, knowledge, and willingness on the part of educational institutions to engage in these collaborations.

*Source:* Epstein, J. L., Coates, L., Salinas, K. C., Sanders, M. G., & Simon, B. S. (1997). *School, Family, and Community Partnerships: Your Handbook for Action.* Thousand Oaks, CA: Corwin Press.

sequential, moving from basic to more complex, and with one building on the other. Let us explore a few examples:

- Suppose that you are the lead teacher in a school-based, inclusive preschool classroom for children ages 3 to 5. You find that some of your preschool teacher colleagues, your teaching assistants, and some of the parents of the children in your room have expressed an interest in learning how to do CPR with very young children, including children who are medically fragile and who have other health and orthopedic impairments. You arrange for a CPR trainer from the local health department to come and do a training workshop over a couple of evening sessions. This is an example of Type 1 involvement.
- As a fourth-grade teacher in your second year of employment, you are beginning to see the unique challenges associated with effective partnering, given that you have more than 100 different sets of families with whom to communicate. In assessing your first year's experience and your own professional development needs, you determine that you need some new ideas on and strategies for written, verbal, and electronic communication. You take a step forward related to your Type 2 obligation by signing up for a graduate summer class on "Practical Communication Skills for Elementary Teachers."
- As a high school special education resource room teacher, you find that your responsibilities for consulting with the general education teachers on behalf of included students is leaving you with insufficient time for some of the direct instruction that you need to do with your students in the resource room. You address this issue by establishing a cadre of peer tutors and community mentors who volunteer time in your classroom (Type 3).
- Your second graders are learning about trees, and it's time to do the collection and classification of leaves project. You develop a guide and a few helpful hints for families as they participate with their children in this homework activity, and you and your first-grade colleagues take turns making yourselves available through the "homework hotline" program to answer questions after school. This is an example of how you as the teacher have contributed to Type 4 involvement.
- As the father of an adolescent daughter who is a student at the local alternative school for children with behavior challenges, you initiate (and get support and assistance from the teaching faculty) a parent–teacher organization (Type 5).
- In your role as a service coordinator, you are responsible for partnering with 30 families in which there is an infant or toddler with a disability that qualifies the child for early intervention services. A number of your families express interest in having access to respite care services. Along with these family members, you and some of your prior, experienced family members develop and distribute a respite care resource guide (Type 6).

## SPECIAL EDUCATION REFORM

Up to this point we have examined general education reform. Let us turn our attention to special education. An examination of the history of parent and family roles in special education and other services for children with disabilities proves to be quite interesting. What comes to mind when one thinks about the parents and other family members of a person with a disability? One's views are significantly affected by their closeness to the family and to the person with the disability. This is especially true if the individual is a member of his or her immediate family. It is reasonable to assume that the closer the personal relationship, the *less* likely one is to hold any of the following historical, stereotypical perspectives. Consider the following widely held historical assumptions:

- Parents are given a child with a disability because they are especially equipped to handle such a challenge.
- Families are given a member with a disability as a form of punishment.
- Families in which there is a member with a disability are stronger and more prepared to cope with adversity.
- Families in which there is a member with a disability tend to be dysfunctional in terms of marital and other intrafamily relationships.
- Parents of children with disabilities have a tendency to be at one extreme or the other, either overprotective of their child or disconnected and distant.
- Parents of children with disabilities go through a highly predictable process in which they experience shock, denial, blame, resistance, and finally acceptance.
- Parents of children with disabilities are adversarial and demanding of school systems and other service programs and are quick to take legal action.
- Parents of children and youth with disabilities want to be the primary teachers and interventionists for their children.

It is likely that some of these statements sound familiar. It is also reasonable to think that elements of truth exist in some of the statements. However, taken as a whole, they represent the inaccurate stereotypes and myths that have hindered our ability to establish and maintain partnerships with families.

With the passage of the Individuals with Disabilities Education Act (IDEA) in 1990 as Public Law 101-476, legislation emphasizing the importance of "person-first" language now exists. This means that an individual's status as a person comes before their special needs. One would refer, for example, to a "child with Down syndrome" rather than a "Down syndrome child." Although it may sound like splitting hairs or political correctness to some, it is not to those persons with disabilities and to their families. They do not want to be primarily defined by their disability status. Richey and Wheeler (2000) suggested that we add the dimension of "family-first" language to the concept of "person-first" language. They pointed out that "we are better served as professionals if our starting point in thinking about and serving families is to view them first as families (like our own families), and then as having uniqueness based on their individual circumstances, including the accommodations needed for a family member with a disability" (p. 12).

What is the relationship between the changes that have occurred over the past 50 to 75 years in the delivery of special education services and the views of and roles of parents and families with children and youth who are the recipients of these services? The reforms in special education over the period noted are intertwined with the actions of parents, professionals' changing views of parents and families, and economic, social, and political changes impacting family life in the United States and the expanding knowledge base regarding causes, prevention, treatment, and intervention for persons with disabilities. This point is validated if you think about your own personal experiences and those of your parents, grandparents, great-grandparents, extended family, and the people with disabilities with whom they have been acquainted. Turnbull and Turnbull (2001) provided a helpful framework for understanding the evolution of parents' and families' place historically—in special education specifically and related to disability generally (Table 2–1). They reported that by understanding this history, we might better understand the present situation and the challenges families face.

Considering how the field of special education has changed over the years, it is reasonable to attribute those reforms to several primary sources, including social, political, and economic factors influencing our attitudes toward and treatment of people with disabilities. Also influencing change has been research regarding causation and best and effective teaching and intervention practices, and the advocacy efforts of many (but especially parents) leading to federal and state legislation and its associated rules and regulations, policies, and financial resources. It is useful at this point to address the relationship between parental advocacy and reforms in special education, especially litigation and legislation.

Yell (1998) stated that the landmark case *Brown v. Board of Education* (1954), which resulted in a victory for the civil rights movement and determined that separate, segregated schools were inherently damaging and not equal and were inconsistent with the Fourteenth Amendment of our Constitution, applied to students with disabilities. The basic position upheld by the Court that racial segregation was stigmatizing and had negative consequences was interpreted to also include persons who were denied opportunity as a result of their disability. The *Brown* decision is important in establishing the rights of persons with disabilities. However, the role of parent advocacy can be associated with a major event that occurred some 44 years prior to the Civil Rights case (Yell, 1998). The first White House Conference on Children took place in 1910. One of the goals of the Conference was to define and establish remedial programs for children with disabilities or special needs. This and related events of the time served as an impetus in the United States to be more responsive to children and youth

**TABLE 2–1**
*Historical and Current Roles of Families*

| Role/Time Frame | Event(s) |
|---|---|
| Parents as the Source 1880–1960 | Eugenics movement and the view of parents as unfit, the need for selective breeding (Barr, 1913) existed. |
| Parents as Organization Members 1930s–Present | Parents take lead in local and national organizing, e.g., United Cerebral Palsy—1949, Autism Society of America—1961, National Association for Down Syndrome—1961, Association for Children with Learning Disabilities—1964, Federation of Families for Children's Mental Health—1988. |
| Parents as Service Developers 1950s–1960s | Largely as a result of the organizations that they developed, parents established service programs. |
| Parents as Recipients of Professional Decisions 1960s–1970s | Parents expected to be passive recipients and appreciative and supportive of the teacher. |
| Parents as Teachers 1960s–1980s | Prompted by the research related to environment and children's intellectual development (Hunt, 1972) and the work of psychologist Urie Bronfenbrenner, Head Start and school-age programs for children with disabilities emphasized parents as extensions of the educator. |
| Parents as Political Advocates 1970–Present | Parents' central role was through advocacy for success of two landmark litigations for rights to treatment and education, leading to passage in 1975 of P.L. 94-142 Education for All Handicapped Children Act. |
| Parents as Educational Decision Makers 1975–Present | Based in P.L. 94-142 and in subsequent reauthorizations 1986, 1990, 1997. |
| Families as Collaborators 1990s–Present | Advanced by Part C of IDEA Infants and Toddlers Program changing focus for parents to families and a family-centered approach. |

Adapted from *Families, Professionals, and Exceptionality: Collaborating for Empowerment* (4th ed., pp. 2–14) by A. P. Turnbull and H. R. Turnbull, 2001, Upper Saddle River, NJ: Merrill/Prentice Hall.

with disabilities in school settings and to establish special education, using segregated classes. The assumption was that this arrangement would provide smaller classes and would facilitate individualized instruction, less competition, and more self-esteem for students with disabilities. Winzer (1993) pointed out that segregated classes and support services increased significantly from 1910 to 1930 and that the placement of children with special needs in segregated special education rooms was restrictive in the same way that custodial placements in institutions had been.

Although the concept of equal opportunity (articulated as a result of *Brown v. Board of Education*) did extend to children with disabilities, it was a number of years after that decision that it was specifically applied in the federal courts to those children. Two landmark class-action lawsuits, the *Pennsylvania Association for Retarded Citizens,* or *PARC* (1972) and *Mills v. Board of Education of the District of Columbia* (1972), along with other cases, were foundational in establishing the right to education for children with disabilities. Prior to *PARC* being argued in court, it was resolved by a consent agreement stating that children who were mentally retarded, ages 6 to 21, had the right to a free public education, and that it was desirable to provide that education in educational settings such as those provided for age peers who did not have disabilities. In a summary of *PARC,* Yell (1998) emphasized four points, including (a) children classified as mentally retarded can and do benefit from education and training, (b) education is more than strictly academic experiences, (c) the State of Pennsylvania can not deny access to public education, and (d) early preschool experiences are important for children with mental retardation and should be provided just as they are for children who are typically developing. Although these statements may seem obvious to us, given where we are today with legislative mandates for special education, it was quite remarkable in 1972.

Like the *PARC* litigation, *Mills v. Board of Education* was a class action. However, it was filed in the District of Columbia by parents and guardians representing a variety of disabilities and children who were denied public education without due process. *Mills* resulted in the federal court mandating that all children with disabilities in the District be provided public education. It also outlined procedural safeguards and due process procedures. Due process has become an established cornerstone of the Individuals with Disabilities Education Act. Families have a right to due process related to the decisions made about their children in special education programs. Earlier in this chapter the role of parents as political advocates was introduced. The central role of parents and families and guardians in advocating for the right to public education for children with disabilities, not discounting the importance of parent organizations as advocates, may be connected to these two lawsuits. *PARC* and *Mills* clearly pointed to the necessity for both federal and state legislation specific to the provision of special education services.

That legislation was forthcoming beginning in the mid-1970s as states and the federal government hastened to pass laws establishing the right to public education for children with disabilities. The legislation education was prompted in part by parent and professional (for example, the Council for Exceptional Children) advocacy groups. Also, a growing understanding from research and model programs about children and youth with disabilities, which showed they were valuable and capable no matter what their disability or its severity, supported legislation. But also, it was clear to politicians and other decision makers from the litigation, especially *PARC* and *Mills,* that legislation was necessary to avoid further lawsuits.

In 1975 P.L. 94-142, the Education for All Handicapped Children Act (EAHCA), was passed, becoming essentially a bill of educational rights for all children with disabilities between the ages of 3 and 18 by September 1978 and up to age 21 by September 1980. This landmark legislation became the foundation for special education services in all 50 states. Its amendments and reauthorizations continue to provide the direction and a significant amount of the resources available today for the provision of special education services, as well as for the preparation of qualified personnel, funding of demonstrations of model service delivery, and the conducting of research in special education. Since it was initially passed as EAHCA in 1975, the legislation has been amended in 1986 as P.L. 99-372, the Handicapped Children's Protection Act, allowing parents to recover attorney's fees and their costs when they prevail in lawsuits. P.L. 94-142 was amended and reauthorized as P.L. 99-457, the Education of the Handicapped Amendments of 1986. In recognition of the established and growing body of research evidence regarding the efficacy of early intervention for very young children with disabilities and resulting from the advocacy efforts of parents, professionals, and others (Safer & Hamilton, 1993), P.L. 99-457 included funds for states to participate, if they chose to, in the development of programs for infants and toddlers (birth to 3 years) and their families. This initiative was Part H (now Part C) of the law and provided funding for 5 years of phasing in, developing, and planning for states to make ready their own models of early intervention.

By September 1991, all states had put in place mandates for early intervention services in compliance with Part H and following the components required in the law. Silverstein (1989) pointed out that a growing recognition of and respect for the importance of family resulted in the inclusion of family-centered and family-focused language and emphasis in Part H. Safer and Hamilton (1993) summarized the importance of families in early intervention by noting that ". . . Part H reflects not only a respect for families and what they know, but also an assumption that the family plays the key role in the development of the young child, and that the responsibility of the service system is to support that role" (p. 5). There is a very significant distinction to be made here between the concepts of supporting families as contrasted with providing services (educational and otherwise) to children. These views might be different based on the age of the child and the nature of the environment, and clearly the family–professional partnership is going to be substantially affected by these factors.

In 1990 the special education federal law was once again amended and reauthorized as P.L. 101-476, the Individuals with Disabilities Education Act (IDEA). As we noted previously, IDEA changed the title of the law to reflect person-first language. P.L. 105-17, the Individuals with Disabilities Education Act Amendments of 1997, reauthorized IDEA and included some changes and refinements, including a greater emphasis on the inclusion of children and youth with special needs in general education (referred to as natural environments for infants and toddlers) and the role of general educators in the planning and implementing of special education. Turnbull and Turnbull (2001) noted that reform in special education has progressed through two phases, including first, the reshaping of how free and appropriate public education (FAPE) is provided and second, reshaping the educational placements of children and youth with disabilities to be more inclusive and to have greater access to the general curriculum. Certainly the basis for this reform in special education over the past 25 years is attributable to the legislative mandates summarized earlier and the changes and refinements associated with their amendments and reauthorization.

### Consider This

- What do you consider significant about the relationship between the federal legislation in special education as a source of reform and the partnership between parents and families of children and youth with disabilities and professionals?
- How might future legislation affect this partnership?

It is important first to remember that the relationship between the reform and partnerships has been reciprocal. That is, parents and families through advocacy, litigation, and in other ways have not only impacted the initial passage of the law (EAHCA) but also the changes that have been made and the ways in which IDEA has been implemented from its regulations at the level of states and local education agencies. Legislation has been the foundation for the establishment and refinement of the family–professional partnership in special education. From the initial passage of the law in 1975, parent involvement has been emphasized as not only positive, but also necessary. If we look at the six **special education principles** that underlie IDEA and that must be met if states are to participate, the relationships between them and both the family-centered focus of Part C early intervention for infants, toddlers, and their families and the parent involvement focus of Part B (special education for children and youth ages 3 years through 21 years) are evident.

## SIX PRINCIPLES UNDERLYING SPECIAL EDUCATION PROGRAMS
### Zero Reject

The principle of zero reject essentially says that children with disabilities, no matter what the disability and without regard for the severity of the disability, have a right to be included in schooling. Consider what this means for a family. The education and special education profession is not that many years past a time when determinations were made about whether or not a child with a disability was educable or not. Now law and public policy says to parents and families of children with disabilities that their children will not be excluded and that their children are entitled to an education, just as all other children. The principle of zero reject applies to children with disabilities who are ages 3 through 21 (Part B of IDEA). However, it does not apply in the same way to children who are ages birth to 3 years (Part C of IDEA) because participation by states is voluntary, and each state determines its own definition for eligibility. For example, some states have rather restrictive definitions that limit the number of infants and toddlers served in early intervention whereas other states have more expansive definitions (including children who are at risk), resulting in a higher percentage of the population of infants and toddlers being eligible.

## Nondiscriminatory Evaluation

The second principle, nondiscriminatory evaluation, requires that the assessment of a child's developmental and educational status be conducted in a fair and unbiased manner and that the parents are a part of the evaluation team. Parents must consent to the evaluation, and "parents have the right to submit and require the evaluation team to consider evaluation and other information that parents themselves initiate or provide" (Turnbull & Turnbull, 2001, p. 248). The step of carrying out an evaluation, whether it is for the purpose of determining eligibility for special education or for identifying a child's strengths and needs to facilitate intervention and teaching, is, of course, early in the process. That makes it especially important to the establishment of a partnership with families, not only with regard to following the letter of the law, but also for professionals to demonstrate an understanding of and commitment to partnering with families. Effective partnering with parents and families during evaluation will set the stage for later success in parent participation. Beyond the fact that parents may expect that their child with a disability will not be denied an education (zero reject) and that the testing of their child will be fair and unbiased (nondiscriminatory evaluation), they may also expect that their child's education be appropriate.

## Appropriate Education

The third principle, appropriate education, maintains that appropriateness of education is based largely on the development and implementation of an individualized plan. You may be familiar with the individualized education program (IEP) for children ages 3 through 21 and the individualized family service plan (IFSP) for infants and toddlers and their families. This textbook introduces a variety of ways in which positive behavior supports for children with disabilities are connected to the goals, objectives, outcomes, and placements included in their IEPs or IFSPs, as well as the use of PBS in the implementation of these plans. Participation in this principle is at the heart of the family–professional partnership. IDEA includes parents in the list of required participants in both the IEP and IFSP processes, and in the instance of the IFSP, other family members as requested by the parent(s) if it is feasible to include them. But simply to require their participation by being at the IEP meeting and signing the document means very little if we as professionals do not value and facilitate their role as partners in both developing the plan and carrying it out. Keep in mind the definition of a partnership.

## Least Restrictive Environment (LRE)

The fourth principle, least restrictive environment, requires that children and youth with disabilities be educated to the maximum extent appropriate in settings with their age peers who do not have disabilities. Schools must provide a continuum of service delivery options from less to more restrictive, for example, from the regular classroom to a self-contained classroom or home-based setting. Inclusion is a practice and process that has been defined (Kerzner-Lipsky & Gartner, 1994) as "the provision of services to students with disabilities, including those with severe disabilities, in their neighborhood schools, in age-appropriate regular education classes, with the necessary support services and supplementary aids for both children and teachers" (p. 36). There is a close connection between the principle of LRE and the practice of including children with disabilities. The principle of LRE is manifested somewhat differently for infants and toddlers and their families being served and supported through Part C early intervention programs and the associated IFSPs. Early intervention programs are family centered rather than child centered, and Part C refers to natural environments rather than LRE. So what about the relationship between family–professional partnerships and LRE, inclusion, and natural environments?

On the basis of many opportunities for partnering with families, it has been the authors' experience that much of what we seek for children with disabilities can be summarized in two statements. First, a parent(s) wishes for their child to experience life and be treated not as an oddity or a disability, but as a child first, having more in common with other children their age than attributes that make them different. Second, parents and families want the specialized needs that their child has to be addressed in a highly individualized and specialized matter by professionals who have experience and expertise related to the disabling condition. Are these two statements consistent or inconsistent with the principle of LRE, inclusion, and natural environments? A cursory understanding might lead one to assume that the first statement is supportive of LRE, but that the second statement suggests the need for a more separate, segregated approach to special education. However, it is a disservice to families with whom we partner if educators and other professionals are unable to support the family's desire to meet these two overriding goals in a manner that makes them congruent as well as in keeping with the principle of LRE.

## Due Process

The due process principle suggests a formal proceeding that is carried out in support of established rules and practices, first at the local level and then appealed to the state level if necessary. It has been a part of IDEA since its inception in 1975 and is a mechanism to ensure that members of the partnership (parents and professionals) are accountable for their behaviors related to both Part B special education services and Part C early intervention supports and services. Due process provides the opportunity for families or professionals to challenge decisions that are made related to evaluation, the IEP or IFSP, and placements. Of course, it is unrealistic to think that carrying out due process will not frequently be adversarial in nature because two parties are in a conflict that requires a formal, legalistic process for resolution. However, with the most recent reauthorization of IDEA in 1997, more emphasis is placed on mediating differences prior to a due process hearing. It is logical that mediation, being an informal, nonbinding discussion, can be more facilitative of the family–professional partnership. It is more challenging to see that connection related to due process. Turnbull and Turnbull (2001) suggested inrelation to the place of due process in collaboration that "due process requirements encourage professionals and families to hold each other accountable and, as each sees what the other is doing to educate the student, to challenge the other" (p. 24). Hopefully, professionals will be able to understand the important place of the due process principle in special education and early intervention and not allow its adversarial nature to interfere with our development of meaningful and lasting partnerships with families.

## Parent Participation

The sixth and last principle underlying the Individuals with Disabilities Education Act is parent participation. This principle specifically addresses parents' rights to have access to the records of their child as well as control of others' access to those records. More generally, this principle may be understood as closely related to the six types of parent participation introduced earlier as a part of the model of home–school partnership developed and researched by Joyce Epstein (1995). The parent participation principle, interpreted somewhat loosely, supports the involvement of parents and families at all levels of special education service development and delivery, including leadership and decision-making roles at the school and school system level. A perspective that has not been sufficiently addressed in research and practice is the understanding of parents and families as being in a developmental process of growth and change, just as their children with disabilities, with regard to their interest in and willingness to be participatory and to be our partners.

## UNIFIED SYSTEMS REFORM

The current movement to restructure schooling and education (including early childhood education) in a way that merges special education and general education and further erases the line between the two is difficult for some professionals to comprehend and accept. McLaughlin (1998) focused on unified systems reform as a means of accommodating and supporting diverse learners and, including those with disabilities, without categorizing students or program resources. She emphasized accountability by schools for the learning of all students. It is reasonable to associate united systems reform with the trends in special education as reflected in the 1997 amendments to IDEA and their emphasis on participation of general education, inclusion for children ages 3 through 21, and natural environments for infants and toddlers and their families. Stichter and Caldicott (1999) discussed some of the issues involved in collaboration between families and schools in the context of the 1997 IDEA reauthorization and amendments and PBS. They emphasized that, whereas IDEA advances the need for personnel preparation that supports partnerships between general and regular educators and partnerships between educators and families, the tendency of preservice programs in special education and general education to maintain distinct boundaries is problematic. It is possible for this separation to make difficult the achieving of a shared vision and the sense of being in a partnership and collaboration, especially as it relates to dealing with challenging behavior and the development and implementation of positive behavior support.

United systems reform has focused attention on the educational needs of all children and has blurred the lines between children who have disabilities and their age peers and classmates who do not have disabilities. The theory and practice of inclusion has gained in acceptance in part as a result of this reform movement. However, there are researchers and leaders in the field of special education who caution that unified systems reform (sometimes referred to as standards-based reform, high-stakes accountability, or minimum standards) has not necessarily been a benefit to children with disabilities, particularly as it relates to assessment and accountability. Some evidence suggests (Vanderwood, McGrew, & Ysseldyke, 1998; Ysseldyke, 2001) that no national data exists for students with disabilities from state-level assessment and accountability systems because those students tend to be excluded. Allington and McGill-Franzen (1992) as well as Ysseldyke and Bielinski (2000) have pointed out that when tests are used for decisions about matters such as graduation and promotion or retention, dropout and referral increases and retention at grade level increases for children with disabilities.

Although it is difficult to pinpoint when reforms in special education and general education converged to become a unified effort, certainly the beginnings could be traced back to the 1980s and early 1990s. It also has been suggested (Kleinhammer-Tramill & Gallagher, 2001) that the National Goals 2000 legislation was the point at which the two converged. In 1989 then-President George Bush and the nation's governors established six national goals. In 1994 they were amended to include two additional goals. These eight goals were intended to provide the framework for reform and improvement in all of our nation's schools and for all of its diverse students. Goals 2000 specifically addressed the importance of including children with disabilities and the necessity for unifying special education and general education reform. The eight goals are focused on (a) children entering school

**FIGURE 2–2**
*National Standards*
*for Parent/Family*
*Involvement*
*Programs*

| | |
|---|---|
| Standard I: | Communicating—Communication between home and school is regular, two-way, and meaningful. |
| Standard II: | Parenting—Parenting skills are promoted and supported. |
| Standard III: | Student Learning—Parents play an integral role in assisting student learning. |
| Standard IV: | Volunteering—Parents are welcome in the school, and their support and assistance are sought. |
| Standard V: | School Decision Making and Advocacy—Parents are full partners in the decisions that affect children and families. |
| Standard VI: | Collaborating with Community—Community resources are used to strengthen schools, families, and student learning. |

Reprinted with permission from National PTA's from *National Standards for Parent/Family Involvement Programs,* Copyright 1998.

ready to learn, (b) improving the high school graduation rate to 90%, (c) children achieving competence in core subjects, (d) excellence in math and science, (e) adult literacy and competing in the workforce, (f) safe, drug-free schools, (g) professional development for educators, and (h) increased parental involvement in learning. Of particular interest here is parent involvement. The full statement of the National Education Goal is as follows: "Every school will promote partnerships that will increase parental involvement and participation in promoting the social, emotional and academic growth of children." The inclusion of this goal specific to parent involvement and partnership came about largely as a result of advocacy efforts by the National PTA (1998). The National PTA developed six comprehensive standards (Figure 2–2) for parent and family involvement with the national educational goal in mind. The National PTA Standards are connected both to research evidence of their impact and to indicators of to what extent they are met. A close relationship between these standards and the work of Joyce Epstein and her associates (Conners & Epstein, 1995), introduced earlier in the chapter, is evident.

The intent associated with Goals 2000 was that the goals would be achieved by the year 2000. That time has come and gone, and most researchers and scholars in education will say that the goals have at best been only minimally or partially achieved. For example, Gerald W. Bracey (2000), in his 10th *Bracey Report on the Condition of Public Education,* suggested that the goals during the period 1989 to 2000 were not achieved. He proposed that the goals were unrealistic and unattainable because of inadequate resources, or they were goals that take more time. Maybe that is the case with regard to parent involvement and participation. Changes with regard to how educators relate to parents and families (and how parents and families relate to schools, teachers, and the system of public education) could take longer to realize. With regard to the goal of increased connections between parents and teachers as partners, Hargreaves (2001) described how the concerns and fears teachers continue to demonstrate and how teachers' and parents' nostalgic views of the way things used to be in education are significant barriers to reform related to parent involvement. He proposed the necessity of a social movement and argued that

> if we want better classroom learning for students, we have to create superb professional learning and working conditions for those who teach them. Perhaps this is the most urgent reason why teachers must overcome the immense and understandable anxieties that many now feel about opening up their practice to parents. Closing the door on parents and trying to control interaction with them is in the worst interests of teachers. It might alleviate teachers' anxiety, but it does so only by mortgaging their own future and that of their students. Moving toward the danger is the more exciting and the only sensible way ahead. (p. 377)

## SUMMARY OF EDUCATIONAL REFORMS

Up to this point in the chapter the intent has been to assist the reader in gaining some perspective on the current status of P–12 education, especially with regard to the relationship of schooling, schools, and teachers to parents and families. Reforms that have occurred in both special education and general education were reviewed, especially over the past three decades or so. How these reform efforts have begun to merge to become a unified systems reform was also summarized. The unified systems reform movement carries with it very significant implications for all stakeholders, including the citizens who fund education, policy makers, researchers and leaders in education and related disciplines, children and youth with disabilities and those who do not have disabilities, and the families of those children and youth. It certainly has ramifications not only for how education is delivered in the United States, but also for how professionals are prepared in teacher preparation and related programs from infancy through high school.

### Consider This

Think about the preservice programs with which you are familiar or the one in which you are currently enrolled. How is the relationship between special education and general education presented in your coursework and by your professors? Are they treated as merged, having some overlap, or as totally separate disciplines with unique and different goals, methods, and desired outcomes? Where might you place the program(s) on this continuum? How is the subject of understanding families and partnering with parents and families treated in those preservice programs? Is there any coursework at all related to families? Or maybe some family content is infused in a course or courses across the curriculum. Maybe the preservice program addresses parents and families in the programs aimed at preparing professionals to teach or intervene with very young children but minimally or not at all in programs at the upper elementary, middle school, or secondary level. Do the courses and field experiences that might be a part of an undergraduate or graduate degree and/or licensure program and that have content and experiences focused on parents and families treat families with children who have disabilities as distinct and separate entities from families with children who do not have disabilities?

These are all important questions and considerations. Education professionals in training need to have a level of confidence that their preservice experiences are reasonably consistent with the expectations that others will have for them in the classroom. Legitimate questions remain about how unified systems reform, despite its potential, will impact all children and their families. From the special educator's perspective, there may be concern not only that students with disabilities might be excluded from the assessment and accountability process introduced earlier, but also that the specialized needs of children with disabilities, especially those with more comprehensive and significant delays, will be unmet or inadequately met in the context of inclusive or natural environments. And from the point of view of the general educator there may be this response: "I am overworked, underpaid, and undervalued, and now you expect me to include students with disabilities (with all the associated paperwork) and to partner with their parents and families! Not only do I now have these children with very specialized, intensive special needs, some of them have behaviors that are very foreign to me, unacceptable in my classroom, and disruptive to the other students!" It is important to acknowledge the challenges and concerns associated with unified systems reform, but it is also important to understand that families are families first, and their status as having a member with a disability is secondary. Finally, it is important to recognize that educators benefit for developing and nurturing a partnership with the parents and families of the children and youth with whom we work.

## BUILDING RELIABLE ALLIANCES—A FRAMEWORK FOR THE FAMILY–PROFESSIONAL PARTNERSHIP

You will encounter a sometimes confusing and seemingly overlapping maze of terminology associated with the relationship of education to parents and families. Some of these terms are *family centered, parent involvement and participation, partnership, collaboration, empowerment,* and *reliable alliances.* In this section of the chapter, the terms are defined and clarified, and the relationships among them are explained. A framework for the partnership between professionals and families is provided. Finally, an examination of the specific connections between PBS and family–professional partnerships is addressed.

In the broadest sense, one of the goals of an educational professional in service to children and youth should be to have an **alliance** with their parents and families. An alliance means a positive connection and bond between two parties. Building reliable alliances suggests that achieving an alliance requires some work, effort, and maintenance (building) and that an alliance is reliable when there is trust and dependability between the two parties. As stated at the beginning of the chapter, a successful **partnership** is one in which a sense of sharing and common purpose, a close, cooperative relationship, and a reasonable balance of rights and responsibilities between the two parties exists. **Empowerment** means to have the ability to get what one wants and needs.

A fundamental question might be, Are we willing, and, if so, do we know how to support parents and families in becoming empowered related to their children's development and education? The term **collaboration** has historically been used to describe what professionals do with each other, rather than to describe the relationship between professionals and families. Collaboration (joint decision making) is more opt to be viewed as a strategy that is appropriate in special education (and especially early childhood special education) than it is in general education. The beliefs and practices associated with **parent involvement and participation** emphasize, especially in general education (for example, in the Epstein model) and in Part B of IDEA, the importance of parents' roles in education in a variety of ways, at different levels, and as associated with their children's achievement and success in educational environments. **Family-centered supports** and services are associated primarily with Part C of IDEA and an approach to planning the IFSP process as well as providing service coordination and delivering early intervention that has developed since the initial passage of the law in 1986. One way to summarize family centered (Richey & Wheeler, 2000) is "services to infants and toddlers with disabilities must not be delivered in a way that fails to consider the child as a part of the family unit, and that the family's participation—in ways that take advantage of their strengths, needs, and wishes—is essential" (p. 8).

How does one make sense of these terms and convert them into an overall statement of recommended practice in relationships with families? As a professional, one believes that an important part of their mission is to establish and maintain a partnership (an arrangement) with parents and families and to carry out that partnership through ongoing collaboration (activities and actions). As a result of this partnership and collaboration, a professional intends to build a reliable alliance with parents and families (a positive connection and bond, i.e., we trust each other and we are in this together). From collaboration and the alliance will come increased empowerment (ability to get needs met) for both the professionals and the parents and families with whom they partner. The approach that is employed will tend to be either that of **parent involvement** and participation (child focused and emphasizing parents rather than the family as a whole) or family centered (family focused and emphasizing the family unit and its needs, strengths, routines, and goals).

The framework for building reliable alliances is taken from the work of Ann and Rud Turnbull (2001). They have provided a framework that emphasizes the importance of taking into account the resources (knowledge and skills and motivation) that both families and professionals bring to the partnership or collaboration. They further described the opportunities that might arise during the process for collaboration, and they listed eight obligations that professionals have to build and maintain a reliable alliance. Figure 2–3 lists and defines the obligations.

**FIGURE 2–3**
*Obligations for a*
*Reliable Alliance*

1. *Know yourself:* involves having accurate self-knowledge—knowing and appreciating your own perspectives, opinions, strengths, and needs

2. *Knowing families:* involves being able to identify the unique aspects of each family's characteristics, interactions, functions, and life cycle and to respond in ways that are personalized and individually tailored to respect families' uniqueness

3. *Honoring cultural diversity:* means relating to others in personalized, respectful, and responsive ways in light of values associated with factors such as ethnicity, race, religion, income status, gender, sexual orientation, disability status, occupation, and geographical location

4. *Affirming and building on family strength:* means identifying, appreciating, and capitalizing on families' strengths

5. *Promoting family choices:* involves selecting the family members to be involved in collaborative decision making, deciding which educational issues should take priority over others, choosing the extent to which family members are involved in decision making for each educational issue, and selecting appropriate goals and services for the student

6. *Envisioning great expectations:* means recognizing that one can have an exceptionality and also have an enviable life

7. *Practicing positive communication skills:* means using nonverbal skills (such as physical attending and listening), verbal communication skills (such as furthering responses, paraphrasing, and summarizing), and influencing skills (such as providing information, providing support, and offering assistance) in ways that most sensitively and respectfully connect with families

8. *Warranting trust and respect:* means having confidence that everyone is pulling in the same direction in a supportive, nonjudgmental, and caring way

From *Families, Professionals, and Exceptionality: Collaborating for Empowerment* (4th ed., p. 50) by A. P. Turnbull and H. R. Turnbull, 2001, Upper Saddle River, NJ: Merrill/Prentice Hall. Copyright 2001. Reprinted by permission of Pearson Education Inc., Upper Saddle River, NJ.

These eight obligations provide a useful guide, without regard for the ages of the children, whether or not they have disabilities, and the level and type of participation of parents and families. Some of these obligations are more focused on personal attributes of the professional, his or her beliefs, attitudes, and behavior style. Others are more specific to skills and abilities as a professional. Another way of saying this is that if one wishes to be successful in family–professional partnerships and to be able to meet these eight obligations, then they must be engaged not only in the development and refinement of their own professional competencies, but also in their personal growth in relationships with others. Some would argue that the distinction between the two is artificial and unnecessary. Think about the traditional view of professionals (specifically teachers for our purpose here) as needing to maintain a "professional distance" and "objectivity," to not get "too close" in their dealings with the parents of their students. One might argue that this view is wise and necessary, but think about how it might impact your ability to carry out the eight obligations for a reliable alliance.

# PARENTS AND SPECIAL EDUCATION—THE PARADIGM SHIFT

The definition for paradigm is a philosophical and theoretical framework of a scientific school or discipline within which theories, laws and generalizations, and the experiments performed in support of them are formulated. In the discipline of education, and more specifically special education, the paradigm over the past three or four decades related to parents and families has been well established. It accepts that the contribution of parents is helpful in the process of evaluation and assessment of their children (even though the inclination may be to give their input less weight, to qualify it with a "parent reports" statement, or to disallow it in formally determining performance scores). Special educators have come to accept and value the important role that parents play in the education of their children. This is evidenced by, for example, the legal mandate for their participation in the planning processes of the IEP and the IFSP. The importance of parents as teachers (even saying that they are the "first and most important teachers") has been emphasized. The need for consistency between the content and methods that we employ in educational settings and the experiences that children have at home and elsewhere with their families has been emphasized. Special educators have stressed that new learning and behavior or the replacement of an unacceptable behavior with a more acceptable one (e.g., learning not to be aggressive toward other children—to refrain from hitting them and to substitute an alternative behavior) requires a commitment to generalization. Generalization, or the generality of behavior change, is described by Martin and Pear (1998) as transferring new behaviors to new settings (including natural environments such as home), making those new behaviors last, and sometimes having behaviors that have been learned lead to the development of new behaviors that have not been learned. Educators and special educators have had the expectation that parents would learn from them what generalization is and why it is important for them at home to be extensions of our behavior change objectives and associated intervention approaches.

Although this is by no means a complete picture of the paradigm that has been employed related to parents of children with disabilities, it does summarize some of the main points. Special educators have considered the active participation of parents as critically important, but they have also tended to view that participation as being subject to the direction of professionals. One could conclude that desirable parent participation to some extent was dichotomized into those parents who were appropriately involved (following the lead of and doing what professionals directed) and those who were not involved (not being responsive to professional direction) or were inappropriately involved (being pushy, demanding, and overstepping their bounds). Education generally and special education specifically are in the midst of a paradigm shift with regard to our disciplines' fundamental position on the relationship between parents and families and professionals. The theoretical and philosophical frameworks that have been employed no longer seem sufficient. However, it is important to note that the suggestion is not being made that there will be no continuing need for parents and families to be educated by professionals. A good example is to be found in the recent professional literature (Delaney & Kaiser, 2001), which described a successful intervention to train parents of preschoolers to support communication and provide positive behavior supports. There are numerous examples in the professional literature in special education of how training and education have been successfully used to assist parents of children with special needs and, in particular, those children and youth with challenging behavior. Maybe it is useful to think of this issue in terms of a balance rather than unidirectional (i.e., professionals training parents). Appropriate times exist for parents and family members to be the providers of training and education for professionals and others concerning their children's disabilities, abilities, needs, preferences, and routines.

Described in this chapter to this point are some of the factors and events that have led to the paradigm shift toward a partnership between professionals and families. Now attention shifts to the application of a new paradigm, the family–professional partnership, related specifically to the provision of positive behavior supports for children and youth who experience challenging behavior in various educational and developmental environments.

## POSITIVE BEHAVIOR SUPPORTS AND THE FAMILY–PROFESSIONAL PARTNERSHIP

Chapter 1 introduced positive **behavior support** (PBS) as an approach to serving individuals with challenging behavior in various educational settings. PBS is founded in the learning, behavioral theory, and research of B. F. Skinner and others such as Sidney Bijou, Albert Bandura, and many who came after them. PBS may be understood as one fundamental means of applying and expanding on the tenets of applied behavior analysis. Like the paradigm shift related to the relationship between the special education discipline and its connection to families, PBS may be viewed as a shift in the paradigm with regard to how behavior theory, principles, and practices are applied to help individuals with challenging behavior. In a significant position paper describing the historical and current relationship between applied behavior analysis and positive behavior support, Anderson and Freeman (2000) concluded that "the approach (PBS) emphasizes using behavior-analytic assessment and treatment strategies to address both challenging behavior and global quality-of-life issues such as helping a person to develop meaningful friendships and participate in the community" (p. 92). This perspective is especially important in understanding the connections between PBS and the family–professional partnership. Considering quality of life, the community, and meaningful relationships, one should recognize that families are frequently at the center of the educator's work. Turnbull and Turnbull (2000) described the contribution of PBS to achieving a "rich lifestyle" for persons with disabilities. They pointed out that although

PBS has made significant contributions to enriching the lives of persons with disabilities, there remains the need for a great deal of research and related improvement and expansion of practice. The goal should be to better use PBS to support persons with disabilities in experiencing a rich lifestyle, as evidenced by the enhanced quality of their lives as individuals and within their families and by their improved abilities and opportunities for self-determination. Self-determination is defined as "acting as the primary causal agent in one's life and making choices and decisions regarding one's quality of life free from undue external influence or interference" (Wehmeyer, Martin, & Sands, 1998, p. 192).

As noted earlier, the 1997 reauthorization of the Individuals with Disabilities Education Act has a central role as it relates to reforms in general education and special education and to its focus on establishing and using the partnerships between parents and families and professionals. Specifically, in the regulations established to guide implementation of the 1997 IDEA amendments, the law is interpreted to "provide an opportunity for strengthening the role of parents, and emphasize that one of the purposes of the amendments is to expand opportunities for parents and key public agency staff (e.g., special education, related services, regular education, and early intervention service providers, and other personnel) to work in new partnerships (Fed. Reg. 1999, p. 12472). So the federal special education law stresses the need for a closer relationship between general education and special education as well as a partnership between parents and professionals, but it also requires that positive behavior supports and interventions be provided when the IEP process determines that challenging behaviors are a concern (i.e., "behavior problems that interfere with his or her learning or that of others" [Fed. Reg. R, 1999, p. 12441]). In summary, the law mandates that positive behavior supports and interventions be provided when appropriate, and it stresses the importance of a team approach, in which parents are partners with educators and other professionals.

The specific relationship between positive behavior supports and the family–professional partnership has only recently been explored and described in the literature. As Chapter 1 stated, positive behavior support is largely an extension of applied behavior analysis and is a conceptual framework that is only about a decade old. Efforts to examine PBS and the partnership between professionals and families are even more recent. One of the primary sources in the literature studying and advocating collaboration and partnership is to be found in the *Journal of the Association for Persons with Severe Handicaps* (JASH). The connection between a professional organization and the advancement of a family–professional partnership seems very logical if one thinks about how parents and families have been participants historically (see Table 2–1) and that often the children and youth with the most complicated, severe, challenging, and lower incidence were the ones most in need of advocacy and political support because they might be viewed as of lesser or even without value (for example, not "educable").

In 1997 JASH devoted a special section of the journal to the development and implementation of PBS as it is influenced by the partnership (collaboration) between parents and professionals. This is important because it is one of the first systematic attempts to examine PBS and partnerships. Goetz (1997) points out that although the articles published in this special section of JASH highlight the important participatory role of families in the process of planning and delivering PBS and taken collectively they should influence our practices and future research, there remain many questions to be answered as we refine the relationship between PBS and families.

In a study designed to employ a community-based and family-centered approach to address the challenging behavior of a 9-year-old boy with severe disabilities, the researchers (Vaughn, Dunlap, Fox, Clarke, & Bucy, 1997) found that partnering with the child's family during the entire process of assessment, **intervention**, and evaluation of effectiveness was very important in reducing problem behaviors, including tantrums, screaming, and aggression. One of the authors of the article reporting this research was the mother of the child who presented the challenging behaviors. Three natural environments were the focus of this study, including a large grocery store, a fast-food restaurant, and a drive-through bank. The researchers indicated that this research is important because it was done with families as partners and to benefit a family's ability to participate in their community. This study was quantitative in nature; that is, they were interested in quantifying changes in disruptive behavior by counting and using percentages to show change as a result of the intervention procedures. In a companion study (with the same family and child) published in JASH employing a qualitative approach (Fox, Vaughn, Dunlap, & Bucy, 1997), both an audio journal kept by the mother and semistructured interviews with both parents and the boy's older brother were conducted over a 10-month period. Two pervasive themes emerged from the research. One was that the child's problematic behavior had a dramatic and pervasive impact on the family as a whole and on their lifestyle. A second theme was that the behavior supports had a powerful and positive impact on the family. The family attributed the success of the intervention to both the nature of the intervention process and the relationship (partnership/collaboration) that developed between the professional(s) and the family.

Three years after publication of the articles summarized in JASH, another event worthy of note here occurred in the special education—positive behavior support professional literature. The editor of the *Journal of Positive Behavior Interventions* invited individuals, including family members, professionals, and others, to contribute articles to the Forum section of the journal in response to the question, What are some important activities that should be encouraged in the next decade to improve the status of assistance and support for families that include a child with severe problem behaviors? The decade to which they referred, of course, was 2000–2010. This invitation produced some very interesting and useful guidance for planning current and future approaches to PBS and family–professional partnerships. Lucyshyn, Blumberg, and Kayser (2000) offered three suggestions, including (a) provide family-centered, home-based positive behavior support services,

**FIGURE 2–4**
*What Can Make a Difference?*

*We must bring more information about positive interventions more forcefully to school administrators, teachers, and staff in every school in the United States.* It is important to substitute for all children positive, preventive, proactive, effective techniques and strategies for negative and punitive approaches.

*There are still universities and colleges that are turning out educators who do not understand and know the science of positive interventions.* In the next decade institutions of higher education must implement programs of hands-on experiences to prepare both general and special education professionals.

*Schools and parents must get on the same page.* Communication is critically important, and programs of positive intervention must cross the child's entire day at home and at school.

*Our collaborative interventions must start when the child is young.* Early intervention is important and necessary. It is harder to impact challenging behavior when the child is older.

*We need to get the pendulum in the middle and keep it there.* Children with disabilities need challenging work and high expectations. They should be required to work hard and experience consequences.

*Finally, I hope that every parent and teacher and friend of a child with a disability takes steps to introduce that child to the community in which they live and integrate them into our schools, churches, and activities.* All elements of the community should know about our children with disabilities so that awareness and acceptance might be raised.

From "Ripple or Tidal Wave: What Can Make a Difference?" by C. Fisher, 2000, *Journal of Positive Behavior Interventions, 2*(2), pp. 120–122. Copyright 2000 by PRO-ED, Inc. Adapted with permission.

(b) expand the unit of analysis and intervention to focus on family routines, and (c) teach professionals to build collaborative partnerships. In the first suggestion, professionals view and treat family members as equals and address challenging behaviors in all relevant contexts, including home. In the second, interventionists must understand problem behavior in the context of the family's daily activities and routines. And finally, university preservice programs, especially at the graduate level, should prepare professionals to be partners and collaborators with families. In an article contributed by the mother of a young adult with autism (Fisher, 2000), six recommendations were provided from the perspective of a parent and family member regarding PBS and the relationships among professionals, schools, families, and communities (Figure 2–4).

## THE BEHAVIOR SUPPORT TEAM

Later chapters in this text address the composition and functioning of the behavior support team specific to planning, implementing, and evaluating PBS. Membership on the team varies widely in both number of members and their roles. The central substantive participation of family members on the team is how a reliable alliance, partnership, and collaboration are manifest. Of course, the manner and extent to which family members served on the team is highly individualized. Cultural differences may also play an important part in how family members view the behavior support team. For example, research shows that cultural background affects the planning process and that traditional Asian and Pacific Island families defer more to service providers (Sileo & Prater, 1998; Sileo, Sileo, & Prater, 1996).

## APPLICATIONS OF PBS AND FAMILY–PROFESSIONAL PARTNERSHIPS

Vignettes 2.1, 2.2, and 2.3 provide a sense of the various ways in which families and professionals might experience PBS. These vignettes come from a combination of the authors' experiences in working with children, educators, and other professionals and in partnering with families over the span of their careers. Also, some ideas have been included from recent literature on applications of PBS. As you read each, you may wish to consider the ways in which they demonstrate both the levels of family involvement (Figure 2–1) and the obligations for a reliable alliance (Figure 2–3). The intent here is not to address the specifics of functional assessment and positive behavior interventions and supports, but rather to present the broad strokes relating family experiences to intervention planning and implementation.

## Vignette 2.1

### Aaron and His Mom, Dad, and Big Sister

Aaron Thompson is 2 years old and is the youngest child of Donna and Horace Thompson. He has a 10-year-old sister, Anna. Aaron was recently diagnosed with autism, and the family has been referred to their state's early intervention system. Aaron has been determined to be eligible for early intervention, and the family's service coordinator, Mrs. O'Connor, feels that they are off to a good start in their partnership. She has made several home visits to get acquainted with the Thompsons before any intervention planning got underway. An Individualized Family Service Plan (IFSP) has been developed for Aaron and his family. The IFSP team includes Mr. and Mrs. Thompson; Mrs. Thompson's mother, who frequently takes care of Aaron; Mrs. O'Connor, a developmental psychologist; Aaron's pediatrician; Aaron's caregiver at nursery school; and an early interventionist representing the local program. In accordance with early intervention public policy and effective practice (Sandall & Ostrosky, 2000), it is family centered and emphasizes natural environments and inclusive experiences for Aaron. Present levels of functioning for Aaron and the family's resources, priorities, and concerns were determined through a functional assessment and through talking with the family to understand their family routines. The family-centered intervention planning routines-based approach developed by McWilliam (1992) was used to better understand the family and their daily activities and to facilitate the embedding of intervention in an activity-based approach (Bricker, Pretti-Frontczak, & McComas, 1998). The IFSP team established major outcomes and associated action steps. One of the outcomes is specific to implementing a PBS plan to address Aaron's pinpointed challenging behaviors. The plan is practical, supported, and understood by everyone and can be implemented across various settings, including home, grandmother's house, Aaron's three-mornings-a-week nursery school room, church, and other places in the community. Another IFSP outcome is that Mr. and Mrs. Thompson want to learn more about autism and especially want to do some reading and perhaps be a part of a parent-to-parent connection. Mrs. O'Connor provides them with a handbook on parent-to-parent programs (Santelli, Poyadue, & Young, 2001), information about autism, and a contact for a local support and advocacy group. Because the grandmother has Aaron during the times that he isn't at nursery school while Mr. and Mrs. Thompson are at work, she wants to volunteer at the nursery school to help out and to observe and get some ideas on how to be more effective with her grandson and to share her knowledge and experience. The early interventionist will consult and help grandmother and the caregiver to facilitate this outcome and help them develop and use a communication plan. Aaron's sister Anna has an understanding of her brother's special needs beyond what might be expected from her developmentally, and she wants to be a part of helping him. Mrs. O'Connor and the early intervention professional trust Anna and her parents that this is a workable idea, find some examples in the literature of how sibling interaction and social play have been facilitated (Baker, 2000), and help them develop activities.

### Reflective Moment

What, if any, special considerations might be made to include the grandmother as a volunteer at the nursery school, and how might her wish to be a resource to others and to share her experiences be accommodated?

When it is time for Aaron's transition to a preschool setting, what will be necessary to maintain the family centered partnership and inclusive nature of her services and supports?

## Vignette 2.2

### Mr. Rodriquez' Kindergarten Classroom

Emilio Rodriquez is in his third year of a job that he loves—teaching in a kindergarten classroom. He teaches in an inner-city school, and the children in his class represent a very heterogeneous group with regard to their families' income levels as well as cultural, ethnic, and religious diversity. He has 18 children in the room and a full-time teaching assistant. Partly as a result of his first 2 years of teaching experience and partly prompted by some graduate coursework in early childhood education in which he is currently enrolled, Mr. Rodriquez wants to address two professional development issues. One is that he wants to merge his understanding of the developmentally appropriate practices of positive child guidance as described by the National Association for the Education of Young Children (NAEYC) with what he has learned about PBS. Second, he wants to further develop and refine the parent involvement program that he has been using for the past 2 years. Mr. Rodriquez sees these two needs as closely related. His parent involvement program has consisted of a parent group that meets monthly (usually low attendance) for the purpose of responding to needs identified by the teacher, such as bringing refreshments for a birthday or chaperoning a field trip. Also, monthly individual parent conferences to review progress, conferences as requested by parents, a weekly newsletter done by the children and taken home, parent attendance at schoolwide functions such as PTA, special occasions (performances, holiday celebrations), and open houses are part of his plan. Mr. Rodriquez wants to improve his parent program to be more comprehensive and collaborative and to have more of a family systems perspective. He has in mind to use the variety and continuum of strategies suggested by Turnbull and Turnbull (2001), including accommodating linguistic and cultural diversity, respecting family preferences, and written strategies of communication. Written strategies will include handouts, newsletters, letters, notes and dialogue journals, progress notes and report cards, and occasional messages. Some of these he had in his old plan. Mr. Rodriquez will also use some nonwritten strategies, including phone contacts, e-mail, maybe a class Web site, and face-to-face interactions. He is planning a series of monthly family meetings to be held at times most convenient for the families and at varied sites, including school, maybe one of the family homes, and elsewhere in the community. The first meeting will be preceded by a letter of explanation of his plan and views on partnership, along with an invitation to the first meeting. It will focus on assessing the interests and needs of families. Two of the families of Mr. Rodriquez' kindergarteners are Spanish speaking, and fortunately, he speaks Spanish. He will develop with each family (of course there will be a good deal of overlap) an individual plan of collaboration and alliance.

With regard to Mr. Rodriquez' positive behavior support plan, he wants to develop a more systematic approach to fostering and maintaining positive behavior and social skills in his classroom, and he wants to be more effective in helping several students who are at risk for problem behavior. At present he does not have in his classroom a child with chronic and intense problem behavior. The behavior support planning that Mr. Rodriquez wants to implement is at two levels. The first is the primary level, which is intended to reduce (prevent) the number of new instances of problem behavior, and the second is the secondary level, which is focused on students who are at risk for problem behavior (Sugai et al., 2000). These are also referred to in the literature (Turnbull & Turnbull, 2001) as Level 1—clear expectations and positive feedback, and Level 2—individualized support in school settings. Mr. Rodriquez intends to merge his new and improved family partnership plan and his PBS plan in several ways. He will present at the first family meeting his preliminary plan for Level 1 positive behavior support, including ideas related to, for example, redesigning the layout of the classroom, organizing materials, centers and tables to facilitate cooperative learning, developing transitions between activities and routines of the classroom, and more consciously providing positive, descriptive praise for desired behaviors. Mr. Rodriquez will incorporate the suggestions provided by families and thereby make the plan more responsive to the uniqueness of the individual children and also foster a shared ownership of the plan with the families. Another thing that he has in mind is to invite the families to begin keeping, and to show them an example of (Hannigan, 1998), a dialogue journal. This will allow families who wish to do so to make daily or periodic written entries in a journal. In addition to being helpful to families, it may contribute to communication between the teacher and families in general and specifically as related to classroom behavior and socialization. For Level 2 positive behavior supports, one of the connections between the classroom and the families that Mr. Rodriquez wants to explore is developing a cadre of classroom volunteers and mentors to provide extra hands, some of whom might learn to do observations to assist in completing functional assessments.

### Reflective Moment

What are some ways in which Mr. Rodriquez might use the work he has done for levels 1 and 2 behavior support planning when he needs level 3 planning for a child with intensive challenging behavior in his class?

To what extent and in what ways do you feel Mr. Rodriquez' parent involvement plan might be used by his kindergarten teacher colleagues in the school?

## Vignette 2.3

### Making Middle School Work for Breela, Her Mom, and Teachers

Breela lives with her mother and her grandmother. She is 12 and just starting seventh grade at Mt. Jackson Middle School. Breela has spina bifida, and her means of mobility is a wheelchair. Breela does have an IEP, as has been the case since she started preschool, but at this point the only issues are related to catheterization and Breela's participation in physical education class. She has done quite well in her academic subjects and routinely makes the honor roll. But this is a new year and a new school for her. Also, there is some concern on the part of her family as well as her homeroom teacher that she is having some difficulty making and keeping friends because she seems to be "bossy" and demanding of them. To address this concern, a behavior support team is established. The membership of the team consists of Breela's mom and grandmother, five of her teachers, the school counselor, the consulting special education teacher, and Breela. Although this is a large team, the need for Breela to learn social skills will allow her to make friendships and better integrate into her school and community. Breela needs Level 2 PBS. That is, intervention is required, but her needs are not comprehensive enough to warrant Level 3 supports. A functional behavior assessment is conducted. Breela, her mother, and her grandmother determine her goals for establishing and maintaining friendships. Family members and professionals agree to use a daily journal summarizing Breela's daily progress. Entries made by everyone (including Breela, who is quite verbal) create communication between school and home. The team agrees on the following strategies. More opportunities will be provided for Breela to co-operate with peers on classroom assignments. Practical aspects of friendship and respect will be addressed in the classroom as curricular content. Breela will be in-structed on replacement behaviors for being bossy and demanding. Also, Breela will use self-monitoring to track her success. All members of the team will gen-uinely praise Breela when she is engaged in behavior that addresses her goals. Directed efforts will be made to help Breela continue the friendships she has made at school through visits at home and outings in the community, such as going to the movies and having sleepovers.

### Reflective Moment

The team will genuinely praise Breela when she is engaged in behavior that ad-dresses her goals. What, in your view, might be the difference for Breela between genuine and disingenuous praise?

How might the daily journal of progress be used effectively? Should some structure be used to facilitate entries, and if so, what should it be?

## SUMMARY

The purpose of this chapter is to introduce the philosophical and theoreti-cal bases for and overview of the history, current status, and future direc-tions and practices associated with family–professional partnerships in a variety of educational environments for children and youth from infancy through high school. Specifically, the goal has been to set the stage for how a partnership with families is integral to successful use of positive be-havior support for children who have challenging behaviors. Partnering with families is a theme that will be carried out in the remainder of the chapters in this text. Views of how parents and families can and should be participants and partners have been influenced in part by the reforms that have occurred in general education and in special education, resulting in what is referred to as unified systems reform. Joyce Epstein's model of six levels of parent involvement has been very influential in the development of general education policies and practices related to parent partnerships. An example of this is found in the standards promoted by the National Parent Teacher Association (Figure 2–2). Reforms in special education spe-cific to parents and families have followed the course described in Table 2–1 and have been promoted by federal legislation beginning in 1975. In particular, the 1986 passage of Part H of Public Law 99-457 (now Part C of IDEA), Early Intervention for Infants, Toddlers, and Their Families, and its subsequent reauthorizations, has brought into focus family empowerment and family-centered supports and services. Indeed, one of the challenges that professionals and families continue to face is the nature of the parents' and families' roles as children with special needs transition from early intervention into preschool environments.

This chapter has defined the various terms associated with the relationships we desire as professionals related to parents and families, including alliance, partnership, empowerment, collaboration, parent involvement and participation, and family centered. As a professional, whether one is a general educator, special educator, early interventionist, therapist, caregiver, counselor, psychologist, or otherwise, it is important to believe that a part of one's mission is to establish and maintain a partnership arrangement with parents and families and to carry out that partnership through ongoing collaboration (activities and actions). As a result of this partnership and collaboration, the professional will build a reliable alliance with parents and families. From collaboration and alliance will come increased empowerment (ability to get needs met) for both professionals and the parents and families with whom they partner. The approach that is employed will tend to be either that of parent involvement and participation (child focused and possibly emphasizing parents more than the family as a whole) or family centered (family focused and emphasizing the family unit and its needs, strengths, routines, and goals). Professionals have eight obligations (Turnbull & Turnbull, 2001) for achieving a reliable alliance, including knowing yourself, knowing families, honoring diversity, affirming and building of family strengths, promoting family choices, envisioning great expectations, practicing positive communication, and warranting trust and respect.

Special education as a discipline and profession, and specifically the area of applied behavior analysis and intervention for children with challenging behavior, has experienced over the past 10 or so years a paradigm shift. Where special educators historically might have thought in terms of the parents (and maybe, in particular, the mother), now they are more likely to view the family as a unit. Where special educators historically might have seen parents as the recipients of training in content determined by the professionals and intended to foster generalization of behaviors into the home setting, now they are more likely to see themselves as in a partnership in which they learn, teach, and share. Where special educators historically might have viewed parent involvement in a more formalized, legalistic way, they are now less likely to be adversarial and more inclined to view families as collaborators, allies, and partners. And finally, professionals are more focused on interventions that meet the criteria of supporting children with disabilities and their families to be self-determining, to function in the community as a whole, and to have a richer lifestyle.

## ACTIVITIES TO EXTEND YOUR LEARNING

1. Interview a respected teacher in your community's school system. Ask about the teacher's plan for parent involvement, what they have found useful, and how their ideas have been developed and refined over time. This could be a general education teacher, a special education teacher, an early interventionist, or a professional from a related discipline.

2. Make arrangements to attend a local meeting of a parent and family organization, such as the school PTA or an advocacy group for children with special needs. Listen to the content of the meeting and attempt to relate what happens in the meeting to the types of involvement and the issues introduced in this chapter.

3. In pairs or small groups in class, study the vignettes provided in this chapter. Identify the ways in which obligations for an alliance and levels of participation are addressed as they are described. Then brainstorm additional potential levels of participation and connections with the obligation for a reliable alliance.

## FURTHER READING AND EXPLORATION

1. This chapter has emphasized the work of Ann and Rud Turnbull and their colleagues related to partnerships and collaboration (building a reliable alliance) with families of children with special needs. Do a literature search to see what you can find out about how the Turnbulls' personal and professional experiences have influenced their ideas on partnerships and their contributions to the literature. You might want to visit the Web site of The Beach Center on Families and Disability at http://www.beachcenter.org.

2. The magazine *Exceptional Parent* recently celebrated its 30th anniversary. Take a look at some sample copies of the magazine. In particular look at the "Editorial Mission" and how the magazine has historically and currently presented the topic of the relationships between professionals and families. How has terminology and emphases changed over time? Do you see any connections between articles found in the magazine and topics introduced in this chapter? Visit the magazine's Web site at http://www.eparent.com.

3. For a focus on early childhood development, at-risk very young children and families, family-centered approaches, and descriptions of models of support and parent training, see the Bulletin of *Zero to Three: National Center for Infants, Toddlers, and Families* at http://www.zerotothree.org. In particular, look for examples of how family-centered approaches have been successfully used with young children at risk and with culturally diverse families.

4. Visit the Web site of the National PTA at http://www.pta.org, review their resources, and get access to a copy of the National Standards for Parent/Family Involvement Programs.

## REFERENCES

Allington, R., & McGill-Franzen, A. (1992). Unintended effects of educational reform in New York. *Educational Policy, 6,* 397–414.

Anderson, C. M., & Freeman, K. A. (2000). Positive behavior support: Expanding the application of applied behavior analysis. *The Behavior Analyst, 23,* 85–94.

Assistance to States for the Education of Children with Disabilities and the Early Intervention Program for Infants and Toddlers with Disabilities: Final Regulations, 64 Fed. Reg. 12, 406–12, 672 (1999). Washington, DC: Department of Education.

Baker, M. J. (2000). Incorporating the thematic ritualistic behaviors of children with autism into games: Increasing social play interactions with siblings. *Journal of Positive Behavior Interventions, 2*(2), 66–84.

Barr, M. W. (1913). *Mental defectives: Their history, treatment, and training.* Philadelphia: Blakiston.

Bengtson, V. L. (2001). Beyond the nuclear family: The increasing importance of multigenerational bonds. *Journal of Marriage and Family, 63,* 1–16.

Bracey, G. W. (2000). The 10th Bracey report on the condition of public education. *Phi Delta Kappan, 82,* 133–144.

Bricker, D., Pretti-Frontczak, K., & McComas, N. (1998). *An activity-based approach to early intervention.* Baltimore Paul H. Brookes.

*Brown v. Board of Education,* 347 U.S. 483 (1954).

Delaney, E. M., & Kaiser, A. P. (2001). The effects of teaching parents blended communication and behavior support strategies. *Behavioral Disorders, 26*(2), 93–116.

Education for All Handicapped Children Act of 1975, 20 U.S.C. § 1401 *et seq.*

Epstein, J. L. (1995, May). School/family/community partnerships: Caring for the children we share. *Phi Delta Kappan, 76,* 701–712.

Epstein, J. L., & Sanders, M. G. (2002). Family, school, and community partnerships. In M. H. Bornstein (Ed.), *Handbook of parenting: Vol. 5. Practical issues in parenting* (2nd ed., pp. 407–437), Mahwah, NJ: Lawrence Erlbaum Associates.

Fisher, C. (2000). Ripple or tidal wave: What can make a difference? *Journal of Positive Behavior Interventions, 2*(2), 120–122.

Fox, L., Vaughn, B. J., Dunlap, G., & Bucy, M. (1997). Parent-professional partnership in behavioral support: A qualitative analysis of one family's experience. *Journal of The Association for Persons with Severe Handicaps, 22*(4), 198–207.

Goetz, L. (1997). Introduction to the special section: Parent-professional partnerships and behavior supports. *Journal of the Association for Persons with Severe Handicaps, 22*(4), 185.

Hannigan, I. (1998). *Off to school: A parent's-eye view of the kindergarten year.* Washington, DC: National Association for the Education of Young Children.

Hargreaves, A. (2001). Beyond anxiety and nostalgia: Building a social movement for educational change. *Phi Delta Kappan, 82,* 373–377.

Henderson, A. T. (1987). *The evidence continues to grow.* Columbia, MD: National Committee for Citizens in Education.

Henderson, A. T., & Berla, N. (1995). *A new generation of evidence: The family is critical to student achievement.* Washington, DC: Center for Law and Education.

Hunt, J. (Ed.). (1972). *Human intelligence.* New Brunswick, NJ: Transaction Books.

Individuals with Disabilities Education Act (IDEA), 20 U.S.C. § 1400 *et seq.*

Kerzner-Lipsky, D., & Gartner, A. (1994). Inclusion: What it is, what it is not and why it matters. *Exceptional Parent, 24*(10), 36–38.

Kleinhammer-Tramill, J., & Gallagher, K. (2001). The implications of goals 2000 for inclusive education. In W. Sailor (Ed.), *Inclusive education and school/community partnerships.* New York: Teachers College Press.

Lucyshyn, J. M., Blumberg, E. R., & Kayser, A. T. (2000). Improving the quality of support to families of children with severe behavior problems in the first decade of the new millennium. *Journal of Positive Behavior Interventions, 2*(2), 113–115.

Martin, G., & Pear, J. (1999). *Behavior modification—What it is and how to do it* (6th ed.). Upper Saddle River, NJ: Merrill/Prentice Hall.

McLaughlin, M. L. (1998). *Special education in an era of school reform: An overview.* Washington, DC: Federal Resource Center, Academy for Educational Development.

McWilliam, R. A. (1992). *Family-centered intervention planning: A routines-based approach.* Tucson, AZ: Communication Skill Builders.

*Mills v. Board of Education of the District of Columbia,* 348 F. Supp. 866 (D.D.C. 1972).

National Commission on Excellence in Education. (1983). *A nation at risk: The imperative for educational reform.* Washington, DC: U.S. Government Printing Office.

National PTA. (1998). *National standards for parent/family involvement programs.* Chicago: Author.

*Pennsylvania Association for Retarded Citizens (PARC) v. Commonwealth of Pennsylvania,* 343 F. Supp. 279 (E.D. Pa. 1972).

Popenoe, D. (1996). *Life without father: Compelling new evidence that fatherhood and marriage are indispensable for the good of children and society.* New York: Free Press.

Richey, D. D., & Wheeler, J. J. (2000). *Inclusive early childhood education: Merging positive behavioral supports, activity-based intervention and developmentally appropriate practice.* Albany, NY: Delmar/Thomson Learning.

Rose, L. C., & Gallup, A. M. (2000). The 32nd annual Phi Delta Kappa/Gallup poll of the public's attitudes toward the public schools. *Phi Delta Kappan, 82,* 41–66.

Safer, N. D., & Hamilton, J. L. (1993). Legislative context for early intervention services. In W. Brown, S. K. Thurman, & L. F. Pearl (Eds.), *Family-centered early intervention with infants and toddlers: Innovative cross-disciplinary approaches* (pp. 1–17). Baltimore: Paul H. Brookes.

Sandall, S., & Ostrosky, M. (Eds.). (2000). Natural environments and inclusion. *Young Exceptional Children Monograph Series No. 2.* Denver, CO: The Division for Early Childhood of the Council for Exceptional Children.

Santelli, B., Poyadue, F. S., & Young J. L. (2001). *The parent to parent handbook: Connecting families of children with special needs.* Baltimore: Paul H. Brookes.

Sileo, T. W., & Prater, M. A. (1998). Creating classroom environments that address the linguistic and cultural backgrounds of students with disabilities:

An Asian Pacific American perspective. *Remedial and Special Education, 19,* 323–337.

Sileo, T. W., Sileo, A. P., & Prater, M. A. (1996). Parents and professional partnerships in special education: Multicultural considerations. *Intervention in School and Clinic, 3,* 145–153.

Silverstein, R. (1989). A window of opportunity: P.L. 99-457. In *The intent and spirit of P.L. 99-457: A sourcebook* (pp. A1–A7). Washington, DC: National Center for Clinical Infant Programs.

Stichter, J. P., & Caldicott, J. M. (1999). Families, school collaboration, and shared vision in the context of IDEA. *Journal of Positive Behavior Interventions, 1,* 252–255.

Sugai, G., Horner, R. H., Dunlap, G., Hieneman, M., Lewis, T. J., Nelson, C. M., et al. (2000). Applying positive behavior support and functional behavioral assessment in schools. *Journal of Positive Behavior Interventions, 2*(3), 131–143.

Turnbull, A. P., & Turnbull, H. R. (2000). Achieving "rich" lifestyles. *Journal of Positive Behavior Interventions, 2*(3), 190–192.

Turnbull, A. P., & Turnbull H. R. (2001). *Families, professionals and exceptionality: Collaboration for empowerment* (4th ed.). Upper Saddle River, NJ: Merrill/Prentice Hall.

Vanderwood, M., McGrew, K. S., & Ysseldyke, J. E. (1998). Why we can't say much about students with disabilities during education reform. *Exceptional Children, 64,* 359–370.

Vaughn, B. J., Dunlap, G., Fox, L., Clarke, S., & Bucy, M. (1997). Parent-professional partnership in behavioral support: A case study of community-based intervention. *Journal of the Association for Persons with Severe Handicaps, 22*(4), 186–197.

Wehmeyer, M. L., Martin, J. E., & Sands, D. J. (1998). Self-determination for children and youth with developmental disabilities. In A. Hilton & R. Ringlaben (Eds.), *Best and promising practices in developmental disabilities* (pp. 191–204). Austin, TX: PRO-ED.

Winzer, M. A. (1993). *History of special education from isolation to integration.* Washington, DC: Gallaudet Press.

Yell, M. L. (1998). *The law and special education.* Upper Saddle River, NJ: Merrill/Prentice Hall.

Ysseldyke, J. E. (2001). Reflections on a research career: Generalizations from 25 years of research on assessment and instructional decision making. *Exceptional Children, 67,* 295–309.

Ysseldyke, J. E., & Bielinski, J. S. (2000). *Factors leading to misinterpretation of trends in the large-scale test performance of students with disabilities.* Minneapolis: University of Minnesota, National Center on Educational Outcomes.

# Chapter 3

# Ensuring Ethical Practices in the Delivery of Positive Behavior Supports

## CONCEPTS TO UNDERSTAND

*After reading this chapter, you should be able to:*

- Define ethics and ethical conduct
- List and describe the nine organizing themes for understanding ethical practices
- Understand accepted standards of ethical conduct
- Understand the unique position of positive behavior supports within an ethical framework
- Evaluate the extent to which behavior interventions are consistent with ethical standards of conduct
- Compare and contrast different professional organizations' standards for ethical conduct

## KEY TERMS

Ethical conduct

Ethics

Person-centered planning

Quality of life

Self-determination

What are ethics and what does it mean to engage in ethical behavior? And what guidance do we as professionals have and use to hold us accountable to ethical practices in our service to children and their families as we plan, implement, and evaluate positive behavior supports? These are the fundamental questions that will be addressed in this chapter. For our purposes, **ethics** are defined as the principles of conduct governing us as individual professionals as well as our particular group or discipline. Whether it is general education, special education, counseling, psychology, the various therapy disciplines, or related areas, there are established principles of conduct that govern ethics. To be ethical as a professional means to conform to accepted professional standards of conduct. You might ask yourself, given your current status with regard to professional development and preparation to be licensed in your discipline and specialty area(s), to what extent are you familiar with the ethical standards of your discipline? Have you taken courses in which ethics were addressed in a substantive manner, either more generally or specific to education and special education? If not, are you aware of a point in your preparation where you will get such a focus? To what extent do your professors and the textbooks used in your classes include ethical standards, guidelines, and practices? Is it simply assumed that textbooks would not include, nor would professors advocate, theories, beliefs, or practices that are unethical?

When you participate in field experiences and other professional development activities, are the standards governing ethical conduct obvious in some manner (e.g., posted somewhere or included in a procedural or policy handbook)? Children with special needs are typically served by at least two and frequently three or more professionals whose disciplines have produced standards or codes of ethical conduct. Do you have an understanding of what those standards might be and the extent to which they are complimentary or possibly incongruent? Of course, much of our focus in this text is on children and youth who have difficult and challenging behavior and who would benefit from positive behavior supports in order to enhance their skills, achievement, self-determination, and inclusion. One might argue that it is especially important to know and adhere to ethical standards of conduct when serving children and youth with challenging behavior and when partnering with their families and other professionals. This is true because there is such a wide variance impacted by factors such as cultural and societal values, religious beliefs, personal beliefs, upbringing and parenting models, theoretical perspectives, and other factors.

In this chapter we will examine the ethical standards governing our professional conduct specifically related to applying positive behavior supports across a variety of educational environments. To do this, we must understand what professional organizations and learned societies believe and advocate with regard to influencing behavior, so we will study content provided by the National Education Association (NEA), the Learning First Alliance, the National Association for the Education of Young Children (NAEYC), the Division for Early Childhood of the Council for Exceptional Children, the Council for Exceptional Children (CEC), and especially the

Subdivision Council for Children with Behavioral Disorders (CCBD) and ethical standards provided by other organizations.

Turnbull and Turnbull (2001) describe how educational systems reform in the future is likely to be unified rather than done with special education and general education on isolated and separate tracks. We might assume that codes and standards of **ethical conduct** will also begin to be somewhat unified. Beyond understanding accepted standards, you will be provided a framework for understanding the elements required in meeting standards and evaluating the extent to which behavior interventions are consistent with ethical standards of conduct. This framework of nine organizing themes will be used to examine relatedness among various sources.

In Chapter 1 the reader was introduced to the primary theoretical models that have been, and continue to be, used to explain human behavior. One useful way to think of ethics and ethical standards in education is to view them as the connector between theory and practice. That is, standards of conduct are outgrowths of one's theoretical point of view, but they also provide at least in a general sense guidance for our practices—what we should and should not do as professionals (e.g., teaching, intervening, playing, and providing therapy). In this chapter we are especially interested in ethical considerations as they apply to behavior theory and the positive behavior support practices with which they are associated (e.g., antecedent-based intervention, functional assessment, behavior support plans, and positive, consequence-based interventions, and evaluation of plans). However, in order to achieve this goal it is necessary for us to overview some of the major professional organizations' statements of ethical conduct and to make some comparisons among them.

## NINE ORGANIZING THEMES FOR UNDERSTANDING ETHICAL PRACTICES

Nine major themes occur as we look at the ethical standards of professional behavior provided by the various professional organizations introduced later. Historically, the preparation of special educators, general educators, and other school personnel (e.g., school psychologists and counselors) in preservice programs has been rather isolated and distinctly separate. That isolation was, of course, reflected in the way we delivered services to children with special needs (with emotional and behavior difficulties or otherwise) in various school environments. Over the past several decades, we have moved toward more inclusive education practices.

Programs preparing teachers and other school personnel have begun to reflect more collaborative approaches and shared content. Standards of ethical behavior have been developed in some respects to reflect the lack of shared philosophy and practice. As we consider ethical standards provided by the organizations included herein, we need to take into account the congruence, or lack of congruence, among them, specifically related to what they have to say regarding how to influence the behavior of children and

FIGURE 3–1
*Nine Organizing
Themes for
Understanding
Ethical Practices*

- Each student as an *individual human being has worth and dignity*, despite the nature or severity of his troubling behavior.
- The *behavior* of children and youth (challenging and otherwise) always *reflects a need*. People respond out of need, and all behavior serves a function.
- Systematic and thoughtful management of learning environments and understanding of individual differences and uniqueness will serve to *prevent* some challenging behaviors. And *early intervention* will serve to prevent or lessen the severity of many challenging behaviors.
- Families, children, and youth should be central to all aspects of PBS, including *active participation* in planning, implementing, and evaluating interventions.
- The uniqueness of children and youth, as reflected by their *family's diversity* (race, ethnicity, religion, and culture) should be taken into account in understanding behavior and responding to challenging behavior.
- Natural environments and *inclusive settings are desirable* for children and youth with troubling and challenging behavior, but school personnel must assume ownership in those settings, and a full continuum of services and settings should be available.
- *Natural and logically occurring consequences* are preferable to extraneous and contrived reward systems, in order to foster self-discipline, independence, and self-determination.
- Behavior interventions should be *positive* and should not include corporal punishment or other punitive measures.
- Actions taken by professionals to either suppress undesirable behavior or to foster desired behavior of children and youth should be associated with meaningful and *functional* attitudes and skills and should be positively related to *quality of life*.

youth. Beyond the degree of congruence, we can relate the various standards to the following themes in terms of emphasis and specificity. Nine organizing themes are presented in Figure 3–1.

Much has been written, especially over the past three decades, about rights of children and youth and ethical conduct in the provision of services to them. It is not our purpose here to undertake an historical review of that literature. It is important that you know that this body of research and writing exists, and it may be seen on a continuum from very broad descriptions of the rights of all children and youth as reflected in social policy to the rights of children and youth, with comprehensive disabilities to specific types of behavior treatment. For example, Garfinkel, Hochschild, and McLanahan (1996), as a outgrowth of the proceedings of the Social Policies for Children conference held at the Woodrow Wilson School of Public and International Affairs at Princeton University in May 1994, suggest that children have rights, which social policy should reflect, in seven arenas, including child care, schooling, transition to work, health care, income security, physical security, and child abuse. Ethics and ethical conduct in the delivery of positive behavior supports will certainly have a beneficial impact on most of these arenas.

At the other end of the continuum, we might consider the position advocated by several of the prominent leaders in applied behavior analysis (Van Houten et al., 1988) at the point in history when the applied behavior analytic approach was being refined and for many restructured to become positive behavior supports. They suggest that individuals in need of behavior interventions have six rights, including a therapeutic environment, services whose overriding goal is personal welfare, treatment by a competent behavior analyst, programs that teach functional skills, behavior assessment and ongoing evaluation, and the most effective treatment procedures available. It may seem challenging to find a fit between two such seemingly disparate statements, but they both provide important guidance about how we as professionals should understand our ethical responsibilities related to children and youth. The point here is that the work that has been done in understanding children's rights, more generally their societal well-being and specifically their rights to helpful responses to their challenging behaviors, is relevant and important as we consider ethical standards and practices in educational environments. Again, these are just two of many ways in which children's rights have been summarized, but you might consider their fit with some of the ethical positions introduced and discussed following. These organization and association ethical perspectives reflect a broader focus on the rights of children in the United States.

## CODES, STANDARDS, AND PRINCIPLES OF PROFESSIONAL GROUPS

Professional organizations and associations in education provide information, support, guidance, and leadership to their members and opportunities for participation through various means of communication, including journals, newsletters, Web sites, and conferences. One central function of these groups is to develop, disseminate, and revise ethical codes of professional conduct that reflect their mission and the standards, beliefs, values, and principles of their organization. These standards provide guidance to teachers and other practitioners as they carry out their professional responsibilities in educating and intervening with children and youth and in working with their families. For purposes of this chapter, some of the most prominent and influential groups have been included. The National Education Association (NEA), the Learning First Alliance (LFA), the Council for Exceptional Children (CEC), the Council for Children with Behavioral Disorders (CCBD), the National Association for the Education of Young Children (NAEYC), and the Division for Early Childhood (DEC) of the Council for Exceptional Children are all introduced in the following pages, and their positions of ethical standards, beliefs, values and principles are considered. Certainly there are a number of associations and organizations that could have been included here but have not been, given constraints of space and scope.

## National Education Association

The National Education Association (NEA) has a membership of more than 2.5 million members who work at various levels of education. NEA was founded in 1857 and is the "largest and oldest organization committed to advancing the cause of public education" (National Education Association [NEA], n.d., para. 1). NEA has considerable influence at the local, state, national, and international levels in all aspects of public education. Many of you may expect to be NEA members as you enter the profession as educators from preschool through university environments or may already hold student membership. In 1975 the NEA (1975) adopted *The Code of Ethics of the Education Profession*. The Code was intended to be the standard by which to judge the professional conduct of its members. See Figure 3–2 for the Preamble to the Code.

Although the Preamble (Figure 3–2) does not provide any specific guidance related to ethical conduct of educators and the behavior of children and youth (students), it does include wording that is important as a foundation for the standards that we consider later in this chapter. Specifically, the phrases, "believing in the worth and dignity of each human being" (i.e., presumably including those with disabilities and/or challenging behavior), "guarantee of equal educational opportunity for all," and "desire for the respect and confidence of students," all seem relevant as we think about our responsibilities related to problematic and challenging behavior.

Two overriding Principles (I: Commitment to Students and II: Commitment to the Profession) with associated standards are the essence of the NEA Code of Ethics. Principle I states that "the educator strives to help each student realize her potential as a worthy and effective member of society." Eight standards are provided under Principle I, and they are presented in Figure 3–3.

**FIGURE 3–2**
*Preamble: NEA Code of Ethics of the Education Profession*

The educator, believing in the worth and dignity of each human being, recognizes the supreme importance of the pursuit of truth, devotion to excellence, and the nurture of the democratic principles. Essential to these goals is the protection of freedom to learn and to teach and the guarantee of equal educational opportunity for all. The educator accepts the responsibility to adhere to the highest ethical standards.

The educator recognizes the magnitude of the responsibility inherent in the teaching process. The desire for the respect and confidence of one's colleagues, of students, of parents, and of the members of the community provides the incentive to attain and maintain the highest possible degree of ethical conduct. The *Code of Ethics of the Education Profession* indicates the aspiration of all educators and provides standards by which to judge conduct.

*Source:* National Education Association (1975). *Code of ethics of the education profession.* Retrieved January 19, 2002, from http://www.nea.org/aboutnea/code.html

**FIGURE 3–3**
*NEA Code of Ethics: Principle I Commitment to Student Standards of Ethical Conduct*

In fulfillment of the obligation to the student, the educator—

1. Shall not unreasonably restrain the student from independent action in the pursuit of learning.
2. Shall not unreasonably deny the student's access to varying points of view.
3. Shall not deliberately suppress or distort subject matter relevant to the student's progress.
4. Shall make reasonable effort to protect the student from conditions harmful to learning or to health and safety.
5. Shall not intentionally expose the student to embarrassment or disparagement.
6. Shall not on the basis of race, color, creed, sex, national origin, marital status, political or religious beliefs, family, social or cultural background, or sexual orientation, unfairly—
   a. Exclude any student from participation in any program,
   b. Deny benefits to any student, or
   c. Grant any advantage to any student.
7. Shall not use professional relationships with students for private advantage.
8. Shall not disclose information about students obtained in the course of professional service unless disclosure serves a compelling professional purpose or is required by law.

*Source:* National Education Association (1975). *Code of ethics of the education profession.* Retrieved January 19, 2002, from http://www.nea.org/aboutnea/code.html

Again, these standards do not specifically address student behavior; however, they may be taken as a start point or foundation for educators. More recently the National Education Association passed a number of resolutions as a part of the process of upgrading and refining their position. One of those resolutions is of particular interest to us here. Resolution B-52 Discipline (NEA, n.d.) includes the following statement:

The National Education Association believes that a safe and orderly environment, in which students are treated with dignity, will provide them with a positive learning experience. Effective disciplinary procedures enhance high expectations and quality instruction, thereby promoting self-control and responsible behavior in students while ensuring the right of all students to due process and an orderly learning environment. (para. 1)

Additionally, the B-52 Discipline resolution states that the Association "promotes the study, development, and funding of a variety of effective disciplinary procedures," "policies and standards that provide the necessary administrative support to education employees for the maintenance of a positive, safe school environment," and "condemns the misuse of discipline as a means of excluding students from the school setting until other means of behavior intervention have been exhausted." Also included in this specific resolution, as well as in other information provided by the National

Education Association, it is made clear that NEA does not believe that corporal punishment should be used as a means of disciplining students (see Web site listings in Figure 3–10).

## Learning First Alliance

The Learning First Alliance was founded in 1997. It is a partnership of 12 leading educational associations who have the shared mission of coming together to improve the learning of students in the United States' public elementary and secondary schools. The Alliance addresses three major goals (Learning First Alliance, n.d., para. 5). The goals are "to ensure that high academic expectations are held for all students; ensure a safe and supportive place of learning for all students, and engage parents and other community members in helping students achieve high academic expectations." Member organizations include the American Association of Colleges for Teacher Education, the American Association of School Administrators, the American Federation of Teachers, the Association for Supervision and Curriculum Development, the Council of Chief State School Officers, the Education Commission of the States, the National Association of Elementary School Principals, the National Association of Secondary School Principals, the National Association of State Boards of Education, the National Education Association, the National Parent Teacher Association, and the National School Boards Association. In 2001 the Alliance published a guide (Learning First Alliance, 2001), endorsed and supported by each of the twelve partners, entitled *Every Child Learning: Safe and Supportive Schools*. In this document four core elements of safe and supportive learning communities, along with associated recommendations, are presented. The four core elements are (a) a supportive learning community; (b) systematic approaches to supporting safety and positive behavior; (c) involvement of families, students, school staff, and the surrounding community; and (d) standards and measures to support continuous improvement based on data.

It is reasonable, although these are not stated as codes of ethical behavior and conduct, to treat and use the core elements published by the Learning First Alliance as such. Of course, of particular interest here is the information provided in the second core element–systematic approaches to supporting safety and positive behavior. Each of the four elements is seen as connected to desired outcomes focused on preventing and/or reducing aggressiveness, violence, delinquency, and drug and alcohol use; increasing social competence and positive behavior; increasing concern for others; improving connection to school and educational aspirations; and improving academic motivation and achievement. It is interesting and encouraging to many professionals to note that these desired outcomes are broad based with regard to the role of schooling and not narrowly limited to academic performance. Major points addressed in Core Element 2: Systematic Approaches to Supporting Safety and Positive Behavior, in particular those most relevant to the provision of positive behavior supports to children and youth who exhibit challenging behavior, are presented in Figure 3–4.

*Schoolwide approaches to improving school climate, safety, and discipline*

Communicate a clear, simple positive message about what students must do to be successful, contributing members of the school.

The rules should be revisited and revised as needed.

The rules should not apply to students alone.

It is important to create an atmosphere in which civility, order, and decorum are the norms and antisocial behavior such as bullying, intimidation, and taunting are unacceptable.

School staff must model and reinforce norms and rules.

The emphasis on rules and norms is particularly important at the beginning of the school year, when staff and students can focus systematically on identifying common behavior problems and helping students identify appropriate alternative behaviors.

Rules should be fairly and consistently enforced according to clearly communicated guidelines.

Students and families should play a central role in determining school rules and how they are communicated and enforced.

All students should have opportunity to learn and practice sound decision making and positive approaches to getting along with others.

*Orderly and focused classrooms*

They are best achieved by actively nurturing students' emerging ability to manage themselves.

Celebrate the success of students who meet behavior expectations.

Explicitly teach clear expectations and routines.

Tend to the arrangement of the physical environment, such as classroom seating and traffic patterns.

Clear rules must be coupled with clear and consistent consequences for violations.

Harsh and punitive discipline styles tend to elicit student resentment and resistance and damage relationships.

Excessive punishment focuses the child on the punishment itself and ways to escape it, rather than on recognizing the behavior that evoked the punishment and understanding why the behavior was inappropriate or harmful.

Teacher should focus on recognizing, celebrating and rewarding appropriate behavior.

*A continuum of supports for the few students who need them*

All schools should have in place mechanisms for early identification, quick and appropriate early interventions, and intensive interventions for troubled or violent students.

Schools should offer a range of services for improving the behavior of students who consistently and significantly misbehave.

To the degree possible, parents and students should be enlisted as active participants in a process of correcting and changing behavior.

In severe cases, an alternative setting within the school or in a separate alternative school is necessary.

Students who bring lethal weapons or illegal drugs to school, or who commit serious, violent assaults against others, should be suspended or expelled.

Effective alternative programs include positive behavior supports, caring staff, mental health services, active family involvement, and the involvement of relevant community agencies.

*Source:* Learning First Alliance (LFA) (2001). *Every child learning: Safe and supportive schools.* Retrieved January 28, 2002 from http://www.learningfirst.org

Several things are particularly noteworthy as we think about the basic tenants summarized in Figure 3–4. One central reason why they are significant is that they reflect agreement among the 12 partnering organizations, which represent the majority of the professional constituency of public education in the United States. Of course, none of the member organizations would have agreed to statements inconsistent with their standards and ethics. There is substantial attention given to the school's role in addressing behavior issues of all students and doing so in a positive way with a focus on prevention, early intervention, student participation, and family involvement. And positive behavior support is specifically identified as a desirable and effective approach.

## The Council for Exceptional Children

The Council for Exceptional Children (CEC) is the primary professional organization for special educators. The mission of the CEC (Council for Exceptional Children [CEC], n.d.) was adopted by the CEC Delegate Assembly in April 1995 and is as follows:

> . . . [T]o improve educational outcomes for individuals with exceptionalities. CEC, a non-profit association, accomplishes its mission which is carried out in support of special education professionals and others working on behalf of individuals with exceptionalities, by advocating for appropriate governmental policies, by setting professionals standards, by providing continuing professional development, by advocating for newly and historically underserved individuals with exceptionalities, and by helping professionals achieve the conditions and resources for effective professional practice. (para. 1–2)

As an international organization that had its beginning in 1922, the CEC has grown to a membership in 2002 of more than 52,000 persons who share an interest in the education of individuals with exceptionalities. Although membership is international, the majority of the members are in the United States and in the Canadian Council for Exceptional Children. CEC currently has 17 divisions providing a structure for members to address more specifically particular exceptionalities or phases of special education. The CEC provides a number of services, many with which the reader may be familiar. Journals (including *Exceptional Children* and *Teaching Exceptional Children*), newsletters, numerous other publications from CEC and its divisions, conventions and conferences, and other professional development opportunities and information services, such as the Educational Resources Information Center (ERIC) Clearinghouse on Disabilities (see Web site listing in Figure 3–10) are provided through CEC. All of the advocacy efforts, publications, and other supports provided through the CEC may be assumed to be largely consistent with and reflective of its ethical code.

On April 16, 1983, the CEC Delegate Assembly adopted the CEC Code of Ethics (CEC, n.d.). The following are several statements that introduce the Code:

We declare the following principles to be the Code of Ethics for educators of persons with exceptionalities. Members of the special education profession are responsible for upholding and advancing these principles. Members of the CEC agree to judge and be judged by them in accordance with the spirit and provisions of this Code. Special education professionals are committed to developing the highest educational and quality of life potential of individuals with exceptionalities. (para. 1–2)

Presented in Figure 3–5 are the seven original ethical principles of the CEC Code of Ethics.

In 1997, 14 years after the passage by the Delegate Assembly of the original CEC Code of Ethics, a revision of the Code was published (CEC, n.d.). This revision is entitled the *CEC Code of Ethics for Educators of Persons with Exceptionalities.* Standards were provided to extend the ethical statements. The standards document is entitled *CEC Standards for Professional Practice Professionals in Relation to Persons with Exceptionalities and Their Families.* It is interesting that only two changes were made in the Code, one having to do with a wording change to reflect person-first language. Statement ii was changed from "exceptional individuals" to "individuals with exceptionalities." The second change was the addition of an eighth statement, which is listed as the first one on the revised Code. It is "Special education professionals are committed to developing the highest educational and quality of life potential of individuals with exceptionalities."

Although it is noteworthy that the CEC Code has stood the test of time, given that a great deal happened in the special education discipline during

**FIGURE 3–5**
*Council for Exceptional Children Code of Ethics*

i. Special education professionals promote and maintain a high level of competence and integrity in practicing their profession.

ii. Special education professionals engage in professional activities which benefit exceptional individuals, their families, other colleagues, students, or research subjects.

iii. Special education professionals exercise objective professional judgment in the practice of their profession.

iv. Special education professionals strive to advance their knowledge and skills regarding the education of individuals with exceptionalities.

v. Special education professionals work within the standards and policies of their profession.

vi. Special education professionals seek to uphold and improve where necessary the laws, regulations, and policies governing the delivery of special education and related services and the practice of their profession.

vii. Special education professionals do not condone nor participate in unethical or illegal acts, or violate professional standards adopted by the Delegate Assembly of CEC.

*Source:* Council for Exceptional Children (n.d.). *Code of ethics.* Retrieved January 29, 2002, from http://www.cec.sped.org/ab/purpose.html

the period 1983–1997, the added statement is very meaningful. It appears to suggest that we should have high expectations for the academic achievement of children and youth with disabilities and that we as professionals are ethically obligated to pay attention to the broader context of the lives of these students. Furthermore, it asks us to understand them as members of families and communities. We are obligated to take into account issues of self-determination, independence, and quality of life. Certainly this focus is very consistent with how we have come to understand the ethical applications of positive behavior supports and interventions.

The *CEC Standards of Professional Practice Professionals in Relation to Persons with Exceptionalities and Their Families* provides specific standards under five headings, including instructional responsibilities, management of behavior, and support procedures (i.e., the nature of expectations placed on special educators in such matters as the administration of medication, parent relationships, and advocacy). The standards of particular interest here are the ones associated with behavior management. The five behavior management standards are presented in Figure 3–6.

What are some of the main points that we might take from these five standards related to behavior management and special education? Certainly one might be that in the management of challenging behavior, professional special educators should see themselves as part of an interdisciplinary team, one that includes parents as valued members and equal partners on the team. Another point is that, without regard for the type or severity of the disability or the nature of the challenging behavior, the child is worthwhile

**FIGURE 3–6**
*CEC Standards for Professional Practice Professionals in Relation to Persons with Exceptionalities and Their Families—Behavior Management*

Special education professionals participate with other professionals and with parents in an interdisciplinary effort in the management of behavior. Professionals:

1. Apply only those disciplinary methods and behavior procedures which they have been instructed to use and which do not undermine the dignity of the individual or the basic human rights of persons with exceptionalities, such as corporal punishment.
2. Clearly specify the goals and objectives for behavior management practices in the IEPs of persons' with exceptionalities.
3. Conform to policies, statutes, and rules established by state/provincial and local agencies relating to judicious application of disciplinary methods and behavior procedures.
4. Take adequate measures to discourage, prevent, and intervene when a colleague's behavior is perceived as being detrimental to exceptional students.
5. Refrain from aversive techniques unless repeated trials of other methods have failed and only after consultation with parents and appropriate agency officials.

*Source:* Council for Exceptional Children (n.d.). *CEC Code of ethics and standards of practice.* Retrieved January 15, 2002, from http://www.cec.sped.org/ps/code.html

and her or his dignity is maintained in the selection and application of behavior management approaches. Behavior management is individualized as reflected by the individualized education program (IEP), so what applies to one child may not apply to another. Punitive and aversive techniques are ill advised and should be undertaken only in rare instances and with strict oversight. It might be useful for the reader to compare these five standards to the information provided so far in the chapter from other organizations that are not focused on children with special needs.

## Council for Children with Behavior Disorders

The Council for Children with Behavioral Disorders (CCBD) is one of the 17 divisions of the Council for Exceptional Children (CEC). According to the CCBD (Council for Children with Behavioral Disorders [CCBD], n.d., para. 1), a group of 13 members attended an organizational meeting in Columbus, Ohio, in 1962 to establish the CCBD. There were 200 members by the time they convened the following year at the 40th annual CEC convention held in Philadelphia. Within two years it had become the largest division of the CEC. It is estimated that the membership for CCBD was approximately 10,000 in 2002. The mission of the CCBD is, of course, to promote the education and welfare of children and youth with behavior and emotional disabilities. Their overriding goals are focused on promoting quality in services and programs, advocating, encouraging research and professional growth, disseminating information, providing support to professionals, reducing biases in the overrepresentation of some children, and promoting awareness and advocacy to foster collaborative relationships among families and professionals.

To accomplish its goals the CCBD undertakes a variety of activities similar to the ones detailed earlier in the description of their parent organization, the CEC. One of the activities of the CCBD is the periodic publication of position papers on topics of interest to professionals and advocates for children with emotional and behavior disorders. For the purposes of this chapter, two of these position papers are particularly relevant. The *Position Paper on School Discipline Policies for Students with Significantly Disruptive Behavior* (CCBD, 1990a) resulted in a recommendation that school districts "create flexible, unified school discipline policies." The position paper further recommends that "a committee of general and special educators should set about the task of creating a school discipline policy." It should be noted that there is an emphasis on a unified effort in which special and general educators collaborate and think about the following six content areas. To some extent the six content areas mesh with the information provided by and summarized previously from the NEA and the LFA. A school discipline policy should include (a) major discussion of the desired school climate, (b) behavior expectations necessary to achieve the climate, (c) instructional methods to teach the expectations, (d) responses taken to violations, (e) procedures that treat all students as individuals to implement those responses, and (f) required administrator records concerning the strategy selection.

A second paper published by the CCBD (1990b) entitled *Position Paper on Use of Behavior Reduction Strategies with Children with Behavioral Disorders* focuses on the appropriateness and usefulness of various procedures. Behavior reduction procedures are defined as "a continuum of strategies employed by practitioners to decelerate the rate or probability of behavior that is judged inappropriate in a particular situation." Seven procedures (defined and described at various points in this textbook) are covered in the position paper, including environmental modifications, differential reinforcement, response cost, time-out, overcorrection, aversive conditioning, and corporal punishment. The conclusions provided in the position paper include an acknowledgement that "progress has been made toward developing less aversive, intrusive, and restrictive alternatives for reducing behavior excesses of behavior disorder youngsters." The CCBD "advocates the continued development of more positive behavior reduction alternatives." Finally, the organization "does not sanction the use of corporal punishment, highly aversive, or non-empirically validated procedures for managing problem behaviors of children and youth with behavior disorders." Eight recommendations were produced as an outcome of the position paper (see Figure 3–7). Consider the preceding quotes and the recommendations in

**FIGURE 3–7**
*CCBD Recommendations for Using Behavior Reduction Procedures*

1. Practitioners planning to use these behavior reduction procedures, especially those involving more aversive, intrusive, or restrictive techniques, should obtain prior consent from the child's parents or legal guardians and from administrators, and clearance from human rights committees.
2. Practitioners should carefully analyze potential target behavior(s) and the factors associated with their occurrence before initiating behavior reduction procedures.
3. As a general rule, practitioners should implement and document the use of appropriate, less aversive, intrusive, or restrictive procedures prior to implementing other procedures.
4. Practitioners should develop and follow appropriate guidelines involved in using behavior reduction strategies.
5. Practitioners should develop and subsequently follow a plan detailing the behavior reduction procedure(s) to be used in a particular case.
6. Once aversive behavior reduction procedures are selected and approved, practitioners should select appropriate procedures for specific situations.
7. Persons responsible for carrying out behavior reduction procedures must be appropriately trained.
8. Practitioners should keep data on the efficacy of the behavior reduction procedures and should communicate these in regularly scheduled staff/parent meetings.

*Source:* Council for Children with Behavioral Disorders (CCBD). (1990). *Position paper on use of behavior reduction strategies with children with behavioral disorders.* Retrieved January 30, 2002, from http://www.ccbd.net/

light of the fact that they are now more than 10 years old. This work was foundational in the movement over the past 10 years toward positive behavior supports.

## PREVENTION AND EARLY INTERVENTION

What ethical codes and standards of professional behavior exist that establish the necessity for prevention, early identification, and early intervention for young children who have or may develop challenging behaviors? Much of the literature related to programs, services, and interventions for children with behavior and emotional disabilities emphasizes the importance of prevention and early response to troublesome behavior. Chapter 4 of this textbook targets the importance of antecedent management as a means of preventing or minimizing challenging behaviors. To assist in understanding the guidance that is provided in this regard and to understand the related issues, two leading professional organizations should be considered. They are the National Association for the Education of Young Children (NAEYC) and the Division for Early Childhood (DEC) of the Council for Exceptional Children (CEC). Recently these two organizations have collaborated on a number of efforts aimed at recognizing and responding to their similarities and common purposes and needs, rather than a distinctness based on whether or not a young child has a disability. It will be important to examine later the shared values and standards specific to positive behavior supports.

### National Association for the Education of Young Children

"The National Association for the Education of Young Children (NAEYC) exists for the purpose of leading and consolidating the efforts of individuals and groups working to achieve healthy development and constructive education for all young children" (National Association for the Education of Young Children [NAEYC], n.d., para. 1). This is the mission statement provided by NAEYC. In 2001 NAEYC celebrated its 75th anniversary. The Association was founded in 1926 and has grown in membership, represented in 450 local, state, and regional affiliates, to over 100,000 members (103,000 members in 2000). NAEYC is the nation's largest and most influential organization focused on the educational, developmental, service, and program needs of children from birth through age eight. NAEYC has published an excellent resource detailing the history of the organization and some of its prominent leaders (NAEYC, 2001a).

NAEYC has a *Code of Ethical Conduct and Statement of Commitment* that was approved, following a five-year development process involving the membership, by the association's governing board in July 1989 (Feeney & Kipnis, 1998). Since that time, the Code has been through two revisions, one in 1992 and the second in 1997. Every five years the Code is reviewed for possible revision. The current version of the *Code of Ethical Conduct and*

*Statement of Commitment* is published in a brochure format from NAEYC. The NAEYC takes the position that a code of ethical conduct and its standards are based on core values, and they provide six such value statements. These are important because they are to a large extent aligned with statements found from other sources and organizations, and they can be readily connected to more specific ethical guidance policies that might be used for dealing with young children and used for responses in preventing or intervening young children's challenging behavior. NAEYC (Feeney & Kipnis, 1998) core values state the following:

We have committed ourselves to:

- Appreciating childhood as a unique and valuable stage of the human life cycle.
- Basing our work with children on knowledge of child development.
- Appreciating and supporting the close ties between the child and family.
- Recognizing that children are best understood and supported in the context of family, culture, community, and society.
- Respecting the dignity, worth, and uniqueness of each individual (child, family member, and colleague).
- Helping children and adults achieve their full potential in the context of relationships that are based on trust, respect, and positive regard (para. 2)

These NAEYC core values are followed in the Code by a description of professional responsibilities in four arenas, including (a) children, (b) families, (c) colleagues, and (d) community and society. Ethical responsibilities in each of the four arenas are divided into those that are ideals (aspirations) and those that are principles (guidance for resolving ethical dilemmas). Excerpts especially relevant to the consideration of positive behavior supports and challenging behavior of young children are provided in Figure 3–8. NAEYC has provided a useful document for understanding and applying all aspects of the Code (Feeney & Freeman, 1999).

In July 2001 the NAEYC Governing Board approved a revision of the *NAEYC Standards for Early Childhood Professional Preparation: Baccalaureate or Initial Licensure Level* (NAEYC, 2001b). These standards, which are intended to provide guidance in the development and implementation of preservice preparation of early childhood professionals, were developed in collaboration with several other professional organizations, including the Division for Early Childhood. In the introduction section of the revised NAEYC standards, it states

NAEYC works especially closely with the Division for Early Childhood of the Council for Exceptional Children to ensure that our standards complement and support one another, so that all early childhood teachers are well-prepared to teach young children with and without developmental delays or disabilities. (p. 2)

In fact, a significant reason for the revision of the standards from the prior version published in 1996 is the recognition that the context of early childhood education is rapidly changing—that early childhood educators have increasing opportunities for serving diverse children and in particular the inclusion of children with a variety of special needs and disabilities.

**FIGURE 3–8**
*Excerpts from the NAEYC Code of Ethical Conduct and Commitment*

Section I: Ethical responsibilities to children

*Ideals:*

I-1.2—To base program practices upon current knowledge in the field of child development and related disciplines and upon particular knowledge of each child.

I-1.3—To recognize and respect the uniqueness and the potential of each child.

I-1.5—To create and maintain safe and healthy settings that foster children's social, emotional, intellectual, and physical development and that respect their dignity and their contributions.

*Principles:*

P-1.1—Above all, we shall not harm children. We shall not participate in practices that are disrespectful, degrading, dangerous, exploitative, intimidating, emotionally damaging, or physically harmful to children.

Section II: Ethical responsibilities to families

*Ideals:*

I-2.4—To respect families' childrearing values and their right to make decisions for their children.

I-2.6—To help family members improve their understanding of their children and to enhance their skills as parents.

*Principles:*

P-2.4—We shall involve families in significant decisions affecting their child.

P-2.11—We shall be familiar with and appropriately use community resources and professional services that support families. After a referral has been made, we shall follow up to ensure that services have been appropriately provided.

Section III: Ethical responsibilities to colleagues

*Ideals:*

I-3A.1—To establish and maintain relationships of respect, trust, and cooperation with co-workers.

I-3B.1—To assist the program in providing the highest quality of service.

*Principles:*

P-3C.1—In decisions concerning children and programs, we shall appropriately utilize the education, training, experience, and expertise of staff members.

Section IV: Ethical responsibilities to community and society

*Ideals:*

I-4.1—To provide the community with high-quality (age and individually appropriate, and culturally and socially sensitive) education/child care programs and services.

*Principles:*

P-4.4—We shall cooperate with other professionals who work with children and their families.

*Source:* Feeney, S., & Kipnis, K. (1998) *Code of Ethical Conduct and Statement of Commitment.* Washington, DC: NAEYC.

The revised standards are intended to represent a shared vision and to be empowering for children and professionals alike (NAEYC, 2001b). These standards, written to be the baseline of what an early childhood educator should know and be able to do at an entry level into the profession, have several sections and specific statements describing the standards that are helpful related to influencing the behavior of young children and preventing and intervening when they experience challenging behavior. However, the most direct guidance provided in Standard 4: Teaching and Learning, Substandard 4b, Using developmentally effective approaches, states that "candidates know, understand, and use a wide array of effective approaches, strategies and tools to positively influence children's development and learning" (p. 17). In the description and supporting explanation provided in these revised NAEYC standards, under Standard 4b—Addressing children's challenging behaviors—the following information is provided:

> "Classroom management" is the greatest difficulty reported by most novice practitioners. Well-prepared early childhood candidates demonstrate understanding of the multiple, underlying causes of children's challenging behaviors. Early childhood candidates demonstrate a varied repertoire of research-based guidance approaches to meet individual needs. Their work shows that they understand the importance of a supportive, interesting classroom environment and relationships as ways to prevent many challenging behaviors. In implementing guidance approaches, candidates aim to develop children's self-regulation and respect for others. Candidates also demonstrate knowledge and essential skills to meet the special needs of children whose behavioral difficulties are related to disabilities, family or community violence, or other stressful circumstances. (NAEYC, 2001b, p. 20)

NAEYC has clearly moved in the direction of having greater expectations for beginning early childhood professionals' ability to understand and influence behavior. Candidates are expected not only to be prepared for typical environmental arrangement and positive child guidance techniques, but also to possess specialized knowledge, skills, and techniques to prepare them to respond to diversity, disability, and challenging behaviors.

## The Division for Early Childhood of the Council for Exceptional Children

The Division for Early Childhood (DEC) of the CEC was founded in 1973. It is "dedicated to promoting policies and practices that support families and enhance the optimal development of children" (Division for Early Childhood [DEC], n.d., para. 1). Like NAEYC the DEC has a focus on children from birth through eight years. DEC, however, describes the population as children from birth through eight and their families. You should note the similarities between the two statements of purpose. Although DEC has contributed significantly through its various activities, including conferences, workshops, and publications, to the understanding of and response to challenging behavior of young children, of particular interest here is the ethical guidance and related standards and principles that they have published to provide guidance to their membership.

In 2000, the DEC issued *DEC Recommended Practices in Early Intervention/Early Childhood Special Education* (Sandall, McLean, & Smith, 2000). This document is important because it gives guidance, consistent with the DEC beliefs and standards, to professionals who work on behalf of young children with disabilities and their families. It is an update and expansion of work done previously by DEC (Division for Early Childhood Task Force on Recommended Practices, 1993) and a text written by Odom and McLean (1996) that extended the underlying concepts. One section of the *DEC Recommended Practices* deals with child-focused interventions. Twenty-seven distinct practices are provided in the section on child-focused interventions. Although all 27 may be seen as being relevant to ethical standards of practice and challenging behavior, 10 have been selected as especially applicable here. They are presented in Figure 3–9.

In October 1999 the DEC adopted a concept paper on the identification of and intervention with challenging behavior (DEC, 1999). The concept paper, endorsed by the NAEYC and the Association for Childhood Education International (ACEI), followed adoption from the previous year, 1998, of a DEC position statement on interventions for challenging behavior. The position statement was reaffirmed by DEC in June 2001. The DEC concept paper and position statement are consistent in addressing three primary principles or beliefs about challenging behavior and young children. The first is that "many young children engage in challenging behavior in the course of early development. The majority of these children respond to developmentally appropriate management techniques" (DEC, 1999, p. 1). The second is that "DEC believes strongly that many types of services and intervention strategies are available to address challenging behavior" (p. 1). The third is that "DEC believes that families play a critical role in designing and carrying out effective interventions for challenging behavior" (p. 3). Each of these three fundamental beliefs is described next.

*Many young children engage in challenging behavior in the course of development. The majority of these children respond to developmentally appropriate management techniques.* It is important to understand the development of young children and to know that most young children engage in behavior that may be viewed by some as challenging. These behaviors are typically amenable to appropriate positive child guidance techniques. With these guidance techniques (e.g., redirecting or physical prompting) most young children will learn appropriate alternative behaviors. DEC (1999) cautions that "care must be taken to consider cultural and community beliefs, developmentally appropriate expectations and one's own beliefs about behavior, in the identification of children's behavior as challenging" (p. 1).

*DEC believes strongly that many types of services and intervention strategies are available to address challenging behavior.* For some young children the use of adult vigilance and developmentally appropriate positive guidance

**FIGURE 3–9**
*Selected DEC*
*Recommended*
*Practices:*
*Child-Focused*
*Interventions*

C1. Physical space and materials are structured and adapted to promote engagement, play, interaction, and learning by attending to children's preferences and interests, using novelty, using responsive toys, providing adequate amounts of materials, and using defined spaces.

C2. The social dimension of the environment is structured and adapted to promote engagement, interaction, communication and learning by providing peer models, peer proximity, responsive adults, and imitative adults; and by expanding children's play and behavior.

C3. Routines and transitions are structured to promote interaction, communication, and learning by being responsive to child behavior and using naturalistic time delay, interrupted chair procedure, transition-based teaching, and visual cue systems.

C16. Children's behavior is recognized, interpreted in context, and responded to contingently, and opportunities are provided for expansion or elaboration of child behavior by imitating the behavior, waiting for the child's responses, modeling, and prompting.

C18. Practices are used systematically, frequently, and consistently within and across environments.

C20. Practices are used that are validated, normalized, useful across environments, respectful, and not stigmatizing of the child and family and that are sensitive to cultural and linguistic issues.

C21. Consequences for children's behavior are structured to increase the complexity and duration of children's play, engagement, appropriate behavior, and learning by using differential reinforcement, response shaping, high-probability procedures and correspondence training.

C24. Prompting and prompt fading procedures are used to ensure acquisition and use of communicative, self-care, cognitive, and social skills.

C26. Recommended instructional strategies are used with sufficient fidelity, consistency, frequency, and intensity to ensure high levels of behavior occurring frequently.

C27. For problem behaviors, interventionists assess the behavior in context to identify its function, and then devise interventions that are comprehensive in that they make the behavior irrelevant (child's environment is modified so that problem behavior is unnecessary or precluded), inefficient (a more efficient replacement behavior is taught), and ineffective (i.e., reinforcement and other consequent events are used).

*Source:* Sandall, S., McLean, M. E., & Smith, B. J. (Eds.). (2000). *DEC recommended practices in early intervention/early childhood special education.* Longmont, CO: Sopris West.

techniques is insufficient to successfully respond to their challenging behaviors. For these children, systematic interventions are necessary (Kazdin, 1987; Wahler & Dumas, 1986). Without systematic intervention, it is likely that chronic challenging behavior will escalate and become more problematic for the child and others (Reid, 1993). Sometimes changing of adult behavior, by examining their behavior and the environment, serves to prevent challenging behavior of children. Zirpoli and Melloy (2001) point out that prevention is the best form of intervention.

DEC suggests that services and strategies might include four areas, including designing environments and activities to prevent challenging behavior, using positive behavior interventions that address both the form and function of behavior, adopting curriculum modification and accommodation strategies, and providing external consultation and technical assistance. Further, DEC believes that effective intervention includes the features of comprehensiveness, individualization, positive programming, multidisciplinary, and data based. *Comprehensive* interventions are those that include more than one strategy. Young children may engage in the same challenging behavior for different reasons. Therefore, it is necessary to *individualize* and understand both how to assess and quantify what (form) the behavior is and why (function) the child is engaging in the behavior. Because many challenging behaviors of young children result from a deficit in social and communication skills, *positive programming* is needed to foster development and learning of those skills. Typically the collaborative efforts of a *multidisciplinary* team (e.g., early interventionist, early childhood educator, behavior analyst, and speech therapist) will result in more effective interventions. Interventions that are *data based* and apply systematic methods of collecting data specific to challenging behaviors will serve best in that they will assist with accountability, facilitate communication, and increase the ability of adults to be consistent in responding to behavior across varied settings.

*DEC believes that families play a critical role in designing and carrying out effective interventions for challenging behaviors.* Recommended practices suggest that early childhood education and early childhood special education should have a strong family focus. A coordinated, team effort between professionals and families is critical for success in behavior interventions. In fact, in early intervention programs and statewide systems for children with disabilities from birth to 3 years, a family-centered approach is legally mandated. The family is the smallest unit of intervention. Historically families have been blamed, especially with regard to children who exhibit challenging behaviors. This is frequently incorrect or at least grossly oversimplified, given the numerous complex factors that typically contribute to the establishment and maintenance of challenging behaviors. Families are best viewed as partners in the process of planning, implementing, and evaluating behavior interventions. This point of view is addressed in Chapter 2.

## SUMMARY OF ETHICAL CODES, STANDARDS, AND PRINCIPLES FROM ASSOCIATIONS/ORGANIZATIONS

Thus far, this chapter has reviewed the ethics, standards, principles, and underlying beliefs of a variety of professional associations and organizations. Although this exercise may have seemed somewhat disconnected from the question of what the ethics are that specifically guide professionals in the area of positive behavior supports, it is important for the reader to understand the broader context of ethics in education and the place of prevention and intervention for challenging behaviors in that context. Further, one may assume that in the future as special education and general education systems continue to unify with regard to reform, the revisions and further development of ethical codes will be more inclusive of varied constituencies.

This brief examination has included the ethical standards, principles, and beliefs provided by the National Education Association (NEA), the Learning First Alliance (LFA), the Council for Exceptional Children (CEC), the Council for Children with Behavioral Disorders (CCBD) of CEC, the National Association for the Education of Young Children (NAEYC), and the Division for Early Childhood (DEC) of CEC. The inclusion of these particular associations and organizations has been purposeful and intended to lead the reader from the broadest perspective on education and ethical codes and conduct to a focus on ethics and conduct specific to positive behavior supports. A number of other associations and organizations could have been included, for example, the National Middle School Association and their mission and position statements, the National Association of Secondary School Principals and in particular the information that they provide about special education, and the Council of Administrators of Special Education. (See Web sites in Figure 3–10.) Also, the Association for Persons with Severe Handicaps (TASH), an organization actively involved in a variety of professional activities aimed at improving the lives of persons with comprehensive and severe disabilities, could have been included.

NAEYC and DEC are included and are especially important because of their focus on early identification, prevention, early intervention, and participation of and partnerships with families. Also, these organizations have demonstrated over time willingness to and success in collaboration, including joint efforts aimed at supporting young children with challenging behaviors and their families. It is understood that the readers are preparing to work with children and youth at various levels from infancy through preschool, middle school, and secondary school as well as in various settings, including regular classrooms and the continuum of special education environments. Despite the grade/age level or educational setting that the reader anticipates for their professional service, it is important to have some foundation in the development and learning of young children and the ethical standards that guide practice in early intervention and early childhood education and child care. Obviously, young children become older. As noted previously, challenging behaviors of young children, in the absence of successful and lasting interventions, frequently become chronic and more severe.

You have also been introduced to nine organizing themes for understanding ethical practices. You may have noted that these themes are found in varied number and intensity in the ethical codes, standards, beliefs, and principles of the organizations and associations. We will come back to the subject of the nine themes after we have dealt with positive behavior supports (PBS) and ethics. The themes will serve as our guide for contrasting and comparing all of the information provided.

## POSITIVE BEHAVIOR SUPPORT AND ETHICAL STANDARDS AND PRACTICES

As introduced in Chapter 1, the field of PBS is comparatively new and is built largely on the history of behavior theory and applied behavior analysis. Numerous books and journal articles (e.g., the *Journal of Applied Behavior Analysis*) focused on behavior change over the past four decades have included ethical considerations related to assessment, planning, delivering, and evaluating interventions. Topics such as use of aversive consequences, control of reinforcement, dependence versus fostering of self-determination and independence, participation of the subjects of intervention and their families, and relevance of interventions to an individual's quality of life have received a great deal of attention. Also, the term *behavior modification* fell into disrepute (Martin, 1974), as its meaning was broadened in the public domain to include techniques potentially harmful that we never intended nor appropriately associated with the term, such as brainwashing and medical/surgical procedures. Sulzer-Azaroff and Mayer (1991) point out that in the use of applied behavior analysis and behavior procedures that ethical responsibility requires that "[behavior interventions] are based on the laws of behavior, use scientific methods of evaluation, and improve the quality of peoples lives and society by helping those persons to enhance their repertoires of constructive and reinforcing behavior options" (p. 103). Sulzer-Azaroff and Mayer further state that the primary sources for professional ethical standards have been the Association for Behavior Analysis (ABA) and The Division of Experimental Analysis of Behavior of the American Psychological Association (APA) and the Association for Advancement of Behavior Therapy (AABT).

AABT (Sulzer-Azaroff & Mayer, 1991) has dealt with ethical issues in the provision of behavior therapy and treatment by posing eight questions. One, have the goals of treatment been adequately considered? For example, have the therapist and client agreed and will serving the client's interest be contrary to the interests of other persons? Two, has the choice of treatment methods been adequately considered? For example, is the method supported in the literature, and is the client made aware of other procedures that might be preferred? Three, is the client's participation voluntary? Four, when another person or an agency is empowered to arrange for therapy, have the interests of the subordinated client been sufficiently considered? Five, has the adequacy of treatment been evaluated? For example, has it been quantified and has the client been kept informed? Six, has the confidentiality of the treatment relationship been protected? Seven, does the therapist refer the clients to other therapists when necessary? Eight, and lastly, is the therapist qualified to provide treatment? Although these eight ethical questions posed by the AABT obviously are from a psychological perspective and focus on treatment provided to clients by therapists, they have relevance for applied behavior analysis and the provision of PBS to children and youth by educators and related professionals in various educational environments.

PBS has its basis in federal legislation. The 1997 amendments to the Individuals with Disabilities Education Act (IDEA) provide for both positive behavior support and functional behavior assessment for children with disabilities and for whom behavior issues impede success in educational settings. It has been pointed out (Turnbull, Wilcox, Stowe, Raper, & Hedges, 2000) that the preference for PBS as a behavior intervention approach represented by IDEA is supported by various foundations in public policy, including constitutional precedents, litigation, legislation, and its moral basis.

However, PBS is viewed much more broadly as having relevance for all children and youth in a variety of educational contexts. Turnbull, Turnbull, Shank, Smith and Leal (2002) discuss the importance of "universal support," or schoolwide PBS for all students to provide a positive learning environment. They suggest that in order to be successful in implementing universal support, schools must meet five criteria. These criteria include (a) clearly defined behavior expectations, (b) teach behavior expectations, (c) frequently acknowledge appropriate behavior, (d) evaluate programs and make adaptations on an ongoing basis through a team approach, and (e) target support to address students who need more intense skill development and practice than is offered through universal support. Another way to think about this is through the systems perspective (Sugai et al., 2000). PBS may be developed and maintained at three systems levels, including primary, or reducing new instances of problem behavior, secondary, or reducing current instances, and tertiary, or reducing the intensity and complexity of current instances. If we are to apply this universal and systems perspective to the uses of PBS in educational contexts, then we must understand the tenets of PBS in relation to other education profession codes, standards, principles, and beliefs specific to facilitating desired behavior, preventing undesirable behavior, and intervening with challenging behavior. Vignette 3.1 shows how PBS was used in one school.

## Vignette 3.1

### Riverdale School

Riverdale is a public elementary school located in a rural, midwestern community. There are 300 students in preschool through fourth grade. The student body is quite diverse and includes children with various ethnic, cultural, socioeconomic, racial, and religious backgrounds. Riverdale has a significant focus on their ESL program, largely to serve a growing Hispanic population. Inclusion of children with special needs is also a priority at Riverdale, and approximately 10% of the children have a variety of types and severities of disability and are included in general education classrooms from preschool through fourth grade. Special education teachers serve as team teachers with general education teachers whereas others are in a consulting role, and on occasion they provide pullout services. For the last five years Riverdale has been recognized annually by the state department of education for excellence as a result of readiness and academic achievement scores, for its model practices in inclusion of children with special needs, for its commitment to children for whom English it not the primary language, and for its program of partnering with parents.

During the last cycle of Riverdale's school improvement planning process implemented during the 2002–2003 school year, the consensus of teachers, administrators, other school personnel, and family representatives in their self-assessment was that an area of needed growth and improvement was specific to fostering desired behavior in school, preventing behavior problems, and intervening more effectively in response to individual challenging behavior. It was agreed that for the 2003–2004 the school improvement focus would be on development of a schoolwide PBS plan, and the target date for implementation would be the beginning of school in the fall of 2004. In the fall of 2003 a series of meetings and workshops open to all stakeholders (Riverdale's parents, teachers, the principal and assistant principal, school psychologist, counselor, bus drivers, dietary staff, office staff, custodians, and even a few of the older students) were held for the purpose of achieving a shared vision, commonly held beliefs regarding behavior, and some broad goals for the schoolwide PBS plan. With this done it would be possible in the winter and spring of 2004 to establish a representative team of 8 to 12 members and develop the specific plan for implementation in fall 2004.

One thing that became clear during the process of the broader participation of all interested stakeholders was that it was important to take into account the ethical standards, codes, and principles related to behavior and provided by the various professional organizations represented by the faculty and other professional staff at Riverdale. It was agreed that a subgroup of these individuals would work on merging content of ethical positions from their organizations and develop an ethics statement for consideration by the larger group. Having this formalized ethical position statement would be an important element of the school's belief system and would help guide the work of the schoolwide PBS team. Borrowing from content on ethics provided by the NEA, the LFA, the CEC, the CEC Division for Children with Behavioral Disorders, the NAEYC, and the DEC of the CEC, the subgroup came up with the following general ethical position statement for Riverdale School:

"We believe in the worth and dignity of all of our students, their access to equal educational opportunity, and we will help each student realize his or her potential. We will avoid the use of disciplinary procedures as a means of excluding students from school settings until all other alternatives have been exhausted. We will not use corporal punishment as a means of discipline. We will give priority to prevention, early intervention, student participation, and family involvement in matters of student behavior. We will take into account the uniqueness of individual children, their family diversity, and their developmental status in any decisions about behavior in school. We will use a variety of positive, proactive methods of influencing behavior, and these methods will be relevant to helping our students develop self-determination, independence, and an improved quality of life. When intervention is required, we will use a systematic, team approach and will always select the least intrusive and most typical response to challenging behaviors. This is our ethical position related to the behavior of students at Riverdale School."

### Reflective Moment

The statements made in Riverdale School's ethics position are related to the various codes and standards of NAEYC, DEC, and other associations or organizations. What are some examples?

How might some of the unique features of Riverdale School affect further development and implementation of its schoolwide plan?

How might the large and growing Hispanic population at Riverdale influence the ethical position statement?

One of the central features of PBS is its emphasis on social values. Sugai et al. (2000) assert that behavior change through PBS, in order to be judged as socially significant, must be *comprehensive*, that is, it has relevance across a child's day in school and in other important social contexts. It must be *durable* in that it is lasting. It must be *relevant* and foster skills that are functional and useful in daily living. The necessity for PBS to result in enhancing the quality of life and the ability of individuals to self-determine has also been emphasized as PBS principles have been articulated. Turnbull and Turnbull (2000) point out that achieving "rich" lifestyles is clearly a central belief and purpose of PBS, but research and practice have yet to fully contribute to the achievement of this goal. One promising and useful tool that reflects the emerging values and principles of PBS related to quality of life, self-advocacy, and community inclusion is person-centered planning. **Person-centered planning** has been described by Kincaid (1996) as a philosophy, practice, and set of techniques that lead to the use of PBS to address five goals or accomplishments in a person's life:

- Being present and participating in community life
- Gaining and maintaining satisfying relationships
- Expressing preferences and making choices in everyday life
- Having opportunities to fulfill respected roles and to live with dignity
- Continuing to develop personal competencies

There are numerous sources of information for educators (as well as for families and other stakeholders) about the ethics, principles, and beliefs associated with PBS and its applications in a broader sense with all children and youth in educational settings as well as with those who have substantial and comprehensive challenging behaviors. Two key sources of information and guidance in this regard are the Technical Assistance Center on Positive Behavioral Interventions and Supports (PBIS) and the *Journal of Positive Behavior Interventions*. The mission of the Technical Assistance Center, which was established by the U.S. Office of Special Education Programs, largely in response to the emphasis in the 1997 amendments to IDEA, is to give schools capacity-building information and technical assistance for identifying, adapting, and sustaining effective schoolwide disciplinary practices (Positive Behavioral Interventions and Supports [PBIS], n.d., para. 1). The *Journal of Positive Behavior Interventions* is a quarterly publication; the premiere issue of this journal was published in winter 1999. In that inaugural issue, the editors (Dunlap & Koegel, 1999) indicated that "the major purpose of this new journal is to provide a publication outlet for the exchange of constructive perspectives and credible information so that the field can move increasingly toward a comprehensive, effective and humane response to the substantial challenges of behavioral adaptation" (p. 2).

### Consider This

As a member of the behavior support team for a 30-year-old man with severe physical disabilities and mental illness, you become aware that his direct-support staff are ignoring his choices and providing only maintenance care for him. You recognize the position of the agency in a time of high turnover, but you want to ensure quality of life and self-determination for this man.

- How do you approach this challenge from an ethical standpoint?
- Whose help do you enlist?

In a recent issue of this journal the authors reviewed the evolution of PBS and suggested a vision for the future that includes changes in at least four major areas, including assessment practices, intervention strategies, training, and extension to new populations (Carr et al., 2002). Assessment could be broadened in terms of who participates in completing the assessment, where it is conducted, possible use of more indirect methods, and use of methods beyond measures of discrete social behavior. One example of how intervention strategies might change is the amount of attention shifting toward comprehensive lifestyle improvement and creating environments that support **quality of life** and prevent challenging behavior. PBS will likely experience a continued expansion to populations beyond persons with developmental disabilities to, for example, as noted earlier in the discussion of universal support, typically developing students who are experiencing discipline problems (Lewis & Sugai, 1999). Lastly, training in PBS is likely in the future to rely less on university-based lecture formats and formal workshops focused on learning specific techniques and more on technology applications, on-site education, practical experiences, and interagency collaboration.

## PBS, ETHICAL STANDARDS, AND PRACTICE: NINE ORGANIZING THEMES

The beginning of this chapter stated that nine organizing themes (see Figure 3–1) would be used as a summary and one representation of how to understand the major domains of ethical standards, beliefs, principles and related practices in the provision of PBS in educational contexts for children and youth with challenging behaviors. These themes also serve as the basis for examination of the common elements and differences across the professional associations and organizations related to their positions on behavior.

## Individual Worth and Dignity

Each student (child or youth) is an individual human being with worth and dignity, despite the nature or severity of his challenging behavior. This is a position that is found, sometimes using different terms such as quality of life or human rights, in essentially all the organization and association references that we have examined. The phrase "despite the nature or severity of her/his challenging behavior," however, is not always articulated, but rather implied. In the Preamble to the National Education Association *Code of Ethics of the Education Profession* emphasis is given to the educator's belief in human worth and dignity. (See Figure 3–2.) One of the five core values of the NAEYC is respecting worth, dignity, and individual uniqueness, and this is reinforced as an ideal in the *NAEYC Code of Ethical Conduct and Commitment* (see Figure 3–8), specifically I-1.3—to recognize and respect the uniqueness and the potential of each child.

Historically in special education advocating for the worth and dignity of children and youth, without respect for the severity or type of their disability, has long been central to the mission. In the Council for Exceptional Children standards, specific to behavior management, the first standard requires that special educators use methods and procedures that do not undermine dignity or human rights. (See Figure 3–6.) In discussing the public policy foundations for positive behavior interventions, strategies, and supports, Turnbull et al. (2000) include Constitutional precedents, that is the Fifth Amendment prohibiting the federal government from denying any person life, liberty, or property. Also included are the right to education and right to treatment legislation and other moral and democratic precedents. These are certainly public policy foundations associated with PBS, but also more generally as a basis for advocating the worth and dignity of persons with disabilities. In the reference cited earlier related to applied behavior analysis and rights of individuals in need of behavior interventions, one of the rights (Van Houten et al., 1988) was the right to services with an overriding goal of personal welfare. Finally, in a review of **self-determination** for children and youth with developmental disabilities (Wehmeyer, Martin, & Sands, 1998) point out that "from its earliest application to people with disabilities, self-determination has meant access to basic civil and human rights" (p. 192).

## Behavior Reflects a Need

The behavior of children and youth (challenging and otherwise) always reflects a need on the part of the individual. People respond out of need, and all behavior has a form and serves a function. The important point here is that the challenging behavior of children and youth is all too often misread, leading to responses that do not facilitate positive behavior. Although this specific theme is not found stated as such in the positions of the associations and organizations reviewed previously, the emphasis on viewing children and youth as individuals supports the theme of behavior reflecting a need. In a sense, all the ethical standards and principles reviewed that focus on behavior suggest that professionals must seek to understand the function (purpose or need) addressed by a discrete behavior to intervene effectively.

## Prevention and Early Intervention

Systematic and thoughtful management of learning environments and understanding of individual differences will serve to prevent some challenging behaviors. And early intervention can serve to eliminate or lessen their severity. The theme of prevention is found in numerous places in the various codes, standards, and statements of principles and beliefs. The second core element of the document provided by the Learning First Alliance targets systematic approaches to supporting safety and positive behavior. Much of it is focused on prevention of challenging behavior in school settings through communication, clear rules, modeling, nurturing student's self-management, celebrating success, arrangement of the environment, and avoidance of harsh and punitive styles.

The NAEYC, in its *Code of Ethical Conduct and Commitment,* provides the Ideal (I-l.5)—to create and maintain safe and healthy settings that foster children's social, emotional, intellectual, and physical development and that respect their dignity and contributions. (See Figure 3–8.) In fact, the NAEYC focus on developmentally appropriate practices with young children and the emphasis on positive child guidance may all be understood as intended to foster desired behavior and to prevent the need for an intervention. In the 2001 revision of the *NAEYC Standards for Early Childhood Professionals,* the section on addressing children's challenging behaviors includes a statement that early childhood educators understand the importance of a supportive, interesting classroom environment and relationships as ways to prevent many challenging behaviors.

It is interesting to note that the practices advocated by the DEC (see Figure 3–9) appear to be similar to the guidance provided by NAEYC. Prevention is associated with environmental arrangement, child initiations, play and socialization, engagement, and communication. DEC emphasizes routines, structure, prompting, consequences, and consistency. The concept paper on identification of and intervention with challenging behavior developed by DEC includes three guiding principles (DEC, 1999). One is that "many young children engage in challenging behavior in the course of development. The majority of these children respond to developmentally appropriate management techniques" (p. 1). A common belief is that an "ounce of prevention is worth a pound of cure." That maxim is clearly underscored in the professional guidance provided to educators in responding to the behavior of children and youth. You are reminded of the continuum of positive behavior support introduced earlier (Sugai et al., 2000) in which universal interventions (schoolwide) serve to reduce the number of new instances of problem behavior and as preventive measures.

## Family Partnerships

Families, children, and youth should be central to all aspects of PBS, including active participation in planning, implementing, and evaluating interventions. Chapter 2 emphasizes the rationale for and recommended practices associated with treating families as team members, collaborators, and partners in all aspects of PBS. Ethical codes and standards have recently begun to reflect this. One of the three overriding goals stated by the Learning First Alliance (LFA) is to "engage parents and other community members in helping students achieve high academic expectations" (LFA, n.d., p. 2). One of their core elements of safe and supportive schools is "involvement of families, students, school staff, and the surrounding community" (LFA, 2001, p. 1). Specifically, in one of the LFA core elements (see Figure 3–4) the family role in determining school rules related to behavior and how rules are communicated and enforced is stated. Also included in the LFA core elements are beliefs that parents should (to the degree possible) be active participants in behavior change, and effective alternative programs should include active family involvement.

The ethical code of the Council for Exceptional Children (CEC) has only one reference to families (see Figure 3–5, ii), and its focus is on activities delivered to families rather than partnerships with families. However, the CEC professional practice standards specific to behavior management (see Figure 3–6) are introduced by a statement suggesting that parents (rather than families) are a part of an interdisciplinary team, along with other professionals in an effort to "manage" behavior. The CCBD in its mission statement includes a part of the mission being to foster collaborative relationships among families and professionals.

Focusing now on early childhood as represented by both the NAEYC and DEC, a number of standards, values, beliefs, and principles associated with the place of families are to be found. The NAEYC, as one of its six core values, commits professionals to value the relationships children and their families have. As addressed earlier in the chapter, NAEYC complimented its core values with the addition of related professional responsibilities in four areas, including families (see Figure 3–8). Respecting family child-rearing values and decision making, helping families learn and grow in parenting skills, and involving families in significant decisions affecting their children are all stated as professional responsibilities. The DEC, as noted earlier, has worked closely with NAEYC over the last 10 to 15 years. In the NAEYC mission statement there is recognition of the role of families in the successful development of children. They state that their policies and practices should support families and ultimately the optimal development of children. In the concept paper produced by DEC, and endorsed by NAEYC, on identification of and intervention with challenging behavior, it also supports the critical role of families related to interventions for challenging behavior. Although some might argue this point, it seems clear that one of the most significant changes that may be seen in the evolution of behavior theory and applied behavior analysis to PBS is the movement away from parents as targets for intervention, extensions of the professional, or trainee and toward families as partners in all aspects of PBS, including functional assessment, planning processes, designing and implementing positive behavior interventions, and evaluation.

## Family Diversity

The uniqueness of children and youth, as reflected by the diversity of their families (race, ethnicity, religion, and culture) should be taken into account in understanding behavior and responding to challenging behavior. As was pointed out earlier in the chapter, Turnbull and Turnbull (2000) have suggested that we have much to do to achieve the goal of rich lifestyles (quality of life) for persons with disabilities through the applications of PBS. This might be true related to our understanding of and respect for diversity as a broader societal issue. There is, however, some guidance in professional codes and standards specific to diversity. In Principle I of the *Commitment to Student Standards of Ethical Conduct* (NEA, 1975) of the NEA code (see Figure 3–3) the following statement is provided:

> . . . [T]he educator shall not on the basis of race, color, creed, sex, national origin, marital status, political or religious beliefs, family, social or cultural background, or sexual orientation, unfairly-exclude any student from participation in any program, deny benefits to any student, grant any advantage to any student. (p. 2)

### Consider This

In partnering with the family of a school-age child, you are confronted with their stringent belief in corporal punishment as a means to discipline the child. These beliefs are strongly held cultural assumptions for this family.

- How do you, as a teacher and part of the behavior support team, deal with this challenge?

- How do you maintain ethical standards for the child and in your partnership with the family?

The NAEYC includes as one of its six core values that children should be understood and supported in the context of family and culture. Also, one of the ideals provided in the NAEYC ethical code (see Figure 3–8) directs early childhood professionals to be respectful of family child-rearing values. DEC includes as one of its recommended practices in child-focused intervention (see Figure 3–9, Recommended Practice C20) that practices not stigmatize the child or family and that they should be culturally and linguistically sensitive.

## Natural Environments and Inclusive Settings

Natural environments and inclusive settings are desirable for children and youth with troubling and challenging behavior, but school personnel must assume ownership in those settings, and a full continuum of services and settings should be available. The literature in education, special education, and related disciplines is rich, both empirically based and position statements, with information about natural environments, inclusion and least-restrictive environment. The consideration here is limited to examining the extent to which these issues are addressed in codes, standards, and statements of principles and beliefs. Although the review of organizations and associations provided in this chapter is certainly not exhaustive, neither in terms of numbers nor the extent to which information provided by the organizations and associations is complete, it is surprising to find that natural environments and inclusion apparently receives little attention in ethical codes and standards. The NEA does provide in its resolution on discipline wording that indicates that "discipline" should not be misused as a reason to exclude children from school settings. However, the resolution does provide that children could be excluded after other means of intervention have been exhausted.

The LFA, in their core elements related to supporting safety and positive behavior, stress the necessity of a continuum of services for children who engage in challenging behavior. When NAEYC revised its standards for early childhood personnel preparation in 2001 from the prior 1996 version, they emphasized the importance of professionals being prepared to teach children with and without developmental delays or disabilities. This, of course, reflects the growing movement, especially for young children, of inclusive processes and environments. DEC in 1999 adopted a concept paper, endorsed by NEA, in which they point out that many young children experience challenging behavior as a part of development and that most of them respond to developmentally appropriate management techniques (positive guidance and PBS). Further, DEC takes the position that, even when specific intervention strategies are necessary to address challenging behavior, sometimes changing adult behavior or the environment (inclusive and natural) serves to minimize or prevent challenging behavior.

## Natural and Logically Occurring Consequences

Natural and logically occurring consequences are preferable to extraneous and contrived reward systems, in order to foster self-discipline, independence, and self-determination. The fundamental question here is, of course, what in general should educators do in response to the behavior (desirable and undesirable) of children and youth? What are the consequences of behavior? There is a common assumption in education and special education that logical and natural consequences are desired. What guidance do educators find for this point of view in the ethical codes and standards that have been introduced in this chapter?

One of the core elements of the LFA is a systematic approach to supporting safety and positive behavior (see Figure 3–4). This core element emphasizes the importance of rules for behavior that are clear, consistent, logical, inclusive of student input in development, and fairly and consistently enforced. This provides the opportunity for use of natural and logical consequences for both desired and undesired behavior. The LFA core element also emphasizes the importance of celebrating the success of students who meet behavior expectations. Although the terms *natural* and *logically occurring consequences* are not found in the material presented from either NAEYC and DEC, it is certainly possible to interpret their recommended practices and codes of ethical conduct as in support of logical and naturally occurring consequences. Carr, Reeve, and Magito-McLaughlin (1996) point out that positive reinforcement, negative reinforcement, and punishment have been the mainstays for consequences associated with problem behavior over three decades, but that circumstance is changing with more attention given to understanding and managing antecedents. PBS brings to professionals the focus on prevention as well as emphasis on positive consequences that are meaningful to children and families (natural and logical).

## Being Positive Rather Than Punitive

Central to the philosophy and practice of PBS is an emphasis on being positive. Behavior interventions should be positive and should not include corporal punishment or other punitive measures. Represented in the various codes and standards is a clear movement toward using positive and avoiding negative consequences. This may be the area in which the largest gap continues to exist between general education and special education. In the NEA *Code of Ethics of the Education Profession* educators are obligated, among other things, to not intentionally expose students to embarrassment or disparagement and to protect students from conditions harmful to learning or to health. Although certainly some will disagree, one reasonable assumption is that the use of corporal punishment and other punitive methods could be inconsistent with these ethical standards.

The LFA, in its core elements for safe and supportive learning communities, states that harsh and punitive discipline styles tend to result in resentment and resistance and that excessive punishment puts the student in the position of trying to find ways to escape and takes attention away from the problematic behavior. This organization highlights the importance of teachers rewarding appropriate behavior and alternative programs including PBS (see Figure 3–4). The CEC standards for professional practice related to behavior management give guidance on this theme. Corporal punishment is given as an example of a violation of basic human rights, and aversive techniques are to be refrained from unless other methods have failed repeatedly and after consultation with parents and appropriate agency officials. The CCBD, in a position paper on behavior reduction strategies, notes that progress has been made in developing less-aversive ways of responding to behavior disorders in children and youth and that the Council does not sanction the use of corporal punishment.

Arguably the most important principle in the NAEYC *Code of Ethical Conduct and Commitment* (see Figure 3–8) is P-l.1—"Above all, we shall not harm children. We shall not participate in practices that are disrespectful, degrading, dangerous, exploitative, intimidating, emotionally damaging, or physically harmful to children." In their concept paper on identification of and intervention with challenging behavior, DEC states that children who require specialized interventions may need positive behavior interventions that address both the form and function of behavior. DEC further advocates positive programming.

## Functionality and Quality of Life

The PBS movement, both as specific practice for children and youth or adults with challenging behavior and as a universal school model, has focused attention on a topic that many researchers and leaders in special education had begun to address in some detail. That topic is the relevance of behavior interventions for how a person functions in the "real world" and how the intervention impacts their quality of life. One prominent writer on the subject of quality of life for persons with mental retardation reviews the evolution of the concept in the 1980s and 1990s and how it might be pursued for persons with disabilities in the immediate future (Schalock, 2000). He provides a definition as follows: "Quality of life is a concept that reflects a person's desired conditions of living related to eight core dimensions of one's life: emotional well-being, interpersonal relationships, material well-being, personal development, physical well-being, self-determination, social inclusion, and rights" (p. 121). This definition serves our purpose as we consider the ethical support for positive behavior support and quality of life.

Early in the chapter the reader is introduced to six rights that persons in need of behavior interventions have (Van Houten et al., 1988). The six rights were described in an article that was written from an applied behavior analysis perspective predating the PBS movement. Two of the rights are that intervention has an overriding goal of personal welfare and functional skills should be its focus. The CEC, when it revised its code of ethics in 1997, added an eighth standard directing that special educators attend to quality-of-life issues of individuals with exceptionalities. Finally, supporting persons with disabilities in achieving a quality of life that is functional for them and assisting them in achieving a "rich" lifestyle (Turnbull & Turnbull, 2000) is certainly a guiding principle in the ethical conduct of PBS.

**FIGURE 3–10**
*Selected Web sites*

Association for Persons with Severe Handicaps (TASH)
http://www.tash.org

Council for Children with Behavioral Disorders
http://www.ccbd.net

Council for Exceptional Children (CEC)
http://www.cec.sped.org

Council of Administrators of Special Education (CASE)
http://members.aol.com/casecec/mbes.htm

Division of Early Childhood of the Council for Exceptional Children (DEC)
http://www.dec-sped.org

ERIC Clearinghouse on Disabilities (ERIC)
http://eric.ed.gov

National Association for the Education of Young Children (NAEYC)
http://www.naeyc.org

National Association of Secondary School Principals
http://www.principals.org/

National Education Association (NEA)
http://www.nea.org

National Middle School Association (NMSA)
http://www.nmsa.org/

The OSEP Center on Positive Behavioral Interventions and Supports (PBIS)
http://www.pbis.org

## SUMMARY

It is important for educators to have knowledge of and be prepared to apply in their professional practices the standards of ethical conduct represented in their discipline. Ethics are defined as the principles of conduct governing us as individual professionals as well as in our particular discipline. To be ethical as a professional means to conform to accepted professional standards of conduct. The intent of Chapter 3 is to introduce the reader to the basic ethical codes, standards, principles, and beliefs of key and representative organizations and associations. More specifically the chapter examines the standards targeting behavior in educational environments and draws some comparisons about the overall guidance provided professional educators regarding fostering desired behavior, preventing problematic behavior, and intervening with challenging behavior. The logic of introducing associations and organizations outside the discipline and subdisciplines of special education is the growing trend toward unified systems reform in public education and the perspective that PBS represents principles and practices that have universal relevance for schools and other educational environments. Nine organizational themes for understanding ethical practices are suggested, and the standards, principles, and beliefs from the selected associations and organizations are related to the themes.

## ACTIVITIES TO EXTEND YOUR LEARNING

1. Interview a faculty member who teaches the course(s) in history and philosophy of education and social foundations at your institution. Ask her to assist you in finding additional references and resource material dealing with ethics and ethical behavior in education and in special education/challenging behavior in particular.

2. In small groups of three to five participants in class, develop together your own code of ethics for the use of PBS first for a schoolwide, universal perspective and then from the standpoint of children and youth with challenging behavior.

3. With fellow class participants, discuss the extent to which ethics and ethical behavior is included in your preparation. At what point in your programs of study and in what courses and to what degree is it covered?

4. If you are in field experiences in schools or agencies or have access to various educational settings, look for evidence of ethical standards being displayed or shared in those settings. Ask teachers and other personnel how they keep abreast of codes of ethical conduct.

5. Look at some textbooks in education, special education, and psychology that were published prior to 1960 and note how they presented ethics and ethical standards. Use this information to compare to current information as introduced in the chapter.

## FURTHER READING AND EXPLORATION

1. Visit the Web sites of the organizations and associations introduced in the chapter and review the content that they provide related to ethical codes, standards, principles, and beliefs. These Web sites are listed in Figure 3–10.

2. The *Journal of Positive Behavior Interventions* is a quarterly journal that premiered in 1999. Review all of *JPBI* and develop an annotated bibliography by the nine themes presented in the chapter.

## REFERENCES

Carr, E. G., Dunlap, G., Horner, R. H., Koegel, R. L., Turnbull, A. P., Sailor, W., et al. (2002). Positive behavior support: Evolution of an applied science. *Journal of Positive Behavior Interventions, 4*(1), 4–16.

Carr, E. G., Reeve, C. E., & Magito-McLaughlin, D. (1996). Contextual influences on problem behavior in people with developmental disabilities. In L. K. Koegel, R. L. Koegel, & G. Dunlap (Eds.), *Positive behavioral support: Including people with difficult behavior in the community* (pp. 403–423). Baltimore: Paul H. Brookes.

Council for Children with Behavioral Disorders. (n.d.). *CCBD grows and changes.* Retrieved January 30, 2002, from http://www.ccbd.net/accomplishments/index.cfm?contentID=22

Council for Children with Behavioral Disorders. (1990a). *Position paper on school discipline policies for students with significantly disruptive behavior.* Retrieved January 30, 2002, from http://www.ccbd.net/

Council for Children with Behavioral Disorders. (1990b). *Position paper on use of behavior reduction strategies with children with behavioral disorders.* Retrieved January 30, 2002, from http://www.ccbd.net/

Council for Exceptional Children. (n.d.). *CEC Code of ethics and standards of practice.* Retrieved January 15, 2002, from http://www. cec.sped. org/ps/code.html

Council for Exceptional Children. (n.d.). *Code of ethics.* Retrieved January 29, 2002, from http://www.cec.sped.org/ab/purpose.html

Council for Exceptional Children. (n.d.). *Our mission.* Retrieved January 29, 2002, from http://www.cec.sped.org/ab/purpose.html

Division for Early Childhood. (n.d.). *Homepage.* Retrieved February 1, 2002, from http://www.dec-sped.org/

Division for Early Childhood. (1999, October). *DEC concept paper on the identification of and intervention with challenging behavior.* Retrieved January 23, 2002, from http://www.dec-sped.org/positions/challenging_behavior.html

Division for Early Childhood Task Force on Recommended Practices. (Eds.). (1993). *DEC recommended practices: Indicators of quality programs for infants and young children with special needs and their families.* Reston, VA: Council for Exceptional Children.

Dunlap, G., & Koegel, R. L. (1999). Welcoming editorial. *Journal of Positive Behavior Interventions, 1*(1), 2–3.

Feeney, S., & Freeman, N. K. (1999). *Ethics and the early childhood educator: Using the NAEYC code.* Washington, DC: National Association for the Education of Young Children.

Feeney, S., & Kipnis, K. (1998). *Code of ethical conduct and statement of commitment* (Rev. ed.). Washington, DC: National Association for the Education of Young Children.

Garfinkel, I., Hochschild, J. L., & McLanahan, S. S. (1996). Introduction. In I. Garfield, J. L. Hochschild, & S. S. McLanahan (Eds.), *Social policies for children* (pp. 1–32). Washington, DC: The Brookings Institution.

Kazdin, A. (1987). *Conduct disorders in childhood.* Newbury Park, CA: Sage.

Kincaid, D. (1996). Person-centered planning. In L. K. Koegel, R. L. Koegel, & G. Dunlap (Eds.), *Positive behavioral support: Including people with difficult behavior in the community.* Baltimore: Paul H. Brookes.

Learning First Alliance. (n.d.) *Learning First Alliance.* Retrieved January 28, 2002, from http://www.learningfirst.org

Learning First Alliance. (2001, November). *Every child learning: Safe and supportive schools.* Retrieved January 28, 2002 from http://www. learningfirst.org/

Lewis, T. J., & Sugai, G. (1999). Effective behavior support: A systems approach to proactive school-wide management. *Focus on Exceptional Children, 31,* 1–24.

Martin, R. (1974). *Legal challenges to behavior modification.* Champaign, IL: Research Press.

National Association for the Education of Young Children. (n.d.). *About NAEYC.* Retrieved February 1, 2002, from http://www.naeyc.org/about/default.asp

National Association for the Education of Young Children. (2001a). *NAEYC at 75 (1926–2001): Reflections on the past—challenges for the future.* Washington, DC: Author.

National Association for the Education of Young Children. (2001b). *NAEYC guidelines revision: NAEYC standards for early childhood professional preparation—baccalaureate or initial licensure level.* Washington, DC: Author.

National Education Association (n.d.). *National Education Association FAQ.* Retrieved January 19, 2002, from http://www.nea.org/aboutnea/faq.html

National Education Association (n.d.). *NEA 2000–2001 resolutions: B-52 discipline.* Retrieved January 28, 2002, from http://www.nea.org/resolutions/00/00b-52.html

National Education Association (1975). *Code of ethics of the education profession.* Retrieved January 19, 2002, from http://www.nea.org/aboutnea/code.html

Odom, S. L., & McLean, M. E. (1996). *Early intervention /early childhood special education: Recommended practices.* Austin, TX: PRO-ED.

Positive Behavioral Interventions and Support. (n.d.). *PBIS mission.* Retrieved February 3, 2002, from http://www.pbis.org/english/main.php3

Reid, J. (1993). Prevention of conduct disorder before and after school entry: Relating interventions to developmental findings. *Development and Psychopathology,* 243–262.

Sandall, S., McLean, M. E., & Smith, B. J. (Eds.). (2000). *DEC recommended practices in early intervention/early childhood special education.* Longmont, CO: Sopris West.

Schalock, R. L. (2000). Three decades of quality of life. In M. I. Wehmeyer & J. R. Patton (Eds.), *Mental retardation in the 21st century* (pp. 116–127). Austin, TX: PRO-ED.

Sugai, G., Horner, R. H., Dunlap, G., Hieneman, M., Lewis, T. J., Nelson, C. M., et al. (2000). Applying positive behavior support and functional behavioral assessment in schools. *Journal of Positive Behavior Interventions, 2*(3), 131–143.

Sulzer-Azaroff, B., & Mayer, G. R. (1991). *Behavior analysis for lasting change.* Orlando, FL: Harcourt Brace Jovanovich.

Turnbull, A., & Turnbull, R. (2000). Achieving "rich" lifestyles. *Journal of Positive Behavior Interventions, 2*(3), 190–192.

Turnbull, A., & Turnbull, R. (2001). *Families, professionals, and exceptionality: Collaborating for empowerment* (4th ed.). Upper Saddle River, NJ: Merrill/Prentice Hall.

Turnbull, R., Turnbull, A., Shank, M., Smith, S., & Leal, D. (2002). *Exceptional lives: Special education in today's schools* (3rd ed.). Upper Saddle River, NJ: Merrill/Prentice Hall.

Turnbull, R. H., Wilcox, B. L., Stowe, M., Raper, C., & Hedges, L. P. (2000). Public policy foundations for positive behavioral interventions, strategies, and supports. *Journal of Positive Behavior Interventions, 2*(4), 218–230.

Van Houten, R., Axelrod, S., Bailey, J. S., Favell, J. E., Foxx, R. M., Iwata, B. A., et al. (1988). The right to effective behavioral treatment. *Journal of Applied Behavior Analysis, 21*(4), 381–384.

Wahler, R., & Dumas, J. E. (1986). "A chip off the old block" Some interpersonal characteristics of coercive children across generations. In P. Strain, M. Guralnick, & H. M. Walker (Eds.), *Children's social behavior: Development, assessment and modification* (pp. 49–91). Orlando, FL: Academic Press.

Wehmeyer, M. L., Martin, J. E., & Sands, D. J. (1998). Self-determination of children and youth with disabilities. In A. Hilton & R. Ringlaben (Eds.), *Best and promising practices in developmental disabilities* (pp. 191–203). Austin, TX: PRO-ED.

Zirpoli, T. J., & Melloy, K. J. (2001). *Behavior management: Applications for teachers* (3rd ed.). Upper Saddle River, NJ: Merrill/Prentice Hall.

# Chapter 4

# Identifying Strategies for Antecedent Management

## CONCEPTS TO UNDERSTAND

*After reading this chapter, you should be able to:*

- Understand the relationship between setting events and antecedents
- Describe the methods used in the assessment of antecedents
- Identify and discuss the methods for preventing challenging behavior through antecedent assessment management strategies
- Discuss antecedent management strategies that can be used, such as environmental strategies, instructional strategies, and quality-of-life enrichment

## KEY TERMS

A-B-C recording

Antecedents

Direct and indirect assessment

Functional behavior assessment

Interval recording

Scatter-plot analysis

Setting events

Structural analysis

Triggers

In recent years the field of applied behavior analysis and its outgrowth, positive behavior supports (PBS) has realized the importance of antecedent management strategies as an effective method for addressing challenging behavior. PBS has assisted professionals in gaining a better understanding of the relationship between distant **setting events** (i.e., physical, social, and environmental variables that serve to establish operations or "set the stage") and **antecedents** (i.e., events that trigger behavior) and problematic behavior. The use of antecedent management strategies provides a mechanism for minimizing the occurrence of these challenging responses. Antecedent management is a departure from previous practices whereby teachers and caregivers would place greater emphasis on consequence events following the occurrence of an inappropriate behavior.

The emphasis on consequence events has traditionally involved the delivery of punishers in the case of inappropriate behavior or positive reinforcers (activities, edibles, attention) following the performance of a desired behavior. With the recent advent of PBS, professionals have begun to address challenging behavior from a more proactive framework that includes the use of antecedent management or control strategies as a mechanism for the prevention of behaviors.

The purpose of this chapter will be to explain the role that antecedents play in precipitating or triggering challenging behaviors in learners and how we can better utilize antecedent management strategies in the design of effective interventions aimed at preventing the occurrence of these behaviors. Such intervention options could include how tasks are presented to the learner by the teacher, the type of instructional cues used by the teacher during the presentation of tasks, the presence or absence of choice-making opportunities, and providing the level of behavior supports needed by individual learners to maximize their performance and better utilize their individual learning strengths. It is intended that the reader will have a fluent understanding of the following concepts after completing this chapter.

## SETTING EVENTS, ANTECEDENTS, AND BEHAVIOR

All behaviors, be they desirable or challenging, are influenced by antecedents. Antecedents are also referred to as discriminative stimuli $S^D$ (prompts that trigger specific behaviors). Setting events are broad contexts that alter antecedent–behavior relationships (Horner & Carr, 1997) and are distant to antecedents, yet can be volatile when paired with the right trigger or (antecedent). Setting events often "set" the stage for problem behaviors to occur.

Carr (1994) identified three major categories of setting events. These include biological, environmental, and social or interpersonal. Biological setting events include such things as thirst, hunger, sleep, medication effects, and level of energy. Environmental setting events refer to the quality of the home setting, classroom, school setting, temperature, climate, dense or overcrowded work area, and level of noise in the classroom. Finally, social/interpersonal setting events include social interactions with peers or significant

**FIGURE 4–1**
*Examples of Setting Events*

**Biological**
- Thirsty
- Hungry
- Poor sleep, not enough sleep, too much sleep
- Drowsy, irritable from medication
- No energy or hyperactivity

**Environmental**
- Clutter in the home
- Not enough play materials in classroom
- Cannot see the blackboard in classroom
- Too hot or too cold
- Crowded environment
- Too loud

**Social/Interpersonal**
- Misunderstanding with store clerk
- Argument with peer or family member
- Personal space infringed upon

others in both home and school environments, friendships, and personal space. Figure 4–1 provides an example of each of these.

It is easy to understand how one or many of these setting events, when combined with a specific **trigger** or antecedent event, can spark the occurrence of challenging behavior. Vignette 4.1 provides a context for understanding these relationships.

## Vignette 4.1

### Setting Events and Antecedents

Annie is a 12-year-old child with chronic allergies and asthma who often must rely on a variety of medications to control her condition. A sudden change in weather conditions can spark an attack that can lead to an infection such as bronchitis or even worse, bronchial pneumonia. She has experienced recurring periods of illness where she will arrive at school not having slept well the previous night because of her respiratory condition. To make matters even more difficult, her school building is in a declining state of disrepair and has very poor ventilation, thus resulting in building temperatures that are often varied extremes such as too hot or too cold. On these days when she is not at her physical best and presented with a difficult task demand by her teacher, she will become agitated and will often get frustrated and place her head on the desk and not complete the assigned work. These behaviors do not occur on days when she has had sufficient rest and is feeling well. Thus, the setting event in this example is that her physical illness has made her sleep deprived, the antecedent is the task demand made by her teacher, and the behavior is Annie's inability to complete the task due to frustration and exhaustion. If Annie's teacher can better understand these relationships, she can utilize a behavior support strategy and alter how the task demands are given on those days when Annie is challenged by her medical condition.

### Reflective Moment

- What you would do if you were the teacher in this situation?
- How could you minimize Annie's frustration?

It is important as a teacher to be sensitive toward identifying the relationships between setting events, antecedents, behaviors, and the consequences that result. These relationships are reflected in the following diagram:

SE————————A——————B—————C
(Setting Event(s)—Antecedent(s)—Behavior(s)—Consequence(s)

An illustration of this diagram, in practice is as follows:

Jason does not go to bed early on school nights, thus he arrives at school very tired each morning (setting event), Jason's first class is rather demanding, and when his teacher places a work demand (antecedent), he refuses and often gets verbally abusive with his teacher (behavior). His teacher later takes him to the office, where he receives a suspension (consequence). In the preceding brief example, Jason is negatively reinforced for his behavior as he has successfully escaped performing the work required of him by his teacher by being removed from class.

In the previous examples we have focused on how setting events can occasion antecedents that result in challenging forms of behavior for both the learner and the teacher. Understanding these relationships can also result in the promotion of positive forms of behavior in the learning environment as well. As an example, if the teacher can better identify the learner's strengths and the level of structure needed by the individual learner for optimal performance, then the teacher can better design effective instructional antecedents to correspond with these distinct learner characteristics. An illustration of this is contained in Vignette 4.2.

## Vignette 4.2

### Promoting Positive Learning Experiences Through the Arrangement of Instructional Antecedents

Aaron is an eight-year-old child with attention deficit/hyperactivity disorder (ADHD) who is easily distracted by extraneous stimuli in his environment and therefore needs enhanced structure during instruction. In an effort to accommodate his learning style and behavior support needs, his teacher utilizes a visual schedule at his desk containing the list of tasks to be completed in their respective order and a filing system of colored folders containing tasks listed on his schedule. Prior to the presentation of new tasks, the teacher reviews the use of Aaron's individualized schedule and color-coded filing system with him. By attending to these instructional antecedents (designing the instructional system around Aaron's learning strengths and the provision of behavior supports to minimize his distractibility), Aaron is afforded a greater likelihood of success and enhanced learning and behavior outcomes.

### Reflective Moment

- What strategies would you as a teacher use in the design of instructional antecedents that would promote a learner's engagement?
- What were some of the strategies used by Aaron's teacher?

It may oftentimes be difficult to identify the distant setting events associated with some behaviors. The teacher may have a limited understanding of the events that may have occurred prior to school or before the learner has entered their respective classroom. In spite of the difficulty to reliably identify a specific setting event associated with a particular behavior, teachers will be better equipped and prepared to address challenging behavior(s) if they understand how setting events can set the stage for problematic behavior(s) to occur.

## METHODS USED IN THE ASSESSMENT OF ANTECEDENTS

**Functional behavior assessment** has many components that assist us in the assessment of antecedents and toward our understanding of how they influence behavior in learners. There are several methods that a classroom teacher can use to help in the identification of antecedents and their relationship to behavior responses in learners (both positive and negative). These include the collection of descriptive data such as structured interviews, behavior rating scales, and observational data. Each method of antecedent assessment will lead to the development of hypotheses related to the design of interventions. The process begins with the following.

### Structured Interview

The process of collecting descriptive assessment data is initiated with the structured interview. Typically, the structured interview is completed by the classroom teacher, other instructional personnel, family members, and any significant others in the learner's life. The content of the structured interview seeks to identify the various elements associated with the behavior(s) of concern. These elements include a description of the behavior, patterns of occurrence/nonoccurrence of the behavior, antecedents and consequences associated with the behavior, life events that may have had a relationship to the behavior, and physical events such as medication changes or health factors that could serve as precursors to the behavior.

There are numerous examples of structured interviews that exist and several that have been adapted by school personnel to accommodate the specific needs of learners within their respective learning environments. Perhaps one of the most commonly used is the Functional Assessment Interview (FAI) developed by O'Neill et al. (1997). Figure 4–2 provides an example of a structured interview form for use in a school setting.

**FIGURE 4–2**
*Functional Assessment Interview Form*

Student _____ Date _____

Completed by _____

### Description of the Target Behavior(s)

1. What are the specific target behaviors in observable and measurable terms?

### Predictability of the Target Behavior(s)

2. Are there events (antecedents) that consistently happen prior to the behavior?
3. What typically happens after the behavior occurs (consequences)?
4. Do the target behaviors occur at predictable times during the day?
5. If you answered "yes" to number 4, please indicate these time periods and the activities that coincide with the occurrence of the behaviors.

### Function(s) of the Target Behavior(s)

6. What are the function(s) of the target behavior(s) or what does the behavior accomplish?
7. What is the communicative intent of the target behavior(s)?

### History

8. Are there any significant life events that could account for the behavior(s) exhibited?
9. Which behavior intervention methods used in the past have been demonstrated to be effective in reducing the target behavior(s)?

### Setting Events

10. Are there medical/physical issues that could account for the target behavior(s)?
11. Does the occurrence of the target behavior(s) coincide with demands placed on the student in instructional settings, transition periods, or while the student is alone?
12. Is there a predictable schedule for the student during the school day?
13. What form does the schedule take (e.g., written, symbol, picture, object)?
14. Are there times and activities in which the behavior(s) does not occur?
15. Please indicate preferred reinforcers that the student enjoys (i.e., activities, tangibles).

Upon completing the structured interview with key informants, the teacher should then collate and synthesize the information. The data obtained from the interview should be analyzed to determine the patterns associated with the behavior such as:

- A description of the target behavior
- Antecedents, or "triggers," that commonly precede the behavior
- Consequences that consistently occur following the behavior
- Life events that could account for the behavior (if a sudden change such as death of a parent or loved one, parental separation, divorce)
- Hypotheses statements related to the function or (purpose) of the behavior, causal factors, and things to consider in terms of remediation

## Behavior Rating Scales

Behavior rating scales represent another tool that can be used to gather preliminary information about the specifics surrounding challenging behavior. There are numerous behavior rating scales designed to identify problem behaviors through the use of questionnaires. One instrument, the Motivation Assessment Scale (MAS), is very helpful in understanding the functions associated with challenging behavior.

The MAS (Durand & Crimmins, 1988) is a relatively easy instrument to use. When combined with other sources of data such as a structured interview and behavior observation, it can be very helpful in the identification of probable antecedents and consequences that are associated with problematic behavior. The MAS is also very helpful in the identification of the function associated with the behavior(s).

The MAS is comprised of 16 items presented on a Likert scale and is designed to assess the functions of challenging behavior, namely attention, tangible, social, and self-stimulation. The MAS examines both antecedents and consequences. The 16 items are equally distributed across the four major functions of challenging behavior, sensory (4 items), escape (4 items), attention (4 items), and tangible (4 items). The items are then tallied, resulting in a total and mean score with the relative ranking of perceived function being the final product. Once the perceived function of the target behavior has been identified, intervention plans can result with an emphasis on the arrangement of antecedents, the teaching of positive alternative behaviors, and/or the modification of consequence events.

Emphasis is given to the development of behaviors that serve the same function as that of the challenging behavior, yet are directed at allowing the individual's needs to be met through the development of appropriate behavior responses. Thus the function of the behavior is never altered; however, the form or what the behavior (looks like) is the focus of the intervention effort.

There are limitations associated with indirect forms of assessment such as behavior rating scales. These methods rely totally on informants to provide information based on memory that could be potentially limiting in terms of a respondent's accuracy. They may also encourage exaggerated responses on the part of respondents, especially where challenging behaviors are concerned.

One method that can lend greater reliability to the use of **indirect assessment** tools such as structured interviews and the MAS is to sample multiple respondents. This allows one to synthesize the comments or ratings across respondents, thus providing feedback in terms of the degree of similarities and consistency across raters.

The best method would be to use indirect assessment methods such as rating scales as part of an assessment package along with behavior observation and other components (Miltenberger, 1998). The benefits of behavior observation as the best method for understanding the relationship of antecedents to behaviors cannot be overstated in terms of reliability. It provides the observer with a hands-on view of the learner within the relevant setting of his natural environment, thus providing an understanding of the interaction that is occurring between the learner and the pertinent environmental variables. This method can, of course, be more time consuming, yet lends itself to ensuring the reliability and accuracy needed to understand the issues surrounding challenging behavior.

## Observational Methods

As previously described, direct observation offers many advantages when attempting to understand the events surrounding behavior, including antecedents and consequences. There are three different methods of behavior observation that are useful to consider in the assessment of antecedents associated with problematic behavior. These methods include (a) scatter-plot analysis, (b) A-B-C (Antecedent-Behavior-Consequence) recording, and (c) interval-based recording of behavior. An additional method that has been quite useful in the assessment of antecedents is structural analysis (Wacker, Cooper, Peck, Derby, & Berg, 1999). Structural analysis is a form of functional analysis that seeks to better understand the relationship of specific antecedent events to challenging behavior through the manipulation (i.e., the adding or removal) of these antecedents and noting the effects on the rate of behavior. Although structural analysis has been used in the study of antecedents that occasion challenging behavior in learners, it has primarily been used in clinical evaluation settings. It also appears to have promise within home and classroom environments (Wacker et al., 1999).

## Scatter-Plot Analysis

**Scatter-plot analysis** (Touchette, MacDonald, & Langer, 1985) is a simple and portable method that provides information concerning the frequency, time, and setting in which the target behavior occurs. It enables us to understand the pattern of behavior over time such as time of day in which the behavior occurs or does not occur, activities or demands associated with high frequencies of the behavior, and also those activities and demands associated with an absence of the behavior. Scatter-plot analysis allows us to correlate high rates of behavior with one or more of these corresponding variables and better identify the important antecedents associated with challenging behavior. It is a relatively easy procedure to implement within educational environments and is preferred by many teachers because of its ease and utility within busy learning environments. A scatter-plot data sheet consists of a series of grids that are associated with time increments and days of the week. The time increments may vary based on the specific needs of the classroom teacher, but generally range from 15 to 30 minute intervals. When the target behavior occurs during the designated time interval, a slash is placed in the corresponding box. If the behavior occurs multiple times during the designated time period, the box is blackened completely through, and if the behavior does not occur at all during the designated time period, the box is left blank.

Typically scatter-plot data are collected over a period of time such as 1 week before trends can be noticeably visible. Most often these trends reveal high rates of problematic behavior corresponding consistently with certain times of days and activities occurring within these time frames. An example of a scatter-plot data sheet is contained in Figure 4–3.

A scatter-plot data sheet allows the teacher to link the high rates of behaviors to specific times of day and to the activities associated with these time periods. In this example, the learner has peak periods of behavior that are associated with math and reading. The remaining portions of the day are relatively free from disruption. Given this information, the teacher can now examine the nature of those activities with the learning style and challenges associated with the learner.

In this example, the child, Peter, has a diagnosed learning disability, and math and reading are two areas that pose significant learning challenges for him. He meets with frustration during these activities. The teacher can now use this information to examine more critically the types of learning tasks and how these tasks are presented to Peter. This type of microanalysis allows Peter's teacher to better understand the instructional antecedents that prompt Peter's work refusal behavior. She can now attempt to modify her instruction and at the same time teach Peter new behaviors that would better accommodate his frustrations and redirect them.

### Consider This

The use of a scatter-plot can assist teachers in not only documenting the frequency of a behavior but also the contextual variables that surround the occurrence of a behavior. An example of these would be the time of day the behavior occurred and the class or activity the student was engaged in.

In the example provided, Peter's outbursts are directly related to his apparent skill deficits in reading and math. Given that his behavior coincides with each of these classes, it would enable a teacher to strategize about instructional methods and curriculum changes needed to facilitate Peter's engagement in each of these areas.

**FIGURE 4–3**
*Scatter-Plot Data Sheet*

Name _____        Behavior _____

|  | Monday | Tuesday | Wednesday | Thursday | Friday |
|---|---|---|---|---|---|
| 8:00–8:15 |  |  |  |  |  |
| 8:15–8:30 | ✓✓✓✓ | ✓✓✓✓ ✓✓ | ✓✓ | ✓✓✓✓ ✓✓✓ | ✓✓✓ |
| 8:30–8:45 |  |  |  |  |  |
| 8:45–9:00 | ✓✓✓ | ✓✓ | ✓✓✓✓ | ✓✓✓✓✓ | ✓✓✓✓ |
| 9:00–9:15 | ✓✓ | ✓✓✓✓ | ✓✓✓ | ✓✓ | ✓✓✓✓✓ |
| 9:15–9:30 |  |  |  |  |  |
| 9:30–9:45 |  |  |  |  |  |
| 9:45–10:00 |  |  |  |  |  |
| 10:00–10:15 | ✓✓ | ✓✓✓ | ✓✓ | ✓✓ | ✓✓✓ |
| 10:15–10:30 | ✓✓✓ | ✓ | ✓✓✓ | ✓✓✓ | ✓✓✓ |
| 10:30–10:45 | ✓✓ | ✓✓✓ | ✓ | ✓✓ | ✓ |
| 10:45–11:00 | ✓ |  |  | ✓✓ |  |
| 11:00–11:15 | ✓✓ |  |  |  | ✓ |
| 11:15–11:30 |  |  |  |  |  |
| 11:30–11:45 |  |  |  |  |  |
| 11:45–12:00 |  |  |  |  |  |
| 12:00–12:15 |  |  |  |  |  |
| 12:15–12:30 |  |  |  |  |  |
| 12:30–12:45 |  |  |  |  |  |
| 12:45–1:00 |  |  |  |  |  |
| 1:00–1:15 |  |  |  |  |  |
| 1:15–1:30 |  |  |  |  |  |
| 1:30–1:45 |  |  |  |  |  |
| 1:45–2:00 |  |  |  |  |  |
| 2:00–2:15 |  |  |  |  |  |
| 2:15–2:30 |  |  |  |  |  |
| 2:30–2:45 |  |  |  |  |  |
| 2:45–3:00 |  |  |  |  |  |
| 3:00–3:15 |  |  |  |  |  |
| 3:15–3:30 |  |  |  |  |  |

## A-B-C (Antecedent-Behavior-Consequence) Recording

**A-B-C** (antecedent-behavior-consequence) **recording** represents another more commonly used behavior observation technique. This method is most helpful and relatively practical for use by classroom teachers and instructional staff. It is also referred to as anecdotal or narrative recording. A-B-C recording is conducted by selecting an observational period, for example 20 minutes of an hour or perhaps one short class period per day. Often the selection of the observation period can be guided by the data from the scatter plot. Upon examining the trends found within the scatter plot, the observer can plan to observe using A-B-C recording during both the peak times when behavior occurs at the highest frequency and also during periods in which the behavior does not occur at all. The contrasting observation periods will shed light on the antecedents and consequences that occasion periods of high-frequency periods with that of the periods in which little or no occurrences of the behavior occur.

When conducting anecdotal or A-B-C recording, the observer is interested in observing a specific learner within the context of her natural environment such as the classroom or home setting. The observer attempts to be noninvasive and records the antecedent–behaviors–consequences as they naturally occur. This is done on a data sheet specifically designed for this type of recording (see Figure 4–4). It is important when conducting A-B-C recording that the observer maintain focus and record the events as they happen in a manner that is descriptive.

Another variation of the A-B-C recording method has been offered (Miltenberger, 2001; O'Neill et al., 1997). It is referred to as the checklist method (Miltenberger, 1998) and involves a data sheet that lists specific antecedents, behaviors, and consequences associated with an individual. This permits the observer to simply check the corresponding box when noting the occurrence of a specific antecedent–behavior–consequence.

## Interval Recording

The third method used in the assessment of antecedents–behaviors–consequences is interval-based recording. Typically a 5- to 10-second interval scoring procedure is used to note the occurrence/nonoccurrence of specific antecedents, behaviors, and consequences as they occur. There are two types of interval scoring procedures to select from. These include whole interval scoring or partial interval scoring. Partial interval scoring is the one most commonly preferred and is most frequently cited within the literature.

Whole **interval recording** specifies that the target behavior must occur throughout the entire interval (i.e., 5 or 10 seconds) before an occurrence is scored. When using partial interval scoring, the target behavior must occur during a portion of the interval in order to be scored as an occurrence. There are some obvious limitations to the use of whole interval scoring

**FIGURE 4–4**
*A-B-C Recording Data Sheet*

Observer: _____

Date: _____

Time: _____

| ANTECEDENT | BEHAVIOR | CONSEQUENCE |
|---|---|---|
|  |  |  |
|  |  |  |
|  |  |  |
|  |  |  |
|  |  |  |
|  |  |  |

within busy classrooms and learning environments. In reality teachers have little time to conduct this level of analysis. One method that could serve to provide teachers with the information they need and allow for more detailed analysis is the use of videotape and subsequent analysis at a later time. Videotaping the interactions within the classroom or learning environment provides a permanent product that can be later scored. See

**FIGURE 4–5**
*Interval Recording*
*Data Sheet*

Name: _____

Behavior: _____

Date: _____

+ = on task

− = off task

| Time | Interval | | | | | | | | | | | | | Percentage |
|------|---|---|---|---|---|---|---|---|---|---|---|---|---|------|
| 1:00 | + | + | + | − | + | − | − | − | + | + | − | + | − | |
| | − | + | − | − | + | + | + | | | | | | | 55% |
| | | | | | | | | | | | | | | |
| | | | | | | | | | | | | | | |
| | | | | | | | | | | | | | | |
| | | | | | | | | | | | | | | |
| | | | | | | | | | | | | | | |
| | | | | | | | | | | | | | | |
| | | | | | | | | | | | | | | |
| | | | | | | | | | | | | | | |

Miltenberger, Rapp, and Long (1999) for an excellent description of how to use videotaped analysis for scoring behaviors in applied settings such as the classroom, home, or community. They describe how through using videotape, behaviors can be scored using the automated counters now commonly found on VCRs, thus making the analysis much easier as the intervals on the screen correspond with those on the data sheet. Figure 4–5 serves as an example of an interval scoring data sheet.

While using an interval recording procedure, the teacher can develop a checklist of probable antecedents, behaviors, and consequences specific to a particular learner and use a checklist while they conduct an analysis of videotaped sessions (Miltenberger, 1998). Another variation is the use of a code sheet that reflects the specific antecedents, behaviors, and consequences relevant to a specific setting. An illustration of this type of data sheet is contained in Figure 4–6. The data sheet reflects specific antecedent, behavior, and consequence variables related to the instruction of a young child with autism.

**FIGURE 4–6**
*Interval Data Sheet with Codes*

Observer: _____

Date: _____

**Conditions:**
P = play
I = instruction
A = alone

**Behaviors:**
+ = hair pulling
✓ = screaming
− = non-occurrence

| Time | Condition | | | | | | | | | | | Interval |
|------|-----------|---|---|---|---|---|---|---|---|---|---|---|
| 10:05 | I | + | + | − | − | − | ✓ | ✓ | + | + | − | − |
| | | | | | | | | | | | | |
| | | | | | | | | | | | | |
| | | | | | | | | | | | | |
| | | | | | | | | | | | | |
| | | | | | | | | | | | | |
| | | | | | | | | | | | | |
| | | | | | | | | | | | | |
| | | | | | | | | | | | | |

## Structural Analysis

**Structural analysis** (Wacker et al., 1999) has been used to evaluate the effects of various antecedent conditions on the behavior of children within clinical settings. It represents a form of functional analysis (the experimental manipulation of antecedent and consequence events to note their effects on behavior). In structural analysis, various antecedents are presented and removed so that the effects of these manipulations on behavior can be noted (Wacker et al., 1999). Antecedent variables include how tasks are presented, the number of tasks presented, the type of instructions used, and in general the instructional delivery. In using structural analysis, we hope to identify the specific antecedent conditions that trigger the target behavior. Conversely, we also hope to identify those antecedent conditions that promote positive behavior in the learner. Structural analysis serves as a mechanism to experimentally validate functional relationships (i.e., cause and effect) between antecedents and behavior. Functional assessment and functional analysis will be presented in greater detail in Chapter 6.

Wacker and colleagues (1999) have used structural analysis to investigate such antecedent events as varying levels of task demands, task preferences, and parental contact on the behavior of children within clinic and home environments. The rationale for the use of this procedure is that it allows the evaluator to gain a better understanding of the learner's behavior through the presentation and removal of specific antecedent variables in a systematic manner. The procedure typically involves the presentation of these various antecedent stimuli in the context of brief conditions lasting approximately 5 minutes in length. A series of reversal designs (i.e., the systematic presentation and removal of specific antecedent variables) is used to experimentally validate the presence of a functional relationship between specific antecedent variables and increased levels of problematic behavior.

Research into the use of structural analysis conducted by Harding, Wacker, Cooper, Millard, and Kovalan (1994) examined the effects of antecedent variables (a) play, (b) general directions, (c) specific directions, (d) choice making, (e) differential reinforcement, (f) preferred activities, and (g) timeout and guided compliance in the design of intervention packages for children ages 4 to 7 years with mild behavior challenges in an outpatient clinic. The structural analysis allowed researchers to identify specific antecedent variables that coincided with high rates of challenging behavior, thus allowing researchers to formulate treatment approaches aimed at using instructional antecedents that promoted positive behavior and subsequently those instructional antecedents that served as triggers for problematic behavior.

The obvious limitations associated with this particular type of assessment is that it requires a level of control (i.e., ability to manage all the variables to the degree of experimental control that is needed to validate results) that is typically not possible within educational settings. In spite of its portability within traditional learning environments, it has been demonstrated to be effective within home settings and shows promise in the assessment of antecedents that frequent problematic behavior.

## Points to Remember

- Antecedent assessment is important for understanding those factors that trigger challenging behaviors in learners
- The most commonly used methods used in the assessment of antecedents include

  1. Structured interview
  2. Scatter-plot analysis
  3. A-B-C recording
  4. Interval recording
  5. Structural analysis

- Antecedent assessment assists in the identification of variables that influence challenging behavior, thus providing essential information used in the development of proactive intervention strategies.
- An antecedent that may serve to trigger problematic behavior in learners includes physical, social/emotional, environmental, and instructional components.

# PREVENTION OF CHALLENGING BEHAVIOR THROUGH THE MODIFICATION OF ANTECEDENTS

The assessment of antecedent influences on challenging behavior allows us to understand how these events trigger problematic behavior in learners. Upon identifying these relationships, we then can design interventions aimed at lessening or preventing their impact on behavior. These interventions can range from modifying instructional practices, learning environments, and/or enhancing the quality of life for the learners we serve. A key point to bear in mind is how environmental variables paired with instructional design and delivery can play a significant role in the behaviors. The way instructional materials are presented, scheduled, and arranged within the physical environment can all have an impact on a learner's behavior (Dunlap & Kern, 1993).

It is essential in our effort to provide effective and meaningful educational outcomes for every child that we understand first how to provide effective behavior supports to children and youth. Antecedent assessment provides us with critical information to aid in the development of learner-centered interventions.

A teacher is first and foremost a facilitator of learning. This includes organizing the learning environment and instructional structure needed by every child to learn and maintaining sensitivity to the individual characteristics and performance strengths and limitations encountered by every child. The outcomes derived from the assessment of antecedents can offer practical considerations in the organization and delivery of instruction, in the design of the learning environment, and to the level of individual supports needed. These various antecedent management strategies including environmental modifications, instructional modifications, and quality-of-life enrichment strategies will be explored in greater depth.

# ENVIRONMENTAL INTERVENTION STRATEGIES

Often problematic behavior can be linked to environmental conditions such as overcrowding, noise, room temperature (too hot or too cold), a lack of visual clarity for learners, and general structure and organization within the classroom. Often the challenging behaviors that occur within learning environments can be attributed to one or more of these factors. These behaviors are often a blend of skill limitations on the part of the learner coupled with an insensitivity found within the environments in which they learn and function (Durand, 1990).

A good illustration of the importance of structuring the environment for learner success can be found in the education of children and youth with autism. Educators of children and youth with autism recognize the importance of structuring the learning environment to compensate for the skill deficits experienced by learners with autism. These challenges include organizational skills, the need for enhanced visual clarity, and the need for enhanced supports through transitions (Lord & Schopler, 1994). Environmental accommodations are therefore made to ensure positive learner outcomes and minimize the occurrence of problematic behavior, thus serving as an example of how environmental antecedents can be managed to promote positive behavior and learning outcomes.

Many environmental variables could potentially influence the occurrence of problematic behavior in learners. Too often these influences may not be apparent to the teaching personnel who continually confront these ongoing behaviors. Some of the more relevant questions to ask with regard to environmental antecedents will now be examined.

## Is the Environment Pleasant?

This may seem too obvious to some. Certainly what is pleasant to some is not to others, and how can one operationally define and measure this variable? One observable and measurable indicator is the degree to which the environment is stimulating. Is the classroom colorful and inviting? Are materials age appropriate and stimulating to the eye? Do the interactions between the learners and the teacher reflect a warm and inviting manner? Is the noise level within the classroom comfortable? Do the learners appear content and engaged in meaningful activities? Other important considerations include the temperature of the classroom: Is it comfortable and seasonably appropriate? Is the classroom well organized and uncluttered? Is the classroom overcrowded, and what is the condition of the learners' desks and chairs? Vignette 4.3 discusses how the environment can influence learning.

## Vignette 4.3

### Environmental Influences on Classroom Behavior

Consider Michael, a fifth-grader who has just begun middle school. He had attended a small neighborhood elementary school prior to his transition to the fifth grade. His school is large and very old with many building problems. Among them are that the classrooms are too hot both in winter and summer, and the restrooms have antiquated plumbing that results in toilet overflows on a regular basis. Aside from these building issues, his year has been one of adjustments with changing classes, new teachers, and a considerably larger school. He has begun to complain to his parents about his dislike for school on a weekly basis. Given these challenges, Michael is an exceptionally gifted and talented student who is very skilled and capable, yet the distress he finds in his school environment has begun to diminish his desire to excel academically.

### Reflective Moment

- Given the apparent environmental challenges that Michael encounters in his classroom, how can his teacher minimize their effects by creating a more inviting learning community for him?

## Are the Environmental Cues Clear and Consistent?

Within most educational classrooms and learning environments cues are found that assist learners with regulating their behavior. These include aisles for walking and negotiating the classroom space, assigned seats and work areas for learners, and often a classroom schedule displayed for all to see. Some teachers use individual schedules for all learners as a method for promoting self-determination skills. Attention to these types of environmental supports is an excellent way to design environments conducive to learning and the support of children and youth.

## Is Ample Space Available?

One of the most overlooked factors that chronically plagues classrooms and schools is the problem of density and overcrowding. There has been much recent debate in the literature on how this topic relates to student performance outcomes. The Student-Teacher Achievement Project (STAR) has been a long-term research study conducted in Tennessee over the past 4 years that has examined the teacher–student ratio and benefits of small class sizes.

Findings from this project have indicated that classrooms of 17 students or less are optimal in terms of performance outcomes and student behavior. Their findings indicate that students from smaller classrooms consistently outperform their peers from larger classrooms in terms of better grades. Longitudinal studies that have followed many of these students beyond high school have indicated better lifestyle outcomes, including higher percentages attending college. Also relevant to these findings were that teachers from the smaller classes that were studied demonstrated an enhanced love for children, had better-developed listening skills, prepared instruction in advance, and were more effective communicators with students and parents than were their peers who were teaching in larger classrooms (Finn & Achilles, 1999).

The research findings have been viewed by many as landmark in that they empirically validate the benefits of small class sizes on learning and learner outcomes. Other potential benefits are that smaller class sizes reduce the stressors for both the teachers and learners, resulting in a more engaged learning environment with fewer behavior problems.

## Instructional Intervention Strategies

Often the behaviors that learners engage in within educational environments can be directly linked to curriculum and instruction. Research has demonstrated the relationship between instructional variables and their influence on the behavior of learners within educational settings (Dunlap, Kern-Dunlap, Clarke, & Robbins, 1991). This body of literature has substantially increased in the past decade and has raised many questions concerning how we teach and what we teach to youngsters. Often behavior problems experienced during the school day are precipitated by instructional demands and teacher/student interactions, not to mention school climate and how students feel about their teachers and principal. The problematic behavior often displayed by learners can be attributed to instructional variables. These problem behaviors can result from an interaction between instructional demands (how instructions are provided, the difficulty of the work, the amount of work) and a lack of congruence with the learning style and abilities of the student.

Generally speaking, there are two major classes of learning problems that learners confront. These are (a) skill deficits or the insufficient level of skill needed to perform the task and (b) motivation problems or a lack of desire to attempt performance. Skill deficits refer to a lack of ability on the part of the learner to perform a desired skill or behavior because they have either not been taught the skill, lack certain prerequisites that are critical for performance of the skill, or lack fluency to perform the skill independently. A lack of motivation on the part of the learner can be linked to many factors including the individual's learning history, the absence of reinforcing consequences present in his classroom, and a general fear associated with performance (Mager & Pipe, 1997). Teachers and educational personnel can promote learner engagement and minimize the occurrence of challenging behavior through careful attention to instructional antecedents and management of those variables that impede learning and behavior outcomes. Many of these fall under the category of preinstructional considerations, in that they should be addressed before instruction is delivered. These preinstructional considerations include

1. *Learning Strength—What learning strengths does the learner have that can be emphasized in the development of successful instructional formats?*

   Too often the learning and behavior challenges experienced by children and youth are addressed from the perspective that remediation is needed to "fix" the academic and social challenges experienced by these individuals without any attention to their individual strengths. Each learner has a set of skills or attributes that if identified can be used in the development of instructional programs directed toward setting the learner up for success. Subsequently, by capitalizing on individual strengths and using a compensatory approach through the design of behavior supports within environments, we can promote enhanced learning outcomes.

2. *Are there successful teaching and response formats that have been used successfully in the past?*

   It is important to confer with the child's former teachers, parents, and family to assist you in the identification of teaching and response formats that have been demonstrated to be successful with the child in the past. Understanding what works for the child is important when teaching new skills. How tasks are presented, the types of cues used in their presentation, and error correction procedures that have been successful are all very important preinstructional considerations.

Language and communication skill levels are also central to this area and identify the communication skills abilities of the learner; their ability to process cues such as gesture, visual, and auditory cues; and their preferred response modes, be they verbal or gesture. Prizant and Schuler (1987) referred to a series of core assessment questions when developing communication-based interventions for children with autism-spectrum disorders. Among these communication assessment considerations were the range and means of communicative functions expressed by the child (both verbal and nonverbal), conventional communication as well as idiosyncratic forms of communication.

**3.** *What is the cognitive level of the learner?*

It is important to understand the cognitive level of the learner before initiating instruction. The presence or absence of cognitive disability (i.e., mental retardation) is an important consideration when designing instructional programs in that it can also have an impact on the language and communication skills of the learner, the rate at which they acquire new information, and their tolerance for sustained instruction over a long period of time.

**4.** *What are the preferred activities of the learner?*

This preinstructional consideration attempts to identify the likes and dislikes of the learner. It is important to identify what subjects the learner enjoys and the type of academic skill instruction (i.e., drill and practice, computer-assisted instruction, creative endeavors, kinesthetic activities, and experiential learning) that is most/least preferred by the learner. It is also important to understand the activities that the learner enjoys for fun.

One important area often overlooked by teachers is the area of homework and promoting engagement and homework completion among learners. Hinton and Kern (1999) found that when student interests were incorporated into homework assignments that the performance rate for the fifth-grade middle school participants increased from 60% to over 95% in terms of completion, thus serving to validate this concept.

Kern, Dunlap, Clarke, and Childs (1994) developed a student-assisted functional assessment interview to assist in the identification of student interests across the curriculum. The interview is administered to students and assesses student rankings (i.e., likes and dislikes) on academic content (English, Math, Reading, Social Studies, Music, PE, and Computers) as well as on areas such as reinforcement, interest level and quality of academic content, and the student's self-perceptions on what area they do their best on and where they do not. A later study conducted by Dunlap, Foster-Johnson, Clarke, Kern, and Childs (1995) demonstrated the efficacy of this procedure in reducing the behavior of three students with learning and behavior challenges while modifying student learning outcomes around student preferences. These studies demonstrate the importance of student input in the development of instruction.

We have examined the major areas of preinstructional considerations when attempting to modify instructional antecedents. The chapter will now explore the use of instructional interventions aimed at antecedent management that also have functional utility across learners and learning environments.

Kern and Dunlap (1998) have synthesized research findings in the area of curricular intervention and broadly define the term *curricular variables* to include (a) content and objectives, (b) materials used in their performance, (c) behaviors associated with performance, (d) scheduling and sequencing, and (e) the ecological and social conditions in which they are presented. Their review points out that curricular modification has been inclusive of three major areas of study.

Namely, these have included (a) task modification (b) instructional modification and (c) modification of setting events. Basically, these equate to how tasks are designed for the learner taking into account the individual's learning strengths, interests, and the selection of socially valid instructional goals. This also takes into consideration how tasks are delivered to the learner in terms of instruction. Tasks need to be presented in a systematic manner, prompts used in the initial stages of acquisition to assist the learner, and reinforcement used throughout as a means to promote engagement on the part of the learner. Lastly, the issue of modifying setting events is difficult within many learning environments; however, teachers can become aware of these distant setting events and their influence on the behavior of learners.

The modification of instructional antecedents by teachers and caregivers represents an effective and systematic method for minimizing the effects of problem behavior across learning environments (schools, day care settings, home, community). The difficulty has been making the methods identified within the research portable and practical for educators within these environments to use. This question has been addressed by the field of positive behavior supports and continues to undergo further study through applied research. Some of these research-based practices will be expanded on in the next section of the chapter.

## MODIFYING INSTRUCTIONAL ANTECEDENTS

This section of the chapter will provide a sample of suggested strategies aimed at the modification of instructional antecedents as a method for minimizing the frequency of challenging behavior. These will be presented within two major categories. These are (a) task design and (b) presentation of tasks. These strategies are also applicable across ages and learning environments.

## Task Design

When designing instructional tasks for learners several intervention strategies can be used to prevent the occurrence of challenging behavior. These are as follows:

- *Make Tasks Relevant to the Learner*—Tasks should be directed toward the learner. They should be age and developmentally appropriate and be socially valid and functionally relevant. Teachers should be mindful to be inclusive of these elements in the selection and design of tasks. Often task demands are not geared for a learner's age or developmental level nor are they socially or functionally relevant to the learner's needs or interests.
- *Matching Tasks to the Learner's Abilities*—Tasks should be modified to the level of the learner. If tasks are too difficult and beyond the skill levels possessed by the learner, frustration can occur and subsequent behavior problems can ensue.
- *Build in Opportunities for Choice*—All learners respond better when they are given choice-making opportunities (Romaniuk & Miltenberger, 2001). Allow time and ample opportunity for learners to select tasks at different intervals throughout their day. One option that is useful is to identify the teaching objective, select three to five tasks and provide the learner with choice-making opportunities from this list of options. For example, the goal might be a language arts activity; the list of task options could include (a) a skills worksheet, (b) a kinesthetic activity requiring the learner to move about the learning area collecting materials, (c) peer buddy activity where more than one child works together, and lastly (d) a computer-assisted instruction exercise. The teacher can allow the students to select two of the four options for completing their activity in language arts during the period. By creating opportunities for choice potential, problem behaviors can be avoided.
- *Determine the Appropriate Length of Activities*—The length of activities is very important across all age groups and levels of ability. Activities should have time limitations that coincide with the age and developmental levels of the learner. Preschool-age children should engage in activities that do not exceed 15 minutes in length such as group story time. Primary-grade-level learners should not exceed 30 to 40 minutes per one activity, middle school youngsters no more than 45 minutes, and high school students no more than 60 minutes per activity.
- *Vary Activities Within the Classroom*—Structure and predictability within the classroom are no doubt important; however, activities should be varied and alternated to control for boredom and fatigue. Alter the types of activities used to teach specific content; provide novelty and alternative activities on an intermittent basis to achieve this goal. The teacher should also be aware of how frequently learners engage in the same task over and over as they fulfill the objectives stated on the learner's individualized education program (IEP). Often, problematic behavior results from children and youth being assigned the same tasks or worksheets every day with no new instruction or activity being offered.

- *Use of Classroom and Individual Schedules*—Classroom schedules are important components of an organized learning environment. The efficacy of this intervention tool as a means of promoting positive behavior in learners within inclusive settings has been documented (Massey & Wheeler, 2000). The schedules can be centrally located in the classroom or learning setting and can include times and written and pictorial listings of the scheduled activities for a given day. It serves as a reference point for both the learner and teacher to refer to. Individualized schedules can also be helpful for promoting self-management skills in learners and for reinforcing organization and task engagement. They have been widely used with children and youth with autism as a learning support mechanism. Individualized schedules are developed for each learner and tailored to her needs in terms of level. They can be developed using objects for learners with intense support needs such as children who are nonverbal and with severe disabilities or for younger children who are at prelanguage stages of development. Schedules can also be developed using photographs, picture symbols, and written words paired with these or alone. The level of visual cue represented on the schedule is an individual decision based on the abilities of the learner. As children age and develop language and sight word reading schedules, they can be graduated to become more abstract and ultimately lead to the use of a daily planner or pocket calendar in many instances.

The importance of task design as a mechanism for the prevention of challenging behavior has been described in detail. However, this concept is explored in terms of its application with a learner having severe disabilities in Vignette 4.4.

## Vignette 4.4

### Structuring Tasks for Learner Success

Josh was a 16-year-old learner with the label of severe mental retardation and was served in a self-contained classroom for adolescents with moderate and severe disabilities. He used functional signs to communicate his needs and was suspected of having auditory processing difficulties. Josh displayed out-of-seat behavior, general agitation, and ultimately aggression toward himself and others. His behaviors would usually escalate in that order if left unattended.

A functional assessment was conducted that consisted of (a) structured interview with his teachers and family, (b) scatter-plot analysis, (c) A-B-C analysis, and lastly (d) 10-sec partial interval recording using videotape analysis. From the data gathered, it appeared the trend was obvious that there were inconsistent teacher cues used during instruction and an absence of environmental cues present in the classroom such as a visual schedule for Josh to refer to. There was also an absence of reinforcing consequences associated with performance. The functions of his behavior appeared to be escape and sensory related.

Further observations revealed an absence of a functional curriculum for Josh. An example was the teacher reading a children's book to Josh and his peers during a group instruction period, at which point Josh left several times. Upon further analysis of Josh's frequency of these problematic behaviors, data revealed that the prevalence of these behaviors corresponded with periods of group instruction. During these periods he averaged approximately 70% of occurrences across 3 days of observation. In contrast, his periods of problematic behavior during individual instruction time averaged less than 25%.

The behavior support team collaborated on the possibilities and concurred that during group instructional periods more auditory cues were used with an absence of visual cues such as gestures. The opposite was true during the individual instructional periods, with more visual cues embedded within tasks thus making the ability to discern performance expectations clearer for Josh. Upon modifying the instructional presentation and developing instructional supports such as a picture schedule, Josh's behavior began to vastly improve.

### Reflective Moment

Why are visual cues so important in helping Josh understand the performance expectations associated with the teacher's instructional tasks?

## Task Presentation

How tasks are presented to learners can serve as antecedents that trigger problematic behavior if not controlled. Often little thought is given to understanding how to modify the presentation of academic demands to facilitate appropriate learner responses. There are several key points to consider when presenting instructional demands. These are as follows:

- *Use of Clear and Consistent Cues*—The selection of instructional cues is important when initiating instruction with learners. The cues that the teacher selects should be geared to the specific learner's needs. They should also be clear and consistent. Often a failure to clarify cues leads to learner confusion and subsequent frustration, resulting in disengagement and the potential for problematic behavior that interferes with instruction and task completion.

  Instructional cues should be direct, brief, and clear. They should also be consistent. In teaching new tasks, these recommendations are most important in that the goal of instruction during the skill acquisition stages of learning is to teach the components of a new skill with minimal error. Also important is the type of cue used. Verbal, gestural, or physical cues may be used or paired with one another. For example, the use of a verbal cue paired with a gesture or physical cue is not uncommon when teaching a new task to a learner. The form of cue used is important and should be determined based on the assessment of the learner's needs and strengths. Some children with some disabilities such as attention deficit disorder need short and direct verbal cues paired perhaps with gesture cues to lend clarity in their presentation.

- *Use Embedded Cues within the Task*—The use of embedded cues within the task is also important. For example, learners can be taught to identify cues embedded within the performance of a task that will serve as a visual stimulus for correct learner performance. Some examples could include when teaching a match-to-sample problem a lined outline of the sample be provided that the learner will use to make the correct match. Another illustration would be the use of highlighted instruction within written text and color-coded cues within tasks.

- *Interspersed Requesting*—One method that has been successful in promoting momentum related to task approach and completion has been interspersed requesting. It is an approach that uses high probability requests throughout the delivery of a task as a means of fostering learner compliance and task completion (Wehby & Hollahan, 2000). An example of this method applied to an academic task such as math problem completion would be to intermittently present math problems that are within the learner's performance range (skills currently in his repertoire) within a group of problems, some being more difficult as a method for promoting task engagement and reducing escape-motivated behavior in learners.

- *Systematic Instruction*—Systematic instruction represents an instructional methodology designed to teach skills in a structured and stepwise manner. It employs the use of prompts and error correction procedures sometimes referred to as prompt hierarchies. Prompt hierarchies vary depending on the type of task to be taught and the needs of the learner. Most often, a system of least-to-most prompts is used in the delivery of instruction. Such a prompt hierarchy would look as follows:

I  = Independent performance—(Teacher allows for the learner to independently perform the task).

V = Verbal prompt—(The teacher initiates the task with a verbal prompt such as "begin working").

G = Gesture prompt—(If after 3 to 5 seconds, the learner does not initiate the task, the teacher may point or use another gesture to help the learner initiate the step in the task that he is working on).

P = Physical prompt—(Again, the teacher allows 3 to 5 seconds to elapse at which point if the learner fails to respond to the component step in the task, the teacher then uses a hand-over-hand procedure to assist the learner).

In using such a system, the teacher would initiate a task with the learner and allow for a 3 to 5-second time delay to occur before initiating the next level of prompt to assist the learner. The prompt hierarchy is structured in such a way that the teacher would proceed through the hierarchy as needed based on the learner's performance.

• *Use of Naturally Occurring Reinforcers*—Often learners approach the performance of a task with greater interest if functional and naturally occurring reinforcers are a consequence for task completion. By this, we are not recommending the extensive use of edibles and stickers and things that are contrived, yet are recommending outcomes that are functional and naturally occurring within the learning environment. Consequences such as free time paired with choice serves as a good example. Upon completion of an activity, the learner is given free time if she completes the task in the allotted time frame. During this free time period, the learner may select from a list of choices such as computer time, library time, reading time, or assisting the teacher in running errands or with classroom organization. This is not to say that the use of stickers and treats occasionally, when paired with verbal praise, are not warranted or meaningful for some children and youngsters. Quite the contrary, these are looked on with favor by children, but an overreliance on them is not recommended.

The use of a preferred activity as a reinforcing consequence is featured in the example provided in Vignette 4.5.

## Vignette 4.5

### Enhancing Learner Performance

Richard is an 18-year-old young man with Down syndrome. He has severe mental retardation and is currently being served for half the school day in a transition program. As part of this program, he is working on a paid job contract for 4 hours each day. His job is to assemble drapery pulleys for a company that manufactures and sells miniblinds. His job-training specialist has noticed that Richard engages in some stereotypical behavior that she has termed "self-cleansing behavior." This behavior is characterized by excessive rocking, licking the palms of his hands, and running his palms through his hair. Following the completion of a functional assessment, the function of this behavior is thought to be sensory related. After direct observations of Richard in his work setting, the behavior support specialist, Ms. Holmgren, determined that the job-training specialist on average provided two verbal cues per 50-minute session to prompt Richard to work. Furthermore, a preassessment of Richard's skills on performance of the job task was not conducted.

Ms. Holmgren developed a systematic intervention that included the use of a system of least-to-most prompts, a task analysis of the job task, and a method for recording data on performance that included a 15-second partial interval scoring procedure. The intervention also used a preferred reinforcer at the completion of the task and a graduated system of increased work units over time. Ms. Holmgren also initiated a teaching method that included a workbasket, which contained the drapery pulleys, a second workbasket containing component parts, an empty basket for completed pulleys, and lastly a small plastic basket containing Richard's preferred reinforcement (a walkman, cassettes, and a digital timer).

**FIGURE 4–7**
*Percent of*
*Intervals Engaged in*
*Self-Cleansing*
*Behavior*

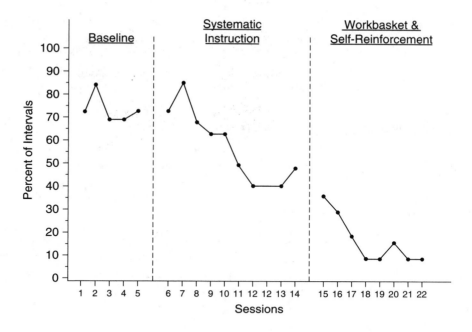

Systematic instruction procedures were implemented following a baseline to determine the percentage of intervals that Richard engaged in the challenging behavior across the conditions. Upon completion of his assigned work found within his workbasket, Richard could select a cassette tape and listen to a song for 3 minutes as set on the digital timer. Ironically, during this time as he listened to his music he would rock to and fro to the music as he enjoyed his favorite activity. The results of this successful intervention are displayed in Figure 4–7. It is also interesting to point out that during the initial stages of instruction, Richard was only able to complete 10 pulleys on average with assistance. Ultimately, as a result of sustained instructional efforts, he was able to assemble 50 pulleys consecutively.

### Reflective Moment

How would you modify the intervention developed by Ms. Holmgren? What could you do to increase the maintenance and generalization of Richard's newly acquired skills?

As you see in Figure 4–7, the percent of intervals that Richard engaged in self-cleansing behavior averaged 75% of intervals observed during baseline. During the first phase of intervention (systematic instruction), Richard's behavior decreased to 55%. The final phase of the intervention (workbasket and self-reinforcement) resulted in a further decrease of Richard's self-cleansing behavior to below 20%. The results of this intervention demonstrate the efficacy of systematic instruction as a means of enhancing the delivery of instruction and as a viable method for reducing challenging behaviors that interfere with learning.

## QUALITY-OF-LIFE ENRICHMENT

There has been emerging research over the past three decades on the significance of quality-of-life factors in the lives of persons with disabilities (Schalock, 2000). This concept is very congruent with the philosophy that underlies positive behavior supports. Quality-of-life factors are often sorely overlooked when designing interventions to address challenging behavior in learners. Although this area may be the most difficult area in which to have an impact on as a teacher, being attentive to the quality of life of learners is nevertheless very important. Schalock (2000) offers eight quality-of-life indicators as identified from extensive studies in the area. These indicators include

1. Emotional well-being
2. Interpersonal relations
3. Material well-being
4. Personal development
5. Physical well-being
6. Self-determination
7. Social inclusion
8. Rights

Schalock (2000) further addresses how these elements can be better attained through the delivery of services and supports to individuals with disabilities. One of these areas is matching persons with their environments as a method for diminishing the discrepancies between a person and his environment (Schalock, Keith, Hoffman, & Karan, 1989). Promoting a goodness-of-fit between and individual and his environment is a basic and important step to ensuring an individual's quality of life.

How does this translate to the concept of antecedent management within learning environments? As previously discussed in the preceding chapters, PBS believes in the engineering of environments as a critical factor in the success of individual learners. Learning environments must be mindful to promote this relationship between learners and their learning environments. Secondly, learning environments can seek to implement educational services and supports that are learner centered and inclusive of quality-of-life features. Enrichment of learning environments and programmatic efforts can result through attention being given to this very important aspect of intervention. Finally, the resulting outcomes from such approaches can be meaningful learning outcomes for all learners, including a sense of happiness, self-determination, satisfaction, safety, and general well-being. Lastly, such practices will lead to a reduction in problematic behavior and a greater sense of belonging on the part of all learners.

Through the material discussed in this chapter we have raised several key factors that directly or indirectly address the quality of life of children and youth within learning environments. As previously mentioned, a sensitivity to the learner and those antecedent variables that influence the behavior of a child or adolescent and the use of proactive assessment and intervention practices will lead to better outcomes for all concerned.

## SUMMARY

This chapter examined the relationship between setting events and antecedents and challenging behavior in learners. We learned from reading the chapter that there are three major categories of setting events: biological, environmental, and social/interpersonal. Biological setting events included thirst, hunger, sleep, the effects of medication, and fatigue factors. Environmental setting events involve factors such as the quality of environments (temperature, density, noise, climate, and design). Lastly, social/interpersonal setting events address the quality and scope of social relationships, friendships, social interactions, and personal space factors.

The assessment of antecedents was also presented with a number of methods for assessing antecedents being described. These methods included the use of a structured interview as used in a functional assessment of behavior. The purpose of the interview is the identification of target behaviors and the development of hypotheses statements related to the causal factors associated with problematic behavior. The use of other indirect forms of assessment such as behavior rating scales was also described. As pointed out in the chapter, the use of indirect forms of assessment used in isolation was considered a limitation, given they rely on secondary sources for information concerning a learner's behavior and not within the context that the behaviors occur. The Motivation Assessment (MAS) was recommended as a method for generating interview data relating to the functions of challenging behavior, especially concerning learners with more severe disabilities.

The section on antecedent assessment contained within the chapter also described observational methods such as scatter-plot analysis, A-B-C recording, and interval-based recording and the merits of each for use within classroom settings. Scatter-plot analysis represents a relatively easy to use method for determining both the frequency of occurrence of target behaviors as well as the time of day in which they occur and more contextual features that are related to their occurrence such as teacher and content area that they correspond with. A-B-C or anecdotal recording was reviewed as a method for identifying antecedents, behavior, and consequences using a narrative recording format. The use of interval-based recording was also described as a means by which to gather observational data related to antecedents and consequences related to behavior. In addition, the use of videotape analysis as a practical method for the analysis of behavior was discussed. Lastly, structural analysis (Wacker et al., 1999) was described as an experimental method for determining functional relationships between antecedents and problematic behavior with discussion on its potential applications. The value of structural analysis in the experimental analysis of antecedents that precipitate behavior is noteworthy; however, the obvious question mark has been the utility of this procedure within classrooms and applied learning environments.

The final section of the chapter addressed the importance of preventing challenging behavior through the modification of instructional antecedents. Research conducted by Dunlap and colleagues (1993) and subsequent research conducted by Kern and Dunlap (1998) were highlighted. The rationale for understanding the relationship between instructional antecedents and problematic behavior was described, and methods for prevention were explored. Other important areas that were introduced included the use of environmental intervention strategies aimed at the enhancement of learning environments and the use of instructional intervention procedures as a means of preventing problematic behavior.

Instructional interventions include preinstructional considerations. These considerations are prior to the implementation of specific strategies and are designed to provide a better understanding of individual learning strengths, challenges, and general characteristics of the learner. Also mentioned were task design (how tasks are selected and designed), task delivery (how instruction is given to the learner), and finally, quality-of-life enhancements such as the development of self-determination skills and the design of environments that interface with the needs and choices of the individual.

## ACTIVITIES TO EXTEND YOUR LEARNING

1. Conduct an assessment of antecedents within an applied setting and use the following methods: (a) structured interview, (b) Motivation Assessment Scale and at least one of the following (c) scatter-plot analysis, (d) A-B-C recording, and (e) interval-based recording. Compare and contrast each method in terms of its utility within the learning environment you selected and the data derived from each approach.
2. Describe one antecedent control strategy that you would consider using within your classroom to address a specific challenging behavior and present your approach to your classmates. Provide the rationale behind your selection.
3. Discuss numerous methods of preventing challenging behavior in learning environments and develop a list of strategies that you as a teacher could employ.

4. Conduct an assessment of a selected learning environment and identify methods for enhancing the learning environment with an emphasis on identifying and controlling for potential antecedents.
5. Conduct a literature search on one of the antecedent management strategies described in the chapter and develop a resource file of those references for future reference as a teacher.
6. Brainstorm how antecedent management strategies could be developed and used schoolwide to prevent discipline problems.

## FURTHER READING AND EXPLORATION

1. Consult the Positive Behavior Supports Web site at http://www.pbis.org and research any citations within the Web site to antecedent management strategies.
2. Examine the text entitled *Antecedent Control: Innovative Approaches to Behavioral Support* by James K. Luiselli and Michael J. Cameron (1998, Baltimore: Paul H. Brookes).

## REFERENCES

Carr, E. G. (1994). Emerging themes in the functional analysis of problem behavior. *Journal of Applied Behavior Analysis, 27,* 393–399.

Dunlap, G., Foster-Johnson, L., Clarke, S, Kern, L., & Childs, K. E. (1995). Modifying activities to produce functional outcomes: Effects on the disruptive behaviors of students with disabilities. *Journal of the Association for Persons with Severe Handicaps, 20,* 248–258.

Dunlap, G., & Kern, L. (1993). Assessment and intervention for children within the instructional curriculum. In J. Reichle & D. P. Wacker (Eds.), *Communicative alternatives to challenging behavior* (pp. 177–203). Baltimore: Paul H. Brookes.

Dunlap, G., Kern-Dunlap, L., Clarke, S., & Robbins, F. R. (1991). Functional assessment, curricular revision, and severe behavior problems. *Journal of Applied Behavior Analysis, 24,* 387–397.

Durand, V. M. (1990). *Severe behavior problems.* New York: Guilford.

Durand, V. M., & Crimmins, D. B. (1988). Identifying the variables maintaining self-injurious behavior. *Journal of Autism and Developmental Disabilities, 18,* 99–117.

Finn, J. D., & Achilles, C.M. (1999). Tennessee's class size study: Findings, implications, misconceptions. *Educational Evaluation and Policy Analysis, 21,* 97–110.

Harding, J., Wacker, D. P., Cooper, L. J., Millard, T., & Kovalan, P. (1994). Brief hierarchical assessment of potential treatment components with children in an outpatient clinic. *Journal of Applied Behavior Analysis, 27,* 267–278.

Hinton, L. M., & Kern, L. (1999). Increasing homework completion by incorporating student interests. *Journal of Positive Behavior Interventions, 1,* 231–234.

Horner, R. H., & Carr, E. G. (1997). Behavioral support for students with severe disabilities: Functional assessment and comprehensive intervention. *Journal of Special Education, 31,* 84–104.

Kern, L., & Dunlap, G. (1998). Curricular modifications to promote desirable classroom behavior. In J. K. Luiselli & M. J. Cameron (Eds.), *Antecedent control: Innovative approaches to behavioral support* (pp. 289–307). Baltimore: Paul H. Brookes.

Kern, L., Dunlap, G., Clarke, S., & Childs, K. E. (1994). Student-assisted functional assessment interview. *Diagnostique, 19,* 29–39.

Lord, C., & Schopler, E. (1994). TEACCH services for preschool children. In S. L. Harris & J. S. Handleman (Eds.), *Preschool education programs for children with autism* (pp. 87–106). Austin, TX: PRO-ED.

Mager, R. F., & Pipe, P. (1997). *Analyzing performance problems* (3rd ed.). Atlanta: The Center for Effective Performance.

Massey, N. G., & Wheeler, J. J. (2000). Acquisition and generalization of activity schedules and their effects on task engagement in a young child with autism in an inclusive preschool classroom. *Education and Training in Mental Retardation and Developmental Disabilities, 35,* 326–335.

Miltenberger, R. G. (1998). Methods for assessing antecedent influences on challenging behavior. In J. K. Luiselli & M. J. Cameron (Eds.), *Antecedent control: Innovative approaches to behavioral support* (pp. 47–66). Baltimore: Paul H. Brookes.

Miltenberger, R. G. (2001). *Behavior modification: Principles and procedures* (2nd ed.). Belmont, CA: Wadsworth.

Miltenberger, R. G., Rapp, J. T., & Long, E. S. (1999). A low-tech method for conducting real-time recording. *Journal of Applied Behavior Analysis, 52,* 119–120.

O'Neill, R. E., Horner, R. H., Albin, R. W., Sprague, J. R., Storey, K., & Newton, J. S. (1997). *Functional assessment and program development for problem behavior: A practical handbook.* Pacific Grove, CA: Brooks/Cole.

Prizant, B. M., & Schuler, A. L. (1987). Facilitating communication: Theoretical foundations. In D. J. Cohen & A. M. Donnellan (Eds.), *Handbook of autism and developmental disorders* (pp. 289–305). Silver Spring, MD: V. H. Winston & Sons.

Romaniuk, C., & Miltenberger, R. G. (2001). The influence of preference and choice on problem behavior. *Journal of Positive Behavior Interventions, 3,* 152–159.

Schalock, R. L. (2000). Three decades of quality of life. In M. I. Wehmeyer & J. R. Patton (Eds.), *Mental retardation in the 21st century.* Austin, TX: PRO-ED.

Schalock, R. L., Keith, K. D., Hoffman, K., & Karan, O. C. (1989). Quality of life: Its measurement and use. *Mental Retardation, 27,* 25–31.

Touchette, P. E., MacDonald, R. F., & Langer, S. M. (1985). A scatter-plot for identifying stimulus control of problem behaviors. *Journal of Applied Behavior Analysis, 18,* 343–351.

Wacker, D. P., Cooper, L. J., Peck, S. M., Derby, M. K., & Berg, W. K. (1999). Community-based functional assessment. In A. C. Repp & R. H. Horner (Eds.), *Functional analysis of problematic behavior* (pp. 32–56). Belmont, CA: Wadsworth.

Wehby, H. H., & Hollahan, M. S. (2000). Effects of high probability requesting on the latency to initiate academic requests. *Journal of Applied Behavior Analysis, 77,* 259–262.

# Chapter 5

# Using Reinforcement to Increase Appropriate Behavior

## CONCEPTS TO UNDERSTAND

*After reading this chapter, you should be able to:*

- Define and discuss reinforcement
- Describe positive and negative reinforcement
- Identify and describe classes of positive reinforcement
- Discuss the principles of effective reinforcement
- List and describe methods for using positive reinforcement within learning environments
- Describe the applications of reinforcement programs within the classroom, such as token reinforcement programs

## KEY TERMS

Chaining

Classes of reinforcers

Contingent reinforcement

Establishing operations

Fading

Interval schedules of reinforcement

Negative reinforcement

Positive reinforcement

Ratio schedules of reinforcement

Reinforcement

Shaping

Stimulus control

One of the major goals of positive behavior supports (PBS) is to foster learning environments and teach skills that promote positive behavior in all learners. Teachers and child caregivers alike can facilitate the development of appropriate behaviors in all learners through the use of positive reinforcement. Positive reinforcement is a critical piece of any instructional package in the development of new behaviors. Previously learned skills can also be maintained through the application of reinforcement procedures. Reinforcement is a vital component of all effective instructional or behavior intervention programs. It is important that teachers be fluent in their understanding of these principles to accomplish desired instructional and learning outcomes aimed at promoting positive behavior change.

Reinforcement is defined as the contingent delivery of a consequence following a behavior that increases the future probability of the behavior (Cooper, Herron, & Heward, 1987). Reinforcement strengthens behavior and can occur naturally within one's environment or can be part of an intervention plan aimed at teaching new behaviors (Sulzer-Azaroff & Mayer, 1991). In this chapter we will examine how positive reinforcement can be used to promote the development of new behaviors and skills in learners.

## WHAT IS REINFORCEMENT?

**Reinforcement** is a consequence that follows a behavior that strengthens the behavior. A formal definition of reinforcement is "the process in which the occurrence of a behavior is followed by a consequence that results in an increase in the future probability of the behavior" (Miltenberger, 2001, p. 496). What this means is that the contingent delivery of the reinforcing consequence must maintain or increase the behavior in terms of its rate, frequency, duration, and/or intensity. If it does not, then the consequence is not considered to be reinforcement.

Reinforcement is a part of everyday life. The term reward comes to mind for many when speaking of positive reinforcement. We all seek rewards in life, be in it our work, leisure-time pursuits, and other major areas of life. The work of B. F. Skinner (1953) has enlightened us on the topic of operant conditioning and the role of reinforcement in this process. Operant behaviors are those behaviors that operate on the environment and generate consequences and as a result are influenced by these consequences (Martin & Pear, 1999). Behaviors that are reinforced over time are strengthened. Reinforcement can occur naturally as part of everyday life or can be planned such as in an educational or learning setting or within the home such as parents providing incentives to their children for picking up their rooms or for assisting with household chores. Unplanned or naturally occurring reinforcement could include a child who works diligently on a class assignment because his teacher has recently commented about how she appreciates his efforts in her class. Planned reinforcement used by a teacher could include developing a point scheme for homework assignments turned in early or on time or the use of verbal praise by a parent for a child's attempt at performing a specific household task.

An individual's behavior is influenced by the interactions between that individual and her environment. These interactions over time result in the development of an individual's reinforcement history (Cooper et al., 1987). A reinforcement history is developed through the culmination of these life and learning experiences that mold and shape what we as individuals define as reinforcing. To be effective, reinforcement should be individualized and take into consideration the preferences of individual learners to the greatest extent possible. Another important point to remember as a teacher or therapist when working with students is to not underestimate the power of reinforcing consequences to change and or maintain desired behavior in learners. However, it is equally as important to understand how reinforcement can be used to enrich the quality of the learning environment, subsequently enhancing the quality of life for the learner. An example of this is illustrated in Vignette 5.1.

## Vignette 5.1

### Quality-of-Life Reinforcement at School

A young adolescent girl who just entered her first year of high school came home from school one day and proclaimed to her parents how much she enjoyed school and what supportive teachers she had. A few days passed, and the young girl again came home ecstatic about her day at school. When asked by her father as to what made her day so special, she replied, "My teachers are simply great! My English teacher told us how special we were and how she looked forward to our class every day because we worked so hard, and that we were wonderful students. And, my history teacher always says how much he appreciates our giving it our best in his class, and my computer science teacher told me how impressed she was with my knowledge of computing." The father smiled and said to his daughter, positive praise goes a long way doesn't it, and do you think this is why you are enjoying school so much this year?" The girl replied, "Absolutely Dad, this is the first time I have ever felt this level of encouragement from my teachers. I actually look forward to going to school each day and what I am going to learn from each of my teachers."

### Reflective Moment

How can a teacher's affect influence the performance of their students? What can you as a teacher do to help learners engage in learning and at the same time contribute to their self-esteem?

Vignette 5.1 shows the significance of enriching a learning environment with positive reinforcement. To begin and end each school day with a statement of positive regard or a kind gesture from one's teacher is invaluable. To receive acknowledgement for one's effort can enhance a child or adolescent's self-esteem and desired behavior to learn. In contrast, consider Vignette 5.2.

## Vignette 5.2

### A Failure to Provide Reinforcement

Consider the following scenario. A six-year-old child named Ethan, with mild cerebral palsy, was given an assignment to color a picture from his workbook that accompanied a story. He worked very hard at selecting the right colors and carefully traced the picture with his crayons, being cautious to color the picture just right. Upon completing his masterpiece, he proudly went up to the teacher's desk and said, "Would you like to see my picture?" The teacher looked up and said, "Oh, you are finished?" "Well, you colored outside the lines didn't you?" Tearfully Ethan went back to his chair and shortly thereafter had a behavior incident that later escalated in more externalized behaviors, thus resulting in a less than positive day at school for him. Sadly, a caring teacher could have avoided the entire situation and that moment in a child's life.

#### Reflective Moment

Describe how you feel the teacher should have responded to Ethan concerning his work. How would you have given feedback to Ethan?

After reflecting on the material covered to this point, decide how you as a teacher could respond to the situation in Vignette 5.2 in a more reinforcing manner. Another important point to consider from the previous example is that the child in this case, Ethan, is attempting to recruit reinforcement from his teacher (i.e., he is attempting to get affirmation or validation from the teacher regarding his work). For the teacher in this instance, it is important to respond favorably to Ethan's attempts at performance, being mindful to recall that he was engaged in completing the task, that he genuinely put forth his very best effort in completion of the task, and that he sought affirmation for his work. It is important to remember how a teacher's response can make or break the spirit of a child.

## POSITIVE REINFORCEMENT

**Positive reinforcement** is perhaps the most well known form of reinforcement procedure practiced among educators. Positive reinforcement is defined as the contingent presentation of a stimulus that increases the probability of the occurrence of the behavior in the future. Translated to practice, what does this mean? If a teacher provides a learner with a choice of preferred activities consisting of library time, computer time, or time with the teacher following the completion of their assigned task and this procedure results in strengthening the behavior (task completion) then positive reinforcement has been demonstrated. Positive reinforcement is widely used within classroom settings and other learning environments. Examples of positive reinforcement can include verbal praise, smiles, teacher proximity, access to preferred activities, and choice. The key points to remember are that reinforcers should be individualized and are valued by the individual in order to be effective. Also, regardless of the type of reinforcers that are selected (e.g., praise or activities) in order to qualify as a positive reinforcer they must increase the occurrence of the target behavior. Positive reinforcement is an effective tool when used by a skillful and caring teacher within any teaching and learning context.

### Consider This

An example of this would be the use of the Premack Principle (Premack, 1959). This has also been referred to as "Grandma's Rule" (Alberto & Troutman, 2002). The Premack Principle states that the opportunity to engage in a high-probability behavior can be used to reinforce a low probability of behavior. Some examples of the Premack Principle are as follows.

"When you complete your dinner, you may have a piece of chocolate pie." The high probability behavior (eating a slice of chocolate pie) will have a greater value, especially if an unpreferred dish happens to be the entrée for dinner that evening.

Another example might be something like this, "when you complete the assignment, you may play your favorite game on the computer." Each example clearly specifies that if the learner performs the desired behavior (low-probability behavior) that they will be reinforced by a desired consequence or a (higher-probability behavior). This technique can be very effective for classroom teachers when attempting to promote task engagement and task completion with learners.

## NEGATIVE REINFORCEMENT

**Negative reinforcement** occurs when an occurrence of the target behavior is followed by the removal or avoidance of an aversive stimulus, ultimately resulting in an increase in the target behavior (Miltenberger, 2001). This procedure is often misunderstood and thought of as a punishment procedure; however, it does not reduce behavior as would be the case with punishment; it strengthens or increases the probability of a target behavior

(Cooper, et al., 1987). One of the most obvious examples that comes to mind is in Vignette 5.3.

## Vignette 5.3

### Strengthening Challenging Behavior Through Negative Reinforcement

Aaron is a 14-year-old learner with an identified learning disability. School has served as a constant source of frustration for him over the past several years, and now with his recent transition to high school he feels more out-of-sorts about it than ever. This is especially the case in math. He is in a prealgebra class and receives some tutoring and assistance from the resource teacher, but is struggling in the regular classroom. Upon receiving his problems to complete during class, he attempts a few and then becomes increasingly frustrated, shouting expletives about how he thinks the work is useless resulting in an exchange of verbal jabs between him and his teacher, resulting in Aaron being sent to the principal's office.

#### Reflective Moment

As a teacher, how would you respond to a learner like Aaron who is obviously "turned off" to school? How can we promote Aaron's success through our instructional efforts and in turn lessen his ill feelings toward school?

In examining Vignette 5.3, it is apparent that Aaron has difficulty completing the task. In response to his frustration, he fails to be able to communicate his need for assistance in an effective manner, resulting in behaviors that are not appropriate, nor helpful to Aaron. The teacher's response in this case is to send Aaron to the principal's office, allowing him to escape the task demand and ultimately serving to negatively reinforce and strengthen this behavior. Often escape behaviors as demonstrated in the previous example are strengthened by negative reinforcement. Escape behaviors are those behaviors that are directed at escaping from an aversive situation, such as the example illustrated in Vignette 5.2. With regard to positive behavior supports, individual and specific classroom supports once identified and implemented can be used to successfully eliminate such problems from occurring.

Avoidance behavior is also associated with negative reinforcement, with the intent being aimed at avoiding an aversive stimulus rather than terminating it (Cooper et al., 1987). Some more prominent examples of avoidance behavior include children who pretend to be ill hoping to stay home from school to avoid a threat from a school bully or having to sit for an exam, children who fail to verbally express their feelings to avoid conflict with a parent or sibling, and losing homework assignments to avoid receiving a poor grade. In each of these examples, the aversive consequence was avoided. When these behaviors are negatively reinforced over time, the individual fails to develop a repertoire of alternative social and communication skills that would address such conflicts in their lives in a more direct and deliberate manner. Many behaviors such as task disengagement and disruptive behavior are aimed at escape or avoidance from instructional tasks (Cipani, 1995). Cipani (1995) recommended the following approaches for determining whether negative reinforcement is maintaining a problem behavior:

1. Does the behavior result in the termination of instructional demands or activities?

2. Does the learner experience difficulties with regard to the instructional tasks or demands in question?

3. Do the behaviors occur most frequently in those academic subject areas that the learner has difficulty with versus those tasks that the learner has greater degrees of ability in?
   (Cipani (1995). Be aware of negative reinforcment. *Teaching Exceptional Children, 27,* 36–39.

There are some potential solutions for addressing behaviors that are linked to negative reinforcement. One of the most obvious is to alter task demands that would result in promoting participation on the part of the learner. A second strategy would be to teach alternative skills or learning strategies to the learner to address the areas of deficiency, and lastly, use of positive reinforcement to acknowledge attempts at performance and for the absence of the problem behavior. These, along with other types of intervention strategies, will be elaborated on in the latter portion of the chapter under "Using Reinforcement."

## SELECTION OF REINFORCERS

Reinforcement is an important element of quality of life for everyone, yet the types of reinforcers preferred by individuals are numerous and varied. Of course the basic human needs such as food, clothing, and shelter are consistent for most people and certainly toys are meaningful to all children. Yet, it is very important to consider the individual preferences of each learner when developing a program using positive reinforcement. It should also be noted that reinforcers often work best when they are paired. The right combination of edibles, activity, tangible, and social reinforcers when paired with one another can have a significant and lasting impact on promoting positive behavior in each of us. Figure 5–1 contains examples of how reinforcers can be paired to promote and affirm positive behavior.

FIGURE 5–1
*Pairing Reinforcers*

- "I like the way you did such a good job of expressing yourself on your essay, I am going to give you an additional 5 bonus points for your hard work."
- "Excellent job cleaning your room, son, how about an ice cream cone for such good work?"
- "Thank you for the beautiful picture that you made," said the mother, giving her child a hug and smiling.
- "I like how hard you are working on your assignment, if there is time remaining when you complete it, choose a free time activity that you would like to do."
- "Great job, here is a bonus for your excellent work."

These examples emphasize how reinforcers can be paired. Usually this means pairing a social reinforcer with an activity, edible, or tangible reinforcer.

## CLASSES OF POSITIVE REINFORCERS

Typically, reinforcement can be classified using the following labels: edibles, activity, tangibles, social, and token reinforcers. Examples from various **classes of reinforcers** include

- *Edibles—Food and Drink Preferences:* Juice, water, milk, fruit, cereal, pudding, peanut butter, crackers, raisins, cookies, popcorn
- *Activity—Preferred Activities Enjoyed by the Individual Within Work, Play, and Leisure-Time Contexts:* Computer games, reading a book, playing with puzzles, playing basketball, listening to music, playing a board game, playing cards, completing an art project, assisting the teacher, free time, swimming, jobs in the classroom, no homework days
- *Tangibles—Preferred Items Such as Toys, Personal Possessions, and Clothing:* Books, backpack, notebooks, pencils, logo apparel such as a jacket or hat, makeup, magazines, miniature cars, action figures
- *Social—Includes Social Praise, Conversation, Hugs, Smiles, Social Attention and Eye Contact. These Can be Applied to Individual Learners or Used Within an Entire Class:* Smiles from the teacher or parent, nodding in affirmation, recognition for attempts at performance, "Good work," "Nice improvement," "Thanks for your efforts," "That's great," "Thank you for being so patient," "I like the way you have gotten your materials out and are ready for work"
- *Token—This Category Includes Token Reinforcers That Can be Exchanged for a Specific Reinforcer that Is Valued by the Learner:* Candy, free time, computer access, bonus points, homework free pass, library time, tickets to a movie, free meal coupons, gift certificate, money

When constructing an intervention plan, it is important to list those reinforcers that have been effective in the past and also those that are preferred by the individual learner. Several methods can be used to identify reinforcers for a specific learner. These methods include

1. Asking the parents and family of the learner what he enjoys most such as favorite toy, activity, social amenity, or other.

2. Asking the learner what he enjoys most. Assessing personal preference is important and everyone likes to be considered. Ask the learner to complete a reinforcer survey where they circle or list their most preferred reinforcers in the following areas: edibles, tangibles, activities, and social.

3. Providing the learner with choice and allowing him to select their preferred reinforcers from a reinforcer menu or by presenting them with various items and allowing them to choose their preferred reinforcers as they are presented. This is known as reinforcer sampling.

4. Performing a review of past educational records is another helpful method for identifying reinforcers that were successfully used in the past.

An important consideration to remember is that for learners who have well-developed communication skills and who are school age, the direct approach is often best when trying to identify reinforcer preferences. Asking the learner is the best and most timely method for ensuring what the learner likes most and what they least prefer. Another method that is often effective is by presenting students with a reinforcer menu and asking them to circle their preference. However, for learners who are young, or for students with significant challenges in communication associated with comprehensive disabilities, the use of parent interviews, record review and presenting the student with choice-making opportunities is recommended.

Reinforcer assessment can be accomplished through allowing a choice-making opportunity for a child. This is done by presenting the student with a choice of two objects (i.e., toys or activities) by using picture symbols or photos of actual activities. Provide a verbal cue paired with a gesture if necessary such as a pointing motion and ask the student to "pick the toy you want to play with" or "choose the activity you want." It is important to recognize how to accommodate individual needs when presenting them with a choice-making opportunity to assess reinforcers. For example, if severe cognitive disabilities and subsequent communication difficulties are present, often allowing the child to point or approximate by pointing to the desired object is sufficient. Bambara and Koger (1996) described a procedure for teaching how to make choices. Their recommendations were formulated from a review of pertinent literature in this area includes the following steps:

1. Provide a student an opportunity to sample the options that are available to her. These options should be based on personal preferences.

2. Present the options before the student and allow her to visually or tactilely scan each option.

3. Verbally prompt the learner to choose, by asking, "Which one do you want?"

4. Wait approximately 5 to 10 seconds to allow the learner to respond.

5. Reinforce immediately if an independent choice occurs by giving the preferred choice to the student with verbal praise.

6. Provide prompting if the independent choice response does not occur immediately.

7. Repair the situation if a student refuses an option, take it away, and never force choice.

8. Repeat steps 2 to 7 for another choice opportunity and continue as long as the student is receptive and vary options, left or right on each trial. (Bambara & Koger, 1996)

## PRINCIPLES OF EFFECTIVE REINFORCEMENT

For reinforcement to be effective, some basic rules associated with delivery of reinforcers should be remembered:

1. *Reinforcement Must be Contingent*—It is important that teachers establish the contingencies or rules related to reinforcement. Clear guidelines concerning classroom behavior need to be established, with contingencies being clearly explained to all learners. Miltenberger (2001) defined **contingent reinforcement** as "a relationship between a response and a consequence in which the consequence is presented if and only if the response occurs" (p. 491). Guidelines for administering reinforcement also need to be clear and concise so that learners understand expectations and consequences associated with desired behavior.

2. *Reinforcement Needs to be Immediate*—For reinforcement to be effective it must be delivered immediately following the desired behavior (Skinner, 1938). When a teacher asks a child to complete a task, the teacher must administer the appropriate reinforcer immediately following performance of the behavior on the part of the learner.

3. *Establishing Operations Will Increase the Value of the Reinforcer*—This term refers to the factors that affect the reinforcing value of a particular stimulus (Michael, 1993). Deprivation and satiation are most frequently cited as examples of **establishing operations** (Martin & Pear, 1999). A reinforcer will be more effective when an individual has been deprived of it for a substantial period of time. An example of this principle is when you have not eaten a favorite food or dessert for a long period of time. You will experience a heightened sense of fulfillment from this favorite food upon eating it. On the other hand, satiation occurs when a previously reinforcing consequence loses its value and is therefore no longer reinforcing. For example, if you eat your favorite dessert following the Thanksgiving meal (pumpkin pie), and then repeatedly snack on it two or three more times before nightfall, it will eventually lose its value, despite how much you like it as a dessert. Or, when you have viewed the same movie more than two or three times, it eventually loses its value and is at that point no longer of interest to you.

4. *Intensity of the Reinforcer Will Result in More Effective Outcomes*—The intensity of the reinforcing consequence will typically be more effective (Miltenberger, 2001). Individuals will be more likely to expend greater amounts of effort if the yield in terms of reinforcement is greater. Consider student–athletes who are willing to work extra hours to perfect

their skill to earn a starting berth on the team (something that they value as a goal). The intensity associated with the consequence could be the enjoyment they derive from playing their chosen sport, the increased social attention that they receive, and generalized emotional and social fulfillment. Another example could be the Academic Dean at a major state university who uses her personal leave time so that she can be compensated financially for teaching a class that she enjoys.

## USING POSITIVE REINFORCEMENT WITHIN LEARNING ENVIRONMENTS

This section will provide examples of how teachers and others can better use positive reinforcement within learning environments. Concepts will be introduced that examine the various facets associated with positive reinforcement programs such as schedules of reinforcement, shaping behavior, chaining, stimulus control, fading reinforcement, and enlistment of naturally occurring reinforcers.

### Schedules of Reinforcement

Reinforcement schedules have been widely written about within the behavior literature. Basically there are two major terms related to reinforcement that one should be familiar with. These are continuous reinforcement and intermittent reinforcement. Continuous reinforcement occurs when a target response is repeatedly reinforced following its occurrence. Consider the following examples:

- Each time Alli, a young student driver, gets into the car and puts her safety belt on, her teacher verbally praises her.
- When Duncan picks up each individual toy and places it in his toy chest, his mother says, "Good job picking your toys up."
- The teacher praises Curt each time he attempts and completes a math problem.
- Ben's father verbally reinforces him for each step that Ben approximates or successfully attempts in his pursuit to learn to ride his bicycle independently.

These examples illustrate the concept of continuous reinforcement. Continuous reinforcement is most frequently used during the skill acquisition stage of learning when a learner is attempting to learn a new skill. Parents and teachers alike can best use this approach to reinforce children when learning a new skill or routine within the home. The more frequently a teacher reinforces desired behaviors the better, as these patterns of responding will be more likely to occur. Sulzer-Azaroff and Mayer (1991) recommended that a dense or continuous schedule of reinforcement (CRF) should be used when the goal of the instructional program is to increase or stabilize a behavior. Teachers and parents should rely on high rates of reinforcement during these first learning stages. By doing so, they will increase the likelihood that the learner will attempt the task or behavior and ultimately result in the acquisition of the skill. As skill acquisition occurs and the behavior is established, reinforcement can be thinned and applied intermittently. Instead of each response being reinforced, every second or third response is reinforced, until ultimately natural consequences associated with completion of the task successfully will ultimately become reinforcing enough.

An intermittent reinforcement schedule is used during the fluency and maintenance building stages of learning. As students become more fluent in performing a new task, intermittent reinforcement is provided at key points during the performance of the task or following the completion of the task. Fluency is the ability of an individual to perform a skill or behavior with minimal or no assistance at a reasonably fast rate with few or no errors. Intermittent reinforcement is typically used during this phase of learning to promote ongoing refinement of the skill and performance maintenance of the skill or behavior over time. Intermittent schedules of reinforcement consist in four different types of schedules. These include fixed interval, variable interval, fixed ratio, and variable ratio schedules of reinforcement (Ferster & Skinner, 1957). **Interval schedules** are connected to periods of time, whereas **ratio schedules** are associated with an average number of responses.

When using fixed and variable interval schedules of reinforcement, a behavior is reinforced after a designated time interval has passed. Fixed interval schedules (FI) utilize the same time period, for instance (FI 30) would mean that the first occurrence of the behavior on or following when the 30 seconds has elapsed would be reinforced. Conversely, when using a variable interval schedule, the amount of time is based on average. An example of this would be a variable interval schedule (VI 30); the behavior would on the average be reinforced at approximately 30 seconds. The obvious difficulty for a teacher in a busy general or special education classroom would be the degree to which they could consistently adhere to such a reinforcement schedule.

Ratio schedules of reinforcement are based on the number of responses that must occur before reinforcement is given. An example of a fixed ratio schedule would be as follows:

> Curtis receives a stamp on his paper after he completes every third problem. His teacher is using a (FR 3) schedule of reinforcement.

Fixed ratio schedules of reinforcement are very effective within classroom settings. Teachers can effectively use this approach when teaching certain academic tasks such as completing math problems. It is also an effective approach for use within job settings in which parts assembly is a required task. An example of this applied to a job setting would be as follows:

> Roger, a young adolescent with Asperger's syndrome, is employed at a grocery store. His primary job is stocking shelves. His work supervisor has worked out a fixed ratio schedule (FI 9) of reinforcement in which Roger is given a token after he has completed stocking the ninth shelf unit in the aisle. He can redeem the tokens for food and beverage items in the store during his break and lunch periods.

Variable ratio schedules also deliver reinforcement based on the number of responses that occur, but are based on average number of responses. Variable ratio schedules can also be used within school settings related to the performance of academic tasks. Classroom teachers would therefore administer reinforcement based on a range of responses. In the case of Lawrence, a fourth grader, who receives a good job stamp for successive problems completed in math, he may receive a stamp every three problems, 6 problems, 8 problems, or 10 problems. The average number of these would constitute the variable ratio schedule being used. One important point to consider when using a variable ratio schedule is that the learner is not "tipped off" as to when the reinforcement will be administered and thus is more likely to continue to be task engaged hoping for the reinforcer to be administered.

## Shaping

When teaching a new behavior or skill, reinforcement is necessary to initiate skill acquisition. One effective teaching method that employs reinforcement in the development of new skills is **shaping**. Shaping is defined as the reinforcement of successive approximations of a target behavior. Cooper et al. (1987) defined a successive approximation as "any intermediate behavior that is either a prerequisite component of the final behavior or a higher order member of the same response topography as the final behavior" (p. 329). The idea is that reinforcement is applied incrementally as the behavior more closely resembles the terminal behavior that you are trying to teach. Another example of this is as follows:

> A father teaching his son to hit a ball begins by first using a soft ball, perhaps a plastic ball in order to minimize injury. He continues by reinforcing his son's crude approximations at holding the bat and continues to reinforce his son's efforts at refining his stance and holding the bat. The father then initiates pitching to his son maintaining a close proximity and slowly pitching the ball underhand so that his son will have a greater chance of striking the ball with his bat. As these steps take place, the father continues to reinforce his son's attempts at approximating a swing and ultimately continues the process until his son does indeed hit the ball. As his son's abilities increase, he will "raise the bar," so to speak, and gradually move further away and pitch the ball slightly harder until his son has ultimately refined his skill to a more advanced level.

To use shaping, the teacher must identify a target behavior. The next step is to then identify a starting point or an initial approximation. The teacher then reinforces the learner for engaging in the approximation. As the learner refines the ability to perform the initial step with ease and proceeds to the next step, the teacher then gets excited at the learner's progress and begins to provide reinforcement for each of those subsequent steps. By doing so, the teacher's use of differential reinforcement in this case is enhancing the learner's desire to proceed to the next step and move closer toward performance of the target behavior as was identified. Consider the example in Vignette 5.4 of shaping applied to teaching a young boy with Down syndrome how to ride his bicycle.

## Vignette 5.4

### Learning to Ride a Bike

Jared, a young boy, aged 7 with Down syndrome wanted desperately to ride a bike but was somewhat fearful and apprehensive when his parents tried to teach him. His parents contacted the motor development clinic at the local university, and they invited Jared to attend to assess how they might help in teaching the skill. They began the session by assessing Jared's ability to perform the desired motor sequence needed for riding a bike. They placed him at first on an exercise cycle to reduce his anxiety and to reinforce his approximation at sitting on a bike. They also wanted to determine whether Jared could independently pedal in sequence, and thus the exercise bike was a perfect answer, given that it was stationary and lessened Jared's fear of falling from the bike. Jared had some obvious difficulty with pedaling independently that became noticeable almost immediately. The clinic's instructional staff began by verbally praising Jared for his attempt at keeping his feet on the pedals, and as each assistant moved Jared's left and then right foot in sequence, repeating the pedaling motion over and over again, they verbally praised Jared's performance. As Jared assumed greater levels of independence in performing the pedaling sequence at the close of the first session, the staff then began to use a timer on the bike to encourage Jared to maintain his pedaling for extended periods of time. At the close of each time period, Jared was given a break and allowed to play basketball. The team began by setting the timer on the bike for one minute in which they praised Jared for pedaling independently during this time period, gradually increasing the timer to 5 and then 10 minutes. At that point, the instructors mounted Jared's bike on an adapted bike rack used by competition cyclists to train indoors during inclement weather. The team continued with the timer and reinforced Jared for his independent pedaling. As Jared began to display less fear on the bike and continued to improve in his ability to pedal independently without physical prompts, the team then proceeded to mount training wheels to Jared's bike. They then used the same shaping method, in which they reinforced Jared for his attempt at each successive approximation of the target behavior such as his ability to sit and independently pedal and steer his bicycle. This process went on for nearly three months weekly, ultimately resulting in Jared learning to ride his real bike independent of assistance and training wheels, which led to a very happy outcome for Jared and his family.

### Reflective Moment

What recommendations would you have in teaching Jared to ride his bike? Was this a socially valid skill to teach, and why?

As a rule, shaping can be used to teach and increase new behaviors and also to systematically reduce excessive or problematic behavior over time. The benefits of shaping as a teaching procedure are many. It is a positive procedure that is learner centered, individualized, and promotes the delivery of reinforcement for successive approximations thus placing other behaviors on extinction (Cooper et al., 1989). Shaping is a long-term and systematic goal-setting process that can often serve to enlist greater degrees of learner participation. The obvious challenge when using shaping procedures within any learning setting is that it is a time-consuming activity that does require a great deal of attention and monitoring on the part of the teacher and other instructional staff. However, the instructional progress that is made possible to a learner through this practice and the ultimate learning outcomes that are likely to ensue provide a great return on the time investment that is required.

## Chaining

When teaching a new skill or behavior to a student, it is important to focus on the entire skill or behavior. This method is referred to as **chaining**. Chaining involves a sequence of related steps or behaviors or discriminative stimuli (SDS) and responses (Rs) that are linked together just as links in a chain. For example, when children arrive home from school, their parents might have a routine comprised of a sequence of behaviors that must be accomplished. These might include having a light snack, completing their homework, washing their hands, and having supper together as a family. Each of these activities can be taught individually or can be linked and taught as a sequence or behavior chain.

How does this apply to a school setting? Consider the behavior chain associated with arriving at school and attending the first-hour class. Upon arriving at school, Kaitlin will go to her locker, retrieve her books and notebooks needed for her first- and second-period classes, go to her first-period class, take her assigned seat, place her instructional materials on her desk, stand for the Pledge of Allegiance, remain standing for the moment of silence, and will then sit down and wait for instructions from her teacher. For Kaitlin, each of these behaviors serves as a discriminative stimulus SD for the next response. A discriminative stimulus (SD) is defined as an antecedent stimulus that influences the occurrence of a particular behavior (Cooper et al., 1989). Martin and Pear (1999) described the individual stimulus response units of a behavior chain as "the 'links' that hold the chain together" (p. 134). Chaining is an important skill in the development of behavior in that it will frequently result in the delivery of reinforcement.

Three methods of chaining have been used in teaching. These include the total task presentation, backward chaining, and forward chaining. However, before a chain can be taught, it is important to develop a task analysis, which is a method designed to break down a complex behavior into small components or steps. Task analysis has been instrumental as a teaching method almost since the inception of special education. It is conceivable that any instructional task can be task analyzed. This can include academic skills, social skills, and functional self-help skills, to name a few of the possible categories. To task analyze a skill one should observe others performing the skill and write down the essential steps of the task, being mindful of the entire process. Next, perform the skill yourself, noting the chain of discriminative stimuli and responses that comprise the task. As noted by Cooper et al. (1989), there are five methods that can be used to validate the sequencing in a task analysis. The authors recommend the following:

1. The behaviors required in the sequence are developed after observation of others performing the task.

2. Consultations with experts or persons who are recognized for their abilities in performing the task are conducted.

3. Perform the task yourself to aid in refining the movements and sequence that are required for optimal performance of the entire task.

4. Sequence the steps in a task analysis in the same order as they will be performed.

5. Lastly, behaviors in a task analysis can be listed in order of difficulty proceeding from less difficult to more difficult.

Whatever the method that you select for validating the task analysis, be sure that attention is given to identifying the most efficient sequence of steps and note the SD for each response to ascertain if the learner will be able to discriminate the individual stimulus–response chains. Figure 5–2 provides an example of a task analysis for going through the lunch line in the school cafeteria.

The various stimulus–response units are easily identified when one examines this task analysis. If any one of these fails to be performed, the entire behavior chain is disrupted and ultimately the reinforcing outcome may not be realized. Task analysis is important in teaching in that it allows a task to be broken down into smaller steps. Skills are more efficiently taught in smaller steps. Another benefit is that it allows the teacher to assess a student's performance on each component of the skill sequence,

**FIGURE 5–2**
*Going Through the*
*School Lunch Line*

1. Enter the cafeteria.
2. Pick up tray and wait in line.
3. Proceed through the line as it slowly progresses forward.
4. Select food items and place on tray.
5. Select desired drink (milk, chocolate milk, or juice).
6. Give student identification number to the cashier.
7. Pick up utensils and napkins.
8. Pick up condiments (mayonnaise, ketchup, mustard).
9. Locate a seat and begin eating.

thus enabling individualized instruction at different skill levels. We will examine how as a teacher you can use chaining with a task analysis for teaching new behaviors.

### Total Task Presentation

The total task presentation method of chaining basically involves allowing the student to attempt each step in the task analysis from beginning to end. In this method, the teacher provides the necessary instructional assistance in the form of instructional cues (verbal, gestural, and physical prompts) as needed to assist the learner in completing the sequence of behaviors. Miltenberger (2001) indicated that graduated physical guidance has been widely used with this type of chaining procedure. Graduated physical guidance is a term used to describe a form of physical prompting that uses a hand-over-hand procedure provided by the teacher to assist the student in completion of the task.

We often witness examples of this form of chaining being used to teach new and complex motor skill behaviors such as feeding oneself, using utensils, drinking from a cup, and also with adult learners such as learning to swing a golf club or a tennis racket. As the student becomes proficient in performing each step in the task analysis, the teacher can begin to back off or fade the use of physical prompts or graduated guidance as a means of promoting independence on the part of the student.

### Backward Chaining

Backward chaining involves teaching a task beginning with the last step first and then moving in a descending order, the next to last step, the third from last step, and so on. Backward chaining has been a successful teaching method for teaching a variety of skills, including dressing, grooming, and feeding. This method was widely used in the early days of applied behavior analysis when teaching functional skills to persons with developmental disabilities living within institutional settings. One advantage to backward chaining is that the student receives reinforcement for completion of the last step, thus reducing the wait time and making the reinforcing consequence more effective.

When using backward chaining, the teacher must first establish the performance criteria that must be attained before introducing subsequent steps. The teacher begins by assisting the student with all of the early steps in the task analysis and continues until the very last step. The student is then instructed how to complete the last step by the teacher. This may require use of a verbal, gestural, or physical prompt on the part of the teacher to assist the student. If, for example, the teacher has established as a performance criteria that the student must perform the last step of the task analysis for three consecutive trials without assistance, then upon meeting that performance criteria, the teacher will then initiate teaching the next to last step in the skill sequence. This pattern continues until each step in the task analysis has been mastered. For example, if we examine the task analysis in

Figure 5–2, we would assist the student in completion of steps 1–8 and then teach step 9 until mastery. The process would then be repeated. We would assist the learner through steps 1–7 and then teach step 8 until mastery, and the learner would complete step 9 independently.

### Forward Chaining

Forward chaining takes the opposite approach from backward chaining. With forward chaining, the first step in the task analysis is taught first. Typically the first step is taught to the student until a predetermined performance criterion is attained before introducing the second step of the task analysis. However, there are variations to this approach as identified by Zirpoli and Melloy (2001). This includes teaching more than one step of the task analysis concurrently. This method is referred to as concurrent task training (Zirpoli & Melloy, 2001). Using this method would allow for the presentation of multiple steps of the task analysis and would afford learners a better instructional context for learning more complex behavior chains.

## Stimulus Control

**Stimulus control** is a process by which a stimulus assumes control of a behavior that has been previously reinforced in the presence of that stimulus. What we are referring to with this concept is the ability of a student to successfully discriminate the antecedent stimulus and voluntarily respond to it in an appropriate manner within the natural environment. When a response receives reinforcement repeatedly over time, it is strengthened and learning occurs. This is a process that occurs over time through repeated practice and through trial and error on the part of the student. Consider some examples of stimulus control from everyday life. When driving a car, most people are prompted to stop at the presence of a red light, or to pull over to the edge of the road when seeing a flashing red light and hearing the sound of a siren from a police car, fire truck, or ambulance. Other examples could be purchasing your favorite soft drink from a vending machine when you see that your choice's button on the machine is lit up and upon depositing the correct change and pushing the button, the can tumbles out the bottom of the machine. Other examples include answering the telephone when it rings or answering the door on hearing the sound of the doorbell. These responses are likely to be reinforced by a voice on the other line or a visitor at your door.

From a teaching and learning perspective, it is important to understand how discrimination training is essential to the learning process. Discrimination training refers to assisting a learner in discriminating the presence or absence of a discriminative stimulus (SD). The discriminative stimulus (SD) basically serves as a cue that the behavior, on being emitted, will be reinforced. For example, when the teacher prompts a child to take out his book, and he complies, the teacher verbally reinforces the student with a statement such as, "Good listening." The chaining techniques previously described in this chapter serve as examples of teaching methodologies that support the development of discrimination in learners as response chains are taught and reinforced within task analyses. If in the event the behavior is emitted in the presence of an antecedent stimulus and it is not reinforced, it is termed an S-Delta (S$\Delta$). These also assist the student with discrimination by identifying those antecedent stimuli that are not associated with reinforcement, thus strengthening the student's ability to discern the correct cues. When attempting to promote stimulus control Martin and Pear (1999) have recommended the following guidelines:

1. Select distinct cues and make them apparent to the learner so that he can readily identify the discriminative stimulus (SD). This will minimize errors and frustration and lead to reinforcing outcomes. One example could include being precise about directions for completing an assignment or operationally defining what constitutes a "clean room." Another could be defining for learners which assignments must be completed before they are "finished."

2. Use errorless learning procedures to control for errors. When and if possible teachers should use errorless learning approaches to teaching as a method for promoting the stimulus–response patterns and avoiding mistakes. As students are first learning to recognize the distinct instructional cues (SDs), attempts should be made to make these as obvious as possible to reinforce correct responding, thus leading to stimulus control.

3. Provide frequent opportunities for practice. When teaching new skills, learners must be afforded numerous opportunities to practice the desired behaviors and to receive reinforcement for appropriate responses before learning can occur. Frequent repetitions or trials are needed during the acquisition and fluency stages of learning to reinforce both the recognition of discriminative stimuli and the refinement of responses. But as the old adage goes, "Practice does indeed make perfect."

4. Use rules and contingencies. When teachers or parents state their performance expectations and are clear and consistent in their reinforcement of these rules or contingencies, children and youth will most likely demonstrate the desired behavior. Recognition of desired behavior through the administration of reinforcement and the withholding of reinforcement for undesired or incorrect responses will assist the learner in making the necessary discriminations provided these rules are maintained and are consistent.

Simply stated, the previous section has attempted to familiarize you with methods for promoting stimulus control. It is the ultimate goal of every teacher to facilitate learning. As we have discussed in this section of the text, the importance of reinforcement used in conjunction with systematic teaching techniques and repeated trials can result in the attainment of desired instructional and learning outcomes.

## Fading

**Fading** is a procedure designed to systematically remove instructional prompts so that the behavior occurs under natural conditions. Fading is a process that teachers frequently use over time to reduce the amount of instructional prompts provided to the learner to allow for independent performance on the part of the learner.

Prompting is a teaching method designed to provide instructional support to the learner in completing a task. Prompt hierarchies, as we have learned, can involve a system of least-to-most prompts or conversely a series of most-to-least prompts depending on the nature of the skill, the skill abilities of the learner, and general complexities associated with teaching the task. Typically when using a system of prompts a time-delay element is also incorporated, which allows for a 3- to 5-second time delay between the presentation of a prompt and a learner's response before initiating the next level of prompt. Time delay can be classified as an errorless learning approach. It involves systematically fading teacher-delivered prompts so that behavior is controlled by naturally occurring contingencies.

Shuster and Griffen (1990) have indicated that two types of time-delay procedures can be used. The first is a constant time-delay procedure that basically uses a 0-second time delay between a teacher-delivered prompt and learner performance. As indicated by Shuster and Griffen (1990), the constant time-delay procedure does not allow for independent performance on the part of the learner, the instructional cue is given by the teacher, and subsequently the teacher assists the learner in performance of the task relying on prompts to assist the learner in task completion. The second type of time-delay procedure is called progressive. The goal of the progressive time-delay procedure is to slowly lengthen the time delay following the instructional cue, thus allowing for independent performance on the part of the learner. As the learner's proficiency increases, the time delay is slowly lengthened to a maximum of approximately 5 seconds before assistance in the form of a prompt is provided by the teacher to the learner. The ultimate goal, of course, is the transfer of stimulus control from teacher-delivered prompts to the naturally occurring contingencies found within the task and environment. Examples of prompting approaches are displayed in Figure 5–3.

Fading procedures allow the teacher to systematically withdraw the level of teacher assistance in the form of prompts over time as the students become fluent in their performance and maintain high levels of performance. Fading can take on many forms such as the reduction of stimulus prompts in terms of their frequency and intensity. Massey and Wheeler (2000) demonstrated a systematic reduction of both the frequency and intensity of prompts delivered to a young child with autism. Their study used a system of most-to-least prompts to teach a young child with autism how to successfully use a picture activity schedule as a method for promoting increased task engagement and reducing problematic behavior. The authors determined that prompts would be systematically faded if the child reached a performance criteria of 80% for task engagement across six consecutive sessions. It is important to gradually

**FIGURE 5–3**
*Prompt Hierarchies*

A least-to-most prompt hierarchy would be as follows:

I—Allow for independent performance on the part of the learner

V—Following a 3- to 5-second time delay, initiate a verbal prompt (e.g., "Pick up the cup.")

G—Allow for a 3- to 5-second time delay for a response to occur, if no response occurs, initiate a gestural cue paired with a verbal cue, "Pick up the cup," while pointing to the cup.

P—Following a 3- to 5-second time delay, initiate a physical prompt (light touch on the hand or graduated physical guidance) paired with a verbal prompt, "Pick up the cup."

In contrast to this, a system of most-to-least prompts would be as follows:

P—Using a graduated physical guidance procedure the instructor would provide hand-over-hand guidance to the learner in performing the task in conjunction with a verbal cue.

G—As the learner acquires the ability to perform the task, the teacher gradually fades physical assistance and relies on a gestural prompt to initiate the learner's performance also being paired with a verbal cue.

V—As the learner exhibits fluency in their ability to perform the desired task, the teacher fades to the use of verbal prompts to assist the learner in task performance.

and systematically change these antecedent stimuli over time in a stepwise fashion based on the performance indicators of the student. A rapid or premature reduction of these important instructional prompts could result in disaster and likely result in having to reteach the skill.

It is important to know when to reduce prompts and subsequently fade them in an effort to transfer stimulus control, thus promoting learner independence. There are some effective strategies that can assist in this process. These include reinforcing correct responses and reinforcing independent performance on the part of the student. Other strategies include using errorless learning strategies such as building embedded cues within the task as much as is possible.

## APPLICATIONS OF REINFORCEMENT PROGRAMS WITHIN THE CLASSROOM

We have examined the principles and guidelines for using reinforcement within instructional programs. The following section will provide examples of reinforcement programs that are classroomwide and are primarily token economy systems.

### Token Economy Programs

Token economy programs have been widespread in a variety of educational and habilitation settings for a number of years (Kazdin, 1982). Originally developed within state institutions for use with adults with mental retardation, this method was designed as an incentive system to promote behavior change within these settings (Ayllon & Azrin, 1968). The token economy has also been extensively used within classroom and school settings, largely within educational programs serving children and youth with special needs. Within these settings token economies have seemed to be most prevalent in serving learners identified with emotional and behavior disorders as a means of promoting positive behavior change.

The basic design of a token economy is that point values are attached to desired behaviors. The tokens or points earned by students can be redeemed later for various backup reinforcers (e.g., food, tangible, social, and activities). There are numerous examples of backup reinforces that can be included within such a program. These could include stickers, pencils, fruit snacks, free time, library time, free time to choose an activity, and so on. A token economy can be applied classwide with individuals and in collaborative learning situations. In establishing a token economy, the teacher must take into consideration several key elements. These include

1. Defining desired behaviors within the classroom. The behaviors that are operationally defined should be those that are expected within the classroom, such as

   - Coming to class on time
   - Sitting in assigned seat
   - Being prepared for class with the appropriate materials
   - Raising your hand for teacher assistance

2. Determining the tokens or other currency used within the classroom. These could include chips, hole punches on a card, stickers, point cards, ribbons, and play money to name a few.

3. Determine backup reinforcers that will be used in conjunction with the tokens. Identify and list those backup reinforcers that are available to you within the classroom or that could be easily developed. Keep in mind, if these backup reinforcers are linked to more naturally occurring consequences, even better, as they will be much easier to implement within the classroom setting. Also, aside from ease of administration, affordability must be taken into consideration. Too often teachers develop token systems out of pocket with limited resources, thus bearing the cost of purchasing backup reinforcers by themselves.

4. Define how the system will be implemented such as the frequency by which tokens will be given and exchanged, the token or point value of backup reinforcers, and how you will maintain records of individual learner performance.

5. Train staff and inform families of the system as a means to ensure consistency and support in terms of implementation

6. Also, develop methods for fading the procedure, maintenance of behavior change, and transfer to naturally occurring contingencies.

**Consider This**

When using token economies, make sure that the token reinforcers used are valued by the learner(s) and that they are efficiently administered contingent on performance of the desired behavior.

## SUMMARY

This chapter has provided you with an introduction and overview of reinforcement and the application of positive reinforcement procedures within instructional programs. Specifically, the use of positive reinforcement procedures within intervention programs designed to increase appropriate behavior in learners were described. The terms *positive* and *negative reinforcement* were also defined and the point made that reinforcement strengthens behavior. The point being that negative reinforcement is not to be confused with punishment as is often the case. Selection of reinforcers was also described with various methods for determining individual preference. These methods included reinforcer sampling, providing opportunities for choice, asking parents and family members if not the learner directly, and reviewing past educational records to obtain insights as to previously effective reinforcers.

Classes of positive reinforcement were also described. These included the following: edibles, activity, tangibles, and social reinforcers. Principles of effective reinforcement were discussed, which included guidelines for administering reinforcement. These principles included: making reinforcement contingent on behavior, administering reinforcement immediately, and establishing operations, including deprivation and satiation. Deprivation is important for reinforcer effectiveness in that when an individual has been deprived of a reinforcer for a period of time, the reinforcer will have greater effectiveness. Satiation, on the other hand, is when the reinforcer has lost its value because the individual has received too much of it.

Schedules of reinforcement were also introduced within the chapter. Continuous reinforcement refers to when each occurrence of a behavior is reinforced, and intermittent reinforcement refers to when a behavior is reinforced on an intermittent basis with either a ratio or interval schedule of reinforcement. Ratio schedules of reinforcement involve reinforcing the average number of behaviors with either a fixed ratio (a fixed number) or a variable ratio (an average number of responses intermittently reinforced). Interval schedules of reinforcement involve administering reinforcement for a fixed time interval (e.g., 2 minutes) or for a variable interval schedule, which would involve intermittently reinforcing a behavior an average of every 2 minutes.

The chapter also introduced the principles of shaping (i.e., reinforcing successive approximations of a terminal behavior) and fading, the systematic withdrawal of instructional prompts and reinforcement. Prompt hierarchies and time-delay procedures were introduced with applied examples of how these instructional procedures are used to teach new behaviors and how they coincide with fading. The importance of systematically fading external prompts and reinforcers was described as it related to transfer of stimulus control to natural contingencies. Lastly, the application of token economies within schools and classrooms were described. The efficacy of such programs and considerations for the implementation of token systems within the classroom were identified.

In conclusion, this chapter introduced important concepts related to reinforcement and tied these with their use within instructional situations. These principles will be elaborated on in later chapters as we explore how to teach positive alternative behaviors and reduce problematic behavior.

## ACTIVITIES TO EXTEND YOUR LEARNING

1. Identify and list within the various classes of reinforcement (edibles, tangibles, activity, and social) your preferred reinforcers. Note the frequency of occurrence of each of these respective reinforcers in your life. And, lastly, identify which activities (e.g., work, leisure, and or school) they are most frequently associated with.
2. Conduct an observation within a classroom and note the presence of reinforcement in the classroom. Identify the types of reinforcers used by the teacher and whether or not they are individualized for each child.
3. Create an assessment tool for use within home, community, and school environments that you live and work in and identify the level of reinforcement found within these settings. Are these environments dense in reinforcement or are they lean? How might these settings be enhanced to provide a more reinforcing environment that could enhance your own quality of life?

## FURTHER READING AND EXPLORATION

1. Develop a database of teaching related articles from such journals as *Teaching Exceptional Children* on reinforcement. Develop these strategies into a file that you can later refer to when you have your own classroom.
2. Visit the Web site http://www.pbis.org and note articles and resources on this Web site related to using positive reinforcement in the development of behavior intervention plans for learners with challenging behavior.

## REFERENCES

Alberto, P. A., & Troutman, A. C. (2002). *Applied behavior analysis for teachers* (6th ed.). Upper Saddle River, NJ: Merrill/Prentice Hall.

Ayllon, T., & Azrin, N. H. (1968). *The token economy: A motivational system for therapy and rehabilitation.* New York: Applegate-Century Crofts.

Bambara, L. M., & Koger, F. (1996). Opportunities for daily choice making. *Innovations* (no. 8). Washington, DC: American Association on Mental Retardation.

Cipani, E. (1995). Be aware of negative reinforcment. *Teaching Exceptional Children, 27,* 36–39.

Cooper, J. O., Herron, T. E., & Heward, W. L. (1987). *Applied behavior analysis.* Upper Saddle River, NJ: Merrill/Prentice Hall.

Ferster, C. B., & Skinner, B. F. (1957). *Schedules of reinforcement.* Upper Saddle River, NJ: Prentice Hall.

Kazdin, A. E. (1982). The token economy: A decade later. *Journal of Applied Behavior Analysis, 15,* 431–445.

Martin, G., & Pear, J. (1999). *Behavior modification: What it is and how to do it* (6th ed.). Upper Saddle River, NJ: Merrill/Prentice Hall.

Massey, N. G., & Wheeler, J. J. (2000). Acquisition and generalization of activity schedules and their effects on task engagement in a young child with autism in an inclusive preschool classroom. *Education and Training in Mental Retardation and Developmental Disabilities, 35,* 326–335.

Michael, J. (1993). Establishing operations. *Behavior Analyst, 16,* 191–206.

Miltenberger, R. G. (2001). *Behavior modification: Principles and practices* (2nd ed.), Belmont, CA: Wadsworth.

Premack, D. (1959). Toward empirical behavior laws. I: Positive reinforcement. *Psychological Review, 66,* 219–233.

Shuster, J. W., & Griffen, A. K. (1990). Using time delay with task analyses. *Teaching Exceptional Children, 22,* 49–53.

Skinner, B. F. (1938). *The behavior of organisms.* New York: Appleton.

Skinner, B. F. (1953). *Science and human behavior.* New York: Macmillan.

Sulzer-Azaroff, B., & Mayer, R. G. (1991). *Behavior analysis for lasting change.* Fort Worth, TX: Harcourt Brace Publishers.

Zirpoli, T. J., & Melloy, K. J. (2001). *Behavior management: Applications for teachers.* Upper Saddle River, NJ: Merrill/Prentice Hall.

# Chapter 6

# Understanding Functional Behavior Assessment

## CONCEPTS TO UNDERSTAND

*After reading this chapter, you should be able to:*

- Describe the importance of functional behavior assessment
- List and discuss assumptions concerning challenging behavior
- Describe the components of functional behavior assessment: identifying and defining target behaviors, conducting behavior observations, understanding the data and generating hypotheses, and conducting a functional analysis
- List, describe, and recommend approaches for the development of an intervention plan

## KEY TERMS

Anecdotal recording

Challenging behavior

Duration recording

Frequency or event recording

Functional behavior assessment

Interval recording

Scatter-plot analysis

Target behavior

Functional behavior assessment has become a more widespread practice across educational settings since the 1997 reauthorization of the Individuals with Disabilities Education Act. This piece of legislation mandated that educational teams use functional behavior assessment (FBA) and positive behavior supports (PBS) in the assessment and development of interventions for students whose behaviors impede their learning and or the learning of others (Armstrong & Kauffman, 1999; Individuals with Disabilities Education Act, 1997).

One outcome from this mandate has been the delivery of training to inservice and preservice educators in the area of FBA and PBS (Asmus, Vollmer, & Borrero, 2002). The training of personnel has been extremely important to the implementation of these practices as educational systems attempt to address this mandate within their respective schools and learning environments.

FBA is a multistep process that is designed to identify causal factors associated with challenging behavior and to generate plausible hypotheses about the functions of problem behaviors and also to develop possible interventions aimed at replacing such behaviors. We have learned through the research that challenging behaviors do serve a function for the individuals who engage in them. This was supported by Skinner (1974), who stated that all behavior had a purpose and promoted the analysis of motivation and purpose through his research in the area of operant conditioning. Subsequent research by Carr (1977) examined hypotheses on the motivation of self-injurious behavior and also on escape-related behaviors (Carr & Newsom, 1985) in persons with developmental disabilities.

Iwata, Dorsey, Slifer, Bauman, and Richman (1982) further studied the functions of self-injury in a landmark study that established the basic model for conducting what is referred to as analogue assessment or functional analysis. Their study presented a new and innovative model referred to as analogue assessment, to be used for the assessment of functional relationships between self-injurious behavior and specific environmental events. This study and subsequent investigations over time have examined these methods and have given us tremendous insight into the factors that contribute to problem behaviors and the functions of these behaviors in a variety of persons with behavior and developmental disabilities. These research efforts have enlightened us in our efforts to understand complex human behavior. As a result, we know, for example, that challenging behavior is not always maladaptive; rather, it often does serve a purpose or function for the individual, such as attempting to gain attention or to meet other needs, whereas maladaptive behavior fails to do so (Carr, Langdon, & Yarbrough, 1999).

Behavior functions associated with problem behavior can include one or more of the following: (a) tangible reinforcement, (b) attention, (c) sensory reinforcement, and (d) escape (Carr & Durand, 1985; Horner, Sprague, O'Brien, & Heathfield, 1990; O'Reilly, 1997). These behaviors often coincide with communication difficulties and are attempts at communicating some basic needs, such as the need for attention from others. Often something as simple as, "I need help," might be communicated with a more externalized behavior that has occurred out of frustration. Another example might be an individual's need for escape from an activity that they find unpleasant, yet they are unable to communicate their need for a break. Given this need coupled with skill limitations in the area of communication, the learner may use those skills currently in their repertoire, resulting in a less-than-appropriate response.

The purpose of this chapter will be to describe the components and process of functional behavior assessment. The chapter will also explore the applications of this methodology across learners and learning environments and how teachers can better use functional assessment to understand the behavior of children and youth and how the information derived from this process can be used in the development of meaningful interventions.

## THE IMPORTANCE OF FUNCTIONAL BEHAVIOR ASSESSMENT

**Functional behavior assessment** (FBA) has been identified as an effective practice in the assessment of **challenging behavior**, as recognized by the 1997 reauthorization of the Individuals with Disabilities Education Act. The reauthorization of this legislation mandated the use of FBA and PBS to address chronic and excessive problem behavior (Dunlap & Kinkaid, 2001).

FBA has been defined by Sugai et al. (2000) as a "systematic process of identifying problem behaviors and the events that (a) reliably predict occurrences and nonoccurrences of those behaviors, and (b) maintain the behaviors over time" (p. 137). One important point to understand about the terms *functional assessment* and *functional behavior assessment* is that the terms are synonymous. Dunlap and Kinkaid (2001) indicated that there is agreement among experts in the field that the terms *functional behavior assessment* and *functional assessment* are one and the same.

FBA combines both direct and indirect forms of assessment, is conducted within natural environments, and relies on multiple data-collection methods. An FBA is completed through a systematic process of data collection consisting of interviews and observations within the learner's relevant environments, including classroom settings, home, and community. The data-collection process usually includes a structured interview paired with observational data collected within natural environments to gain a contextual understanding of the behavior in relevant environments. This is important in that the FBA will assist us in understanding how environmental variables influence problem behavior.

The goal of FBA is to understand the factors that occasion or reinforce problematic behavior and the subsequent function(s) that this behavior serves for the individual. This information allows educational personnel to generate hypothesis statements concerning the relationship between these events and behavior. In turn, the outcomes of FBA should translate into effective learner-centered interventions designed to ameliorate the problem behavior. In contrast, traditional forms of assessment have often relied on secondary reporting through the use of indirect methods such as interviews, checklists, and rating scales to identify the frequency and severity of problem behavior. Behavior rating scales have been frequently used in school settings, given the high volume of children and youth served within these environments and because of the ease and efficiency for completing these types of instruments.

The adoption of FBA procedures has not been an easy transition for many school systems despite the mandate. These problems have been largely due to limited training and experience with these procedures and partly due to philosophy, in addition to how challenging behavior has been traditionally viewed within these settings. Most educational systems have maintained discipline policies that are punitive in their response to challenging behavior and view such behavior as intolerable, such as evidenced by "zero-tolerance" policies. There are, however, exceptions, with some school systems having adopted school-wide behavior support programs that have resulted in a reduction of office referrals and incidents of problem behavior (Horner & Sugai, 2000).

FBA provides practitioners with a systematic method for understanding challenging behavior and offers effective procedures that schools need to readily embrace as a part of their regular practice when addressing problem behaviors (Scott & Nelson, 1999). FBA is aimed at understanding the variables that contribute to challenging behavior and gathering information that lends itself to the development of effective interventions. It provides a constructive framework for understanding problematic behavior and addressing these problems from a solutions standpoint. Such a viewpoint is necessary, given that too frequently within classrooms and schools, children who fail to exhibit desired behavior for whatever reason are viewed as the problem without any concern as to why these behaviors occur. The burden most often falls entirely on the learner without any consideration being given to other contributing factors. FBA offers teachers and families research-based practices that are user friendly and effective in understanding behavior and the factors that influence it.

## ASSUMPTIONS CONCERNING CHALLENGING BEHAVIOR

Frequently, when professionals encounter learners who display challenging behavior, they conjecture about the causes of these behaviors, which often translate into false assumptions. Many times, this results in blame for why a particular child has such difficult behavior to manage. Often the child or family is made the scapegoat. This type of practice is wrong and counterproductive, as it offers nothing in terms of a solution to address the problem behavior.

Chandler and Dahlquist (2002) synthesized these assumptions into five major areas. These areas include (a) the bad child (the child misbehaves because he is bad, (b) the child's disability (problem behavior occurs as a direct result of the child's disability), (c) the bad family (problem behaviors are the result of ineffective parenting and poor family dynamics, (d) the bad home (problem behaviors occur because of problems in the home), and (e) trauma suffered earlier in the child's life (the child's behavior can be attributed to some form of trauma such as abuse, neglect, or sexual abuse). Many factors influence problem behavior, such as previous learning, stress within the home or family, academic or social skill challenges, and physical factors, to name just a few. It is important to view problem behavior from a comprehensive perspective and take into account the many variables that can trigger and maintain such responses. Care must be taken to consider all these factors if we are to be effective in the delivery of positive behavior interventions and supports.

FBA maintains that all behavior is purposeful, including challenging behavior. This is especially true for young children and individuals with disabilities who are often challenged by developmental limitations that may prevent them from effectively communicating their needs to caregivers. If caregivers and family members are insensitive to these attempts, frustration ensues on the part of the child, and a problem behavior could result. It is extremely important for parents and professionals to recognize these communicative attempts as a means of preventing challenging behavior. Also, behavior does often serve as a basic form of communication. For example, when a child cries or has tantrums, these behaviors may result from increased levels of frustration that have not been addressed or anticipated by caregivers, fatigue on the part of the child, or frustration at not being able to obtain her basic needs.

### Consider This

- Does challenging behavior have communicative intent and represent an attempt on the part of the learner to communicate a need? Think of some examples from your own experience.

Behavior is not only purposeful but also may represent a lack of congruence between the demand being placed on the learner and the skill limitations they experience. For learners with disabilities, challenging behaviors should not be viewed as abnormal responses because these behaviors reflect the skill limitations frequently experienced by the learner and a lack of sensitivity on the part of the environment (Durand, 1990). Demchak and Bossert (1996), in a synthesis of the research on FBA, offered the following principles concerning challenging behavior: (a) challenging behaviors serve a specific purpose or function for the individual, (b) challenging behaviors have communicative intent, (c) challenging behavior is directly related to events in the environment that influence or reinforce such behaviors, and (d) a single challenging behavior can serve multiple functions. FBA is a process that seeks to understand these behaviors and the factors that underlie them so that effective interventions can be designed. The goal of positive behavior supports is to promote supportive environments, the teaching of replacement behaviors that increase the learner's options, and intervention practices that address the overall quality of life of the individual.

## COMPONENTS OF FUNCTIONAL BEHAVIOR ASSESSMENT

As previously stated, FBA is a multistep process. Although some sources vary in their presentation of the specific number of steps, the basic components of an FBA consist of (a) gathering descriptive information or data concerning the target behavior through a structured interview and or use of behavior rating scales, (b) conducting behavior observations to determine the antecedents and consequences associated with the target behavior and any patterns that might exist, (c) formulating hypotheses related to the function(s) of the behavior and variables that are contributing to the behavior, and last, if necessary, (d) conducting a functional analysis consisting of systematic manipulations of antecedent and consequence variables to validate their relationship to the behavior and also to confirm the function of the behavior (Demchak & Bossert, 1996; O'Neill et al., 1997).

## Identifying and Defining Target Behaviors

The initial step of a functional behavior assessment is identifying and defining the **target behavior** of concern. The best method for this is through a structured interview that is posed to relevant individuals in the learner's life such as her teacher, teaching assistants, principal, parents, and family. An example of a structured interview form is contained in Chapter 4. The structured interview should inquire about the following:

- What time of day does the behavior typically occur?
- How often does the behavior occur?
- Does the behavior coincide with specific events such as particular classes, academic or social activities?
- Are there antecedent events that consistently coincide with occurrences of the behavior?
- What typically happens after the behavior has occurred?
- What does the behavior accomplish for the individual?
- What is the communicative intent of the behavior?
- Are there significant life events that could account for a change in behavior?
- Are there any medical or physical problems that could be contributing to the behavior?
- Is there a predictable schedule for the learner each day?
- Is the learning environment pleasant and safe?
- Are classroom expectations clear and consistent?

Once the structured interview has been conducted, the results should be compared and contrasted across raters resulting in the identification of the target behavior, characteristics of the behavior, the probable antecedents and consequences associated with the behavior, and other relevant points. Behavior rating scales might also be used in conjunction with the structured interview, as we learned in Chapter 4. Another option that could be used is a student-assisted interview. In some cases this type of assessment would be most conducive to understanding triggers within the environment and behavior from the learner's own perspective. Target behaviors should be defined in terms that are measurable and observable so that data collection can occur and there is reliable agreement among professionals on what the target behavior looks like. When identifying the target behavior, it is important to be specific in your description:

### Effective Behavior Definitions

- When presented with a written task, Laura will push the materials aside and place her head on her desk.
- Emily will manipulate assigned task materials consistent with their use.
- Brenda will wipe with a sponge both the front and back of each cafeteria tray and then rinse each side before sending it through the dishwasher.
- Jacob's competing behaviors are defined as verbal or physical aggression including name-calling and slapping, noncompliance with teacher requests as evidenced by refusal to comply with teacher directives, and tantrums when presented with a task demand.

These definitions are characterized by a description of specific observable behaviors that can be identified and measured by observers. In the last example, we see how a class of related behaviors can be grouped for purposes of data collection. In this case, we see several behaviors referred to as competing behaviors or behaviors that compete negatively with instruction. Often, teachers within busy classrooms will employ this strategy if there is more than one target behavior of concern, provided these behaviors are related. If there are multiple target behaviors that cannot be grouped, you should prioritize them by their level of severity. If certain behaviors pose an eminent risk or threat to the safety of the individual or others, then that behavior should take priority over others. Contrast the previously stated examples with the following:

### Ineffective Behavior Definitions

- Bob will behave in class.
- Julie will be kind to others during recess.
- Josh will be compliant during classroom instruction.
- Bob will wait his turn during instruction.

These examples are vague and ambiguous. The reader is left with questions about what the desired behaviors really consist of. They also fail to provide the needed detail for an observer to reliably and accurately measure and observe the behaviors.

## Conducting Behavior Observations

As we previously learned in Chapter 4, behavior observations are necessary for understanding the relationship between behavior and environmental events. Observations provide us with baseline data so that we may document the severity of the problem behavior (Dunlap et al., 1993). Behavior observations begin after the initial interview is conducted. Chapter 4 described the various methods used to collect data. These included the following.

### Anecdotal Recording or A-B-C Analysis

The **anecdotal recording** form of data collection is effective for identifying the (a) antecedent variables that serve as triggers for the behavior, (b) the actual behaviors exhibited by the learner in response to these triggers, and (c) the consequences that are maintaining these behaviors.

### Frequency or Event Recording

**Frequency or event recording** is used to determine how frequently a learner engages in a behavior. It is often used by teachers within classroom settings because of its relative ease for use within these busy environments. Frequency or event recording is most effective when the behavior has a clear beginning and end that can be distinguished. This method of data collection can also be paired with permanent product recording. Permanent product recording is useful in classroom settings as it simply involves collecting work samples (or a permanent product) from learners. These work samples can include homework assignments, writing samples, and in-class work assignments. Frequency or event recording can be coupled with this method to monitor how frequently a student completes homework or in-class assignments and hands them in to the teacher.

Frequency data is typically converted to rate, which is calculated by taking the frequency or number of times that a behavior occurs and dividing it by the amount of time the behavior was observed (see Figure 6–1). An example of calculating the rate of behavior is as follows:

The frequency of Richard's out-of-seat behavior during a 6-hour school day totaled eight times. To calculate the rate of his behavior you would do the following:

Frequency of out-of-seat behavior = 8 times

Total observation time = 6 hours = Rate = 1.3 per hour

**FIGURE 6–1**
*Frequency/Event Recording Data Sheet*

Student _____     Observer _____

Target Behavior _____

| Date | Start Time | End Time | Frequency of Occurrence | Total |
|------|-----------|----------|------------------------|-------|
|      |           |          |                        |       |
|      |           |          |                        |       |
|      |           |          |                        |       |
|      |           |          |                        |       |

When using frequency/event recording, the following points should be remembered:

- Select an observation time that is consistent in time length so that data can be easily computed.
- Select behaviors that have a clear beginning and end.

### Scatter-Plot Analysis

**Scatter-plot analysis** (Touchette, MacDonald, & Langer, 1985) is an effective method for measuring not only the frequency of the behavior but also the pattern of these behaviors, such as setting, time of day, the presence or absence of certain people, an activity, or a contingency of reinforcement. Use scatter plot in half-hour intervals or less throughout the course of the day and record the frequency of the behavior. The data is then transferred to a scatter chart (see Chapter 4), and the code is used to designate the frequency of the behavior. The code indicates whether or not the behavior occurred at a high, low, or zero frequency.

### Duration Recording

**Duration recording** is used to determine the length of time that a student engaged in a behavior. Duration recording involves making a notation of when the behavior begins and ends and computing the amount of time that has elapsed from beginning to end (see Figure 6–2).

**FIGURE 6–2**
***Duration Recording Data Sheet***

Student _____    Observer _____
Target Behavior _____

| Date | Start Time | End Time | Total Duration |
|------|-----------|----------|----------------|
|      |           |          |                |
|      |           |          |                |
|      |           |          |                |
|      |           |          |                |
|      |           |          |                |
|      |           |          |                |

### Interval Recording

**Interval recording** involves breaking down an observation period into smaller and equal intervals. There are two major methods of interval recording, as were discussed in Chapter 4. These include whole interval and partial interval. Whole-interval recording involves noting the occurrence of a behavior with a plus (+) if the behavior occurs throughout the entire interval and a minus (−) if it does not. Partial interval recording, on the other hand, would score an occurrence of the behavior (+) if it occurred at any point during the interval and a (−) if it did not occur at all during the interval (see Figure 6–3).

### Momentary Time Sampling

This method of data collection is similar to interval recording in that it breaks a large period of time into smaller time units; however, unlike the interval recording methods previously described, less time is required of the teacher in carrying out the procedure. Momentary time sampling requires that a teacher observe a student at the end of an interval and record an occurrence (+) or nonoccurrence (−). Vignette 6.1 provides an example of this method of data collection.

**FIGURE 6–3**
*Interval Recording Data Sheet*

Student _____     Observer _____
Target Behavior _____
Interval Length _____

**INTERVALS**

| 1 | 2 | 3 | 4 | 5 | 6 | 7 | 8 | 9 | 10 |
|---|---|---|---|---|---|---|---|---|----|
|   |   |   |   |   |   |   |   |   |    |
|   |   |   |   |   |   |   |   |   |    |
|   |   |   |   |   |   |   |   |   |    |
|   |   |   |   |   |   |   |   |   |    |
|   |   |   |   |   |   |   |   |   |    |
|   |   |   |   |   |   |   |   |   |    |
|   |   |   |   |   |   |   |   |   |    |
|   |   |   |   |   |   |   |   |   |    |
|   |   |   |   |   |   |   |   |   |    |

## Vignette 6.1

### Momentary Time Sampling

Mr. Harrison, a secondary transition teacher, spends much of his day in the community monitoring the performance of his students in various community job settings. His most recent supported employment placement involves Peter, a young man age 17 with developmental disabilities, who is employed at a local pizza restaurant. Peter's job is to load the commercial dishwasher each shift, and in order to complete the task, he must work at a steady rate without stopping. Mr. Harrison wants to assess his progress in staying engaged in his work task and will use momentary time sampling to collect task engagement data. Mr. Harrison begins by observing Peter at the end of each 1-minute interval and continues for the 20-minute time period. At the end of the 20 minutes, he examines the data. He notes that Peter was engaged in performing his task for 14 of the 20 observations. Mr. Harrison converts this to a percentage by taking 14 occurrences and dividing it by 20, or the total number of occurrences, and multiplying it by 100, thus equaling 70%, or $(14/20 = 0.7 \times 100 = 70\%)$. Mr. Harrison can now graph Peter's percent of task engagement for that day (see the following figure).

Student: *Peter Smith*          Observer: *Mr. Harrison*
Target Behavior: *Task engagement*
Interval Length: *1 minute*

**INTERVALS**

| 1 | 2 | 3 | 4 | 5 | 6 | 7 | 8 | 9 | 10 |
|---|---|---|---|---|---|---|---|---|---|
| + | + | + | − | + | + | + | − | + | + |
|   |   |   |   |   |   |   |   |   |   |

| 11 | 12 | 13 | 14 | 15 | 16 | 17 | 18 | 19 | 20 |
|---|---|---|---|---|---|---|---|---|---|
| − | − | − | + | + | + | + | + | + | − |
|   |   |   |   |   |   |   |   |   |   |
|   |   |   |   |   |   |   |   |   |   |
|   |   |   |   |   |   |   |   |   |   |
|   |   |   |   |   |   |   |   |   |   |
|   |   |   |   |   |   |   |   |   |   |

$$\frac{14 \text{ occurrences}}{20 \text{ total opportunities}} \times 100 = 70\%$$

### Reflective Moment

Why is it important for the teacher to collect performance data on Peter's level of task engagement? How would you use such data to improve Peter's performance?

It is important that teachers select an observational method that fits comfortably within their schedule so that they will be amenable to it. A simple rule of thumb for teachers to consider when in the data process is to be consistent when conducting behavior observations so that comparisons can be made across observations. Data should be taken for a minimum of 1 week because at this point trends in the data will be most likely to appear. O'Neill et al. (1997) recommended gathering data for 2 to 5 days or until a minimum of 10 to 15 occurrences of behavior have been documented.

### Consider This

Many teachers often remark that they feel constrainted when it comes to having the necessary amount of time to collect data on problematic behavior. It is important to remember that indeed there is an initial investment of time on the front end, but with persistence and the selection of appropriate data collection methods, the investment will be worth it over time for both you and the learner.

## UNDERSTANDING THE DATA AND FORMULATING HYPOTHESES

At the conclusion of the FBA, the data will be summarized and hypotheses statements will be generated regarding the environmental events associated with the behavior and the function(s) of these behaviors. Interventions are then developed that address the hypotheses and whether there are consistent triggers that elicit the target behavior, and finally, the consequences following the behavior should be examined to ascertain if they maintain the response. Figure 6–4 shows examples of hypotheses culminating from FBAs.

The hypothesis statements provided offer a description of the antecedents and consequences associated with each target behavior. These examples were derived from FBAs conducted within school settings by the first author. The information contained in the hypothesis statements

**FIGURE 6–4**
*FBA Hypotheses Statements*

---

*Student:*   Jacob                         Grade Level:   3
*Target Behavior:*   Refusal to Complete Assigned Work
*FBA Components:*   Structured Interview
  A-B-C Analysis
  Scatter-plot Analysis

*Hypothesis:*   When Jacob is presented with worksheets and prompted to complete them, he fails to make any attempts at completing his assignments, and upon receiving a second prompt from his teacher, he will turn away and ignore the teacher. The teacher will then attend to Jacob, thus providing him with negative attention.

*Function:*   Attention
  Escape/Avoidance

*Intervention Strategies:*   These would include conducting a criterion-referenced assessment to determine if Jacob can indeed perform the work he is being asked to do or if he has a skill deficit in this area. Secondly, modify the task by presenting fewer problems and worksheets at one time, use a red light/green light card on each student's desk, and instruct the students to display red on their card if they need teacher assistance and green if they are not in need of teacher assistance as a method of antecedent management. Teach Jacob the necessary skill requisites for task completion and also how to appropriately seek teacher assistance. Lastly, use redirection techniques if Jacob engages in work-refusal behavior and provide him with differential reinforcement for attempts at task engagement and immediate verbal praise for task attempts and completion.

*Student:*   Sharon                         Grade Level:   7
*Target Behavior:*   Cursing in Class
*FBA Components:*   Structured Interview
  A-B-C Analysis
  Scatter-plot Analysis

*Hypothesis:*   Sharon will frequently curse in class. This behavior coincides with teacher-delivered instruction or when assignments are given. The behavior will consist of an impulsive outburst that will result in laughter from other students and a reprimand from the teacher, including a verbal warning that if Sharon persists she will be sent to the principal's office.

*Function:*   Attention

*Intervention Strategies:*   Teach Sharon how to appropriately communicate her frustrations when in class. Use a self-recording form for Sharon's talk-outs and establish goals for changing the behavior over time. Pair this approach with a point structure for appropriate behavior and a plan for redeeming the points. Consequence-based strategies include the use of differential reinforcement in the form of teacher attention for appropriate communication and consistent consequences for engaging in the behavior, such as point loss. Develop a point system for the entire class for appropriate classroom communication and conduct as a means of promoting a positive peer culture.

*Student:*   Ray                         Grade Level:   HS/CDC
*Target Behavior:*   Rocking and Hand Flapping
*FBA Components:*   Structured Interview
  Motivation Assessment Scale
  A-B-C Analysis

*Hypothesis:*   During functional skills training while in the classroom, Ray will frequently engage in rocking and hand flapping if he is not actively engaged in an activity.

*Function:*   Sensory Stimulation

*Intervention Strategies:*   Provide Ray a picture schedule of his daily activities so that he can anticipate his daily routine. Provide instruction on new tasks, and develop a systematic method of structuring tasks so that Richard can work independently on maintaining the skills he has already learned. Enrich his environment with new opportunities for learning (novel skills or routines), and allow him opportunities for choice within his daily routine. Redirect him prior to the onset of the stereotypical behavior, and provide intermittent verbal reinforcement in the form of praise for task engagement.

provides us with insights that would be most helpful in the development of interventions.

Consider Vignette 6.2 for an example of a completed functional assessment.

## Vignette 6.2

### A Functional Behavior Assessment

*Student:*  David

*Diagnosis:*

*Educational Placement:*

*Age:*  13

Emotional/Behavior Disorders

Self-Contained Class and Inclusive Art, Physical Education, and Lunch

*Description:* David's classroom teacher referred him for an FBA because of his chronic behavior problems within the self-contained and inclusive classroom settings. These disruptive behaviors have been ongoing and persistent and have disrupted David's ability to learn and also that of his classmates.

*FBA Components:*    Structured Interview

Scatter Plot

A-B-C Analysis

*Target Behavior:* David will speak out in class without raising his hand and not engage in assigned tasks for extended periods of time. During these frequent periods of task disengagement, David will interrupt the work of other students with ongoing chatter until they tell him to stop, which results in a hostile verbal exchange from David. Summarized results from the structured interview conducted with his teachers revealed the following comments:

*Structured Interview*

1. *What are the specific target behaviors of concern?* Excessive talking out in class, negative attention-seeking behaviors such as his "cartoon voices" that consists of David imitating the voices of his favorite cartoon characters for attention and general off-task behavior.

2. *Are there antecedent events that consistently happen prior to occurrences of the behavior?* His behavior escalates when given a written assignment unless he receives teacher assistance on the front end. If he does not prefer a task or has any difficulty, he will lose his patience and go off task, and then it becomes increasingly more difficult to redirect him.

3. *What typically happens after the behavior occurs?* David will continue to talk and chatter, which causes a great deal of frustration on the part of his classmates, until one of them will boldly tell him to "shut up," which makes him very angry, at which point he yells at them. He has been dismissed and sent to time-out on repeated occasions and has also been sent to the principal's office.

4. *Do the target behaviors occur at predictable times of day?* His worst periods are during the midmorning and early afternoons. These occur during math and physical education during the morning and during English in the afternoon.

5. *What are the functions of these behaviors?* Attention seeking.

6. *Are there significant life events that could account for the behavior?* Nothing new or different has occurred in David's life. These behaviors have been chronic for a long period of time, and past reports indicate that many of these same issues were unsuccessfully treated in his past educational placements.

7. *What behavior interventions have been used in the past to address the behavior?* Time-out, loss of privileges, and in-school suspension.

8. *Are there medical or physical issues that could account for the behavior?* No, he currently takes no medications.

9. *Are there times in which the behavior does not occur?* It does not occur during art, which is his favorite subject, nor does it occur during social studies as long as the class is on a topic of interest to him.

10. *Please indicate activities that the student enjoys.* He enjoys art, creative activities, music, his vocational education class, and he loves computers and technology.

Results from the A-B-C analysis reveal that David has some consistent antecedents and consequences that occasion his off-task and disruptive behaviors. A sample of these comments is illustrated below:

**Observer:** *Mrs. O'Brien*
**Date:** *11/14/03*
**Time:** *1:15–1:45 P.M.*

| ANTECEDENT | BEHAVIOR | CONSEQUENCE |
|---|---|---|
| Teacher prompts class to take out work materials | David continues to talk and interact with others | Teacher again prompts David |
| Teacher delivers instructions for the activity | David places head down and taps on his desk with a pencil | Teacher attempts to redirect him with a verbal cue |
| When confronted by the teacher to begin working | David mutters under his breath and attempts task | Teacher turns and walks about the room |
| When "time up" is announced by teacher | Students turn in work, David hands in an empty sheet | Teacher reprimands him for not completing his assignment |

*Hypothesis:* When presented with task demands in specific courses—math, English, and physical education—David will frequently engage in off-task behaviors, including excessive talking and general noncompliance (an ability to redirect back on-task given an instructional cue by the teacher). During these periods, he will engage in many negative attention-seeking behaviors, including whispering to his classmates and the use of "cartoon voices" that causes some laughter (negative attention) and serves to create more disruption in the classroom.

*Function:* Attention

*Intervention Strategies:* The following intervention strategies were generated from David's team after reviewing the data from the functional behavior assessment. (a) *Prevention Strategies:* Modify the presentation and delivery of tasks in math and English. This includes providing David with preinstructions on each assigned task, the use of guided instruction, and high probability requests embedded within the math problems and written assignments. (b) *Behavior Change Strategies:* The use of self-monitoring and self-recording to enhance David's task engagement in math and English, and direct instruction in how to appropriately request teacher attention. (c) *Consequence Strategies:* Use of differential reinforcement for appropriate classroom behavior, a point system for task engagement paired with the self-monitoring and self-recording program that would enable him to earn privileges such as computer access, increased art lab, and a free pizza upon the accrual of the necessary points depending on his choice.

Evident in this example is how data can reveal an obvious trend that will assist us in the formation of hypotheses statements and intervention strategies.

However, if in the event the trends in the data are not clear and you have collected additional data (i.e., 7–10 days) and you still cannot identify the causal factors associated with the target behavior or the function, then you should consider conducting a functional analysis (O'Neil et al., 1997).

### Reflective Moment

What intervention strategies might you recommend other than those suggested? What is the rationals for using a comprehensive plan that identifies antecedent management, replacement behavior, and consequence strategies simultaneously?

## CONDUCTING A FUNCTIONAL ANALYSIS

The efficacy of functional analysis procedures for identifying the function of challenging behavior across settings has been well documented in the literature (Carr et al., 1999; Iwata, 1994; Iwata et al., 1982; O'Neill et al., 1997). However, most functional analysis procedures reported in the literature have been conducted in clinical or other highly controlled settings using analogues. For instance, it was reported by Peck Peterson (2002) that 33 of 46, or 71.6%, of experimental studies that used functional assessment/functional analysis procedures in the *Journal of Applied Behavior*

*Analysis* during the years 2000–2001 were conducted in controlled settings such as clinics or residential facilities for persons with developmental disabilities. Many of these studies employed the analogue assessment model. An analogue assessment (Iwata et al., 1982) is when a functional analysis is conducted within a controlled setting (such as an unused classroom or clinic room) with experimental conditions being similar to those found within natural settings such as school (Asmus et al., 2002) and home environments (Peck Peterson, Derby, Berg, & Horner, 2002). Some have argued that analogue assessment is not as socially valid, given that the target behavior is not exposed to the same level of contingencies operating in the natural environment when in such a contrived setting (Conroy, Fox, Crain, Jenkins, & Belcher, 1996). Despite these limitations, research in the area of functional analysis has helped advance our understanding of how to experimentally validate hypotheses concerning the functions of challenging behavior.

A functional analysis is conducted by changing various environmental events or situations to determine their effect on behavior (O'Neill et al., 1997). These manipulations are designed to test the hypotheses that we arrived at through the functional assessment process. Demchak and Bossert (1996) suggested that when conducting a functional analysis within a school setting, the manipulations should be selected for their potential to invoke the target behavior of concern. An example of this would be selecting manipulations based on the hypotheses and perceived function of the target behavior. This would require setting up brief conditions, approximately 10 minutes in length, to assess the behavior that would coincide with the perceived function, such as Attention, Access to Tangibles, Escape, and Sensory Stimulation as described by Iwata et al. (1982). Functional analysis, therefore, serves to validate and confirm what function the problem serves for a learner. When conducting a functional analysis, the following conditions are typically assessed using a multielement design, and the effects of these manipulations on the target behavior are noted (Asmus et al., 2002; Wacker, Cooper, Peck, Derby, & Berg, 1999).

## Conditions Associated with a Functional Analysis

1. *Attention:* If you suspect that a learner is engaging in a problem behavior for the purpose of gaining attention, use the 10-minute time period and set up a series of activities for the learner to engage in while you sit in the room totally preoccupied on some other activity. Each time the learner engages in the target behavior, provide him with attention. If the behavior occurs at a high rate of occurrence, one could assume that a probable relationship exists with attention serving as the function for the problem behavior.

2. *Escape:* If you believe that the learner's behavior is related to escape, then you could provide the learner with a nonpreferred task. Instruct the learner to work on the task for the duration of the 10-minute period. If the learner should engage in the target behavior, allow him to stop

working, have a brief break, and then resume the task. If the problem behavior should reoccur, then repeat the procedure, allowing the child to take a brief break and then returning to the task. Note the occurrences of the behavior to determine the relationship between task presentation and the learner's behavior. High frequencies of escape behavior from the task would indicate that the function of the target behavior was escape.

3. *Sensory Stimulation:* This condition allows the learner to be alone without any reinforcing materials, toys, or other forms of stimulation. If the child's behavior is aimed at providing sensory stimulation, the behavior should occur within this condition.

4. *Access to Tangibles:* Assess whether or not the learner's behavior is directed at obtaining tangibles such as a preferred toy, food, drink, or other item. Select a preferred toy and place it in view of the learner. When the learner engages in the target behavior, allow the child to interact with the preferred object for a brief, period, and then have the learner resume the task. Repeat the procedure again until the brief 10-minute period has elapsed and note the occurrences of the behavior. If the target behavior occurred numerous times, the behavior is aimed at obtaining tangible reinforcement.

5. *Play:* This condition is characterized by the learner being given noncontingent access to high-interest materials and attention, with the expectation being that the problem behavior will not occur. The play condition also serves as a control condition (Carr et al., 1999; Demchak & Bossert, 1996).

Most functional analyses are conducted using either a multielement or reversal design. These research designs as well as others will be described in greater depth in Chapter 9. The multielement design (Iwata et al., 1982; Sidman, 1960; Ulman & Sulzer-Azaroff, 1975) has also been referred to as the alternating treatment design (Bailey & Burch, 2002). The point behind this design is to assess the effects of a variety of stimuli that are thought to precipitate or maintain problem behavior (Alberto & Troutman, 2003; Bailey & Burch, 2002). Figure 6–5 depicts the use of a multielement design in a study conducted by Zarcone and colleagues (1994). In this study, the authors were examining whether or not a decrease in instructional trials would result in reductions of self-injurious escape behavior and maintainence over time with instructional fading.

O'Neill et al. (1997) recommended guidelines to be considered for conducting experimental manipulations as part of a functional analysis. These include: (a) conduct manipulations only when you can control relevant situations, (b) determine the level of potential risk involved for learners and staff, (c) obtain permission and approval to conduct systematic manipulations (d) use protective procedures and equipment as necessary for learner and staff safety, (e) consider assessment of "precursor" behavior as alternative strategies, and (f) use manipulations to evaluate specific ideas or hypotheses about the situations that are related to challenging behaviors and the functions they serve.

**FIGURE 6–5**
*Use of a Multielement*
*Design for Use in a*
*Functional Analysis*

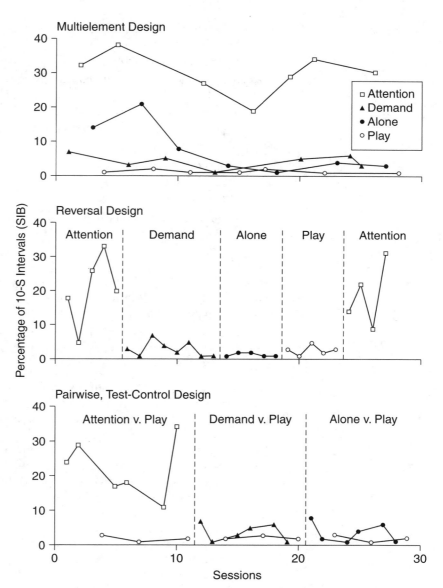

*Source:* Zarcone, J. R., et al. (1994). "Reemergence and Extinction of Self-Injurious Behavior During Stimulus (Instructional) Fading," *Journal of Applied Behavior Analysis, 27,* 307–316. Copyright 1994 by The Society for the Experimental Analysis of Behavior. Reprinted by permission.

## DEVELOPMENT OF AN INTERVENTION PLAN

Following the completion of the functional analysis, it is time to develop a comprehensive intervention using the data derived from the assessment. When developing an intervention, it is important to consider the data that has been gathered (O'Neill et al., 1997). These data include some of the following elements:

1. An operational definition of the target behavior.

2. Factors that could be influencing the behavior, including a change in major life events, medication, physical illness, or other such factors.

3. Setting events and antecedents that consistently serve as triggers for the problem behavior: Are they settings, tasks, individuals, time of day, instructional cues, and/or others?

4. Events that follow the behavior that serve to maintain the behavior such as negative reinforcement.

5. The function of the behavior and how it serves the individual.

6. Potential replacement behaviors that would serve the same function as that of the problem behavior.

7. A list of attempted interventions that have been used in the past to address the target behavior.

8. Quality-of-life variables that may need to be addressed as part of a comprehensive intervention package. These could include enriching environments, providing increased opportunities for choice, scheduling changes, and other environmental supports designed to increase the individual's quality of life.

9. Socially valid data from the learner or learner's parents and family concerning their perspectives on the problem behavior and input on the development of a behavior support plan.

The development of a behavior support plan requires that we consider the type of intervention that will best address the problem behavior. Therefore, the hypothesis statements are important in helping us determine how to intervene.

When addressing challenging behavior, perhaps the best place to begin is at the antecedent and setting-event stage. To address these behaviors on the front end, so to speak, is a proactive approach that will hopefully result in the prevention of these problem behaviors or at least their significant reduction in the future.

Bambara and Knoster (1998) offered research-based strategies for antecedent and setting-event modifications. Their recommendations include (a) avoid giving assignments that are repetitive or overly difficult in an area that the learner has problems with, (b) modify a problem event such as adapting lessons or instructional cues, (c) intersperse difficult and less-difficult tasks, (d) add tasks and learner preferences that promote desired behavior, and (e) block or neutralize the impact of events that trigger challenging behavior (Bambara & Knoster, 1998).

Other strategies to consider when modifying antecedents and setting events as part of a behavior support plan include the following:

### Modifying Setting Events and Antecedents

- How can changes in the environment help to prevent occurrences of the problem behavior?

- What can be done to alter specific antecedents that trigger the problem behavior?
- How can daily schedules and routines be enriched to increase the likelihood of appropriate alternative behaviors?

Teaching alternative replacement behaviors that serve the same function is also a critical element of a good behavior support plan. This is accomplished through the identification of some essential skills that could assist the learner in obtaining her needs as well as eliminating the need for the problem behavior. Bambara and Knoster (1998) defined three areas from the available research on teaching replacement behaviors. These areas include (a) replacement skills—behaviors that are designed to serve the same function as the target behavior; (b) general skills—skills that build on current competencies and expand and generalize the skills that enable the individual to have greater options and thus reduce the need for problem behavior to occur; and (c) coping Skills—coping strategies for the individual to use when challenging and difficult situations are encountered.

Other questions to consider when selecting alternative replacement behaviors could include some of the following:

## Teaching Positive Replacement Behaviors

- What positive, alternative behaviors would be acceptable replacement behaviors that would serve the same function?
- Does the learner have strengths that could assist him in acquiring alternative behaviors?
- What are some specific self-management skills that would enable the learner in coping with difficult situations?
- What are the specific areas of intervention needed to teach replacement behaviors (social or communication skills, self-management skills such as self-instruction, self-monitoring, or other)?

Traditionally, behavior change programs within schools have placed a great deal of emphasis on consequence-based approaches with the administration of reinforcers or punishers. Although important to the behavior change process, they are part of a larger, more comprehensive approach toward the development of a behavior support plan. Some important considerations in the use of consequence-based intervention practices are as follows:

## Consequence-Based Interventions

- How can consequences be altered to reduce the frequency of the problem behavior?
- What type of strategy will be used (differential reinforcement, redirection, planned ignoring)?
- How will positive alternative behaviors be reinforced so that they will become more efficient than the problem behavior?
- Have crisis intervention procedures been identified to protect the child or others in the event that they are needed?

Finally, an area of great importance in the design of a behavior support plan is the individual's overall quality of life. This point cannot be overstated, as the major goal of positive behavior supports is the enhancement of an individual's quality of life (Horner, 1999). Concern for the quality of life of the persons we serve through the design and delivery of positive behavior supports is consistent with the promotion of self-determination skills. Self-determination skills are essential for promoting happiness and self-fulfillment among all people.

Self-determination represents a basic human right and was defined by Wehmeyer, Martin, and Sands (1998) as "acting as the primary causal agent in one's life and making choices and decisions regarding one's quality of life from undue external influence or interference" (p. 191). Many times, these rights have been denied persons with disabilities because of challenging behavior and often because of an identified disability that has served to label these individuals as being incapable of performing such skills. The tools that enable us to assist individuals in obtaining such outcomes include positive behavior interventions and supports. The FBA and functional analysis are tools by which we can assess these enhanced lifestyle avenues. Functional behavior assessment offers us an applied technology to facilitate positive life changes through the design and implementation of behavior support plans with enhanced quality of life serving as the ultimate outcome.

## SUMMARY

This chapter described the process of functional behavior assessment (FBA). The importance of FBA was identified given the 1997 reauthorization of the Individuals with Disabilities Education Act. One major point from this piece of legislation is that it called for the use of FBA and PBIS. These assessment and intervention tools have been mandated to address the behavior support needs of children whose behavior negatively affects their learning and/or the learning of others (Tilly et al., 1998). Also addressed within the chapter were the assumptions that are often made by professionals and others concerning challenging behavior. Such false assumptions are simply conjecture and are not based on fact nor are they supported by data and thus serve no purpose in addressing the problem. However, it is important to remember that challenging behavior serves a function or purpose, and quite often these behaviors are communication based. Behaviors often have communicative intent and are directed at getting one's needs met. As we also learned in the chapter, the process of FBA provides us with a systematic method for obtaining information that will lead us to a better understanding of challenging behaviors, the factors that influence its occurrence, the variables that reinforce it, and the function such behavior serves. The components of functional behavior assessment were also described and applications of these methods provided. The final portion of the chapter discussed how to conduct a functional analysis. Questions of the utility of functional analyses within school settings were addressed, as was how the experimental manipulation of variables could serve to validate the function of problem behavior. Finally, the chapter described how information compiled from an FBA could translate into the development of behavior support plans and the various types of intervention alternatives available.

## ACTIVITIES TO EXTEND YOUR LEARNING

1. Select a series of target behaviors and operationally define these behaviors in measurable and observable terms.
2. Conduct a series of behavior observations within your practica setting while focusing on the target behaviors you selected and practice each of the observational methods described within the chapter, such as interval recording and time sampling.
3. While in your practica setting, observe your cooperating teacher and other educational professionals as they conduct an FBA.
4. Interview a teacher, behavior support specialist, and school psychologist concerning their perspectives on conducting an FBA. Compare and contrast their viewpoints and approaches.

## FURTHER READING AND EXPLORATION

1. Consult the following Web sites for more information on functional behavior assessment:

   http://www.pbis.org—This site is the link to the Office of Special Education Programs on Positive Behavioral Interventions and Supports.

   http://www.rrtcpbs.org—This link connects you with the NIDRR Rehabilitation Research and Training Center on Positive Behavior Support, the OSEP Technical Assistance Center of Positive Behavioral Interventions and Supports, and the Florida Positive Behavior Support Project.

   http://www.air.org/cecp—This site is affiliated with the Center for Effective Collaboration and Practice and offers many excellent examples of materials related to positive behavior interventions and supports, including functional assessment materials and data collection tools.

2. Develop a resource file on materials related to FBA that includes data collection forms, interview forms, and information that you can use to inform both yourself and families of these approaches.

## REFERENCES

Alberto, P. A., & Troutman, A. C. (2003). *Applied behavior analysis for teachers* (6th ed.). Upper Saddle River, NJ: Merrill/Prentice Hall.

Armstrong, S. W., & Kauffman, J. M. (1999). Functional behavior assessment: Introduction to the series. *Behavioral Disorders, 24,* 167–168.

Asmus, J. M., Vollmer, T. R., & Borrero, J. C. (2002). Functional behavioral assessment: A school based model. *Education and Treatment of Children, 25,* 67–90.

Bailey, J. S., & Burch, M. R. (2002). *Research methods in applied behavior analysis.* Thousand Oaks, CA: Sage Publications.

Bambara, L. M., & Knoster, T. (1998). Designing positive behavior support plans. In *Innovations* (Vol. 13). Washington, DC: American Association on Mental Retardation.

Carr, E. G. (1977). The motivation of self-injurious behavior: A review of some hypotheses. *Psychological Bulletin, 84,* 800–816.

Carr, E. G., & Durand, V. M. (1985). Reducing behavior problems through functional communication training. *Journal of Applied Behavior Analysis, 18,* 11–126.

Carr, E. G., Langdon, N. A., & Yarbrough, S. C. (1999). Hypothesis-based intervention for severe problem behavior. In A. C. Repp & R. H. Horner (Eds.), *Functional analysis of problem behavior* (pp. 9–31). Belmont, CA: Wadsworth.

Carr, E. G., & Newsom, C. D. (1985). Demand-related tantrums: Conceptualization and treatment. *Behavior Modification, 9,* 403–426.

Chandler, L. K., & Dahlquist, C. M. (2002). *Functional assessment: Strategies to prevent and remediate challenging behavior in school settings.* Upper Saddle River, NJ: Merrill/Prentice Hall.

Conroy, M., Fox, J., Crain, J., Jenkins, A., & Belcher, K. (1996). Evaluating the social and ecological validity of analog assessment procedures for challenging behaviors in young children. *Education and Treatment of Children, 19*(3), 233–256.

Demchak, M. A., & Bossert, K. W. (1996). Assessing problem behaviors. In *Innovations* (Vol. 4). Washington, DC: American Association on Mental Retardation.

Dunlap, G., Kern, L., dePercezel, M., Clark, S., Wilson, D., Childes, K. E., White, R., & Falk, G. D. (1993). Functional analysis of classroom variables for students with emotional and behavioral disorders. *Behavioral Disorders, 18,* 275–291.

Dunlap, G., & Kinkaid, D. (2001). The widening world of functional assessment comments on four manuals and beyond. *Journal of Applied Behavior Analysis, 34,* 365–377.

Durand, V. M. (1990). *Severe behavior problems: A functional communication training approach.* New York: Guilford.

Horner, R. H. (1999). Positive behavior supports. In M. Wehmeyer & J. Patton (Eds.), *Mental retardation in the 21st century* (pp. 181–196). Austin, TX: PRO-ED.

Horner, R. H., Sprague, J. R., O'Brien, M., & Heathfield, L. T. (1990). The role of response efficiency in the reduction of problem behaviors through functional equivalence training: A case study. *Journal of the Association for Persons with Severe Handicaps, 15,* 91–97.

Horner, R. H., & Sugai, G. (2000). School-wide behavior support: An emerging initiative. *Journal of Positive Behavior Interventions, 2*(4), 231–232.

Individuals with Disabilities Education Act. 20 U.S.C. § 1401 *et seq.* National Association of State Directors of Special Education (1997). IDEA information: A reauthorized IDEA is enacted: Comparison of previous law and Pub. L. No. 105-17 (1997 Amendments). Unpublished document.

Iwata, B. A. (1994). Functional analysis methodology: Some closing comments. *Journal of Applied Behavior Analysis, 27,* 413–418.

Iwata, B., Dorsey, M., Slifer, K., Bauman, K., & Richman, G. (1982). Toward a functional analysis of self-injury. *Analysis and Intervention in Developmental Disabilities, 6,* 1–4.

O'Neill, R. E., Horner, R. H., Albin, R. W., Sprague, J. R., Storey, K., & Newton, J. S. (1997). *Functional assessment and program development for problem behavior.* Pacific Grove, CA: Brooks/Cole.

O'Reilly, M. F. (1997). Functional analysis of episodic self-injury correlated with recurrent otitis media. *Journal of Applied Behavior Analysis, 30,* 165–168.

Peck Peterson, S. M. (2002). Functional behavior assessment in natural settings [Special issue]. *Education and Treatment of Children, 25,* 1–4.

Peck Peterson, S. M., Derby, M. K., Berg, W. K., & Horner, R. H. (2002). Collaboration with families in the functional behavior assessment of an intervention for severe behavior problems. *Education and Treatment of Children, 25*(1), 5–25.

Scott, T. M., & Nelson, M. C. (1999). Using functional behavioral assessment to develop effective intervention plans. *Journal of Positive Behavior Interventions, 1,* 242–251.

Sidman, M. (1960). *Tactics of scientific research.* New York: Basic Books.

Skinner, B. F. (1974). *About behaviorism.* New York: Knopf.

Sugai, G., Horner, R. H., Dunlap, G., Hieneman, M., Lewis, T. J., Nelson, C. M., et al. (2000). Applying positive behavior support and functional behavior assessment in schools. *Journal of Positive Behavior Interventions, 2,* 131–143.

Tilly, W. D., Knoster, T. K., Kovaleski, J., Bambara, L., Dunlap, G., & Kincaid, D. (1998). *Functional behavior assessment: Policy development in light of emerging research and practice.* Alexandria, VA: National Association of State Directors of Special Education.

Touchette, P. E., MacDonald, R. F., & Langer, S. M. (1985). A scatter plot for identifying stimulus control of problem behaviors. *Journal of Applied Behavior Analysis, 18,* 343–351.

Ulman, J. D., & Sulzer-Azaroff, B. (1975). Multi-element baseline design in educational research. In E. Ramp & G. Semb (Eds.), *Behavior analysis areas of research and application* (pp. 377–391). Upper Saddle River, NJ: Prentice Hall.

Wacker, D. P., Cooper, L. J., Peck, S. M., Derby, K. M., & Berg, W. (1999). Community-based functional assessment. In A. C. Repp & R. H. Horner (Eds.), *Functional analysis of problem behavior* (pp. 32–56). Belmont, CA: Wadsworth.

Wehmeyer, M. L., Martin, J. E., & Sands, D. J. (1998). Self-determination for children and youth with developmental disabilities. In A. Hilton & R. Ringlaben (Eds.), *Best and promising practices in developmental disabilities* (pp. 191–203). Austin, TX: PRO-ED.

Zarcone, J. R., Iwata, B. A., Smith, R. G., Mazaleski, J. L., & Lerman, D. C. (1994). Reemergence and extinction of self-injurious behavior during stimulus (instructional) fading. *Journal of Applied Behavior Analysis, 27,* 307–316.

# Chapter 7

# Planning Behavior Supports

## CONCEPTS TO UNDERSTAND

*After reading this chapter, you should be able to:*

- List and describe the seven components of the planning process.
- List and describe the five factors that influence the success or failure of a plan.
- Describe two planning processes typically used in programs for children, youth, and families.
- Compare and contrast individual education programs (IEPs), individualized family service plans (IFSPs), and person-centered planning (PCPs).
- Discuss generally the role of planning in each of the three levels of positive behavior support (PBS).
- Outline a schoolwide support plan for a preschool, middle school, and high school.
- Outline a level 2 behavior support plan for a preschooler and school-age child with challenging behavior.
- Outline a level 3 behavior support plan for a preschooler and school-age child with challenging behavior.

## KEY TERMS

Behavior support levels 1, 2, 3

Behavior support planning

Competing behaviors model

Constraints

Developmentally appropriate management techniques

Evaluation

Goals

Group action planning (GAP)

Impeding behavior

Implementation

Individual Education Program (IEP)

Individualized Family Service Plan (IFSP)

Objectives

Person-centered planning (PCP)

Primary, secondary, tertiary prevention

Rationale/mission

Resources

Schoolwide positive behavior support

Stakeholders

Strategies

Whether it is in our everyday lives or our roles as professionals in education and other disciplines, we are constantly in the process of assessing, planning, implementing, and evaluating. Often, this process occurs rather informally and even unconsciously, but it certainly impacts the quality of our lives and the lives of those we care for as well as the lives of the children and youth we serve as professionals. At one end of the continuum, some individuals appear to have an aversion to planning, preferring, rather, that events unfold as they will without any structure imposed by making a plan. Other individuals appear to enjoy spending an inordinate amount of time in the development of formal plans, sometimes to the detriment of carrying out the plan. Perhaps you know someone who fits one of these extremes. Maybe you know someone who might state that they have no plan for the day, just that they will let it unfold, take whatever it brings, and make the best of it. On the other hand, maybe you know someone who starts every day with a list of things that they intend to do, the order in which they will be undertaken, and the criteria by which successful completion of each task will be measured. The point here is that everyone has a different perspective on planning and its place in our everyday lives. Given this fact, it is important to keep in mind that professionals, families, and persons targeted for a behavior support plan will also have differing views about the place of planning in their work and lives.

## THE PLANNING PROCESS

Frequently, planning processes have been described in seven components—a rationale or mission, goals, objectives, strategies, constraints and resources, implementation, and evaluation (Figure 7–1).

Although it is not our intent here to go into detail about these components of planning (evaluation is addressed in Chapter 8), it is useful to briefly introduce and illustrate each. The relevance of each component will be clear as you progress further in the chapter and give consideration to the means by which behavior support planning is successfully done. The first component of a plan is the **rationale/mission**, sometimes thought of as a philosophy. Suppose we use a rather mundane subject to illustrate what is intended—having a meal. You are thinking about and planning for lunch. Your mission is to eat lunch, given that your body requires nutrients and your stomach is telling you that you are hungry. It is your belief that lunch should be the more substantial meal of the day and that it is preferably taken in a relaxing, quiet environment with people about whom you care and with whom you can converse comfortably. These statements might represent at least a partial mission–rationale–philosophy for your plan to have lunch.

What about goals? **Goals** are broad statements of intent associated typically with what one believes. The goals for the lunch plan might be to enjoy a pleasant lunch in a relaxed, quiet setting with a friend, to eliminate your feeling of hunger, to avoid high-fat and high-cholesterol foods while having lunch be the big meal of the day, to stay within your budget, and to not take too much time from your busy schedule.

**FIGURE 7–1**
*Components of a
Planning Process*

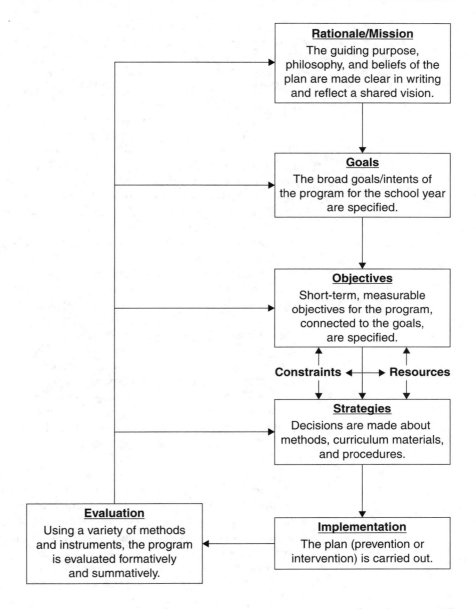

**Rationale/Mission**
The guiding purpose, philosophy, and beliefs of the plan are made clear in writing and reflect a shared vision.

**Goals**
The broad goals/intents of the program for the school year are specified.

**Objectives**
Short-term, measurable objectives for the program, connected to the goals, are specified.

Constraints ← → Resources

**Strategies**
Decisions are made about methods, curriculum materials, and procedures.

**Evaluation**
Using a variety of methods and instruments, the program is evaluated formatively and summatively.

**Implementation**
The plan (prevention or intervention) is carried out.

**Objectives** are more specific and measurable subsets of goals. How will you know that you have met the goals that you have in mind? One objective might be that you will be done with lunch by 1:00 P.M. and that the meal will cost no more than $5. Another objective might be that you will feel satisfied but not overly full, and the fat and cholesterol content of the meal will be within the limits that you have established.

The **strategies** are the actions that you might choose to meet your goals and objectives. Some of the strategies available in our example might be related to transportation. Will you walk, drive, take public transportation, have food delivered? Another strategy choice might be related to location. Will you go to a restaurant, eat the brown bag lunch you brought to school in the office or student lounge, or go home for lunch? Another strategy decision might be associated with costs and how you will pay. Do you want to use cash, check, or a credit card, or maybe it will be food that you prepared and brought from home?

The strategies that one chooses to address their goals and objectives are always affected by the presence of **constraints** and **resources**. Constraints and resources may be thought of as things that limit what one can do (constraints) and the things that support and assist what one can do (resources). Of course, constraints and resources are frequently different sides of the same coin. That is, for example, money is a constraint if you do not have more than $5 for lunch, but it is a resource because you do have $5 to spend on lunch. Obviously, we take into account our resources and constraints as we select strategies to meet goals and objectives. For the lunch example, maybe you have class at 1:00 P.M., so you are limited to 1 hour for lunch, and you have only the $5 in cash to spend. You want to go with your friend to a nearby restaurant, but most of those within walking distance are fast-food places with choices that will load you up on fats and cholesterol. You have easy access to your vehicle (resource), and there is a nice salad bar in 5 minutes' driving time. The salad bar is buffet style, so time efficient, it is all you care to eat, and your $5 will cover lunch. And, it is relatively quiet with no loud music, so you can talk with your friend. You have assessed the constraints and resources associated with meeting your goals and objectives, and you have considered various strategies. Now it is time to go have lunch (or maybe all this planning has taken away your appetite!). In the planning process, this is referred to as **implementation**—you drive with your friend to the restaurant with the salad bar that is 5 minutes away and have lunch.

The last of the seven components of the planning process is **evaluation**. How will you evaluate whether or not you have met your goals and objectives for lunch? Can you quantify or measure the outcomes of lunch? Of course you can! Did the $5 cover your meal? Are you satisfied and do you have a feeling of being full? Did the meal meet your requirements for nutrition? Did you get back in time for the 1:00 P.M. class? Did you and your friend have a pleasant conversation and are you free of any need for antacids? The seven components of the planning process have been applied in our lunch example. Each is important and interconnected. Planning is not something that we impose on clients; rather, it is best understood as something that we all do in various ways and to various degrees to improve the quality of our lives.

## FACTORS INFLUENCING A SUCCESSFUL PLAN

The seven components just introduced are useful in understanding the typical process, or cycle, of planning. What are the factors that might be associated with a successful or unsuccessful plan? You might think about some of the factors that have influenced the success or failure of a plan in your personal or professional life. Following are five such factors.

First of all, one might consider whether or not all the seven components are sufficiently taken into account. For example, one might have a plan that is heavy on constraints and limited on resources, and therefore not probable for success. Maybe a plan is well conceived from a strong rationale, has meaningful goals and objectives, has strategies based on consideration of constraints and resources, and is implemented, but there are no means of evaluating how the plan worked. So one factor associated with a successful plan is the extent to which it includes all the components.

A second factor is the question of how much emphasis is given to collaboration and teamwork, the partnership, among the members responsible for designing and carrying out a plan. (The lunch plan in the example provided is also going to be important to the friend who accompanied you. Was she involved in the process?) Plans are often doomed from the start if they do not provide for the meaningful involvement and participation of all who are stakeholders and who care about and will be impacted directly by the result of the plan. Related to the functions of a planning team, it is obvious that if they do not have a shared vision, a comparable philosophy and mission in mind, they will have difficulty from the start of the process. Therefore, the second factor associated with successful planning is the use of a team approach in which members have a stake in the plan and the ability to influence decisions through meaningful contributions based on their knowledge and expertise.

A third factor is the extent to which the plan is a real, practical, and useable document that is applied as opposed to one that is produced to satisfy an imposed requirement. This plan is likely to be filed away and forgotten, used only in the event of a need to provide documentation. Is the plan active or passive? Is it used as a road map over the period of time that it is intended to address? Is it updated, changed, and revised as circumstances dictate?

The fourth factor associated with the success or failure of a plan is the role played by the person(s) who is (are) the target(s) of the plan. To the extent possible, have the individual who will be most impacted by the plan directly involved in making decisions regarding all components of the process. After all, if an individual is the target of changes specified in a plan, then that person will hopefully feel an ownership and investment in carrying out the plan. Further, the person targeted in a plan should experience it as an effort to advocate, support, and facilitate for them, rather than an adversarial effort intended to require, force, and mandate changes that are imposed on them.

A fifth and final factor is the question of how doable the plan is and its sustainability. It is possible, considering the establishment of goals and objectives based on constraints and resources, to make a plan that is too hard and impossible to achieve or one that is too easy and represents insignificant or irrelevant change. For example, it might be difficult for someone to sustain a plan in which his objective was to lose 25 pounds in 1 month.

Conversely, the objective of losing 1 pound over the period of 1 month might also make the plan of limited use.

To summarize, one might understand the success of planning as dependent on five factors: (a) including all components of the planning process; (b) using a collaborative team approach; (c) having a meaningful, relevant, and useful document; (d) involving the person who is the target of the plan; and (e) making the plan challenging while doable and sustainable.

## PLANNING FOR CHILDREN AND YOUTH AND THEIR FAMILIES

As you are undoubtedly aware, there are numerous required or recommended planning formats and documents associated with the myriad services and programs for children and youth and their families. Although the focus here is specifically on planning as it relates to children and youth in educational environments (and especially, of course, those manifesting or at-risk for challenging behavior), it is useful to also consider briefly some of the planning approaches in related areas. It is important for us as professionals to keep in mind that these various plans are frequently mandated and required for individuals to gain access to needed services and resources. So in some respects, they are imposed, and that fact creates circumstances associated with the successful development and implementation of a plan. Following is a brief introduction to various planning formats, some of which you are most likely familiar with, possibly in a similar form.

In the authors' state, the program that delivers services to children, youth, and families in poverty and is the welfare reform plan, replacing the Aid to Families with Dependent Children (AFDC), requires that participants must early in the process develop with their caseworker their own personal responsibility plan (PRP). The PRP states that recipients must make sure their children receive immunization shots and health checks, make sure their children attend school regularly, and agree to work, if not exempt. Further, teen parents under age 18 must stay in school and attend regularly and live at home with parents or other responsible adult(s). Another component of the PRP is that it requires the individual to work full time or part time and take classes to prepare for work. Failure to comply with the PRP may result in loss of cash and other benefits.

Persons receiving counseling and mental health services are frequently expected to have individual treatment plans (ITPs). Adults with developmental disabilities living in community-assisted living environments and working in supported environments may have an Individual Support Plan (ISP), emphasizing the means by which they will acquire and maintain self-sufficiency, self-determination, and an improved quality of life. When children or youth are removed from their birth families in instances of child maltreatment and placed in foster care, there is often the legal requirement for a foster care plan in which the circumstances and criteria under which the child may return to his home are specified. At the university where the authors are employed as professors, there is an Office for Students with Disabilities.

**Consider This**

For any college student who has a verified disability and who requires and wishes accommodation or adaptation in her classes, the university must participate in a plan designed to address the individual needs of the university student with a disability. This plan is referred to as the Accommodation Plan (AP).

- Do you know anyone at your university who has a disability and a related plan for their classes?
- What does that person think of how her plan was developed?

The purpose here is to remind you that there are numerous planning formats and requirements across a variety of human service disciplines, targeting individuals (and families) who must meet established goals, objectives, and criteria to retain or receive desired outcomes. For example, if a parent has been the perpetrator of physical abuse toward his child, the foster care plan might require that the parent meet the objective of learning more acceptable disciplining skills as a condition for return of the child to the home. Although it is not a criticism of the aforementioned plans, it is important to keep in mind that one of the factors associated with a successful plan is the extent to which the targets of the plan have a sense of ownership and investment in carrying it out. And of course, it is fair to state that it is frequently more difficult to carry out a plan that has been imposed on someone than a plan that they have chosen for themselves.

## PLANNING FOR CHILDREN AND YOUTH WITH DISABILITIES

The two prominent plan requirements in special education are the **Individualized Family Service Plan (IFSP)** and the **Individual Education Program (IEP)** plan. The reader is most probably to some extent familiar with these two plans. The IFSP is required for infants and toddlers (from birth to 3 years) with disabilities and their families who meet the various state definitions for early intervention services provided under Part C of the Individuals with Disabilities Education Act (IDEA). The IFSP is different from the IEP in several significant ways, including its emphasis on services in natural environments, the expectation that a quality IFSP will be family centered and include outcomes and action steps focusing on the family unit, and the participation of professionals and disciplines outside education. The IFSP is completed on an annual basis, is reviewed at 6 months, and requires a transition plan be done 1 year before the child moves to a preschool setting. Compared to the IEP, the development, refinement, and evolution of the IFSP is rather brief, having begun with its inclusion in the IDEA reauthorization of the Education for All Handicapped Children Act Amendments of 1986 (PL 99-457).

The IFSP remains a work in progress, as does the IEP, but it is important to note that the differences between the two planning documents and their associated processes continue to be a source of contention between early interventionists and school personnel. Two reasons for this are the family-centered nature of the IFSP and the use of family-stated and often less-measurable objectives (referred to as outcomes) in the IFSP and the inclusion of more broadly stated action steps in the IFSP, rather than curricula and specific strategies as often found in the IEP. It should be noted here that states may choose to use the IFSP for preschool-age children with special needs if they so choose.

In contrast to the IFSP, the Individual Education Program (IEP) plan is child focused and intended to exclusively address the special educational needs of children who are eligible to receive special education services. Rather than the family-centered emphasis of the IFSP, the IEP has a focus on parent involvement and their participation as one of several stakeholders (note later discussion in the chapter of this term). The IEP is required to be done on an annual basis, including a reevaluation of the child's or youth's eligibility and need for special education services. IEP plans tend to include more measurable and educationally stated objectives than one will typically find in the IFSP. The IEP is applied for children receiving special education through age 21, and a transition plan, beginning at age 16, is required as a part of the process.

### Consider This

When appropriate and desired, the student for whom the IEP is written should be a part of the team responsible for writing and implementing progress toward achieving the goals and objectives stated.

* In what ways might this impact the planning process?

Although both the IEP and the IFSP require that the plan be the result of the efforts of a multidisciplinary team including professionals and family members, the IEP team is child focused and interested in educational matters only. The central mission and beliefs underlying these planning processes, the different roles of parents and families, and the different perspectives related to the approach of measurable outcomes are all important factors to be considered in using behavior support plans for children and youth of all ages in various educational environments.

Before getting into the specifics of behavior support plans, it is helpful to consider a few additional planning processes targeting children and youth with special needs. **Person-centered planning (PCP)** has been defined (Turnbull & Turnbull, 2001) as "a process that was created to listen to the great expectations of individuals with disabilities and their families and to tailor lifestyle support to actualize those great expectations" (p. 296). A primary example of PCP is the *McGill Action Planning System* (MAPS) (Forest & Lusthaus, 1990). The MAPS process provides the opportunity for a student with a disability, his or her friends, and teachers, parents, and siblings to get together and to develop a vision, as well as creating an action plan for the student to achieve the vision.

Turnbull and Turnbull (1996) advocated another example of a planning process, referred to as **group action planning (GAP)**. The emphasis in the group action plan is on the family unit's need for positive behavior support, rather than exclusively the child's, and more broadly on inclusive lifestyle change rather than behavior change. GAP is intended to provide comprehensive family support. Turnbull and Turnbull (1996) have suggested that, as compared to the IEP process, which tends all too often to be routinized, somber, tense, and distant, the key to group action planning is "to create a context in which people can enjoy themselves, feel a sense of renewal and rejuvenation, and obtain personal gratification and validation that they are making a difference in someone's life" (p. 107). GAP contains five elements—inviting support, creating connections, envisioning great expectations, solving problems, and celebrating success. In its emphasis on the family and natural and inclusive lifestyles, GAP may be seen as quite similar to the intent of the IFSP. However, there remains an emphasis frequently in the development of the IFSP on child-centered behavior outcomes to the exclusion or deemphasis of family-centered and family-guided inclusive lifestyle actions and outcomes. Certainly, the GAP process is quite different from the intent and actualization of the IEP plan. Unlike GAP, the IEP tends to be formal (even quasi-legal), exclusively child centered and focused only on education, time limited, paper driven, and requiring highly measurable outcomes.

The purpose here is not to be critical of the IEP process. Certainly since its beginnings and the inception of the IDEA in 1975, the IEP has been a significant tool to ensure that children and youth with disabilities receive the individualized education programs that they need. Rather, the purpose is to help the reader understand that there are various planning formats and processes, and that they have different missions, emphases, and content. We have briefly considered the IFSP, the IEP plan, PCP and the related MAPS process, and GAP.

Numerous other planning approaches could have been included. The question remains for the future. What should and will be the connections among these various planning approaches, especially as they relate to the needs of children and youth with challenging behavior? Will children and youth with special needs and their parents or families be subject to participation in planning processes (often because professionals have said they ought to) that are quite different and even seen to be at cross purposes? Are there significant discrepancies in the various planning approaches, for example, with regard to child versus family focus, outcome measurability, education versus broader lifestyle, that create barriers, block progress, and create distance for children and youth with disabilities and their families? An example of the potential for incompatibility of plans may be seen when children in early intervention programs transition to preschool or school-based classrooms. Because there is a great deal of difference between the two, educators, parents or families, and other stakeholders sometimes experience difficulty in successful transition planning. Finally, what about the connection between the planning approaches introduced here and behavior support plans? The point is that the planning approaches and processes that we use as professionals, although not needing to be uniform, should have sufficient consistency and unity of purpose that children and youth and their families are well served and can have a sense of partnership and ownership in the plan.

## INTRODUCING BEHAVIOR SUPPORT PLANNING

As the reader has learned, the need for **behavior support planning** is an outgrowth of the recent focus on positive behavior support. The emphasis on positive behavior support may be seen as originating from both a concern about increasing disciplinary problems in schools (Sugai et al., 1999) and the specific focus on challenging behavior and children and youth with special needs. In the 1997 reauthorization of the IDEA is the following statement: "In the case of a child whose behavior impedes his or her learning or that of others, the child's IEP team must consider, when appropriate, strategies, including positive behavior intervention strategies and supports to address that behavior" (Sec. 1414 (d) (3) (B) (i). A definition of **impeding behavior** has emerged (Turnbull & Turnbull, 2000) and is provided in Figure 7–2.

Thinking back to the beginning of this chapter and the discussion of the components of program planning and evaluation, you will recall that, prior to the establishment of a plan, the components include the mission–rationale–philosophy, the goals and objectives, the constraints and resources existing that impact the choices of goals and objectives, and the associated strategies

**FIGURE 7–2**
*A Definition of Impeding Behavior*

---

**The term *impeding behavior* means those behaviors of a student that:**

1. Impede the learning of the student or of others and include those behaviors that are externalizing (such as verbal abuse, aggressions, self-injury, or property destruction); are internalizing (such as physical or social withdrawal, depression, passivity, resistance, social or physical isolation, or noncompliance); are manifestations of biological or neurological conditions (such as obsessions, compulsions, stereotypes, or irresistible impulses); or are disruptive (such as annoying, confrontational, defiant, or taunting behavior)

2. Could cause the student to be disciplined pursuant to any state or federal law or regulations or could cause any consideration of a change of the student's educational placement

3. Are consistently recurring and therefore require functional behavior assessment and the systematic and frequent application of positive behavior interventions and supports

---

Source: *Free Appropriate Public Education: The Law and Children with Disabilities* (6th ed.), by H. R. Turnbull and A. P. Turnbull, 2000, Denver, CO: Love Publishing Co.

needed to carry out the plan should be considered. Applying this perspective to positive behavior supports (PBS) and behavior support planning, we know that the philosophy of PBS emphasizes schoolwide relevance, positive methods, teamwork and collaboration, parent or family partnerships, and quality of life and lifestyle improvements that are quantifiable. If those participating in the plan development do not share this point of view, success will be limited or nonexistent. Goals and objectives to be included in a behavior support plan should be the result of a collaborative team effort and a partnership with parents or families and should be functional, meaningful, and foster a sense of ownership by the children or youth targeted and their families. Further, the goals and objectives of the plan should be derived largely from the findings of a functional behavior assessment (see Chapter 6), especially for children and youth with more substantial and troublesome challenging behaviors.

It is very important to systematically take into account the constraints and resources available prior to the development of a behavior support plan. Certainly these are not constant and will change over time. In fact, the successful beginnings of implementation of the plan will frequently increase the resources. For example, the plan might lead to more prosocial behavior, which gives a child access to more peer support and friends (resources). Consider that the behavior support plan for a student is being done in the context of the multidisciplinary team and the IEP meeting. Traditionally, IEP meetings have failed to give much attention to the constraints and resources associated with accomplishing the stated goals and objectives, except maybe to emphasize the placement option. In summary, one would desire that the behavior support plan be the result of a shared vision (mission—rationale–philosophy); include quantifiable objectives based on goals that are functional, meaningful, related to improved quality of life; be the result of information provided by a functional assessment; and use a process of considering and delineating constraints and resources in determining goals, objectives, and intervention strategies.

Positive behavior support (Turnbull & Turnbull, 2001) has been described as having relevance and usefulness for all children and youth in various educational environments, delivered at three levels of support. These three levels will now be briefly introduced, then used as the basis for the vignettes and examples of behavior support planning provided later in this chapter. **Level 1** support targets all students, emphasizes prevention of troublesome behavior by making expectations clear, including students in decision making and ownership of rules, teaching expectations, and providing positive feedback and regard for desired behavior. The percentage of students in a school for whom level 1 support will be sufficient to establish and maintain desired behavior will vary substantially by the nature of the school and its population. But certainly, the failure to have a schoolwide behavior support plan will increase the number of students who will need more intensive behavior supports.

**Level 2** supports are individualized and more intense than level 1 and are the result of functional assessments in school settings. A variety of individualized strategies might be used as a part of level 2 supports. Turnbull and Turnbull (2001) suggested, for example, environmental changes, predictability of schedule, increased choices, curricular adaptations, more attention to rewarding positive behavior, and teaching replacement skills. **Level 3** supports are intended for children and youth with the most comprehensive and pervasive challenging behaviors. Supports at this level would be for a relatively small percentage of students, applied across learning and living environments and resulting from a systematic functional behavior assessment.

Children who require level 3 supports have impeding behavior that negatively impacts their quality of life across multiple environments. Another way to understand the three levels of PBS is by levels of prevention (The National Center on Education, Disability and Juvenile Justice, n.d.) as they have been used to describe the prevention of juvenile delinquency. Figure 7–3 defines the three levels of prevention. **Primary prevention** corresponds to level 1 PBS, **secondary prevention** corresponds to level 2, or targeted PBS, and **tertiary prevention** to level 3, or intensive PBS. Sugai et al. (1999) further connected these two perspectives. They indicate that primary prevention (schoolwide, level 1) typically includes 80% to 90% of students without serious behavior problems, secondary prevention (level 2) includes 5% to 15% of students at risk for problem behavior, and tertiary prevention (level 3) is focused on the 1% to 7% of students with chronic/intense challenging behavior and in need of specialized and highly individualized interventions.

In addition to understanding PBS planning by the levels introduced, it is helpful to consider planning by age ranges associated with typical educational environments. For purposes here, those environments would include

**FIGURE 7–3**
*Three Levels of Prevention*

| | |
|---|---|
| **Primary** | Focuses on avoiding the initial occurrence of a problem. Involves the application of universal strategies; that is, strategies that are applied to intact groups or populations, such as a schoolwide discipline plan that is used to help all students in a school meet behavior and academic expectations. |
| **Secondary** | Provides additional support when universal preventative efforts are not sufficient. The focus here is on preventing repeated occurrences of problem behavior through more targeted interventions. For example, students who have more than one disciplinary referral in a given month for fighting may be provided with special instruction in conflict resolution or social skills. |
| **Tertiary** | The most intensive level of support and intervention that attempts to reduce the impact of a condition or problem on the individual's ability to function in the least-restrictive setting. For example, the needs of students identified as having an emotional/behavior disability are addressed through special education services and behavior intervention plans so that they may benefit from the educational program. |

*Source:* National Center on Education, Disability, and Juvenile Justice: http://www.edjj.org/prevention/LevelsPrevention.html

infant and preschool settings, early elementary and middle school settings, and high school/secondary environments. There are, of course, a number of factors that contribute to the uniqueness of PBS and associated plans, dependent on the ages of the children and youth and the chronological ages associated with the settings. Some of those factors, for example, are the relative importance of peers, the role of parents/families, developmental ages and abilities of the child or children for whom planning is done, the nature and composition of the planning team, and the different standards, goals, and practices associated with each environment. For the remainder of this chapter, we will consider all three levels of plans, taking into account some of the special considerations associated with typical age-level educational environments.

## PLANNING FOR LEVEL 1 SCHOOLWIDE POSITIVE BEHAVIOR SUPPORTS

Although most of the literature related to PBS planning describes efforts to prevent or intervene at levels 2 or 3 for individual children or youth in a specific context, comprehensive **schoolwide positive behavior support** (PBS) also requires systematic planning. It has been noted (Turnbull & Turnbull, 2001) that The National Center for Positive Behavioral Interventions and Supports (http://www.pbis.org) is a primary source for current information about the design and implementation of schoolwide models of positive behavior support. In many respects, schoolwide positive behavior support includes the basic elements that have long been considered desirable in education. Students know and understand what is expected and are provided opportunities to learn the expectations. Behavior expectations are stated positively, and students are acknowledged and rewarded for adhering to the expectations significantly more than they are sanctioned for not adhering to them. Additionally, the development, implementation, and evaluation of the schoolwide behavior support plan are the result of a team collaborative effort that (to the maximum extent possible) includes participation by the persons (students) who are the targets of the plan.

Consider the five factors introduced at the beginning of the chapter and associated with successful planning. The first factor is that all components of planning are included—that it is comprehensive. If, for example, a school develops what seems to be a good plan but does not specify the means by which it will be evaluated, then it will be difficult to determine when and if it has succeeded.

The second factor is the extent to which teamwork is used. Suppose that a high school-wide plan includes the participation at all levels of high school students as members of the team; this obviously has the potential to improve the plan.

The third factor is the extent to which the plan is real, practical, and useable. Who are the primary persons (the stakeholders) directly affected by a schoolwide behavior support plan? They would include the teachers and other school personnel, the students in the school, and the parents or families of the students. Of course, having a comprehensive plan (factor one) that includes representation from all of the stakeholders as members of the team (factor two) is going to contribute to the plan being real, practical, and useable (factor three). Suppose, for example, that a large, diverse, and urban high school, without the participation of the student body, determines that their schoolwide plan will include a strict dress code requiring a uniform. The students are the targets of this plan, so if they are represented in decisions about the dress code, then they are more likely to have a sense of ownership and commitment to successful implementation of the plan (factor four).

The fifth factor is the extent to which the plan is doable and sustainable. To summarize, all these factors are connected. A schoolwide behavior support plan that is comprehensive, is developed by a team, is relevant, involves meaningful participation by the persons targeted by the plan, and is doable and sustainable is most likely to be successful. Horner and Sugai (2000) provided seven key themes regarding the implementation of schoolwide behavior support (see Figure 7–4). These themes provide the framework for the development of a schoolwide PBS plan.

## Level 1 Behavior Support Planning for Very Young Children

In planning PBS for very young children, it is especially important to keep in mind the guidance related to behavior provided by both the National Association for the Education of Young Children (NAEYC) and the Division for Early Childhood (DEC) of the Council for Exceptional Children (CEC). As stated in Chapter 3, DEC adopted a concept paper (Division of Early Childhood [DEC], 1999) reaffirmed in 2001 and endorsed by the NAEYC. One of the primary principles and beliefs about the challenging behavior of young children is that "many young children

**FIGURE 7–4**
*Seven Key Themes Regarding the Implementation of Schoolwide Behavior Support*

1. Schoolwide behavior support procedures were designed by local teams.
2. Successful schools relied on clear administrative direction and support.
3. Schools identified a small number of behavior expectations that defined the culture of the school.
4. The behavior expectations were taught to all students.
5. Performing to the behavior expectations was rewarded through an ongoing recognition system.
6. Dangerous and disruptive behavior resulted in corrections. Problem behaviors were neither ignored nor rewarded.
7. Information on student performance was collected continuously and summarized for decision making by local teams.

*Source:* From "School-wide Behavior Support: An Emerging Initiative," by R. H. Horner and G. Sugai, 2000, *Journal of Positive Behavior Interventions, 2*(4), 231. Copyright 2000 by PRO-ED. Reprinted by permission.

engage in challenging behavior in the course of early development. The majority of these children respond to **developmentally appropriate management techniques**" (p. 1). This points to the importance of planning that is done by infant, preschool, and other early childhood educators related to establishing and maintaining learning and developmental environments (such as Head Start, preschool classrooms, home-based settings, and nursery schools) that facilitate desired behaviors. Fox and Little (2001) described the successful development and implementation of a schoolwide behavior support plan in an inclusive, NAEYC-accredited, community preschool. The seven themes provided in Figure 7–4 were used as a guide for development of the plan.

In general, we might conclude that an effective preschoolwide behavior support plan will include the characteristics to follow. It is the result of a collaborative team process that includes meaningful input from all the "**stakeholders**," including, for example, teachers/caregivers, family members, administrators, specialists, assistants/paraprofessionals, and other relevant individuals. The plan is written in a manner that is clear and understood by all the stakeholders. It represents what is known as best and effective practice (for example NAEYC, DEC, and the state's standards and guidelines) related to positive child guidance and positive behavior supports. Although everyone will most certainly not agree, to the maximum extent possible the plan reflects a shared vision and agreed-upon beliefs, goals, and actions. And last, the plan is available, referenced, and used on a regular basis, making it an active plan rather than one that is filed away and forgotten.

## Level 1 Behavior Support Planning for School-Age Children and Youth

It is useful here to consider the distinctions that may be made among prevention, support, and intervention as they relate to schoolwide behavior support planning in elementary, middle school, and secondary school educational environments. Schoolwide plans are intended to support the desired behavior of all students and to prevent acute or chronic challenging behavior of students by providing positive environments and supports, thus avoiding the necessity of interventions at level 2 or level 3. The assumption is that the development and implementation of a sound schoolwide plan will decrease the numbers of students who will require intervention. Schoolwide behavior support is proactive and preventive as opposed to a reaction to an occurrence of challenging behavior. Intervention is, after all, an intrusion, and the more intensive the intervention, the more it draws attention to differences and potential exclusion rather than similarities and inclusion. This is not to say, of course, that interventions do not have nor achieve the objective of facilitating a student's learning of more acceptable behaviors and therefore more inclusion with their peers and in the classroom. Keep in mind that the mission of PBS is to improve quality of life, including independence and inclusion.

Successful schoolwide systems of positive behavior support have been characterized (Beech Center on Families and Disability, 1998; Fitzsimmons, 1998) as including the following. They define expectations without overwhelming students with too many, and they teach students about these expectations throughout the school year. All students have opportunities to learn self-control and social skills. There is a creative and individualized system for rewarding desired behaviors, and immediate feedback is provided for undesirable behavior. Problematic behavior has clear consequences, but much more emphasis is given to rewarding desired behavior. Settings that prove to be problematic are changed. All school employees are involved. The plan includes a clear means of monitoring and evaluating whether or not the schoolwide system (plan) is achieving the desired intents. Last, there is the recognition that approximately 5% of students have chronic challenging behavior and will benefit from level 2 or 3 PBS.

PBS may be thought of as a continuum of support for children and youth in educational environments, from systemic, schoolwide supports to highly individualized and intensive interventions. The approaches, formats, and purposes of planning may also be understood as occurring on this continuum. Planning for schoolwide systems of PBS are distinct from level 2 and level 3 planning, but they, too, include the idea of focusing on inputs, process, and outputs as part of planning. Input is the assessment and collection of information needed to develop the plan. It might include the school mission and beliefs, quantifiable data regarding retention rate, referrals related to behavior, staff turnover, information on classroom behavior incidences, and suspensions. It might also include the points of view of families, teachers, administrators, and students. These are examples of the input needed to develop a plan. Process is the implementation of the plan and ongoing efforts to monitor how it is going. Continued reference to and use of the plan during the process of implementation is important. It might be necessary to make adjustments and refinements as experience dictates during implementation. Outputs are the outcomes of implementation of the schoolwide behavior support plan. Outcomes (outputs) may be used to sum up (summative) what and how much has been accomplished by the plan or may be used to formulate new and revised plans (formative). Sugai, Lewis-Palmer, Todd, and Horner (2001) have provided an instrument useful in evaluating and assessing the critical features of a schoolwide behavior support plan. The Systems-Wide Evaluation Tool: School Wide (SET-SW) applies multiple steps to gather information from multiple sources, including review of permanent products (such as school improvement plan goals or discipline handbooks), observations, staff and student interviews, and surveys.

Weber (2002) provided an outline for efforts to develop a schoolwide behavior support plan. Although procedures will, of course, vary according to variables such as student age, school setting, and characteristics of the population and community, eight procedures are typically needed in the planning and preparation stages. Figure 7–5 outlines these eight steps. The plan should be developed by a committee that includes both a lead group and a

**FIGURE 7–5**
*Eight Steps in
Planning a Schoolwide
Behavior Management
System*

1. Form committees to start work on the plan.
2. Develop an all-encompassing statement of purpose.
3. List a set of valued and important beliefs/principles.
4. Create a list of clearly defined expectations for behavior.
5. Develop a program that helps students to understand and display the behaviors that are desired.
6. Devise a sequence of consequences.
7. Develop total staff commitment to the new approach.
8. Engage in an awareness training program.

*Source:* maxweber server, Hunter College, New York. http://maxweber.hunter.cuny.edu/pub/eres/EDSPC715_MCINTYRE/SchoolWideSystem.html

secondary group that participates periodically to provide feedback. A statement of purpose and an associated set of values or beliefs and principles should be developed. Next, a list of clearly defined behavior expectations for all students in the school should be developed. Development of a program that helps students understand and display the desired behaviors should be articulated as a part of the plan. A sequence or continuum of consequences should be devised to apply when students violate the behavior expectations. Fostering of a total staff commitment and a sense of common purpose is necessary. Last, there should be an awareness and teaching effort designed to help the students understand and also feel ownership of the behavior support plan and system.

Scott (2001) described the impacts of a schoolwide PBS in an inner-city elementary school. He found that a schoolwide system of PBS resulted in both a decrease in the number of problem behaviors of students, specifically decreasing those excluded from classrooms for problem behaviors, and a clearer focus for intervention on the students with needs for intense support and intervention. Specifically with regard to the planning process, this study applied the principles of effective schoolwide PBS introduced earlier. The commitment of school personnel was gained through a process of three meetings, resulting in a unanimous vote to adopt a schoolwide PBS plan for the upcoming year.

School personnel then participated in a process that generated a list of predictable problem behaviors in the school and the places, times, and conditions under which they would occur. Next, groups of school personnel worked to brainstorm prevention strategies and develop a consensus regarding strategies to be applied. Finally, the school personnel determined schoolwide expectations predictive of student success and agreed to consistently reinforce compliance with behavior expectations and to enforce and reteach for students who were not complying. From the school personnel participating in the planning process, a schoolwide team was created to meet monthly, look at data, report to others on progress, and facilitate changes as needed.

## PLANNING FOR LEVEL 2 POSITIVE BEHAVIOR SUPPORTS

Remember that although level 1 PBS is comprehensive, schoolwide, and limited in intensity, level 2 PBS is of moderate intensity, is for some students in school settings, and frequently is developed from data gathered though a functional assessment conducted in the school environment (Turnbull & Turnbull, 2001). There is limited data about the numbers of students who require positive behavior support at the three levels. However, in general it is reasonable to assume that a successful schoolwide system of PBS might reduce the number of students needing level 2 or level 3 support from 20% to between 10% and 15%. For that 10% to 15%, perhaps half of them might benefit from level 2 PBS. There will consistently be about 5% of the population in a given school that will require level 3 intensive PBS. We therefore may estimate that the population of students that will benefit from level 2 PBS will be 5% to 10%. Of course, this percentage varies as a result of the success of the schoolwide plan, the nature of the population, the skill of the teachers, and other factors.

A primary distinction between level 1 and level 2 PBS is that level 2 supports are individualized and are primarily interventions rather than focused on groups and on prevention. Level 2 supports, although not in every instance, will frequently be a part of a child's or youth's IEP or a very young child and her family's IFSP. So the level 2 PBS plan might be merged with a broader special education or early intervention planning process and documents. However, there are many circumstances in which young children or school-age children and youth need individual support of moderate intensity, but have not been classified as having a disability and as a result are not entitled under IDEA to positive behavior intervention and support to address behavior that impedes the child's learning or the learning of others. Here the authors think of the many preadolescent and adolescent youth with whom they are familiar who have been removed from school and placed in an alternative school environment, who have not been classified as having serious emotional disturbance or any other disability but nonetheless are in need of level 2 (and frequently level 3) PBS. For students who require level 2 PBS, but who have been identified as having a disability, the behavior support plan may be the single document and guide for addressing the student's challenging behavior(s). One obvious difference is that the law does not mandate the development and implementation of a plan.

### Consider This

Children and youth in a sense might "fall between the cracks" because level 1 support isn't sufficient, but they do not have a disability, and their challenging behavior(s) may not be chronic and intense to the extent that level 3 intervention and support is required.

- How might you, as an educator, provide the support and reinforcement that children in this category need to replace their present behavior with more acceptable behavior(s) in your setting?

In a comprehensive review of the effects of level 2 PBS for individuals with disabilities, Carr and others (1999) looked at outcomes. Their synthesis of the research yielded some important findings and conclusions. Beyond the finding that level 2 supports made a significant difference in reducing the impeding behaviors of most of the instances, other findings are useful in guiding planning. Functional behavior assessment was important to planning, adults significant in a child's life must also change their behavior, environments should frequently be reorganized, and people who have central and meaningful relationships with the person targeted for behavior change are most important. One might think of these factors as they relate to successful IEP planning. The plan is based on multiple sources of assessment data (including frequent functional behavior assessments), it is undertaken and monitored by a team of people who care about the child, and it includes a focus on how others (for example, teachers, family members, or classmates) might change and how the environments might also change. We now turn our attention to some of the considerations associated with level 2 PBS planning in either preschool or school-age educational environments.

## Level 2 Behavior Support Planning for Very Young Children

The myriad of effective positive child guidance techniques that are typically applied by parents, caregivers, and preschool teachers are, of course, not always sufficient to address the challenging behaviors of young children. When these usually effective strategies, specified as a part of schoolwide (preschool) PBS planning are not sufficient, it is necessary to respond by developing plans that are more individualized and that apply different strategies or more intense versions of existing strategies. In the development of behavior support plans, it is important to keep in mind that intervention is by nature intrusive and that it focuses on differences rather than likenesses between children. Therefore, it is desirable to plan level 2 positive behavior interventions and supports only at the level of intensity needed to affect desired behavior change. Vignette 7.1 illustrates how level 2 planning might be applied in a preschool classroom environment.

## Vignette 7.1

### Alyshea

Alyshea is a 3 ½-year-old girl who is enrolled in Noah's Ark, a community-based and church-affiliated private preschool. Her classroom has 15 children ages 3 to 5, reflecting the movement in early childhood education and the benefits associated with multiage grouping. Alyshea is chronologically the youngest child in her room. She is also developmentally the youngest because she functions in general more like a child of 3 years of age. Alyshea has been described by her pediatrician as immature and may be showing some indications of attention deficit/hyperactivity disorder. There is a lead teacher and teaching assistant in the room, which is organized into activity centers. Emphasis is placed on child-initiated and directed activities. Noah's Ark is accredited by the National Association for the Education of Young Children, and the beliefs and principles of developmentally appropriate practice are followed.

In this child- and family-friendly environment, Alyshea functions quite well, with one notable exception. Each morning there is a circle time when for 15 minutes the teacher reads a book to the group. The children are seated on a rug in a semicircle and listen to the teacher as she reads. The teacher engages the children by asking them questions and having them name and describe characters in the book. The teacher's plan (level 1) for all the children to achieve the desired behaviors/outcomes of listening to the story, interacting, increasing attention span, increasing vocabulary, appreciating books, and fostering preliteracy skills include the following. She selects books that are of high interest and developmentally appropriate, she introduces the children to the book the day prior to reading it, she provides frequent opportunities for the children to interact as she reads, and she has her teaching assistant circulate and verbally prompt and redirect children as needed. This works reasonably well for all of the children—except Alyshea. She has difficulty sitting for more than a few minutes, so she stands up and runs around the room. She also has verbal outbursts that interrupt the teacher and the other children. With the support and technical assistance available from the local school behavior specialist for young children and with the support and acceptance of the parents, the teacher, teaching assistant, and director, a team is established to develop a plan for Alyshea.

### Reflective Moment

The reader will note that Alyshea does not have a formal disability diagnosis, so she is not eligible for an individual education program as a part of special education services. What implications might this fact have, either positive or negative, for the planning and delivering of positive behavior support for Alyshea? What might be some of the alternative strategies chosen by the team to include in a plan to improve Alyshea's circle time behavior?

## Level 2 Behavior Support Planning for School-Age Children and Youth

Consider the forms that the challenging behavior of school-age children from kindergarten through high school might take. It might be noncompliance, refusal to follow instruction or do assignments, aggressive behavior or bullying toward peers, verbal outbursts, cursing, other forms of class disruption, withdrawn, overly shy behavior, and many other impeding behaviors. Also, think about the children and youth who exhibit those behaviors. They might be students who have been classified as having a disability, emotional/behavior disorders, another type of disability, or a combination of all three. Or they might be students who are not classified as having special needs, but who do have an acute challenging behavior that is not responsive to the broader structure and approach (level 1) to preventing misbehavior and fostering desired behavior in school settings.

As has been noted previously, when students exhibit challenging behavior that is not successfully addressed by schoolwide behavior support, they will frequently require and benefit from a more individualized and systematic intervention, based on data gathered from a functional behavior assessment. Keep in mind the distinction (albeit it is frequently difficult or even unnecessary in practice to do so) between levels 2 and 3 of positive behavior intervention and support planning. Level 2 targets challenging behavior that is singular, is more situation specific, and necessitates interventions of moderate intensity. Level 3 targets challenging behavior of fewer students, requires more intensive interventions, and is comprehensive in nature. That is, it occurs across various environments and suggests the need for persons representing all those environments as participants in the planning (as well as implementation and evaluation) process. One might argue that although children and youth experiencing challenging behavior at either level will have a diminished quality of life, those for whom level 3 PBS and interventions are needed will predictably experience a more substantial and comprehensive negative impact on their quality of life and that of their families, teachers, classmates, and others.

Carr et al. (1999), in a synthesis of the research on level 2 PBS, reached several conclusions that have direct relevance for the planning process. Interventions and supports are more successful when functional behavior assessments are the basis for the plan when significant individuals, in addition to the student targeted, change their behavior when the environment is reorganized and when intervention is carried out by persons with whom the student has an ongoing and meaningful relationship. All these dimensions of successful level 2 PBS should be evident in the planning process and documents. In a position paper provided by the ERIC Clearinghouse on Disabilities and Gifted Education (Fitzsimmons, 1998), the importance of conducting functional behavior assessments and including behavior intervention plans as a part of the development of IEP is stated. This is consistent with the 1997 IDEA amendments in which the relationship between learning and behavior for students with disabilities is stressed. The paper provides the following overriding guidance regarding behavior intervention plans:

> The student's behavior intervention plan should include positive strategies, programs or curricular modifications, and supplementary aids and supports required to address the behaviors of concern. It is helpful to use the data collected during the functional behavior assessment (FBA) to develop the plan and to determine the discrepancy between the child's actual and expected behavior. Intervention plans that emphasize skills needed by the student to behave in a more appropriate manner and that provide proper motivation will be more effective than plans that simply control behavior. Interventions based on control often only suppress the behavior, resulting in a child manifesting unmet needs in alternative, inappropriate ways. Positive plans for behavioral intervention, on the other hand, will address both the source of the problem and the problem itself and foster the expression of needs in appropriate ways. (pp. 2–3)

A number of behavior support plan formats and processes are described in the literature (Alberto & Troutman, 2003; Anderson, Russo, Dunlap, & Albin, 1996; Florida Department of Education, 1999; Jackson & Veeneman-Panyan, 2002; Janney & Snell, 2000; Knoster & Tilly, 1999; O'Neill et al., 1997; Rehabilitation Research & Training Center on Positive Behavioral Support, n.d.; Scott, Liaupsin, & Nelson, 2001). These forms and processes vary somewhat and must, of course, be individualized to address the unique circumstance of a particular student, family, and school environment. They do, however, have the following components and emphases largely in common in varying amounts.

They are frequently entitled "behavior support plan," "positive behavior support plan," "plan for positive behavior support," or "behavior intervention plan." Jackson and Veeneman-Panyan (2002) used the term *Solution-Focused Behavior Intervention Planning Form* to guide what they describe as a "different planning and implementation format that is inspired by solution-focused concepts, grounded in theories of discourse and collaborative processes for the construction of shared knowledge, and structured as an ongoing guided inquiry activity" (p. 215). Most planning forms and formats include either the complete results of the functional behavior assessment or a summary of that assessment. Most forms and formats include a description of the challenging behavior(s), and some differentiate in the description between the form and function of the behavior(s). Stated another way, what does the behavior look like (form) and what purpose does it serve for the child in meeting his needs (function)? Essentially all plans and formats require the inclusion of an operational definition of the behavior(s). The definition must be operationally defined and easily understood by everyone. Some plans include a section in which previous strategies are described or summarized. Most plans and formats include a hypothesis regarding the function of the behavior. This might be a brief description of what individuals believe is the function of the behavior. The hypothesis might be specific, global, or both. It might be argued that in practice and with a number of team members involved, the global hypothesis is more useful. It is generated from data attained through the functional behavior assessment and might be described as an "educated guess" about how the challenging behavior is associated with the child's having his needs met.

Most approaches apply some version of what O'Neill and others (1997) and the Florida Department of Education (1999) referred to as the **competing behaviors model**. In the competing behaviors model, the following elements are used to identify desirable and replacement behaviors to compete with the impeding, challenging behaviors. Setting events associated with the challenging behavior are described when possible. Antecedents associated with the challenging behavior, the desired behavior, and/or replacement behavior are stated. The desired behavior is stated in the plan. The consequences assumed to be reinforcing the challenging behavior and those to be associated with the desired or replacement behaviors are stated. Frequently in plans one finds summaries or descriptions of antecedents including changing environmental arrangements and teaching strategies.

Also, plans may include detail about the reinforcing consequences of desired behavior. Some plans include a section on written behavior objectives, but most treat them as part of the implementation and do not include them in the plan. Other components that are occasionally included in planning formats and forms are descriptions of long-term prevention strategies or crisis plans (what to do if the student experiences a crisis that has an acute potential for endangering himself, others, or property). Although most plans provide a place where names and roles of team members might be stated and signatures provided, less provide information about action planning (who will do what, when, and where) and what supports will be given to particular team members. Last, some forms and formats include a section that allows for formative and summative evaluation (see Chapter 8) of the plan's implementation. They are largely focused on outcomes of the intervention and answering the question about whether desired behaviors increased or undesired behaviors decreased.

In summary, there are numerous planning forms and formats for PBS. Some are simple and straightforward. Others are more complex and comprehensive. Some include content that addresses the team and collaborative nature of PBS assumed especially in level 3 interventions and supports. Figure 7–6 illustrates one example of behavior support plan forms for level 2 or level 3 positive behavior intervention and support planning.

## PLANNING FOR LEVEL 3 POSITIVE BEHAVIOR SUPPORTS

Remember that children and youth who require level 3 PBS are those for whom the planning and implementation of levels 1 and 2 are insufficient to address their challenging behavior. That is, level 3 PBS is used only when there is a need for an intensive and comprehensive plan that is not provided by less-intrusive approaches. Planning for level 3 PBS is complicated by the fact that the challenging behavior(s) occur across multiple settings (home, school, and community), requiring a high level of coordination and collaboration from individuals who are especially concerned about the well-being of the child.

We intentionally avoid use of the term *stakeholders*, simply because that seems to suggest that the child is an object or a commodity. Also, the family should certainly be seen and understood as more than just one of several stakeholders. The teaming and shared beliefs necessary to successfully plan level 3 support suggest the need for intraschool (between and among personnel, and possibly students, in the school or preschool) connections as well as between school personnel and others, such as family members and other persons who are significant in the child's life (for example, minister or coach). The difficulties here are obvious. It is challenging in many schools to find time, opportunity, and willingness for teachers to meet and plan together. Also, it has been noted (Turnbull & Turnbull, 2001) that most schools do not have comprehensive services, so the important connections between a student (who needs a level 3 PBS plan) and her life at home and in the community are possibly not understood or addressed by teachers and other school personnel.

**FIGURE 7–6**
*Behavior Support Plan Forms*

Child's Name:   Daniel E.                                                    Date: 03/16/04

Age: 6
E/BD w/communication delays

Review/Revision Date(s): 09/01/04

Team Members: Classroom Teacher                                *Miss Hasenfuss*

S/L Therapist                                                            *Laura Logan*

Parents                                                                  *Bill and Pam Eshler*

---

**Functional Assessment Summary (attach complete assessment):**

Structured interview completed by classroom teacher, speech language therapist, and parents.
Motivation Assessment Scale—Completed by teacher and S/L Therapist; Scatter plot—Completed by teacher.

| **Behavior Description:** | **Behavior Definition:** |
|---|---|
| Verbal and physical aggression, destructive behavior, tantrums, and noncompliance | Incidents of challenging behavior are defined as any acts of verbal or physical aggression (yelling at teacher, hitting, kicking), tantrums as evidenced by crying and shouting at the teacher, and noncompliance. |

**Summary of Previous Strategies:**

Daniel appears to be a "visual learner" and performs well when working one-on-one with the teacher or in small groups of less than three children. Daniel can also display appropriate behavior when working on preferred tasks.

**Hypothesis—Function of Behavior:**

| Global | Specific |
|---|---|
| Primary Function—Attention; Secondary Function—Escape/ Avoidance | When presented with nonpreferred tasks, Daniel will display one or more forms of challenging behavior. |

**ABC:**

| Antecedents | Behavior (desired) | Consequences |
|---|---|---|
| Setting Events: Large group or classwide setting event | To consult his schedule as a means of promoting task engagement and to communicate his need for teacher assistance by raising his hand. | Use of differential reinforcement in the form of praise for approximations at "task engagement," appropriate use of schedule, and for raising his hand to seek teacher assistance. Present Daniel with increased opportunities for choices in tasks during the day. |
| Antecedents: Unpreferred tasks presented by teacher | | |
| Strategies: Develop a picture schedule to serve as a cue to help Daniel in understanding task sequences. | Strategies: Actively teach Daniel in using his schedule and raising hand. | |

**FIGURE 7-6**
*Continued*

**Implementation Notes (including behavior objectives):**

*Antecedent Management Strategies*—Use of picture/word schedules, advanced prompts, and verbal reinforcement for approximating compliance and task engagement.

*Replacement Behaviors*—Actively teach and reinforce "how to" seek teacher assistance appropriately. Use a system of least-to-most prompts and modeling.

*Consequences*—Using differential reinforcement, verbally praise Daniel for attempts at desired behavior in the absence of challenging behavior.

**Team Action Plans:**

| Who | What | When | Where | Support |
|---|---|---|---|---|
| Classroom Teacher | Picture/word Schedule + | Daily | Classroom Setting | Daniel's team will provide support if needed. |
| Speech/Language Therapist | Use of Differential Reinforcement + Opportunities for Choice | | | |

**Long-Term Prevention Strategies:**
Use of creative scheduling and interspersed requesting by building in opportunities for choice and performance of preferred activities.

**Crisis Plan:**
If Daniel's aggression is perceived as invasive or as a threat to the well-being of his classmates, he will be escorted to the principal's office.

**Tentative Evaluation Plans:**

| Inputs<br>(looking at the plan) | Processes<br>(looking at the implementation) | Outcomes<br>(looking at the results) |
|---|---|---|
| Are the behavior expectations stated in the plan developmentally appropriate for Daniel? Plan reviewed and commented on by teacher's first-grade colleagues and by parents. | Team meeting, including parents, after 2–3 weeks of implementation to discuss progress to date and consider any needed adjustments to plan. | At 6 weeks, observation and frequency count of increase in raising hand and consulting schedule and decrease in aggressive behaviors.<br>Also, meeting with parents to determine satisfaction with plan and possible impacts at home. |

Finally, with regard to level 3 positive behavior support, planning always is based on the results of a functional behavior assessment. Refer to Chapter 6, "Understanding Functional Behavior Assessment," for specific procedures, processes, and instruments useful in conducting functional behavior assessments for children in need of comprehensive and intensive plans. The next two sections address considerations associated with level 3 planning for either preschool-age children or school-age children and youth.

## Level 3 Positive Behavior Support Planning for Very Young Children

The preschool period refers to children whose ages range from birth through kindergarten. NAEYC takes the position that kindergarteners are preschoolers. Therefore, very young children may be understood as including newborns, infants, toddlers, preschoolers ages 3 to 5 and kindergarteners. What are the considerations associated with planning level 3 positive behavior interventions and supports for very young children?

The fundamental components of successful planning (see five factors described earlier in the chapter) apply, and the need for a systematic functional assessment, in which the form and function of challenging behavior are identified and operationalized, also applies. Collaborative teamwork aimed at producing a comprehensive, individualized plan with measurable outcomes applies. However, some considerations are largely unique when planning level 3 supports and interventions for very young children. Beyond considerations such as the developmental status of young children related to, for example, the ability to communicate and their level of dependence on adults, here are three such considerations. One is that although certainly not all (see, for example, Alyshea's Vignette 7.1), many of these children will have been formally identified and certified as having special needs. As a result, they will have an early intervention (IFSP) or a special education (IEP) plan.

The IFSP or IEP might vary from having a great deal of focus on behavior support planning to none. If the primary disability is specific to behavior, one would certainly expect the IEP or IFSP to be the basis for behavior support planning. So one consideration associated with very young children is the nature of and formats for the legally mandated planning in early intervention and preschool special education. Stated another way, the IFSP is different from an IEP and is focused on children from birth to 3 years and their families, and the IEP for a preschool-age child is different from an IEP for a school-age child.

A second consideration has to do with living, learning, and developmentally appropriate environments. We have learned that level 3 interventions and supports are comprehensive; that is, they apply across all the settings relevant to an individual child. Obviously, the typical environments in the life of an infant, toddler, or preschooler are different from a school-age child. For a very young child, it might be more focused on home, child care center, grandparents or extended family, and neighborhood settings such as the grocery market. For school-age children, school, afterschool programs, and group environments (for example, the soccer team) are more typical. These varied environments are inhabited by different individuals requiring different approaches to their participation in level 3 planning. The reader is aware that there is a significant emphasis on natural environments and early inclusion practices for very young children with special needs, including challenging behaviors. Therefore, planning might require more attention to the fit between the interventions and supports planned, the realities of the natural and inclusive environments, and the willingness of the persons in those environments to participate in planning and delivering the level 3 interventions and supports.

Suppose in our example in Vignette 7.1 that Alyshea's challenging behavior is somewhat more extreme and not responsive to level 2 supports. She runs around the room throughout much of the day and also hits other children, and these behaviors occur across other environments (home, Sunday school, etc.). Alyshea needs comprehensive, intensive level 3 intervention and support. Historically, the caregiver or preschool teacher might have felt that Alyshea is now beyond his responsibility and expertise and should be referred for evaluation, special education, and a placement outside the preschool classroom. The challenge is clearly how to plan level 3 support in a manner that is individualized, intensive, and measurable; works across environments; and fits with the natural and inclusive setting.

A third consideration is the role of parents/families in planning level 3 supports for very young children. Most of the professional literature addressing interventions for children and youth experiencing challenging behavior will include a discussion of the importance of parents as part of a multidisciplinary team or as partners in a collaborative team effort. However, distinctions might be made between the focus on parents versus families and on family-centeredness versus parent involvement. For school-age children and youth (with special needs related to challenging behavior), the focus is clearly on parent involvement as a part of the team planning and delivering intervention and support to achieve education-specific objectives—that is, to change behavior that impedes educational progress.

On the other hand, for very young children and especially for early intervention, the emphasis will likely be on families rather than just parents, on family-centered practices, and on challenging behavior as it impacts all aspects of a young child's quality of life, not just their academic performance. Neilsen and McEvoy (2004) suggest that, when linking the results of functional behavior assessment to intervention for young children with challenging behavior, interventions selected must be acceptable to families and consistent with their values, skills, and resources. Understanding the role of families and knowing how to facilitate their empowerment and accepting their increased influence related to level 3 planning proves challenging for many of us as educators.

## Level 3 Positive Behavior Support Planning for School-Age Children and Youth

The PBS planning forms and formats appropriate for level 3 school-age planning are essentially the same as those described earlier as appropriate for level 2 school-age PBS. However, there are some unique considerations associated with level 3 school-age planning. Remember that level 3 interventions and supports are intended for students who have a need for intensive and comprehensive interventions that are delivered by multiple individuals (team members) across a variety of settings. Turnbull and Turnbull (2001) suggested that a distinguishing characteristic of level 3 support planning and implementation is the necessary link among home, school, and community and the pervasive collaboration among them. Peck Peterson, Derby, Harding, Weddle, and Barretto (2002) pointed out that "facilitating parental input in behavior support plans is especially valuable when children reach school age because of the variety of settings in which they must participate (e.g., home, classroom, bus, child care)" (p. 303). Consider how this complicates the planning process, given what was introduced at the beginning of the chapter as factors associated with successful planning. One such factor is the extent to which the plan is comprehensive and includes all the elements of planning (rationale or mission, goals, objectives, strategies, constraints and resources, implementation, and evaluation).

Development of a comprehensive plan that results from the meaningful contributions of team members representing home, school, and community takes substantial coordination, time, and effort, and it is dependent on a process of team building, establishment of trust, and problem solving over time. A second factor associated with successful planning is the extent to which it represents a partnership and a shared vision among the team members. Level 3 planning (and implementation) will be unsuccessful or minimally successful if all members of the team do not feel themselves a part of the plan. It is, of course, insufficient to just include stakeholders in the planning meeting and have them sign the form as team members.

The extent to which the plan is real, practical, and doable (third factor associated with success) certainly will impact success in level 3 planning. Intervention plans have long failed because they did not have these attributes for parents, family members, and other persons in the child's life. Too often historically we as educators and behavior interventionists have expected parents and others to plan and implement interventions that were not a good fit for them. Rao and Kalyanpur (2002) described this as developing plans with a good conceptual fit. That is, all aspects of the intervention, including the means of reinforcing the desired behavior and the individual styles of the persons and unique aspects of the environment, should be individualized. They pointed out that "interventions that do not consider parental values or resolve the differences between parents and professionals may not address the problem behavior at all" (p. 232).

A fourth factor associated with successful planning is the role of the person who is targeted for behavior change. A worthwhile goal in the development, implementation, and ongoing assessment of level 3 planning is to work toward increased participation of the student. Remember that no one likes to have a plan imposed on them and that ownership of the plan increases likelihood of success. Certainly it is dependent on the developmental and cognitive status of the child or youth, but in most instances she can be supported to feel a sense of ownership of the plan. Because the student is the only one who is to be found in all of the settings relevant to the plan, she can become an important part of ensuring continuity across environments.

The last factor associated with successful planning is making the plan challenging but doable. Consider this as it is associated with level 3 school-age planning. Given that plans and interventions at this level are intense and comprehensive, they are also more complicated and more difficult to manage. Whether it is a teacher in the general education classroom, a parent or, for example, a Sunday school teacher, their roles as part of the intervention may seem overwhelming and not doable. So it is important in the planning to take into account that the persons involved believe that, as a part of the team and with the team's support, they can do their part and be successful.

## SUMMARY

Planning is something that we all include in both our personal and professional lives. There is, of course, a great deal of variance among people with regard to how they view planning and how they use it to improve the quality of their lives. Sometimes planning is systematic, formal, and written, and at other times it is unsystematic and done with few if any behavior manifestations. Planning is applied in formal ways across a variety of human service disciplines and areas, such as social services, mental health, and child welfare. As professionals in education, it is important for us to think of planning as something that we do *with* people rather than something that is done *to* people. Many special educators, for example, might concur that all too often the IEP process is more consistent with the latter.

The planning process has been described as having seven components, including a rationale or mission, goals, objectives, strategies, constraints and resources, implementation, and evaluation (evaluation is covered in detail in Chapter 8). Five factors may be associated with successful planning, including comprehensive inclusion of all components; a teamwork/collaborative approach to planning; having a meaningful, relevant, and useful planning document involving the person(s) who is (are) a target of the plan; and making the plan challenging while doable and sustainable. These components of the planning process and the five factors associated with success are applicable to behavior support plans across multiple settings and at three levels of intensity.

Although the literature in behavior support planning is largely focused on meeting the individual needs of children with challenging behaviors, behavior support planning has a broader application in supporting PBS. Three levels of behavior support planning are introduced and examples provided. Level 1 is planning that is associated with comprehensive, schoolwide plans. It includes all students in a particular school environment, is limited in intensity, and does not include the use of functional assessment as a means of establishing the plan or evaluating its success. Level 2 behavior support plans are for a limited number of students who experience moderate levels of challenging behavior. It is typically confined to implementation in school settings and includes the use of functional assessment. Level 3 behavior support planning is for fewer students, often associated with their IFSP or IEP, is more intense, typically extends beyond the school environment to home and community, and results from a functional assessment.

This chapter has not focused on providing you with a recipe for what a behavior support plan should look like. There are many examples in the literature in which different planning processes, formats, and documents have been successfully applied (see Further Reading and Exploration for sources). The chapter has emphasized the importance of planning at the three levels of positive behavior support and the elements typically included for successful planning at each level. There are few examples in the literature of what a level 1 schoolwide PBS plan looks like. Rather, the emphasis is on the desired process and the elements that should be included. If one looked at comprehensive plans across a number of schools, undoubtedly some would be limited to one or two pages, whereas others might take up a volume or more to detail the plan. For levels 2 and 3 positive behavior intervention and support, largely as a result their connection to special education, it is likely that the plan will be rather standardized and will be written to include the elements described earlier. No matter what the level of planning, it is important for professionals to know what planning is, what makes it succeed, and how it should be applied to support children and youth to learn and exhibit the behavior that will help them succeed in learning environments.

## ACTIVITIES TO EXTEND YOUR LEARNING

1. This activity might be done over the period of several class sessions. Divide the class into small groups (teams) of four to eight members. Each team should develop a hypothetical school environment (including preschool, elementary, middle, and high school) and specify characteristics and uniqueness of the school (setting, diversity, emphasis, etc.). Establish roles for each member of the team (for example, teacher, parent, administrator, student, other). Develop a schoolwide behavior support plan, using the guidance provided in the chapter. Complete this exercise by sharing with the class as a whole.

2. Generate as a class a list of agencies, disciplines, or programs in which there exists a formal and required planning process and document (see discussion of this in the chapter). Either individually or in small groups, select one planning approach. Review guidelines or talk with professionals who use the plan to gain an understanding of its application. Compare your planning process and document to the criteria provided in the chapter for a quality plan. Also compare your planning process and document to behavior support planning, IEP planning, and IFSP planning.

3. Review your state's guidelines for development of both the IEP and the IFSP as well as the documents. Consider how behavior support planning might fit well or not so well, given its desired components, in your state's IEP and IFSP.

4. Identify a school in your community that has successfully implemented for 2 or 3 years a schoolwide behavior support plan, and invite a member or members of the team to come and share with your class.

5. Identify a behavior specialist, special education consulting teacher, school psychologist, school counselor, or special education supervisor in a local education agency who is the most experienced professional related to understanding and developing PBS plans. Invite this person, and possibly, if appropriate, a parent or family representative to provide a guest lecture to the class. Ask the guests to contrast their planning approach to the practices recommended in the chapter.

6. Several level 2 or 3 behavior support planning forms and processes are referenced on page 220. Go to the sources for these plan forms and processes and examine each to see what they have in common and how they are unique. Consider how they might work for level 2 planning as compared to level 3.

## FURTHER READING AND EXPLORATION

1. Go to the Web site of the National Association of School Psychologists (http://www.nasponline.org) and look for projects and initiatives that NASP is undertaking related to safe and responsive schools and to prevention of violence.

2. Go to the Web site of the Center for Positive Behavioral Interventions and Supports (http://www.pbis.org) and look for information, articles, sources, and links that will provide you with models for both schoolwide planning as well as levels 2 and 3 PBS planning.

3. Go to the Behavior Management Advice site (http://www.BehaviorAdvisor.com) and use the bulletin board to get information from teachers and other practitioners regarding formats and models for planning and experiences with their use.

4. Look at the *Facilitator's Guide: Positive Behavior Support* developed by the staff of the Positive Behavioral Support Project with support from the Department of Child and Family Studies, Louis de la Parte Florida Mental Health Institute, University of South Florida, and the Rehabilitation Research and Training Center on Positive Behavioral Support. The guide may be accessed at http://www.fmhi.usf.edu/cfs/cfspubs/pbsguide/facilitatorguide pbs.htm. In small groups or the class as a whole, study Step 4: Designing Support Plans and compare the content to the information provided in this chapter.

5. Go to the Web site of the Rehabilitation Research and Training Center on Positive Behavior Support at the University of South Florida and review any resources provided through that site or its links related to PBS planning.

# REFERENCES

Alberto, P. A., & Troutman, A. C. (2003). *Applied behavior analysis for teachers* (6th ed.). Upper Saddle River, NJ: Merrill/Prentice Hall.

Anderson, J. L., Russo, A., Dunlap, G., & Albin, R. W. (1996). A team training model for building the capacity to provide positive behavioral supports in inclusive settings. In L. K. Koegel, R. L. Koegel, & G. Dunlap (Eds.), *Positive behavioral support: Including people with difficult behavior in the community* (pp. 467–490). Baltimore: Paul H. Brookes.

Beach Center on Families and Disability. (1998). *School-wide PBS: School-wide positive behavioral support systems*. Retrieved October 1, 2002 from http://www.pbis.org/english/Schoolwide_PBS.htm

Carr, E. G., Horner, R. H., Turnbull, A. P., Marquis, J. G., Magito-McLaughlin, D., McAtee, M. L., et al. (1999). *Positive behavior support as an approach for dealing with problem behavior in people with developmental disabilities: A research synthesis*. Washington, DC: American Association on Mental Retardation Monograph Series.

Division for Early Childhood. (1999, October). *DEC concept paper on the identification of and intervention with challenging behavior*. Retrieved January 23, 2002, from http://www.dec-sped.org/position/challenging_behavior.html

ERIC Clearinghouse on Disabilities and Gifted Education. (1998). *Functional behavior assessment and behavior intervention plans*. Retrieved October 3, 2002, from http://ericec.org/digests/e571.html

Fitzsimmons, M. K. (1998). *School-wide behavioral management systems*. Reston, VA: Council for Exceptional Children. (ERIC Document Reproduction Service No. ED417515)

Florida Department of Education. (1999, November). *Facilitator's guide: Positive behavioral support*. Tampa: Rehabilitation Research and Training Center on Positive Behavioral Support, University of South Florida.

Forest, M., & Lusthaus, E. (1990). Everyone belongs with the MAPS action planning system. *Teaching Exceptional Children, 2*(22), 32–35.

Fox, L., & Little, N. (2001). Starting early: Developing school-wide behavior support in a community preschool. *Journal of Positive Behavior Interventions, 3,* 251–254.

Horner, R. H., & Sugai, G. (2000). School-wide behavior support: An emerging initiative. *Journal of Positive Behavior Interventions, 2,* 231–232.

Individuals with Disabilities Education Act, 20 U.S.C. § 1400 *et. seq.* (1975).

Jackson, L., & Veeneman-Panyan, M. (2002). *Positive behavioral support in the classroom: Principles and practices*. Baltimore: Paul H. Brookes.

Janney, R., & Snell, M. E. (2000). *Behavioral support: Teachers' guide to inclusive practices*. Baltimore: Paul H. Brookes.

Knoster, T., & Tilly, D. (1999, September 29). *Designing effective behavior support plans for students with problem behavior*. Presentation at video satellite conference. (Available from National Association of State Directors of Special Education, Inc., 1800 Diagonal Road, Suite 320, Alexandria, VA 22314.)

National Center on Education, Disability and Juvenile Justice. (n.d.). *Prevention: Levels of prevention.* Retrived October 3, 2002, from http://www.edjj.org/prevention/LevelsPrevention.html

Neilsen, S. L., & McEvoy, M. A. (2004). Functional behavioral assessment in early childhood settings. *Journal of Early Intervention, 26*(2), 115–131.

O'Neill, R., Horner, R., Albin, R., Sprague, J., Storey, K., & Newton, J. S. (1997). *Functional assessment and program development for problem behavior* (2nd ed.). Pacific Grove, CA: Brooks/Cole.

Peck Peterson, S. M., Derby, K. M., Harding, J. W., Weddle, T. & Barretto, A. (2002). Behavioral support for school-aged children with developmental disability and problem behavior. In J. M. Lucyshyn, G. Dunlap, & R. W. Albin (Eds.), *Families and positive behavior support: Addressing problem behavior in family contexts* (pp. 287–308). Baltimore: Paul H. Brookes.

Rao, S., & Kalyanpur, M. (2002). Promoting home-school collaboration in positive behavior support. In J. M. Lucyshyn, G. Dunlap, & R. W. Albin (Eds.), *Families and positive behavior support: Addressing problem behavior in family contexts* (pp. 219–239). Baltimore: Paul H. Brookes.

Rehabilitation Research & Training Center on Positive Behavioral Support. (n.d.) *Behavior support plans.* Retrieved October 4, 2002, from http://rrtcpbs.fmhi.usf.edu/bsp-index.htm

Scott, T. M. (2001). A schoolwide example of positive behavioral support. *Journal of Positive Behavior Interventions, 3,* 88–94.

Scott, T. M., Liaupsin, C. J., & Nelson, C. M. (2001). *Behavior intervention planning: Using the functional behavioral assessment data: Users Guide.* Longmont, CO: Sopris West.

Sugai, G., Horner, R. H., Dunlap, G., Hieneman, M., Lewis, T. J., Nelson, C. M., et al. (1999). *Applying positive behavioral support and functional behavioral assessment in schools* (Technical Assistance Guide). Available from the OSEP Technical Assistance Center on Positive Behavioral Interventions and Supports Web site: http://pbis.org/english/default.htm

Sugai, G., Lewis-Palmer, T., Todd, A., & Horner, R. (2001, November). *Systems-wide evaluation tool.* Educational and Community Supports, Eugene: University of Oregon.

Turnbull, A. P., & Turnbull H. R. (1996). Group action planning as a strategy for providing comprehensive family support. In L. K. Koegel, R. L. Koegel, & G. Dunlap (Eds.), *Positive behavior support: Including people with difficult behavior in the community* (pp. 99–114). Baltimore: Paul H. Brookes.

Turnbull, A. P., & Turnbull, R. (2001). *Families, professionals, and exceptionality: Collaborating for empowerment* (4th ed.). Upper Saddle River, NJ: Merrill/Prentice Hall.

Turnbull, H. R., & Turnbull A. P. (with Stowe, M., & Wilcox, B. L.). (2000). *Free appropriate public education: The law and children with disabilities* (6th ed.) Denver, CO: Love Publishing Co.

Weber, M. (2002). *Developing a school-wide behavior management system.* Retrieved October 3, 2002 from http://maxweber.hunter.cuny.edu/pub/eres/EDSPC715_MACINTYRE/SchoolWideSystem.html

# Chapter 8

# Evaluating Positive Behavior Supports

## CONCEPTS TO UNDERSTAND

*After reading this chapter, you should be able to:*

- Describe evaluation as a general concept, including definitions of formal versus informal evaluation, summative and formative evaluation, input, process, outcome and context evaluation, and program versus individual evaluation

- Describe the place of evaluation as a component of positive behavior supports (PBS)

- Discuss the issues associated with evaluating PBS, especially related to family and community participation, self-determination, and quality of life

- Compare evaluation methods appropriate for schoolwide behavior support to methods used for individual child interventions

- Create a matrix illustrating the issues and practices associated with input, process, and outcome evaluation for both school-age and levels 2 and 3 PBS

- List and describe five issues or future directions associated with evaluation of PBS

## KEY TERMS

Accountability-driven evaluation

Assessment of needs

Competing behaviors model

Context evaluation

Continuum of behavior support

Ecological validity

Empowerment evaluation

Implementation fidelity

Individual and program evaluation

Informal versus formal evaluation

Inputs, processes, and outcomes

Multicomponent interventions

Multiple outcome measures

Performance-based outcomes

Product evaluation

School climate

Shared vision

Single-subject and multiple-baseline designs

Summative and formative evaluation

Third-party or external evaluation

Transdisciplinary team evaluation

Treatment integrity

To evaluate is to determine the value or significance of something. As was briefly discussed in Chapter 7, evaluation is an activity done on an ongoing basis in both our personal and professional lives. Evaluation may also be understood as part of a process that includes planning, implementing, and evaluating. Once more, we use our example of this process from Chapter 7. We make a plan to go to lunch, based on our personal needs, on our beliefs, and on meeting our goals and objectives. Then we carry out our plan by going to lunch. Evaluation follows naturally to determine if we met our goals and objectives. The joint evaluation of your lunch experience with the person who accompanied you will not only determine the value and usefulness of this event, but it will also potentially help guide you the next time you plan to go to lunch.

This simplistic example of evaluation makes two important points. One is that evaluation is not something we do to someone in a professional–student relationship, but rather is an ongoing part of our personal as well as professional lives. Second, evaluation may be understood as part of a process that includes assessing (e.g., functional assessment), planning (e.g., behavior support), and implementing (e.g., intervention). Additionally, evaluation is best done *with* someone rather than *to* someone. The purpose of this chapter is to overview evaluation, to examine the place of evaluation at all levels of positive behavior support, and to introduce some useful perspectives, methods, and procedures for implementing evaluation.

## OVERVIEW OF EVALUATION

Before we consider evaluation specific to the delivery of positive behavior support (PBS) in educational environments, it will be helpful to provide a framework for what is meant by evaluation. According to Worthen, Sanders, and Fitzpatrick (1997), evaluation may be considered either **formal** or **informal**. Formal evaluation tends to be structured, systematic, thorough, and based on explicit criteria for what is being evaluated. Informal evaluation tends to be more subjective and not connected to the relative merits of varied alternatives. Both formal and informal evaluations are relevant in our personal and professional lives. We are, of course, more interested here in the formal applications of evaluation that will improve the lives of children and youth who are participants in approaches to positive behavior supports. But it is important to recognize that, intended or not, informal perspectives will be present and should be recognized, valued, and included.

We have already noted that evaluation may be formal or informal. **Summative and formative evaluation** (Scriven, 1967) are additional terms often encountered in the literature to differentiate between two primary purposes for evaluation. Summative evaluation refers to the acquisition of information that allows determination at a specified end point of whether goals and objectives have been met or to sum up the impact of effectiveness of (for example) an intervention. Formative evaluation refers to information that is gathered for the purpose of formulating additional goals, objectives, and intervention or teaching practices and to inform future decisions and actions. In practice, of course, the things that we evaluate typically have varying amounts of both types of evaluation. Both are important; their differences are at times blurred, and their purposes are frequently intertwined (Scriven, 1991).

### Consider This

A teacher finds that her cooperative learning approach (providing students opportunities to work in pairs) has resulted in improved on-task behavior.

- What kind of data might she have to demonstrate the positive impact of the strategy?

- How might she use her data summatively? Formatively?

Another way to understand the evaluation process is to differentiate among evaluation of **inputs, processes, and outcomes**. For understanding PBS evaluation in this chapter, these three types of evaluation will be used. However, in the literature on evaluation, and especially program evaluation, four types of evaluation (Stufflebeam & Shinkfield, 1985) are frequently included. In addition to the three stated earlier—inputs, processes, and outcomes—**context evaluation** is included. The objective of context evaluation (Stufflebeam & Shinkfield, 1985) is "to define the institutional context, to identify the target population and assess needs, to identify opportunities for addressing the needs, to diagnose problems underlying the needs, and to judge whether proposed objectives are sufficiently responsive to the addressed needs" (pp. 170–171). Context evaluation serves to inform planning decisions and may be thought of, in general, as a form of needs assessment. In this chapter context evaluation and input evaluation are merged for the purpose of understanding evaluation of PBS. Finally, the evaluation model provided by Stufflebeam and Shinkfield (1985) applied the term **product evaluation**. Product evaluation allows judgments about outcomes of a program and relates outcomes to inputs and processes. For purposes of this chapter and text, product evaluation and outcome evaluation are synonymous.

The study of this textbook as well as other education sources shows that there is growing emphasis on accountability in general education and special education as expressed by measurable outcomes. In the example, the evaluation of lunch is completed after we are finished eating, and it is used to judge the outcome of going to lunch. What about the amount of food, its nutritional value, the cost, and the amount of time it took to be engaged in lunch? These are all outcome measures or indicators.

The point made here is that although outcomes are certainly always important, it is also frequently important as a part of the evaluation process to examine the inputs and processes. Inputs are the elements that go into the plan before it is implemented. Development of the behavior support plan itself would be an example of inputs. Processes are the events and actions that occur as a part of implementing the plan. Vignette 8.1 provides an example of how these elements of evaluation are integrally related.

## Vignette 8.1

### Classroom Evaluation of Reading Skills

A classroom teacher is interested in determining how much gain his students both as a group and individually have made in their reading skills. He is interested in outcomes, that is, what are the quantifiable scores in reading at the end of a specified period of instructional time? He is also interested in outcomes associated with how both the student(s) and parents experienced the reading program. However, the curriculum that he chose (inputs) was not very effective for teaching reading, and he is not very pleased with the way he organized and presented his reading lessons (process). The reading test scores and other outcome measures are disappointing.

### Reflective Moment

It is frequently difficult to effectively evaluate outcomes without also evaluating inputs and processes. Evaluation of inputs and processes should be done substantially during the time that they are occurring, rather than as a look back at the end. Of course, it is easier to focus on outcomes because they are often specific and quantifiable. Can you think of ways that the teacher might have conducted input and process evaluation related to the reading instruction? In what ways might the children and their parents or families have been involved in input and process evaluation?

In addition to understanding evaluation as either summative or formative and as focused on inputs, processes, and outcomes, another distinction is that which is made between **individual and program evaluations**. This distinction is certainly an important one as we consider the varying needs for evaluating the three levels of PBS. Program evaluation, as the term suggests, is aimed at determining the effectiveness of a programwide or schoolwide plan and the implementation of that plan. Program evaluation has been defined by the Joint Committee on Standards for Educational Evaluation (1994) as "activities that are provided on a continuing basis" (p. 3). This definition would certainly apply to the schoolwide behavior support plan. Individual evaluation is aimed at making judgments about the impact of (in this case) PBS on the behavior of individual children and youth. As is the case with summative and formative evaluation, these two purposes sometimes overlap.

## EVALUATION AND PBS

It is important to keep in mind as methods and practices for evaluation of PBS are discussed in this chapter that no one especially likes to have their behavior judged and evaluated. Just as in collaboration, teamwork, and partnerships among professionals, families and others are viewed as important in the process of planning behavior supports at all levels and in carrying them out. They are equally important in determining how the inputs, processes, and outcomes will be evaluated. As discussed in previous chapters, the PBS movement over the past decade, largely as an extension of applied behavior analysis, has broadened behavior principles to include all children and youth. As a result, attention is given to preventing challenging behavior by attending more to setting events and antecedents and by emphasizing a partnership between professionals and families.

PBS is applied at three levels. Each of these levels presents unique opportunities and considerations for evaluation. Historically, evaluation in applied behavior analysis has focused primarily on measurement of outcomes through quantifiable data resulting from **single-subject and multiple-baseline designs** that impacted targeted challenging behaviors. Certainly these approaches continue to be important tools for evaluation, especially levels 2 and 3 of PBS. However, this chapter, although it includes these applied research approaches, also provides information and suggestions for additional means to evaluate PBS. Evaluation methods and practices are multifaceted and often require a period of time for team members to think divergently about possible ways to evaluate inputs, processes, and outcomes and also the opportunity to discuss and problem solve to arrive at a shared view of how the usefulness of PBS (at any level) may be determined.

Carr et al. (1999) have pointed out that one of the distinguishing features of the PBS approach is that it requires **multicomponent interventions** that address the many factors that might influence behavior. Multicomponent interventions require multiple means of assessment and evaluation and might focus on antecedents, setting events, intervention process, outcomes, or broader community, family, and quality-of-life variables.

Another important connection to be made related to the evaluation of PBS is with the concept of **ecological validity**. Ecological validity refers to the meaningfulness and usefulness of behavior supports in the context of an individual's life and daily routines, experiences, and settings. Singer (2000) stated that to advance ecological validity, PBS must in the future "either create PBS service systems that can deliver a variety of services, or we need to team up with more comprehensive service agencies" (p. 124). Doing so will better allow for addressing impeding and challenging behaviors in relevant contexts, such as home and family. Obviously, broadening the contexts, service systems, and professionals involved will require expanding our ways of evaluating effectiveness.

Finally, it is helpful to understand that in most new initiatives in education and other human service delivery models, attention to methods of evaluation tends to lag behind implementation. Keep in mind that PBS as a means of preventing and responding to impeding or challenging behavior is still early in its development and reflects changing and expanding views of behavior interventions (Dunlap & Koegel, 1999). Means of evaluating the effectiveness of PBS have only more recently been addressed in detail in the literature.

One way to understand the relationship between PBS and evaluation is to examine the different purposes of program evaluation and individual evaluation (introduced earlier) as they are applied in PBS. Historically, applied behavior analysis has emphasized focusing on the impact of intervention on individuals' discrete challenging behaviors using quantifiable outcome measures. Systems serving groups of individuals (such as school environments), when formal evaluation was desired or mandated, have tended to use various program evaluation designs in which a broader variety of indicators of success have been applied. Often program evaluation designs include measurable outcomes, but may also include more subjective indicators. Some focus on inputs and processes and the intent of generalizing evaluation findings beyond the group targeted. Part of the PBS movement is to work toward bringing together these disparate approaches and intents of evaluation to best serve its delivery at the three levels of PBS.

In a discussion of the evolution of PBS as an applied science, Carr et al. (2002) pointed out that one is required to change and expand their view of assessment practices (the means by which the success of PBS is determined). The authors suggested that in the future the who, where, how, and what of assessment–evaluation is likely to change as a function of further experience with PBS. Because of the PBS focus on quality of life, life span development, community, various stakeholders, and social validity, persons other than experts will be increasingly involved directly in evaluation (i.e., the who). Schoolwide applications of PBS, rather than only focusing on individuals in specific environments, certainly represents a change in evaluation (i.e., the where). Use of indirect and less-formal and quantifiable means of evaluation will be applied (i.e., the how). And the tools of assessment and evaluation (i.e., the what) are likely to change; for example, they might include an analysis of documents and sociometric measures to determine impacts of PBS.

In a study designed to evaluate the impacts of PBS in a broader sense related to quality of life, social validity, and behavior and ecological outcomes, Kincaid, Knoster, Harrower, Shannon, and Bustamante (2002) applied both survey and interview methods to ascertain the views of 397 individuals on 78 child-centered behavior support teams across three states. The researchers found that the behavior support plans demonstrated social validity and were believed to positively impact quality of life (interpersonal relationships, self-determination, social inclusion, personal well-being, and emotional well-being). We suggest the need for future expansion of collaboration among policy makers, practitioners, and stakeholders and the use of varied research and evaluation methods (such as interviews, rating scales, and checklists that are family and practitioner friendly). The point is that the advancement of PBS at all levels requires rethinking the manner in which professionals design and carry out evaluation.

Not only is it important to think about the relationship between individual evaluation and program evaluation as elements of PBS when conducting

**FIGURE 8–1**
*Evaluation of Positive Supports: Examples of Foci at Input, Process, and Outcome Phases*

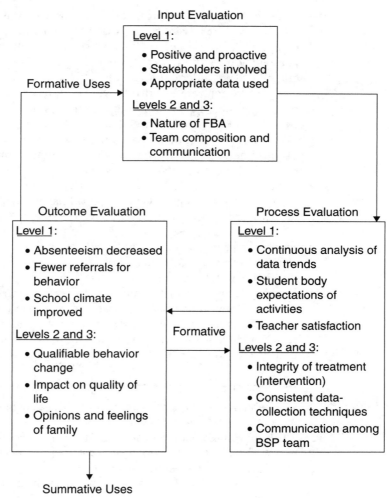

it at the different levels, but it is also important to understand that level 3 PBS requires that the context of evaluation be broadened to demonstrate social validity and to include other stakeholders, family, and community. We will next examine issues and practices in PBS evaluation, using the three levels of PBS and the distinction among input, process, and outcome evaluation as the structure on which to base understanding (see Figure 8–1).

## EVALUATING SCHOOLWIDE POSITIVE BEHAVIOR SUPPORTS

The evaluation of level 1 PBS requires the use of a program evaluation design rather than an individual evaluation approach. That is, we are interested in the quality of the plan (inputs), the ways in which it is implemented (processes), and the extent to which it impacts the behavior of a group of students in a school environment outcomes. As was stated in Chapter 7, an effective and successful schoolwide behavior support plan is assumed to be comprehensive, be developed by a team, be relevant, involve meaningful participation by the persons targeted by the plan, and be doable and sustainable. The federal Office of Special Education Programs Technical Assistance Center on Positive Behavioral Interventions and Supports (OSEP, n.d.) suggested that schools that are successful in developing proactive approaches to schoolwide discipline (schoolwide PBS approaches) are those that develop procedures to accomplish seven actions (Figure 8–2). For our purpose here, it is especially important to note item 5: *Program evaluation and adaptations are made by a team.*

Further, the OSEP Technical Assistance Center on Positive Behavioral Interventions and Supports (OSEP, n.d.) has listed six steps that are prerequisites to the success of a schoolwide system of discipline (Figure 8–3). Note step 6: *Establish a data system that permits the regular and efficient monitoring and evaluation of the effectiveness of the implementation of the schoolwide system of discipline.*

What is important here is the focus on the role of a schoolwide behavior support team in evaluation and on an ongoing process (formative evaluation) of monitoring, based on data (formal evaluation). In describing the consistent themes of schoolwide behavior support efforts, Horner and Sugai (2000) included "information on student performance was collected continuously and summarized for decision making by local teams" (p. 231). These

**FIGURE 8–2**
*Seven-Step Proactive Approach to Schoolwide Discipline*

1. **Behavior expectations are defined.** A small number of clearly defined behavior expectations are defined.

2. **Behavior expectations are taught.** The behavior expectations are taught to all students in the building and are taught in real contexts.

3. **Appropriate behaviors are acknowledged.** Once appropriate behaviors have been defined and taught, they need to be acknowledged on a regular basis.

4. **Behavior errors are corrected proactively.** When students violate behavior expectations, clear procedures are needed for providing information to them that their behavior was unacceptable and preventing that unacceptable behavior from resulting in inadvertent rewards.

5. **Program evaluations and adaptations are made by a team.** Schoolwide systems of behavior support involve ongoing modification and adaptations.

6. **Administrative support and involvement are active.** Schoolwide behavior support involves the active and ongoing support and involvement of key administrators.

7. **Individual student support systems are integrated with schoolwide discipline systems.** Schoolwide behavior support is a process for establishing a positive culture in a school.

*Source:* Adapted from "School-wide PBIS" by OSEP Technical Assistance Center on Positive Behavioral Interventions and Supports, n.d., http://www.pbis.org/english/SchoolwidePBS.htm

**FIGURE 8–3**
*Six Prerequisites for a Schoolwide Discipline System*

*Step 1:* Establish a schoolwide leadership or behavior support team to guide and direct the process. This team should be made up of an administrator, grade-level representatives, support staff, and parents.

*Step 2:* Secure administrator agreement of active support and participation.

*Step 3:* Assess the status of schoolwide discipline or positive behavior support(s) and define short and long-term goals for improving the schoolwide system.

*Step 4:* Secure a commitment and agreement from at least 80% of the staff for active support and participation.

*Step 5:* Establish an implementation action plan that is based on the status assessment and emphasizes the adoption of research validated practices.

*Step 6:* Establish a data system that permits the regular and efficient monitoring and evaluation of the effectiveness of the implementation of the schoolwide system of discipline.

*Source:* Adapted from "School-wide PBIS-FAQs" by OSEP Technical Assistance Center on Positive Behavioral Interventions and Supports, n.d., http://www.pbis.org/english/SchoolwidePBS.htm

considerations all lend themselves to program evaluation, along with judgments made about the desired outcomes (for example, a reduction in the number of students referred to the office for disciplinary action or the percentage of student absenteeism).

## Empirical Evidence for Schoolwide Behavior Supports

Research on schoolwide behavior support plans and the associated methods used to evaluate those plans, especially for elementary and middle school–age students, have recently become more prevalent in the literature. In a longitudinal study of the impacts of a schoolwide behavior support plan in a middle school setting, Luiselli, Putnam, and Sunderland (2002) found substantial benefits over a four-year period. Student detentions issued for disruptive–antisocial behavior, vandalism, and substance abuse decreased, and student attendance increased each year as well as the portion of students earning positive reinforcement. A unique feature of this study was the fact that it was a long-term, four-year effort. The exclusive means of evaluation of effectiveness in this study were quantitative outcome measures, that is, the frequency (increase or decrease) of behaviors measured at the end of each of the three years. Because a team approach was applied (students, teachers, administrators, parents, and community members), this program met the criteria stated previously for an effective schoolwide plan. However, the evaluation criteria did not include any methods other than student-specific outcomes.

Scott (2001) studied the effects of a schoolwide PBS plan in an inner-city kindergarten through fifth-grade school characterized as a school in crisis with students at-risk. A process of obtaining unanimous school personnel commitment, identifying predictable problem behavior contexts, brainstorming prevention strategies, developing consensus, and determining schoolwide expectations and teaching was used. Following that process, a behavior support team representing all job responsibility groups, as well as the principal and a school-based student services coordinator, was established. The plan focused on decreasing the number of SAFE referrals and on decreasing suspensions. SAFE is an acronym for suspension and failure eliminated, and in this school was a room used much like an in-school suspension site. Many proactive prevention strategies targeting the environments of most concern—cafeteria, halls, stairs, and gymnasium—were agreed on and implemented. Results of the program after one year indicated that both SAFE referrals and suspensions were substantially reduced in number. As with the study summarized previously (Luiselli, et al., 2002), the evaluation of effectiveness was limited to quantitative outcome measures. The team did not include family, community, or student representatives, and it is not clear how the team was involved in making judgments about the program's effectiveness.

In a position statement and program description, Fox and Little (2001) delineated the elements of a successful preschoolwide behavior support plan. One of the elements is "evaluating and adjusting team programs," which suggests the central role of the behavior support team in formatively evaluating the impacts of the plan and making adjustments. Fox and Little reported that over the three years of this effort, process and outcome measures suggesting success included maintenance of a healthy organizational climate reflected by high scores on teacher satisfaction scales, national reaccreditations, positive annual parent evaluations, and a long waiting list.

Sailor, Edmondson, and Fenning (2002) described the results of implementing schoolwide positive behavior support in urban settings, including high schools. The outcome measures that they used were attendance, grades, standardized test scores, disciplinary referrals and actions, school safety data, surveys, observations, interviews, and documents. Ongoing and outcome evaluations indicated that what worked was highly engaged students, avoidance of worksheets, engaged students from bell to bell, and avoiding power struggles.

Numerous reports in the literature describe schoolwide behavior support plans. Some describe programs and methods, whereas others provide empirical data from formal research or evaluation efforts. The three references given earlier (Fox & Little, 2001; Luiselli, et al., 2002; Scott, 2001) characterize to some extent how schoolwide plans at various levels (preschool, primary, and middle school) include approaches to evaluation. Teams, sometimes including parents or families and other stakeholders, are frequently cited as responsible for development and overseeing implementation, but it is often unclear how their role might be related to evaluation. Reports of schoolwide behavior support programs focus largely on measurable outcomes, often at an end point, such as the end of the school year.

### Input Evaluation for Schoolwide PBS

Remember that input evaluation is evaluation of the contexts, actions, events, documents, attitudes, and beliefs that precede the plan as well as evaluation of the development of the plan itself. Input evaluation, the precursor to implementation (and process evaluation) of a schoolwide behavior support plan, is the assessment of needs and contributions to the plan. It is evident that insufficient and bad information will limit the ability to develop a good schoolwide behavior support plan. The questions become the following: *Who* are the participants in the input phase and its evaluation? *What* inputs should be evaluated? *Why* are they important? *How* might they be evaluated (criteria, methods of evaluation)? Figure 8-4 provides a summary of how these questions might be answered.

A concern central to determining the quality of input evaluation in schoolwide behavior support planning is to what extent and in what ways the primary stakeholders are participatory. *Who* might those individuals be? They should be the persons most directly impacted by the benefits of having a workable schoolwide behavior support plan (or negatively impacted by the absence of a plan). Schoolwide personnel might be those persons who would be helpful resources and have expertise and experience with behavior support planning. Parent or family representation and participation may be solicited in a variety of ways, including individual contacts, parent–teacher organizations, newsletters, phone surveys, e-mail distribution, class parent meetings, and parent-to-parent networks.

Keep in mind the distinction between input prior to the plan and input as a part of development of the plan. The individuals noted previously are appropriate for the broader context, that is, the **assessment of needs** for the schoolwide plan and the formulation of a **shared vision** regarding the

---

**FIGURE 8–4**
*Elements of Schoolwide PBS Input Evaluation*

*Who are the individuals (input evaluators) on the team?*

The stakeholders will most likely include school personnel (teachers, administrators, supervisors, specialists, teacher assistants, cafeteria workers, custodians and other volunteer and support staff), students, parent/family representatives, and potentially schoolwide personnel and community representatives.

*What are the inputs to be evaluated?*

Inputs include the needs assessment document and results, evidence of a shared mission and consensus, frequency of team meetings, and a complete planning document signed by team members.

*Why are the inputs important for evaluation?*

Success of the schoolwide plan begins with a systematic and thorough effort to involve all stakeholders, build consensus, assess needs, and write a plan directed to the needs.

*How might the inputs be evaluated?*

Use both quantitative and qualitative methods (e.g., questionnaires, interviews, document analysis, focus groups) to examine opportunities for participation, documents, satisfaction, and fit of plan with recommended practice.

overall mission, goals, and objectives of the plan. Shared vision refers to the efforts of a group (for example, the stakeholders noted earlier) to come to a reasonable level of agreement about what the major mission, principles, and goals of a program (schoolwide behavior support plan)—and the schoolwide behavior expectations—should be. That is, they have a shared view of why this is being done, generally how it is being done, and what goals will be achieved. It is, of course, unrealistic to assume that a large group of diverse stakeholders will arrive at full consensus, but the extent to which this is accomplished will affect the success of the development of the plan and its subsequent implementation.

### Consider This

A team develops a schoolwide plan for their high school, and the team arrives at a shared vision and agrees on content. The plan is reviewed by outside experts, including local university faculty and other school districts in which plans have succeeded. Everyone concurs that it is a sound plan. However, no students are involved in plan development.

- What might the students say about the plan (input evaluation)?
- Will they feel ownership of the plan?

As has been stated, the success of schoolwide behavior support planning is partially dependent on the establishment and continuous functioning of a team. Who should be on the team that develops the plan? The membership should include representatives from all the stakeholders noted. How many members should it have? Although there is much variance in team size, it is reasonable to assume that at least 6 to 8 members would be needed and as many as 12 to 15 are possible. The challenges associated with too few or too many team members are obvious. Too few will limit the perspectives and possibly not represent all the stakeholders. Too many will make the team unwieldy and possibly disrupt the team's ability to reach consensus and make decisions. So the input evaluation question related to *who* is broadly stated as follows. Are the appropriate persons included in the wider context, and are the stakeholders represented on a behavior support team?

*What* are the inputs that should be included in the evaluation effort? Prior to establishing the team and development of the plan, several inputs are especially important and should be the focus of formative evaluation. The ethical standards and codes and guidelines for best and effective professional practice (see Chapter 3) related to discipline and behavior in schools would certainly constitute one possibility for inclusion. The points of view of students of what will contribute toward positive behavior and learning and minimal conflict in their school is important. The beliefs, values, and preferences of parents and family members should, of course, be included.

And the beliefs, values, and experiences of school personnel related to behavior expectations in school and effective methods of fostering desired behavior and preventing challenging behavior are important.

Finally, data from a needs assessment process in which all stakeholders are given an opportunity to provide input on plan content should be included. Once the schoolwide behavior support team is established, what should one look for in the plan? Is the plan a written, public document, widely available to all, produced from contributions of all team members? Does the plan have a clear statement of the school's PBS mission, goals, and objectives? Do the mission, goals, and objectives reflect content from the broader stakeholder group? Is the plan based substantially on quantifiable data related to goals and objectives and measurable benchmarks to judge success?

*Why* are the inputs noted of importance as targets for evaluation? If there is to be a partnership among various stakeholders in which collaboration and teamwork are demonstrated toward the development of a sound schoolwide behavior support plan, then everyone with an interest must have a genuine opportunity for input. Primarily the input evaluation is to examine the extent to which relevant persons (who) had opportunity to contribute (what) to the preliminary steps and development of the plan.

*How* might these inputs be evaluated? As with all forms of evaluation, one can apply both quantitative and qualitative methods. With regard to the quantitative dimension and input evaluation, the questions might primarily be simply yes or no. Did the specified stakeholders have an opportunity to contribute to the preliminary planning? Did these stakeholders arrive at a specified level of consensus? Was a preliminary set of school behavior expectations developed? Was one representative from each stakeholder group elected or appointed to serve on the schoolwide behavior support team? Did the team meet multiple times? Was a schoolwide behavior support plan written? Are the objectives in the plan measurable?

How to evaluate input qualitatively is somewhat more complicated and time consuming, but still very useful in getting off to a good start. Qualitative methods might include using interviews, focus groups, or questionnaires to get at the beliefs, values, and preferences of various stakeholders; asking teachers, parents, and students if they are satisfied with their opportunity to provide input; comparing the plan to other plans (considered model plans) for inclusion of the desired elements; and comparing the plans, goals, and objectives to established professional ethical codes, standards, and guidelines for behavior and school discipline.

### Process Evaluation for Schoolwide PBS

Frequently schoolwide behavior support plans are implemented on an academic year calendar. That is, they are carried out as planned for one school year, and judgments are made about the extent to which goals and objectives were met (outcomes). The successes or failures of the implementation (summative evaluation) are used to inform decisions about the future (formative evaluation). The process, or implementation, lends itself to numerous opportunities for evaluating how the methods and strategies applied are working to address the mission, goals, and objectives of the plan. Evaluation of the process allows for any midcourse adjustments and fine-tuning as needed to keep the plan on track. Evaluation of the process of implementing schoolwide behavior support plans can also be understood by examining the who, what, why, and how questions. Figure 8–5 provides a summary of how these questions might be answered.

*Who* are the key persons related to the evaluation of the process of implementing a schoolwide behavior support plan? For the most part, they are the same individuals and groups that participated during the input phase. Certainly the schoolwide behavior support team must have a central role in the ongoing evaluation of the effectiveness of the plan. Feedback from the students about how the implementation of the plan is working for them is necessary. Provide a mechanism for the larger stakeholder group to continue to influence implementation. Finally, parents or families of the students should not only be kept abreast of the progress of the plan but should also have opportunity to provide formal or informal evaluation information along the way. These four groups—the team, students, stakeholders, and parent or family members—are the key to ongoing evaluation of the process.

**FIGURE 8–5**
*Elements of Schoolwide PBS Process Evaluation*

*Who are the evaluators of the process?*

The same group as in the input phase, including the schoolwide team, students, parents and family representatives, and community members.

*What are the processes to be evaluated?*

The processes include the written plan, data trends relating to behavior change, school social climate, and evidence that the plan has been communicated consistently and continuously to school personnel and students.

*Why are these processes important for evaluation?*

Ongoing evaluation (formative) will allow for changes and improvements along the way. Data on trends (e.g., how absenteeism is being impacted) will be helpful.

*How might the processes be evaluated?*

The means of evaluation should be consistent with the answers to the who, what, and why answers introduced previously. Some of the likely means of doing process evaluation are ongoing quantifiable measures such as frequency and percentage of behavior; structured, semistructured, or unstructured interviews of students, teachers, family members, or other stakeholders; focus groups; analysis of documents; and questionnaires related to knowledge, attitudes, and beliefs.

*What* are the processes, products, actions, documents, and behaviors that should be part of the process evaluation? What should be evaluated during implementation of the schoolwide plan? The written plan itself should be periodically reviewed, discussed, and modified as needed, so that it becomes, as intended, a working and useful document rather than a perfunctory exercise. The data reflecting trends related to the goals and objectives of the plan should be analyzed by the team and by others. This might occur monthly or even quarterly, but it will be useful in making adjustments and changes in strategies. For example, given the goal of reducing suspensions, are the data showing a trend toward a decrease in the number of students suspended? Changing attitudes and beliefs of the various stakeholders should be assessed as a part of the process, as well as attitudes and beliefs of the students about the schoolwide plan. Although the notion of **school climate** may be somewhat abstract and difficult to measure, it is nonetheless important, and it will be useful to ask the teaching staff and support staff of the school to evaluate how it has been affected by the behavior support plan.

*Why* are the process evaluation activities important and desirable? As stated earlier, process evaluation will allow for fine-tuning and making adjustments as the plan is implemented. It also provides for strengthening and advancing the shared vision that was fostered as a part of the initial development and planning effort. Documenting the experiences of implementing the plan in a qualitative and descriptive fashion will potentially be useful as formative information when plans are made for a subsequent year's plan. Stated in a straightforward manner, it is not only necessary to judge what we intended to do (input) and what we did (outcome), but also to consider carefully how we got there (process).

*How* might these processes be evaluated? Numerous methods, strategies, and instruments might be developed or applied to evaluate the process of implementing schoolwide positive behavior support. They are, of course, situation specific and dependent on the needs and goals of the school, team, and other stakeholders.

### Outcome Evaluation for Schoolwide PBS

Outcome evaluation is the judgment made about the results of a schoolwide behavior support plan, usually after a period of one year. In a study reported by Scott (2001), the results of an inner-city elementary school PBS plan were provided after one year of implementation, and two dependent variables were addressed. These variables (referral to an in-school suspension room and suspension from school) were seen to be dependent on the success of the behavior support plan. Desired outcomes were, of course, for both variables to decrease in frequency over the period of the year. The outcome evaluation in this instance consisted of monthly and end point quantifiable measures of frequency. This example likely represents the most frequently applied and traditional means of outcome evaluation. Others might serve to compliment and expand this strategy. Outcome evaluation,

**FIGURE 8–6**
*Elements of*
*Schoolwide PBS*
*Outcome Evaluation*

*Who are the evaluators of the outcomes?*

The evaluators are the schoolwide team, an outside evaluator(s), or a combination of both.

*What are the outcomes to be evaluated?*

Measurable intended outcomes to be evaluated include absences, suspensions, discipline referrals, and student, teacher, and family attitudes about the school, based on goals and objectives in the plan. Unintended outcomes, such as promoting interest of some teachers to learn more about PBS, should also be evaluated.

*Why are these outcomes important for evaluation?*

Outcome evaluation serves the dual purpose of providing end-of-the-year evidence of the impact of the schoolwide effort (summative) and information useful for formulating a new plan for the next year (formative).

*How are outcomes evaluated?*

Evaluation tools include group trend data analysis, behavior observations, interviews, focus groups, and questionnaires.

like input and process evaluation, may be understood by considering who, what, why, and how (see Figure 8–6).

*Who* might be the participants in the evaluation of the outcomes of a schoolwide behavior support plan? Three approaches to this question are presented. It is logical and appropriate for the schoolwide PBS team to be primarily responsible for the formative and summative evaluation of the outcomes of the effort. A second approach is sometimes applied in the use of a **third-party or external evaluation**. Third-party or external evaluation is the use of a presumably unbiased evaluator or team from outside the school and school system. There are advantages to both external and internal evaluation approaches. Internal evaluators (for example, the PBS team) presumably have more contextual information and are familiar with the implementation. Having an outside evaluation does not necessarily ensure objectivity and credibility (Scriven, 1993). A third approach to who evaluates outcomes of a schoolwide plan is to use a combination of the behavior support team and representatives from other schools experienced in PBS and possibly university professors experienced in program evaluation and PBS.

*What* are the elements that might be evaluated at the outcome stage? The extent to which the mission or vision of the plan, its overriding goals, and its specific objectives are accomplished should be evaluated at the end of an established period (often one school year). Although the mission and goals tend to be less measurable and lend themselves to more qualitative analysis, the objectives should be written in a manner that makes them quantifiable and measurable. For example, the objectives might have been to reduce (perhaps by an established percentage or frequency) measurable behaviors such as in-school suspensions, suspensions, discipline referrals, disruptive behavior incidents, or absences.

*Why* is outcome evaluation important? Keep in mind that schoolwide PBS requires a program evaluation approach rather than a focus on individuals. Program evaluation targets program (school) processes and outcomes, aggregate data, judgments about achieving goals, and producing data for decision makers. It has been pointed out in the evaluation literature (Patton, 2002) that "outcomes evaluation has become a central focus, if not the central focus, of **accountability-driven evaluation**. The accountability movement is not so much about achieving quality as it is about demonstrating responsible use of public funds to achieve politically desired results" (p. 151). The trend toward accountability and **performance-based outcomes**, although certainly having advantages, has the potential weakness of minimizing or excluding important outcomes that do not fit well with the objectives or do not lend themselves to quantitative methods. Kibel (1999) has noted

> For programs engaged in healing, transformation, and prevention, the best source and form of information [outcomes] are client [teachers, students, families] stories. It is through these stories that we discover how program staff interact with clients, with other service providers, and with family and friends of their clients [students] to contribute to outcomes, and how the clients, themselves, grow and change. . . . It is only for a story not worth telling, due to its inherent simplicity, that numbers will suffice. (p. 13)

*How* might one evaluate outcomes of a schoolwide behavior support plan? Suppose that the stated objectives of the plan are to reduce in-school suspension referrals, school suspensions, discipline referrals to the office, and absences and to increase student, faculty and staff, and parent satisfaction with the school climate related to behavior and discipline. All these variables may be evaluated quantitatively as outcomes using data counts taken on a monthly basis and questionnaires using a Likert-type scale to measure attitudes and beliefs related to the changing school climate. Interviews and focus groups may be used to add qualitative data, targeting any or all stakeholders.

## EVALUATING LEVEL 2 AND LEVEL 3 POSITIVE BEHAVIOR SUPPORTS

Crone and Horner (2003) pointed out that evaluation is essential to successful PBS and that it should be a part of the initial design of PBS. They suggested that evaluation procedures should be simple and efficient and that they include three elements—the assessment of changes in behavior, the feasibility and acceptability of the plan, and the satisfaction with the plan and implementation of students, parents, and teachers. Also, evaluation of PBS should conclude with plans for maintenance of behavior improvement. This point of view is consistent with the position taken in this chapter that PBS should be evaluated at all points, including inputs, processes, and outcomes. Further evaluation must go beyond being limited to assessing behavior change.

Because levels 2 and 3 PBS both focus on individuals and their challenging or impeding behavior, they both require individual evaluation (as opposed to program evaluation) approaches. Also the input, process, and outcome elements are very similar, with the distinctions mainly related to the intensity and comprehensiveness of the interventions. The methods of evaluation at all phases are comparable. For example, antecedents, setting events, and functional behavior assessment and analysis are likely to be important to both. The process of delivering levels 2 and 3 PBS will require evaluation of progress by collection of ongoing measurable impacts. Using observation of discrete behaviors, multiple baselines, and collaboration among persons responsible for implementation will help. The evaluation of outcomes for levels 2 and 3 will both include quantifiable data and issues of self-determination and social or ecological validity. Following are some issues and ideas related to evaluation at the three points in the process.

## Input Evaluation for Level 2 and Level 3 PBS

What are the input variables associated with individual positive behavior supports, and how might they be evaluated? Keep in mind that the objective is to evaluate them prior to the process and outcome stages to establish the best start possible. This is opposed to waiting until the implementation is in process or is completed, then looking back to consider whether the inputs were appropriate and useful.

Inputs for level 2 and level 3 positive behavior planning typically are identifying goals, gathering information, developing a hypothesis, and designing the support plan (Florida Department of Education, 1999). Each of these four steps involves specific actions. *Identifying goals* includes establishing a team, establishing rules and guidelines for the team's functioning, formulating a picture (profile) of the child or youth, consideration of the broader goals or enhancement of quality of life for the child or youth, and defining the target behavior(s). *Gathering information* is conducting a functional behavior assessment (see Chapter 6). O'Neill and others (1997) posited five primary outcomes for functional behavior assessment. They are (a) describing the problem behaviors; (b) identifying events, times, and situations that may predict problem behavior across daily routines; (c) identifying consequences that maintain problem behavior; (d) developing summary statement(s) that describe behaviors, situations in which they occur, and the consequences maintaining them; and (e) collecting data from direct observations (for example, scatter plots) that support summary statements. Interviewing, reviewing records, and other forms of assessment may also be useful as a part of the functional behavior assessment process.

Developing a *hypothesis* is the third step. The information gathered by the team is analyzed to identify patterns of behavior that may help clarify the contexts of challenging behavior (antecedents) and the functions of behavior (consequences). Patterns of behavior allow for the development of a hypothesis (summary statement) related to the challenging behavior. Setting events may also be relevant in developing the hypothesis. Testing the hypothesis (for example, functional analysis) may be desirable. The fourth and last step in the input phase is *developing* and *designing* the plan (see Chapter 7 for planning formats). One prominent and recommended strategy (Florida Department of Education, 1999) is the **competing behaviors model** (O'Neill et al., 1997). "This model uses summary statement information (setting events, antecedents, behaviors, and maintaining consequences) to identify specific replacement skills and other desired behaviors" (Florida Department of Education, 1999, p. 53). Intervention strategies that are positive, educational, and functional are specified in the plan specific to the desired behavior.

One important means of evaluating the inputs described is simply to have a checklist to record whether or not these actions have been taken, on what date, and by whom (individual, team as a whole, other). Another method is to determine whether specific documents, such as the list of team members and the team functions and guidelines, exist. These are quantifiable measures.

### Consider This

There are also important qualitative questions in evaluating inputs.

- Is the team representative of the "stakeholders"?
- Does each of the team members feel that they had an opportunity to provide input, and were their ideas taken seriously and considered?
- Are the team members (and other relevant persons) satisfied with the portrait of the child or youth?
- Is it clear how the planning is connected to broader goals of the family and the child's quality of life?
- Is the conduct of the functional behavior assessment consistent with the literature's description of recommended practices?
- Are setting events adequately represented in development of the hypothesis?
- Is the plan itself written in a way that communicates clearly and effectively with all members of the team, other members of the family, and the child or youth who is targeted?
- Do the interventions selected to facilitate the replacement behavior meet the criteria of being positive, educational (or developmental), and functional?
- Are the planned interventions socially valid?

Qualitative questions are frequently more difficult to answer and may require methods with which behavior planners have limited experience and expertise. For example, semistructured and unstructured interviews, questionnaires, document analysis techniques, focus groups, and third-party judgments might be applied.

## Process Evaluation for Level 2 and Level 3 PBS

When the PBS plan has been implemented and is ongoing, how might progress be evaluated? Crone and Horner (2003) suggested that numerous methods can be used, but that frequency counts, individualized behavior rating scales, and observations are more common methods. Evaluation of the ongoing intervention procedures (also referred to as treatment, particularly in applied behavior analysis single-subject and multiple baseline research designs) may be thought of as efforts at ensuring **treatment integrity** and **implementation fidelity** (Crone & Horner, 2003).

Treatment integrity refers to the ethics and functionality as well as the honesty of the intervention directly related to the child or youth. Implementation fidelity has been used to describe a broader perspective on how positive behavior support implementation is progressing, as it impacts the child but also the team, the family, and other partners and collaborators. Just as with input evaluation, both quantitative methods, such as the ones listed, and qualitative methods are important in ongoing assessment and evaluation of the implementation of PBS. These evaluations are formative, in that they are used to make adjustments and formulate new directions as needed in the intervention strategies to better address the goals and objectives of the plan.

Although it is efficient and appropriate for one member of the behavior support team to take primary responsibility for keeping track of the process evaluation and informing the remainder of the team, it is very important that all members of the team have meaningful input into determining what the process evaluation components are and how they will be continuously evaluated. It is also important that all members of the team take part in the collection of process evaluation data. For example each team member might keep a journal describing their role and how they view their contributions.

## Outcome Evaluation for Level 2 and Level 3 PBS

To evaluate outcomes is to make judgments at the end of a specified period of time about whether behavior change has occurred related to the objectives stated in the plan. Attention has been given (Clarke, Worcester, Dunlap, Murray, & Bradley-Klug, 2002) to the importance of using **multiple outcome measures** in the evaluation of PBS. In a single-case study of the use of positive behavior intervention and support (PBIS) with a 12-year-old female student having challenging behaviors and diagnosed with autism and other medical/developmental conditions, Clarke et al. (2002) found that, in addition to direct measures of change in challenging behaviors, indirect measures such as pre- and post-quality-of-life surveys completed by teachers, parents, and peers, as well as PBS satisfaction ratings completed by various stakeholders, were, very important in evaluation.

Questions to be answered in outcome evaluation are the following: Were the goals and objectives met? Was the intervention carried out as designed? In what ways might the intervention(s) be changed if it is to be continued? Outcome evaluation has the dual purpose of summing up the impacts of the intervention (summative) and contributing to the formulation of new, revised plans (formative). The use of objective measures, such as frequency counts, duration of behaviors, or intensity of behaviors, have long been useful outcome measures for applications of applied behavior analysis and PBS. Criticisms of the PBS movement have not been focused so much on the relevance of including dimensions such as social validity, quality of life, self-determination, person-centered planning, and impacts on family but rather on the difficulties associated with quantifying those dimensions. A reasonable assumption would be that a combination of subjective, qualitative methods and objective, quantitative methods of outcome evaluation are necessary to establish a useful picture of how the intervention impacted these variables.

## ISSUES AND FUTURE DIRECTIONS IN PBS EVALUATION

Following are five selected issues related to the future of evaluation of PBS. They include (a) the behavior continuum, (b) empowerment evaluation, (c) partnerships with families, (d) measurable outcomes, and (e) unifying disciplines and fostering professional collaboration. Certainly others could have been included here. These have been selected because they are consistent with the content presented in this chapter and other chapters of the text.

### The Behavior Continuum

Sailor et al. (2002) reported that "typical" and inner-city schools look quite different related to the percentage of students on the continuum of behavior. Typical schools might have 9% of students with chronic or serious behavior problems, 15% who are at risk for behavior problems, and 76% with mild or no behavior problems. Inner-city schools might have an additional category of extreme behavior problems (11%), then 21% with chronic or serious behavior problems, 30% at risk for behavior problems, and only 38% with mild or no behavior problems. Consider how this impacts the way we establish and evaluate behavior support plans. A growing trend (OSEP, n.d.) treats PBS in a given educational environment (such as a school) as a **continuum of behavior support** for all students, from those who have no challenging behavior to those who might have extreme challenging behavior. It is expected that for schools in which there is a high percentage of students with specific challenging behaviors or at-risk factors, there will be a much greater emphasis on individual, measurable outcome evaluation and possibly a schoolwide focus on intervention.

Fox, Dunlap, Hemmeter, Joseph, and Strain (2003) described a model for supporting social competence and preventing challenging behavior in young children. They presented a teaching pyramid in which a continuum progresses from the least to the most intensive approaches. Positive relationships with children, families, and colleagues are at the base, followed by classroom prevention strategies, then social and emotional teaching strategies, and at the top of the pyramid, intensive individualized interventions. This pyramid is one way of describing the connection in a learning environment among the three levels of PBS. Given that implementing these practices depends to a large extent on the positive attitudes and abilities of teachers, the question is in what ways should evaluation focus on the teachers' behavior and attitude changes (input and process evaluation) in addition to the evaluation of outcomes for groups of children or individual children?

## Empowerment Evaluation

McCart and Sailor (2003) described the advantages of **empowerment evaluation** to establish and sustain schoolwide PBS. Empowerment evaluation "enables the partnerships of school personnel, families, and community members to come to perceive ownership of the process, to take an active role in structuring goals and objectives for implementation of PBS and, over time, to become skilled in methods of data collection and evaluation" (p. 27). Helping all stakeholders make decisions based on evidence and feel ownership and helping schools become more self-evaluating and self-reliant are goals of empowerment evaluation. Recent emphasis on school-based improvement teams, often including various stakeholders and also goals associated not only with academic achievement but also discipline and school behavior climate, are encouraging indicators that empowerment evaluation could translate from theory to practice.

## Partnerships with Families

The future with regard to how professionals will and should partner with families in the development, implementation, and evaluation of positive behavior intervention and support is rather complicated and unclear. This discussion is limited to considerations of parent or family roles related to evaluation of PBS. Lucyshyn, Horner, Dunlap, Albin, and Ben (2002) pointed out that a basic tenet of PBS is that families be seen in a positive light and from a strength (rather than deficit) perspective and that the evaluation of PBS be a continuous process in which parents or families are participants. They suggested that "evaluation of child and family outcomes is made family friendly by including parents in the selection of evaluation procedures, by choosing or designing measures that are relatively easy to use, and by ensuring that instruments not only measure problems but also child progress and family success" (p. 28).

Some of the factors that contribute to the complexity of partnerships are (a) the ages and developmental status of the children and youth targeted, (b) the developmental status of the parents and other family members, (c) the preferences of families for participation, (d) the difference associated with various levels of PBS evaluation (for example, individual versus program evaluation), (e) the attitudes and skills of professionals, and (f) the perceptions and policies of schools and school systems regarding partnerships with parents or families. Following is a brief consideration of each of these six factors.

The age of the child affects the partnership with parents or families in evaluating PBS. Consider the differences among toddler, preschool, elementary, middle school, and high school environments and potential parent or family roles. Peck Peterson, Derby, Harding, Weddle, and Barretto (2002) pointed out that, because of the variety of settings and related communication issues, the input of parents is especially valuable when children reach school age. What about the developmental status of parents related to participation in evaluation? Parents and family members are at different places developmentally regarding their ability to contribute to the evaluation process. How are decisions made in this regard, and how is parent or family change and growth taken into account in the process? And what about the preferences of parents or families for participation? How might professionals accurately and continuously assess parent or family preferences for levels and types of participation in schoolwide and individual behavior support planning? One size for all does not work for children, and of course it also does not work for parents.

Turnbull and Turnbull (2001) noted that families are important participants in all aspects (including evaluation) of level 1 PBS, but that their involvement should be pervasive at level 3 and more significant than at level 1 or level 2. Pervasiveness would suggest that parents or families should be integral team members in evaluating PBS at the input, process, and outcome phases of evaluation. Yet there continues to be something of a view of parents or families as recipients of a schoolwide plan rather than as team members and as simply one of many stakeholders, responsible mostly for seeing to the consistency and generalization of intervention plans made and implemented by professionals for level 2 and level 3 PBS.

## Consider This

Think about the difference between parents as evaluators when the PBS plan is for all the students in school as opposed to when the evaluation is focused on their child (and her challenging behavior).

- What about the attitudes and skills of professionals?

- As an educator or educator to be, how do you feel about the roles of parents or families in PBS and especially as part of assessment, evaluation, and making judgments?

- Are you being prepared to value parents as team members, and are you gaining skills and practices that will make that possible?

Last is the issue of school and school system policy and procedure related to parent or family representation on behavior support teams. It is useful to look at a school's improvement plan. Increasingly, public schools are being expected to engage in a process of continuous improvement through a formalized plan. This plan typically includes means of measuring progress toward goals. Does the school (or system) value the role of parents or families by supporting their meaningful participation in all aspects of evaluating school improvement (input, process, and outcomes)? Specifically, are there formalized position statements and guidelines promoting the roles of parents as members on schoolwide or individual PBS teams? Professional literature is replete with arguments, empirically based and otherwise, in favor of parent or family partnerships, but it can be assumed that these practices are not yet realized.

## Measurable Outcomes

A central consideration in the evolution of positive behavior support from its origins (Carr et al., 2002) in applied behavior analysis, the normalization–inclusion movement, and person-centered values has been how to address the need for measurable, quantifiable outcomes, given the emphasis in PBS on quality of life, life span development, ecological and social validity, and family and other stakeholder participation. For professionals in applied behavior analysis, this has been especially troublesome, given the tradition in applied behavior analysis of strict adherence to scientific methods ensuring systematic and measurable examination of child-focused outcomes.

To evaluate outcomes such as quality of life, school climate, impacts on the family, and social validity, it is often necessary to pair qualitative methods and instruments, for example, interviews, questionnaires, scales, focus groups, and document analysis, with quantitative methods. Certainly these social validity and quality-of-life outcomes are sometimes amenable to observation and measurement. Kincaid et al. (2002) recommended that future research include "longitudinal and empirically robust evaluations of assessment instruments that are sensitive to quality of life and social validity issues," but they pointed out that the field of PBS should also be "evaluating the impact of PBS through less labor-intensive methods, including rating scales and interviews" (p. 116). A guiding principle is that the evaluation of outcomes should be done in a logical, clear, and straightforward manner that is understood and agreed upon by team members and that includes measurable child outcomes as well as the broader contexts of the plan. For all members of the team, the evaluation of outcomes should come as a natural progression from their roles in input and process evaluation activities.

## Unifying Disciplines and Fostering Collaboration

There has been, over the past decade or so, a great deal of discussion about the need for various disciplines to be more collaborative in the planning and delivery of educational programs, in particular as they relate to children with special needs. An example is the **transdisciplinary team evaluation** approach. The basis of transdisciplinary team evaluation is that a group of professionals conducts evaluations together, transcending their individual disciplines. Benner (2003) suggested that, though transdisciplinary teaming is a desirable and promising practice, it is time consuming, may require numerous professionals, may be expensive, and requires a level of professional collaboration that may be foreign to many professionals. From the family and child perspective, however, this approach has the potential of saving time and effort, fostering communication with professionals, and eliminating the volume of professional jargon that they must interpret. The team approach advocated in behavior support planning can be a mechanism for transdisciplinary evaluation at the input (planning), process (implementation), and outcomes stages of PBS. However, it will require that professionals in different disciplines (for example, psychology, general education, and special education) find ways to speak the same language and merge their evaluation instruments and methods. If the behavior support team is transdisciplinary for the development of the plan based on evaluation of needs for behavior change, then it should continue to function in that manner as process and outcomes are evaluated.

Another future consideration related to evaluation of PBS is the question of differences among professional organizations (see Chapter 3, Ethical Considerations) in terms of the way they view discipline and challenging behavior in various learning environments. Consider, for example, the different points of view on the acceptability of punitive approaches for children and youth reflected in the ethical codes, standards, and guidelines of the National Education Association, the Learning First Alliance, the Council for Exceptional Children, the National Association for the Education of Young Children, and the American Psychological Association. As has been noted repeatedly, an effective behavior support plan requires consensus building not only between professionals and family, but also among professionals representing varied disciplinary perspectives. To function as a behavior support team and to monitor and evaluate interventions on a continuous basis, professionals are required to resolve differences and reach consensus about target behaviors, intervention methods, and desired outcomes.

## SUMMARY

To evaluate is to determine the value or significance of something. Certainly it is important that we develop and apply effective ways of evaluating positive behavior interventions and supports. Just as planning (Chapter 7) is a process applicable in both our personal and professional lives, so too is evaluation. It is important to keep in mind that evaluation is not exclusively a professional tool—something that we might use *on* someone—but rather that it is a process that is best done collaboratively *with* others, including the person who is the subject of the evaluation.

Evaluation may be characterized as either **formal** or **informal**. Formal evaluation tends to be structured, systematic, thorough, and based on explicit criteria for what is being evaluated. Informal evaluation tends to be more subjective and less planned. Evaluation may also be understood as a part of a **system** that includes planning, implementing, and evaluating.

The two purposes of evaluation are **formative** and **summative**. Formative evaluation refers to information that is gathered for the purpose of formulating additional goals, objectives, and intervention or teaching practices and to inform future decisions and actions. Summative evaluation refers to the acquisition of information that allows one at a specified end point to determine whether goals and objectives have been met or to sum up the impact of effectiveness of an (for example) intervention. In practice, often the same evaluation data is used for both purposes.

Evaluation may be further understood as one of two types, **program evaluation** or **individual evaluation**. Program evaluation is aimed at determining the impact and effectiveness of a program (school) for a group. Individual evaluation is aimed at making judgments about the impact of (in the case of this textbook) PBS on the behavior of individual children with challenging, impeding behavior.

Finally, to understand broadly what evaluation is, it is necessary to think of it as occurring as a part of a process that includes **inputs** (for example, contexts, setting events, environmental arrangements, and antecedents), **processes** (for example, intervention strategies or teaching methods), and **outcomes** (the results of intervention and teaching). These basic elements of evaluation are important to the understanding of evaluation as it is applied to all levels of PBS.

Evaluation of PBS at all levels is a topic of increasing interest in the literature. A number of issues are yet unresolved with regard to how to apply evaluation methods and instruments in PBS. One issue concerns the difference between schoolwide positive behavior support and positive behavior support and intervention for children and youth with impeding or challenging behavior. The former requires a program evaluation approach whereas the latter necessitates an individual evaluation approach. The two are distinct and require different methods and instrumentation.

Another issue is specific to the relative focus on inputs, processes, and outcomes as part of an overall evaluation plan for each of the three levels of PBS. Although each is important and relevant, current emphasis in public policy is focused almost exclusively on outcomes. Finally, in examining the evolution of PBS from its roots in applied behavior analysis, questions arise about broadening evaluation beyond quantifying child behavior outcomes to using a variety of both qualitative and quantitative approaches to answer questions of, for example, social validity, impacts on parents or families, and relationships to self-determination and other aspects of quality of life.

This chapter introduced some of the fundamental issues and practices associated with evaluation of both schoolwide PBS programs and PBS targeting individual children and youth (both those classified as having special needs and those not classified) who have impeding, challenging behavior and require a more intensive and systematic approach. Evaluation is an important and necessary component of any educational endeavor. Evaluation is more than merely determining what has occurred at the end point. It is best connected to inputs, processes, and outcomes. Finally, evaluation is most effective when it reflects both quantitative and qualitative information from a variety of sources.

## ACTIVITIES TO EXTEND YOUR LEARNING

1. Invite the school district behavior specialist or behavior support team chair(s) to come to class and share how they go about evaluating the effectiveness of their plans.
2. Invite family representatives to class to serve on a panel to share their perspectives on how they evaluate the behavior support plan in which they are participants (team members or partners for levels 1, 2, and 3). Discuss at a follow-up class meeting the connections among their perspectives and the points made in this chapter.
3. Divide the class into four research groups, with each group being assigned one of the following topics: social or ecological validity, person-centered planning, quality of life, and self-determination. Research professional literature on these topics, specific to what is being said about how each topic should be evaluated or measured. Share findings across groups and have discussions related to input, process, or outcome evaluation and methods for quantifying.
4. Use a role-playing exercise in class to learn more about the development, implementation, and evaluation of a schoolwide behavior support plan. Divide the class into stakeholder groups (students, parent or families, teachers, other school staff, and administrators). Using a hypothetical (or real) school, have the groups engage in the preliminary process of discussion and consensus building related to the desired behaviors in the school. After this is completed, have each group select one or two members to serve on a behavior support team. The team can develop an outline of a plan and present it to the class, with particular attention to the means of evaluation (use the chapter content for assistance in choosing the who, what, why, and how of the evaluation).
5. For a perspective on issues, practices, and instruments related to the evaluation of processes and outcomes when applying person-centered planning as a part of quality of life with adults having comprehensive disabilities, read and discuss the article by Steve Holburn and others in the *American Journal on Mental Retardation* (2000), Vol. 105(5), 402–416.

6. Identify faculty members at your university who teach, do research, and are experts on school and program evaluation, applied behavior analysis and single-subject design, and qualitative research. Establish interview teams in class and conduct interviews with each of these individuals, focusing on their views about comparing program and individual evaluation and evaluation of PBS. Report your interview findings in class or invite these professors to serve on a panel for a class presentation.

## FURTHER READING AND EXPLORATION

1. Using the eight articles in the Forum section of the *Journal of Positive Behavior Interventions* (Fall 2000), Vol. 2(4), examine the ways in which schoolwide PBS has been applied in various educational environments.

2. Go to the Web site of the Center for Positive Behavioral Interventions and Supports (http://www.pbis.org) and look for references and descriptions of methods of evaluation of PBS at all three levels.

3. Survey schools in your community, city, county, or area, and find out how many have established schoolwide behavior support plans. Collect as many plans as possible and compare them, using the evaluation criteria introduced in the chapter.

4. Look in professional journals in education and educational leadership or administration to find articles describing models of schoolwide behavior support plans. Study and compare the evaluation methods provided in each article. To what extent do these evaluation methods meet the standards for practice detailed in this chapter?

5. For additional perspective on means of evaluating the impacts of levels 2 and 3 positive behavior support(s) for young children with challenging behavior, visit the Web site of the Center for Evidenced-Based Practice: Young Children with Challenging Behavior (http://www.challengingbehavior.org).

6. Developing, implementing, and evaluating schoolwide behavior support plans are often seen in the context of broader, comprehensive schoolwide reforms. Go to http://www.wested.org/csrd/guidebook/get2.htm and review the step related to use of evaluation for continuous school improvement. Consider how this fits with what you have learned about PBS evaluation.

7. Obtain the *Facilitator's Guide: Positive Behavioral Support* developed by the PBS staff at the University of South Florida for the Florida Department of Education. Look specifically at the "Self Check" section at the end of each step described in the guide. Consider how a team might use this information as the basis for evaluation at the input and process phases of individual PBS planning and delivery.

8. To get a perspective on different views of parent/family participation in PBS evaluation, study the contributed chapters in the book *Families and*

*Positive Behavior Support: Addressing Problem Behavior in Family Contexts*, edited by Lucyshyn, Dunlap, and Albin, 2002, published by Paul H. Brookes.

# REFERENCES

Benner, S. (2003). *Assessment of young children with special needs: A context-based approach.* Clifton Park, NJ: Thomson/Delmar Learning.

Carr, E. G., Dunlap, G., Horner, R. H., Koegel, R. L., Turnbull, A. P., Sailor, W., et al. (2002). Positive behavior support: Evolution of an applied science. *Journal of Positive Behavior Interventions, 4*(1), 4–16.

Carr, E. G., Levin, L., McConnachie, G., Carlson, J. I., Kemp, D. C., Smith, C. G., et al. (1999). Comprehensive multisituational intervention for problem behavior in the community: Long-term maintenance and social validation. *Journal of Positive Behavior Interventions, 1*, 5–25.

Clarke, S., Worcester, J., Dunlap, G., Murray, M., & Bradley-Klug, K. (2002). Using multiple measures to evaluate positive behavior support: A case example. *Journal of Positive Behavior Interventions, 4*(3), 131–145.

Crone, D. A., & Horner, R. H. (2003). *Building positive behavior support systems in schools: Functional behavioral assessment.* New York: Guilford.

Dunlap, G., & Koegel, R. L. (1999). Welcoming editorial. *Journal of Positive Behavior Interventions, 1*, 2–3.

Florida Department of Education. (1999, November). *Facilitator's guide: Positive behavioral support.* Tampa: Rehabilitation Research & Training Center on Positive Behavioral Support, University of South Florida.

Fox, L., Dunlap, G., Hemmeter, M. L., Joseph, G. E., & Strain, P. S. (2003). The teaching pyramid: A model for supporting social competence and preventing challenging behavior in young children. *Young Children, 58*(4), 48–52.

Fox, L., & Little, N. (2001). Developing school-wide behavior support in a community preschool. *Journal of Positive Behavior Interventions, 3*(4), 251–254.

Holburn, S., Jacobson, J. W., Vietz, P. M., Schwartz, A. A., & Sersen, E. (2000). Quantifying the process and outcomes of person-centered planning. *American Journal on Mental Retardation, 105*(5), 402–416.

Horner, R. H., & Sugai, G. (2000). School-wide behavior support: An emerging initiative. *Journal of Positive Behavior Interventions, 2*(4), 231–232.

Joint Committee on Standards for Educational Evaluation. (1994). *The Program Evaluation Standards* (2nd ed.). Thousand Oaks, CA: Sage.

Kibel, B. M. (1999). *Success stories as hard data: An introduction to results mapping.* New York: Kluwer Academic/Plenum.

Kincaid, D., Knoster, T., Harrower, J. K., Shannon, P., & Bustamante, S. (2002). Measuring the impact of positive behavior support. *Journal of Positive Behavior Interventions, 4*(2), 109–117.

Lucyshyn, J. M., Dunlap, G., & Albin, R. W. (Eds.). (2002). *Families and positive behavior support: Addressing problem behavior in family contexts.* Baltimore: Paul H. Brookes.

Lucyshyn, J. M., Horner, R. H., Dunlap, G., Albin, R. W., & Ben, K. R. (2002). Positive behavior support with families. In J. M. Lucyshyn, G. Dunlap, & R. Albin (Eds.), *Families and positive behavior support: Addressing problem behavior in family contexts* (pp. 3–43). Baltimore: Paul H. Brookes.

Luiselli, J. K., Putnam, R. F., & Sunderland, M. (2002). Longitudinal evaluation of behavior support intervention in a public middle school. *Journal of Positive Behavior Interventions, 4*(3), 182–188.

McCart A., & Sailor, W. (2003, January/February). Using empowerment evaluation to establish and sustain schoolwide positive behavior support. *TASH Connections, 29,* 25–27.

O'Neill, R. E., Horner, R. H., Albin, R. W., Sprague, J. R., Storey, K., & Newton, J. S. (1997). *Functional assessment and program development for problem behavior: A practical handbook.* Pacific Grove, CA: Brooks/Cole.

OSEP Technical Assistance Center on Positive Behavioral Interventions and Supports. (n.d.). *School-wide PBIS.* Retrieved January 16, 2003 from http://www.pbis.org/english/SchoolwidePBS.htm

Patton, M. Q. (2002). *Qualitative research and evaluation methods* (3rd ed.). Thousand Oaks, CA: Sage.

Peck Peterson, S. M., Derby, K. M., Harding, J. W., Weddle, T., & Barretto, A. (2002). Behavioral support for school-age children with developmental disabilities and problem behavior. In J. M. Lucyshyn, G. Dunlap, & R. W. Albin (Eds.), *Families and positive behavior support: Addressing problem behavior in family contexts* (pp. 287–304). Baltimore: Paul H. Brookes.

Sailor, W., Edmondson, H., & Fenning, P. (2002, October). *Implementing schoolwide positive behavior support in urban settings including high schools.* Paper presented at the meeting of the Implementers' Forum on Systems Change, Naperville, IL.

Scott, T. M. (2001). A schoolwide example of positive behavioral support. *Journal of Positive Behavior Interventions, 3*(2), 88–94.

Scriven, M. (1967). The methodology of evaluation. In R. E. Stake (Ed.), *Curriculum evaluation* (American Educational Research Association Monograph Series on Evaluation, No. 1, pp. 39–83). Chicago: Rand McNally.

Scriven, M. (1991). Beyond formative and summative evaluation. In M. W. McLaughlin & D. C. Phillips (Eds.), *Evaluation and education: At quarter century* (pp. 19–64). Ninetieth Yearbook of the National Society for the Study of Education. Chicago: National Society for the Study of Education.

Scriven, M. (1993). Hard-won lessons in program evaluation. *New Directions for Program Evaluation,* No. 58, 1–107. San Francisco: Jossey-Bass.

Singer, G. H. S. (2000). Ecological validity. *Journal of Positive Behavior Interventions, 2*(2), 122–123.

Stufflebeam, D. L., & Shinkfield, A. J. (1985). *Systematic evaluation.* Boston: Kluwer-Nijhoff.

Turnbull, A., & Turnbull R. (2001). *Families, professionals, and exceptionality: Collaboration for empowerment* (4th ed.). Upper Saddle River, NJ: Merrill/Prentice Hall.

# Chapter 9

# Teaching Positive Alternative Behaviors

## CONCEPTS TO UNDERSTAND

*After reading this chapter, you should be able to:*

- List and describe the factors that contribute to skill deficits
- Describe and discuss the methods for selecting positive replacement behaviors
- List and describe the considerations for design of an instructional plan
- Identify and explain the methods for engineering learning environments to enhance student performance outcomes
- Describe methods for formulating goals and objectives
- Identify and describe how to design a plan to teach replacement behaviors

## KEY TERMS

Differential reinforcement

Engineering learning environments

Functional communication training

Instructional goals and objectives

Positive replacement behaviors

Self-management

Skill deficits

A major goal of positive behavior interventions and supports is to identify and teach alternative behaviors that will result in enhanced educational and lifestyle outcomes for students. These lifestyle outcomes might include increased satisfaction with school, improved academic skills, increased social opportunities, and success on the job or in the community. Irrespective of the outcome, the major focus of positive behavior supports (PBS) is to facilitate greater degrees of personal and lifestyle freedoms for the individual. There are several factors to consider in the selection of alternative skills and in the creation of an intervention plan aimed at teaching these new behaviors. This chapter will examine these factors and describe how PBS can facilitate such behavior change. The chapter will also identify how these outcomes can be realized through the use of systematic instruction to foster meaningful behavior change on the part of all students. Finally, the chapter will explore the following topics related to the development of positive alternative behaviors in learners with challenging behavior.

## UNDERSTANDING SKILL DEFICITS EXPERIENCED BY STUDENTS

Students who engage in challenging behavior may often experience skill deficits in one or more areas as a result of a disability or a lack of learning experience. **Skill deficits** often result when students have not been taught the targeted skill, or they have failed to develop mastery of the skill before instruction on that skill was terminated. A simple illustration of this concept is when a student fails to master the requisite skills in a content area such as math, and yet the work proceeds at a faster and more complex level over time. Given that the student has failed to learn the necessary requisite steps, they fall further and further behind as the skill demands continue to accelerate. This often occurs because the student did not fully master a specific skill set before instruction on that skill was terminated and the new material introduced.

Thus a failure to learn a skill can occur because the student did not develop fluency (i.e., high rate of performance with minimal or no errors) or because a lack of time was designated for promoting generalization and maintenance of the skill before terminating instruction. Another plausible explanation is that there was a failure to employ naturally occurring reinforcement from within the learning environment during instruction that would help maintain the rate of behavior and result in durability of the skill for an extended period of time.

### Reasons to Explain Skill Acquisition Failures

- The student was never fluent in the skill before skill instruction was terminated.
- The activity was too challenging, given the developmental level of the student.
- A lack of emphasis was given to promoting maintenance and generalization during instruction.
- The instructor failed to employ naturally occurring reinforcement during instruction.

- The skill was not functional or relevant in the life of the student.
- Inconsistent use of cues and teaching techniques were employed during instruction.

When students experience skill deficits, other forms of behavior fallout occur. One common side effect for many children and youth is frustration. Chronic frustration resulting from a failure to achieve desired learning outcomes often leads to problematic behavior such as noncompliance, interpersonal problems with teachers and peers, and school refusal behavior. These behaviors begin to develop over time and are often directly related to performance problems in school stemming from specific skill deficits.

Communication skill deficits are also a common cause of challenging behavior among children and youth with disabilities (Durand, 1990; Weatherby & Prizant, 2000). This is more commonly the case with students who experience moderate and severe disabilities and who also may have limited communication abilities such as in the case of children and youth with autism, mental retardation, and other forms of developmental disabilities. Communication skill deficits often result in behaviors that are neither socially acceptable nor functional in the long run to obtain their needs. Yet these behaviors may have been efficient for the individual, given an absence of socially appropriate responses in their behavior repertoire from which to select. These problematic behaviors persist for several reasons, which may include one or more of the following:

- A failure by educational or related professionals to understand and modify the triggers or antecedents associated with the problem behavior
- An inability on the part of the student to select alternative responses due to a limited skill repertoire
- Behaviors continue to be reinforced unknowingly by persons in their environments and therefore persist and are frequently used by the learner

### Consider This

Remember as a teacher that when learners fail to perform a desired behavior, it is your responsibility to first examine whether or not you are using teaching strategies that are sufficient for the individual child.

- What are some methods that you as a teacher can use to minimize failure on the part of your students?

In light of these factors, it is important in such cases to identify **positive replacement behaviors** that can serve as alternative responses for many reasons. These reasons include

- Positive replacement behaviors promote the best overall interests of the student.
- The presence of these skills afford the student increased lifestyle options.

- Replacement behaviors reduce the likelihood that challenging behaviors will occur.
- The development of functional replacement behaviors can lead to a greater sense of independence and self-determination on the part of the student.

Bambara and Knoster (1998) asserted that skill instruction aimed at replacing challenging forms of behavior can be grouped into the following categories: (a) teaching replacement skills and behaviors, (b) teaching general skills, and (c) teaching coping strategies. Replacement skills refer to socially acceptable behaviors that serve the same function as the target behavior of concern yet in a positive form. Therefore, emphasis is given to teaching alternative forms of the behavior that are also socially acceptable. When teaching replacement skills, the focus of an intervention is directed toward changing the form of the behavior to that of a more socially acceptable behavior and maintaining the function, thus allowing the students to obtain their needs but in a socially acceptable manner.

An example of this would be anger associated with frustration. Everyone experiences anger related to frustration when they fail to perform a particular task in a desirable manner. If you were to consider anger placed on a continuum from basic to refined forms of responding, then one can see how replacement behaviors can serve the same function but look different.

Examine Figure 9–1 and reflect on how many ways one can express their anger associated with frustration. At the basic end of the continuum, one could choose some form of aggression, whereas at the refined end of the continuum, a person could express their anger in a calm and rational manner by communicating their feelings through self-talk, "That really makes me angry," or to another, "You know I got so frustrated by that problem that it made me so incredibly angry that I just could not come up with the answer." The function of the behavior is the same across the range of options, and only the form varies.

One aspect to consider when examining Figure 9–1 is the range of behavior options available; however, the presence of skill deficits in the areas of social coping skills may not exist in a student's behavior repertoire. As evident from this example, the importance of teaching replacement behaviors to broaden the behavior options for the individual learner is most important.

**FIGURE 9–1**
*Behavior Continuum for Expressing Anger*

1. Aggression toward self, others, or property destruction and use of profanity, screaming, crying, and withdrawal
2. Attempts at communicating one's feelings and resolution
3. Calm and rational communication concerning one's anger with self or others

Bambara and Knoster (1998) also pointed out that general skills can be defined as broader based skills that alleviate the need for problem behaviors to occur. Therefore, the emphasis in intervention is devoted to developing new skills, thus providing the student with expanded behavior options to select from and hopefully resulting in the reduction of problem behavior. Consider the previous example highlighted in Figure 9–1. The final option recommended in the review by Bambara and Knoster included teaching coping skills to students to assist them in redirecting their behavior. Later in the chapter we will discuss the use of self-management skills as one form of intervention for behavior self-regulation and as an intervention tool to facilitate the development of coping skills.

When attempting to determine your course of action as a teacher, it is important to consider research-based practices that have been documented in the literature to be effective in the development of acceptable and alternative forms of behavior. The choice of *how* to intervene would obviously be determined by evaluating the specific needs of the student. To aid in understanding some of the intervention options that are available and that are recognized as best and effective practice, examine the following methods identified from the literature as options to select from in this area.

Carr and colleagues (1999) conducted a research synthesis of PBS for persons with developmental disabilities that identified two major categories of PBS interventions from the literature. These categories of intervention approaches included (a) stimulus-based interventions, such as antecedent-management and environmental modifications, and (b) reinforcement-based interventions that were directed toward replacing behavior skill deficits.

Antecedent-based strategies (i.e., stimulus-based interventions) have been previously described at length in an earlier chapter. For the purposes of this chapter, reinforcement-based interventions designed to teach replacement behaviors will be highlighted.

## METHODS FOR SELECTING REPLACEMENT BEHAVIORS

Carr and colleagues (1999) described three prominent methods identified within the literature that have been successfully used to teach replacement behaviors to learners with challenging behaviors. These include

- Functional communication training
- Self-management
- Differential reinforcement of alternative behavior (DRA)

**Functional communication training** (FCT) was first described by Carr and Durand (1985) and involves teaching a functionally equivalent communication behavior to a student with challenging behavior. The functionally equivalent communicative response is designed to serve the same function yet replace the challenging form of behavior. As indicated by Durand (1990), FCT consists of two primary components. These include (a) teaching learners an alternative communicative response that serves the same function as the problem behavior and (b) making the problem behavior nonfunctional for the individual. Obviously, the first component of FCT is directed toward the development of new skills, and the second component is directed toward teaching the student that the problem behavior no longer controls the environment and is no longer efficient in obtaining their needs. An example of how to use FCT in teaching a replacement skill would include teaching a child to communicate the need for a break by using a sign or by raising their hand and asking the teacher for a short break, depending on the communicative abilities of the learner, rather than having a tantrum. The use of FCT to communicate these needs eventually reduces problem behavior (aggression) as a means of obtaining teacher attention. The child's needs are now met in an efficient and socially acceptable manner using functional communication. Vignette 9.1 provides another example of how FCT can be used to teach replacement behaviors.

## Vignette 9.1

### Eliminating Challenging Forms of Behavior

Samantha, an 8-year-old child with autism, will frequently engage in extended periods of screaming as a way of escaping the demands associated with instruction. Essentially, over the course of time, this has become her way of regulating the environment around her, given that she has limited communication abilities. She becomes increasingly agitated as her teacher attempts to provide her with instructions for completing a task. She screams very loudly and continues to persist. Her teacher continues to offer instructions as a means of redirecting Samantha and not reinforcing her screaming by allowing her to use it as a means to escape instruction. Her teacher initiated a functional communication training program to teach Samantha how to communicate when she needs assistance and or when she is in need of a break from instruction. The program consists of teaching Samantha to approximate simple verbalizations paired with picture symbols, such as "I need help," or "I need a break, please." The object of functional communication training (FCT) in this example is to teach Samantha that when she attempts to use positive alternative behaviors to meet her needs, persons in her immediate environments will respond accordingly, and she will obtain her needs and be reinforced for engaging in the replacement behavior.

### Reflective Moment

What are some examples of how you could use functional communication training for learners who engage in challenging forms of behavior?

A second type of reinforcement-based intervention strategy identified by Carr et al. (1999) is **self-management**. Self-management is a cognitive–behavior intervention method designed for teaching learners to self-direct their behavior (Kanfer, 1975; Kanfer & Karoly, 1972; Mahoney, 1974; Meichenbaum, 1974). Self-management is composed of three major types of interventions that include self-monitoring, self-instruction, and self-reinforcement. Self-management became popular in the 1970s and has been widely documented in the literature in terms of its efficacy and widespread applications with children and youth with emotional and behavior disorders (DiGangi & Maag, 1992; Dunlap et al., 1995; Miller, Miller, Wheeler, & Selinger, 1989), learning disabilities (Webber, Scheuermann, McCall, & Coleman, 1993), and also with persons with mental retardation (Agran, 1997; Wheeler, Bates, Marshall, & Miller, 1988). Self-management promotes the central involvement of the individual in the selection of goals, monitoring of behavior, and implementation of the intervention procedures (Sulzer-Azaroff & Mayer, 1991).

One of the most popular forms of self-management intervention that has been used extensively within school settings has been self-monitoring. Self-monitoring is directed toward teaching students to monitor their behavior, noting the occurrence or nonoccurrence of the behavior through self-recording. This is often done using some form of cue as provided by either a wristwatch or an audiotape set at varying intervals and designed to deliver an auditory prompt such as a beeping sound or bell (Dunlap, Dunlap, Koegal, & Koegal, 1991). Upon hearing the auditory cue, the student self-records the occurrence or nonoccurrence of a specific target behavior with a plus (+) or minus (−) on a data sheet. Another example of self-monitoring could include monitoring the completion of class assignments as reflected on a to-do list (Figure 9–2) and recording the occurrence or nonoccurrence of the behavior on a checklist. In this example, the checklist becomes the cue, and completion of a task marks the point at which the learner would then self-record, thus placing a check next to the completed task listed on the checklist.

Dunlap et al. (1991) have outlined the essential steps in developing and using a self-monitoring program in the classroom. These include the following:

1. Operationally define the target behavior. This requires the teacher to operationally define the target behavior in specific terms that the child can understand, such as "having class materials out and ready," "remaining seated while in class," or "raising hand for teacher assistance."

**FIGURE 9–2**
*To-Do List of Assignments*

| | |
|---|---|
| **Name:** Trevor **Date:** 10/2/03 | |
| 1. Math Problems—Nos. 10–25, pages 45–47 | ☑ |
| 2. Language Arts—2-page essay on your favorite food | ☑ |
| 3. Social Studies—Color and label the map of Europe | ☑ |
| 4. Science—Complete short-answer questions at the end of Chapter 3 | ☐ |
| 5. Chorus—Bring $10.00 for the chorus T-shirt tomorrow (Friday, 10/3/03) | ☐ |

2. Identify functional reinforcers. The teacher then needs to identify reinforcers that are functionally relevant to the child and setting. These can be activities or other tangibles that are appropriate within the setting. Identifying preferred reinforcers can be accomplished through observation of the child, by asking their parents, and even by allowing the child choice-making opportunities. Reinforcers could include free time, access to the library or computer, fruit snacks, or assisting the teacher.

3. Design the self-monitoring method or device to be used. As the authors recommend, these devices should be nonintrusive and portable. They recommend small notebooks or checklists and wrist counters as examples. Attention should be given to what is functional (whether or not it gets the job done) and what is developmentally appropriate, given the child's age and abilities (e.g., using picture symbols and single functional vocabulary words for a child with moderate mental retardation who has difficulty reading).

4. Teach the child how to use the device. The teacher should provide the learner with direct instruction in how to use the self-monitoring device. The teacher should model how to use the device for the child and then provide them with opportunities to rehearse or practice the skill, with the teacher providing instructional feedback.

5. Fade the use of the self-monitoring device. It is important to fade the self-monitoring device as a method for increasing independence. The authors recommend that this be accomplished in two ways. First, thin the schedule of reinforcement, thus gradually increasing the number of responses required before the child obtains the preferred reinforcer. The second method is to reduce or fade the use of cues provided by the self-monitoring device. Examples of this could include fading the number of embedded instructions on the checklist or reducing access to the self-monitoring device.

In a study conducted by Wheeler et al. (1988) on a self-monitoring checklist, a young man with mental retardation was instructed in the use of a self-monitoring checklist while in a supported employment setting. The checklist contained the target behaviors that were being addressed through the self-monitoring intervention, and as performance criteria were attained, each behavior would then be systematically removed from the checklist, ultimately fading each subsequent behavior until a criterion had been reached on each target behavior, thus eliminating the need for the checklist.

Self-instruction (Meichenbaum and Goodwin, 1971) is another form of self-management and involves teaching a learner a set of instructional steps related to (social, academic, vocational, community living) tasks. An early reference to self-instruction and behavior regulation was offered by Luria (1961) in his book entitled *The Role of Speech in the Regulation of Normal and Abnormal Behaviour,* whereby he explained how in typical child development, a child is first exposed to verbal cues by adults as a means of regulating their behavior. As children age, they then begin to use overt verbalizations as a way to self-regulate their behavior. As they continue to grow and develop, these processes become internalized and result in covert verbalizations as a means for self-directing their behavior. Imagine how you apply this process in your own life related to such behaviors as studying. As a child develops, parents provide support for their children to encourage studying behavior, such as organizing assignments, following a schedule, and allotting time for this important activity through verbal cues paired with some modeling. As children begin to learn these processes, they practice them by using overt self-verbalizations to serve as cues and reinforcement until these patterns become learned and more internalized, eventually eliminating the need for external verbal directives from their parents.

With self-instruction, students are taught a set of statements related to the task that they recite to themselves when in certain situations (Zirpoli & Melloy, 2001). This process is initiated first through models provided by the teacher; the learner then practices the self-instruction sequence through overt verbalization. As acquisition occurs, the learner gradually replaces the overt verbalization with "quiet speech," followed by "whispers," until eventually these become covert speech.

The final form of self-management intervention is self-reinforcement. Self-reinforcement emerges as a method for teaching students to self-administer their preferred reinforcement on performance of a desired behavior. Many examples of how this process works can be found in our daily lives, such as treating ourselves to a cold drink after mowing the yard, playing a game after finishing work, or choosing a favorite television show after completing homework. Within educational settings, self-reinforcement could involve any number of things, including self-administering a token reinforcer for completion of a task or using a system of self-checks for each step of the task that has been completed. This procedure can be most effective within educational settings with children and youth when trying to develop a student's ability to sustain and tolerate performance of a task that he may not be fond of.

Goal-setting strategies, skills instruction, and the opportunity for a student to select a preferred reinforcer are powerful tools for teaching alternative behaviors and warrant the use of self-reinforcement in certain instances. Some key points to consider when using self-reinforcement in the classroom are as follows:

- Involve the student in goal-setting activities related to performance of the target behavior and selection of preferred reinforcers.
- Ensure that the student is fluent in performing the procedure (i.e., self-monitoring and self-reinforcment).
- Evaluate progress and fade the intervention over time as the student meets the preestablished goals.

In summary, self-management interventions are designed to promote the acquisition of replacement behaviors through engaging the student in the behavior change process and by teaching a learning process that can promote self-sufficiency and consistency. Through the successful use of self-management procedures, individual students can be taught a method that will result in increased task engagement, personal independence and less reliance on teacher delivered instructional cues and reinforcers.

**Consider This**

Self-management interventions can be effective in promoting academic task engagement and greater degrees of independence in students, including the development of self-determination skills. List and describe some applications of these procedures with various academic tasks.

The final consequence-based intervention identified by Carr et al. (1999) was **differential reinforcement** of alternative behavior (DRA). DRA is a procedure designed to increase the frequency of a desirable behavior and to reduce challenging behavior through the delivery of reinforcement for positive alternative behavior (Miltenberger, 2001). The problem behavior is thereby placed on extinction and is no longer reinforced when using a DRA procedure resulting in a decrease of the future probability of the problem behavior. Differential reinforcement will be discussed in greater detail in Chapter 10.

## Guidelines for Selecting Positive Replacement Behaviors

When selecting positive replacement behaviors, it is important to take into consideration the function of the challenging behavior that you are seeking to replace. As discussed in an earlier chapter, challenging behavior occurs for a reason and is linked to skill deficits. Once the function of these behaviors has been determined, a replacement behavior can be better identified for instruction. Replacement behaviors serve as functional equivalent responses in that the replacement behavior should serve the same function (be functionally equivalent) as that of the target behavior. Our intervention goal in positive behavior supports centers around teaching the student an alternative form of the behavior (what it looks like and the outcomes it results in), rather than changing the function for the learner. Reichle et al. (1996) described functional equivalent responses as being socially acceptable behaviors serving the same function as that of the problem behavior.

Consider when a child pulls his hair as a means of obtaining attention from his teacher. Teaching that same child to raise his hand for teacher assistance or to communicate a need for teacher assistance in some other alternative form of communication would better meet the child's needs and in turn be more socially acceptable. One key point about teaching functionally equivalent responses that should be noted is that the replacement behavior has to be efficient in meeting the learner's needs. That is, it needs to be as effective and efficient to use for the child as was the challenging form of the behavior. Failure to meet the learner's needs in an efficient manner results in the learner being less likely to rely on the replacement behavior and more apt to revert to the challenging behavior. This occurs because the challenging behavior has been more efficient over time for the child in obtaining their needs.

A central component to this phase of the intervention process is teaching the new skill or behavior to the student. This may be a timely process, and direct instruction should be used to encourage acquisition of the new skill. Scott and Nelson (1999) provided three recommendations for facilitating the development of positive replacement behaviors. These include

1. Select a functionally equivalent replacement behavior (a behavior that serves the same function).
2. Use direct instruction in teaching the behavior to the student.
3. Facilitate access to the same functional outcome for the student, thus making the replacement behavior efficient for meeting the learner's needs.

In summary, it is important to remember that when selecting positive replacement behaviors, they should

- Ideally serve the same function as the target behavior
- Facilitate the desired outcome for the learner within a positive context
- Be efficient in meeting the needs of the student
- Be systematically taught to the learner using direct instruction methods

Some examples of positive replacement behaviors are shown in Figure 9–3.

**FIGURE 9–3**
*Examples of Positive Replacement Behaviors*

**Target Behavior:** Getting out of seat and avoiding work
**Function:** Escape
**Replacement Behavior:** Raising hand for teacher assistance and allowing a short break on completion of the task
**Target Behavior:** Verbally refuses to complete the task, thus resulting in being sent out of class
**Function:** Escape from completing the task
**Replacement Behavior:** Direct instruction on the requisite skills per content area and teaching self-management skills aimed at increasing task engagement; access to free time on completion of assigned work
**Target Behavior:** Taking toys or materials away from peers
**Function:** Social attention from peers
**Replacement Behavior:** Teaching appropriate requesting behavior and contingent access to preferred toys when playing with peers
**Target Behavior:** Stereotypical rocking while at seat and task disengagement
**Function:** Sensory feedback
**Replacement Behavior:** Contingent access to music on completion of short tasks, gradually increasing task engagement time

**Consider This**

Remember when selecting replacement behaviors, they should serve the same function as the problem behavior. Yet, they should be in a socially acceptable form, and consideration should be given to the efficiency of replacement behaviors in addressing the needs of the individual.

## DESIGNING AN INTERVENTION PLAN

The next step in the process is designing an instructional plan that will systematically address all relevant factors related to promoting the successful acquisition of positive replacement behaviors on the part of the student. Within the intervention plan are several components that must be taken into consideration.

Albin, Lucyshyn, Horner, and Flannery (1996) described a concept referred to as contextual fit when developing PBS plans or, in this case, the intervention plan. Their model consists of three major classes of variables that should be considered by professionals while in the formative stages of developing a behavior support plan or intervention plan. These are (a) characteristics of the individual for whom the plan is being designed, (b) variables related to the people responsible for implementing the plan, and (c) features of the environments in which the plan will be implemented. These same considerations also apply when considering the development of an intervention plan to teach positive replacement behaviors. Specific items to consider when constructing an instructional plan aimed at teaching replacement behaviors are the following:

1. *What are the desired learning outcomes that you hope to achieve?*

   Identify the goals that you hope to achieve with the intervention. By first identifying the outcome measures that you seek to attain as a result of the intervention, it can provide a social validity check of whether the goals are relevant and significant to the student. It also provides clarity as you formulate the components of an intervention plan.

2. *What specific skills does the student currently have that can be expanded in teaching the new behavior?*

   Identify the student's strengths and current skills and abilities that could assist in acquiring the new behavior. Also, the individual's learning style and primary input mode (how they process information during instruction) are relevant to the design and ultimate success of the program and therefore should be considered.

3. *Are the replacement behaviors socially valid and functional for the student's needs? Do they serve the same function?*

   Be sure to consider whether or not your selected behaviors are socially valid, given the student's needs, and that they serve to provide the student with an expanded repertoire of behavior options.

4. *How do parents and family members feel about the intervention? What type of input have they had in the planning process? Will there be a home and school component for teaching replacement behaviors across both environments?*

Seek family partnerships in the development of the intervention so that family and school environments are in harmony in terms of intervention goals and in carrying out the procedures. Also, be conscious of the degree of family involvement in carrying out procedures based on where individual families are developmentally. The interests and ability levels of family members in carrying out procedures should be considered.

5. *Who are the professionals who will be implementing the intervention, and what level of expertise to do they have?*

Identify who will be delivering the intervention (i.e., teachers or teaching assistants or other educational and related services professionals). Have they had experience in the area of PBS? Will they need training and support in the implementation and delivery of the intervention? Is there support among professionals for implementing the procedure?

6. *Is additional training needed to equip the staff with skills to implement the instructional program?*

Determine the extent of training required and how training will be provided. Will a skilled professional need to model how to implement the intervention with the learner? Design feedback loops so that professionals carrying out the intervention will have opportunities to share feedback and address any concerns.

7. *What are the specific contexts in which instruction on replacement behaviors will occur?*

Will the intervention be carried out exclusively at school or across multiple environments such as school, home, and the community?

8. *Identify the environmental strengths and barriers that will facilitate and or impede instruction.*

Are there any environmental variables that serve to support the delivery of the intervention, and consequently, what are the environmental limitations that could hinder the intervention from being successfully carried out? Is the student-to-teacher ratio manageable, or will teaching assistants be required to assist in the delivery of instruction? Is the classroom organized environmentally to facilitate ease in the delivery of the intervention?

9. *What are the specific formal and informal supports available to the learner within home, school, classroom, and community environments that will facilitate successful acquisition and generalization of the replacement behaviors?*

Identify existing supports (both formal and informal) that are currently available to the learner in home, school, classroom, and community environments that will assist the learner in the acquisition and generalization replacement behaviors. Also, identify the significant others in the life of the individual that will play an instrumental role in the development of replacement skills.

**10.** *Identify the student's typical daily classroom routine and plan how instruction can be best included within natural contexts.*

Identify whether or not the learner has a current schedule within the classroom. If so, what form does the schedule take (object, picture, written)? Is the schedule individualized to the needs of the learner, or is the schedule for general classroom use? Identify the time periods that coincide with activities that would be conducive for teaching the replacement behavior.

**11.** *Will the intervention plan receive support from all team members and the administration?*

Does the intervention plan have the unanimous support of all parties who are directly or indirectly involved? This includes teacher, family, related school personnel, and administrators. If not, what level of communication needs to occur to facilitate this level of commitment?

## ENGINEERING LEARNING ENVIRONMENTS

The concept of **engineering learning environments** has been synonymous with PBS since the inception of this methodology. The existing research literature has extended our knowledge base concerning the importance of school, home, and community environments in the design and delivery of PBS (Sailor, 1996). Some illustrations of this philosophy include an emphasis on enriching the lifestyles of individuals, promoting opportunities for choice, and social inclusion within educational and community settings.

Systems change within schools and classroom settings continues to be a slow and evolving process with regard to the implementation of PBS. Many reasons could explain this reluctance to change how schools view and respond to challenging behavior, especially when one considers the task faced by schools in meeting the diverse educational needs of all students. Another factor critical to change within educational environments is staff development. Too frequently, this has involved in-service training for teachers and related school personnel that involves very little in terms of content connected to school reform or change. Follow-up evaluations and debriefings are rarely conducted following this form of training, resulting in little or no lasting impact. Guskey (2000) has noted that traditional in-service training seminars have failed to understand what motivates teachers and is unlikely to produce meaningful change within school settings. With the advent of PBS, states have recently initiated programs designed to tie the use of PBS to schoolwide improvement strategies (Utley & Sailor, 2002). These initiatives have encouraged school systems to self-examine and focus their energies on understanding how learning and educational environments can positively impact student behavior and learning from both an individual and group perspective. Most people would agree that all learning environments should be designed to be safe, inviting, and supportive for the learners who use them.

The emergence of PBS as part of the 1997 reauthorization of the IDEA has advanced the concept of how to make learning environments more conducive to promoting positive behavior and learning outcomes through the process of engineering and redesign of these learning environments. The concept of engineering learning environments to promote successful performance outcomes can take on a broad (schoolwide) perspective or a more focused (individual classroom) perspective, depending on the goal of the intervention and whether or not it is aimed at schoolwide levels or focused on a specific individual.

PBS within schoolwide environments has broadened our understanding of how to address problem behavior before it begins, in many cases through activities that promote awareness and prevention. Within PBS are three major strata in terms of schoolwide behavior supports. Sugai et al. (2000) referred to these strata as (a) primary prevention (designed for the largest percentage of students, 80% to 90%, who do not experience serious problem behavior), (b) secondary prevention (directed toward those students, approximately 5% to 15%, who are at risk for problem behaviors) and (c) tertiary prevention (targeted for those students, approximately 1% to 7%, with chronic and intense levels of problem behavior).

The most noticeable areas of school environments that embrace a philosophy of positive behavior interventions and supports are school culture and climate. Schools with effective cultures and climates have the best interests of every child as their primary goal, an emphasis is placed on prevention of problem behavior, and school-based teams are in place to promote positive and proactive interventions that are designed to promote enhanced learning and quality-of-life outcomes for *all* children. These environments also emphasize team-based approaches to problem solving, have active and committed administrations, and direct their efforts on multisystems perspectives that include the district, schoolwide, nonclassroom, classroom, learner, family, and community environments (Sugai et al., 2000).

As Sugai et al. (2000) have indicated, effective learning environments are characterized by the following qualities:

- Behavior expectations are defined and shared among administrators, teachers, families, and students.
- Expectations are published and visually apparent within all areas of the school. Students are aware and informed of the expectations. Subsequently, these expectations are taught to students and reinforced throughout the child's day. The skills are modeled and reinforced time and again by teachers and school personnel on a daily basis.
- Appropriate behaviors exhibited by students are frequently acknowledged and celebrated within these environments by teachers within classrooms and at schoolwide assemblies and functions.

Sugai and colleagues (2000) have also noted that schools that are successful in promoting this type of learning environment typically reflect a pattern of interactions between adults and students that uses four times more positive feedback than negative. This pattern of interaction within schools among teachers and students characterizes the adage that a child will rise or fall to the level of expectation before them and the amount of support provided in meeting that expectation. This type of environment serves as a model for school improvement.

Some examples that can be tried when designing optimal learning environments include a change in seating, lighting, modulating noise in the classroom, and changes in classrooms or teachers to facilitate a better goodness of fit between the student and instructor. More specific modifications within the environment should be considered when attempting to promote acquisition and maintenance of replacement behaviors among learners.

Jolivette, Scott, and Nelson (2000) recommended two major strategies to employ relative to environmental design to promote the successful acquisition of replacement behaviors. These strategies are to manipulate the environment to increase the probability of success and to minimize the likelihood of failure. This is best accomplished by designing the learning environment to reinforce the replacement behavior. This can be accomplished through the careful design of settings, individuals, and tasks. Minimizing the probability of failure is best accomplished by removing barriers that would prevent the replacement behavior from occurring within the appropriate context. Jolivette et al. termed this "removing the predictors of failure." Other types of barriers sometimes exist and could include the level of distractibility within the classroom, the density (number of children within the class), and social interactions with specific students or staff. Any number of these factors could serve as potential barriers to the performance of replacement behaviors, ultimately resulting in a missed opportunity for reinforcement of the replacement skill (Jolivette et al., 2000).

One specific strategy directed at engineering supportive learning environments includes the use of individualized activity schedules. Activity schedules provide students with enhanced structure and also a means by which the daily routine of activities can be clearly and consistently communicated to the student. Activity schedules serve to reinforce the acquisition of new behaviors.

Activity schedules have been widely used with children and youth with autism as a means of communicating instructional demands, showing the sequence of activities, promoting increased task clarity, and communicating performance expectations. They have also been used as a tool to aid in the prevention and reduction of challenging behavior in children with autism (Massey & Wheeler, 2000).

Massey and Wheeler's (2000) investigation used a photo activity schedule with a young child (age 4) with autism in an inclusive preschool classroom as a method for increasing task engagement and minimizing the occurrence of challenging behavior. The primary behavior of concern was the child's difficulty with unplanned transitions between activities, which resulted in periods of crying and noncompliance. Following a period of instruction in the use of a photo activity schedule that consisted of photographs of activities arranged in sequential order on a schedule, the young child demonstrated acquisition and fluency in his use of the activity schedule. This was apparent when examining the decrease in teacher-delivered prompts across work, leisure, and lunch settings. During the work condition, the child needed a total of 265 prompts, which included 170 verbal prompts, 25 gestural prompts, and 70 physical (hand-over-hand) prompts. These figures were noticeably less during the leisure condition, where a total of only 190 prompts were needed. This number included 118 verbal prompts, 69 gestural prompts, and 3 physical prompts. The number of prompts used in the lunch condition consisted of 0 verbal prompts, 9 gestural prompts, and 23 physical prompts. This study demonstrates the child's ability to generalize the use of the schedule across settings as reflected by the systematic reduction in teacher prompts. The child also demonstrated increased levels of task engagement across three distinct conditions, which included work (performing developmentally appropriate class work and activities), leisure (unstructured play), and lunch.

Activity schedules have also been successful in preventing the occurrences of challenging behavior, facilitating successful transitions between activities, and fostering increased levels of independence in learners (Mesibov, Browder, & Kirkland, 2002). The use of individualized activity schedules has long been advocated by Division TEACCH, a comprehensive diagnostic and treatment program for individuals with autism, housed at the Department of Psychiatry of the Medical School at the University of North Carolina at Chapel Hill. Mesibov and colleagues (2002) pointed out that activity schedules serve multiple needs such as assisting students during transitions, fostering independent performance of tasks and activities by learners, teaching students to follow a prescribed schedule within school and home environments, and structuring leisure time. Schedules also promote independence when designed around the learning strengths of an individual.

Activity schedules should also be matched to the literacy level of individual learners (Mesibov et al., 2002). The model recommended by Division TEACCH includes the following hierarchy of forms: (a) objects—actual objects that are used within activities, such as a toothbrush, a bar of soap, or toilet paper; (b) symbolic miniature objects that represent the activity, such as magnets; (c) photographs of the activity; (d) line drawings of an activity or an object used in an activity; (e) sight words, such as *Restroom, Exit,* and *Entrance;* and (f) short phrases pertinent to an activity (Mesibov et al., 2002).

Of course, learners will need to receive individualized instruction in the use of an activity schedule in terms of understanding the symbolic representations of the various objects, pictures or symbols, and written phrases included on the schedule. Other considerations include determining the complexity of a student's schedule, given age and developmental levels. Division TEACCH has coupled the use of other types of environmental supports, such as structured work systems, to foster task initiation and engagement on the part of children and youth with autism.

In summary, it is important to be sensitive to the idea of structure within the learning environment specific to the behavior support needs of individual learners. The need for engineered learning environments and environmental supports, such as the presence of a routine within a classroom and an individualized activity schedule, cannot be overstated. These serve as mechanisms for ensuring meaningful learning outcomes, preventing challenging behaviors, and promoting a stimulating and supportive environment for every student to learn and grow in.

## FORMULATING GOALS AND OBJECTIVES

After selecting a replacement behavior or new skill to be taught, the teacher must develop a set of goals and objectives before proceeding with instruction. Goal statements are simply broad encompassing statements that identify the skill area or behavior and whether the goal will be to increase, decrease, or maintain the identified skill or behavior. Aside from serving as statements of directionality, they also define the level of performance to be attained. Frequently, goals are confused with instructional objectives, yet objectives are substeps or subgoals that contribute to the broader goal. One important component of developing goals is to use goal-setting strategies. Goal setting is an important step when developing an instructional program because goals define the instructional outcome we are trying to obtain.

Martin and Pear (1999) identified some basic elements of goal-setting strategies to consider in promoting the attainment of goals. Among their suggestions were to (a) set realistic and attainable goals; (b) establish clear consequences for meeting or not meeting the goal; (c) develop goals that are of short, intermediate, and long-term duration; (d) establish performance deadlines for meeting the desired goal; (e) provide team-based support to facilitate attainment of goals on the part of the student; (f) evaluate progress toward goals through a system of monitoring; and (g) provide encouragement and positive reinforcement to the student throughout the process (Martin & Pear, 1999). If at all possible, it is advisable to encourage student participation in establishing goals. This enables the student to be engaged in the behavior change process, and thereby the student is more likely to attain the goal. Some guidelines to consider when formulating instructional goals are as follows:

- Consider why the behavior should be taught. Provide a clear and concise rationale as to the importance of the goal in terms of the overall development of the student.
- Is the skill a logical replacement behavior? Will the skill serve as an efficient means by which the student can meet their needs?
- Will the replacement behavior provide the student with needed skills that are consistent with demands found in his or her current and future environments?

- Must prerequisite skills first be taught to ensure overall success?
- Can the goal be accomplished, given the competencies of the teaching staff, or will additional training be required of the teachers?
- Is the goal socially valid, given the needs of the student, and will such a goal positively impact the quality of life of the child?

These considerations are meant to serve as guideposts to enable teachers to carefully plan and consider the instructional goals they develop for students. These considerations stress the importance of goals related to the learning and behavior needs of the individual child, the capacity of educational environments to nurture and foster acquisition of these goals, and the impact of the instructional goals that we as teachers develop in the lives of children and their families.

### Consider This

Goals are broad and encompassing statements of desired learning outcomes.

- How do objectives relate to goal statements?

Goals are dependent on the development of objectives or substeps that approximate components of a goal. Figure 9–4 provides an illustration of how objectives formulate a stepwise development of these subskills that are directly linked to the broader goal. Also relevant to understanding the

**FIGURE 9–4**
*Elements of Effective Instruction*

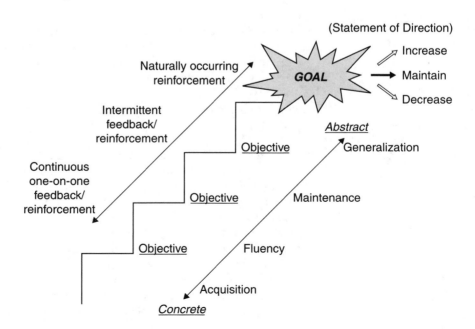

relationship of goals to instructional objectives are the four stages of learning. These are (a) skill acquisition, (b) fluency, (c) maintenance, and (d) generalization. Each of these stages serve as a building block for subsequent stages in the learning process.

Acquisition is the introductory phase associated with the initial learning process. It is concerned with the development of new skills, and accuracy of performance generally improves during this phase because students are presented with multiple opportunities for performing the desired skill or behavior. The goal of acquisition is to embed the basic steps of performing a new skill in the repertoire of the student and subsequently move to a more refined performance of the skill over time. Reinforcement is generally on a one-to-one ratio during this phase and is directed at reinforcing successive approximations of correct performance of the target skill.

The second stage of learning, fluency, is directed toward increasing the learner's accuracy of skill performance as well as speed or rate of performance. It is at this stage of the learning process that reinforcement becomes intermittent, with the intention that performance associated with the task and performance outcomes will replace externally administered reinforcement. However, verbal praise and corrective feedback are important to ensure performance accuracy and the rate associated with performing the target skill.

The maintenance stage that follows is devoted to facilitating use of the newly learned skill over time in relevant learning contexts. This phase of the process is aimed at promoting durable and lasting behavior change or learning that will stand the test of time and ultimately be retained in the student's repertoire.

The final stage of learning is generalization. This stage is concerned with promoting the transfer of skills to untrained settings and situations such as various classrooms or learning environments with different teachers and materials. Generalization is a critical and often-overlooked portion of the teaching and learning process. If students are taught a particular skill or behavior that cannot transfer beyond the specific setting or conditions that were used to teach that skill, it serves no lasting purpose in the life of the students. This can often occur when teachers teach the skill from a tight and narrow focus. It is important to introduce students to sufficient exemplars, such as the range of stimulus and response variations when learning a new skill. An example to consider would be the following. Consider the stimulus and response variations that exist in terms of teaching a child to put on shoes. There are shoes that lace up and tie, shoes with zippers, and shoes with hook-and-loop straps. The subtleties of these stimulus-and-response variations should be taught to the child to promote generalization in learning how to independently put on shoes.

Mager (1997) asserted that objectives are useful for providing both measurable instructional results and also a means by which to realize instructional efficiency. Typically when developing objectives, we begin with the most concrete of skills and move to the more complex or abstract as acquisition and fluency in the skills occur. In Figure 9–4, notice that the first objective in the sequence is also the most concrete step in the sequence of skills that comprise the goal. It is interesting to note that as students proceed through all the objectives, they reach a point in the learning process whereby they have the ability to generalize across variations of the task. A simple example might be teaching a child to use scissors to cut paper.

**Goal:** To Increase Fine Motor Skills

(Several activities could be used with a young child; however, for this example, we will use cutting paper with scissors.)

In terms of objectives, we will list them in descending order to be consistent with the information in Figure 9–4.

**Objective:** Cutting out shapes (Abstract)
(square, circle, triangle)

**Objective:** Cutting curved lines

**Objective:** Cutting angled lines

**Objective:** Cutting straight lines

**Objective:** Holding the paper and using the scissors to cut (Concrete)

If you examine the list of objectives relative to the goal statement, it is evident that the targeted skill (i.e., using scissors to cut lines) moves from the very basic, or concrete (holding scissors and paper, cutting straight lines), to the abstract (cutting curved lines and shapes) as the objectives ascend. We also can see that as the children learn and acquire the basic elements of the task and begin to generalize and refine their skills, they are then able to move to more complex levels of performance, thus mastering the task and its variations.

When developing instructional objectives, note that objectives should contain three important criteria. They should specify the *conditions* that surround the performance, state the *performance* or behavior in measurable and observable terms, and indicate the performance *criteria*. When writing behavior objectives, it is important that the objective be clearly stated, be succinct, and reflect observable and measurable behaviors. Some examples of behavior objectives are as follows:

**Objective**

Jennifer, when confused by math problems that she does not understand, will stop, raise her hand, wait, and ask for teacher assistance 100% of the time.

**Objective**

Sam, when given a toothbrush, toothpaste, and the instructional cue to brush his teeth, will initiate and complete each step of the task analysis 90% of the time for five consecutive trials.

**Objective**

Louis, when needing teacher attention during vocational/technical education class, will say, "Please excuse me, I need your help," rather than interrupting, for 10 consecutive trials.

**Objective**

Jacob, when asked by his teacher or peer during cooperative play, "Please share your toy with me," will share his toy without prompts from his teacher for five consecutive sessions.

**Objective**

When given a written assignment by the teacher, Susan will outline the lesson using the previously learned skill strategy designed for outlining 100% of the time, with performance feedback and praise being provided by the teacher.

Examine each of these objectives and review them to determine if the three components (conditions, performance, and criteria) are reflected. Identify these elements within each of the example objectives. Critique these examples and offer your input on how they might be modified or improved.

## Key Points to Consider When Developing Objectives

When developing behavioral objectives, be sure to include

- *Conditions:* What are the conditions (equipment, materials, aids) that the student will be allowed to use during the performance of the behavior?
- *Performance:* What is the measurable and observable behavior that the learner will be asked to perform?
- *Criterion:* The criterion measure should communicate to the student how well they have performed the skill against a performance standard. An example would be scoring 92 points on an exam with a maximum score of 100 points. When constructing performance criterion related to an objective, the teacher should consider the practical importance (Baer, Wolf, & Risley, 1968) to determine whether behavior change has occurred.

When developing your objectives, pay particular attention to the following:

- Be sure to consider whether or not the objective clearly communicates to the student what, when, how, and where the behavior is to be performed and specifies the performance expectation for the learner.
- Ensure that the objective is written in terms that are measurable and observable and that each objective contains the three elements (conditions, performance, and criteria).
- Consider the social relevance of the objective to the learner's needs.
- Assess how the objectives relate to one another and to the attainment of the overall goal.

Careful consideration of the relationship of goals and objectives in the design of the instructional plan can ensure a greater probability of success when teaching replacement behaviors. The following section will address how to design an instructional plan for teaching replacement behaviors.

# DEVELOPING A PLAN FOR TEACHING REPLACEMENT BEHAVIORS

A systemic instructional plan for teaching replacement behaviors should be comprehensive, with careful consideration given to all aspects of ensuring acquisition and ultimately generalization of the new behavior. There are numerous varieties of instructional program formats from which to choose, and often school districts will have their own for teachers to use. Some basic elements should be inclusive of any instructional plan, regardless of format. Overall, the instructional plan should give consideration to the following basic elements:

## Elements of an Instructional Program

A. *Rationale:* The instructional program should provide a brief rationale of why the skill should be taught, its overall importance to the well-being of the student, and implications of the skill in terms of longitudinal learning outcomes. Parental input should be sought concerning the development of any instructional plan. When selecting replacement behaviors, consideration should be given to individual, family, and cultural values that should be honored in the planning process. The selection of any replacement behavior should also consider the long-term implications of the behavior in terms of future planning for the individual.

B. *Identify the Learner:* The program should be designed and individualized to the needs of a specific child or adolescent. List and describe any of the individual's learning strengths and relevant educational or behavior challenges that should be considered. Also, individual student likes and dislikes should be factored into the development of the plan. Record review should be used to ascertain this information, as well as parental input. Asking for student input into the process is a means of promoting self-determination.

C. *Materials:* List and describe any instructional materials that will be needed as part of the instructional program.

D. *Describe Instructional Antecedent Arrangement:* Provide a description of instructional antecedents, such as how materials will be presented to the learner, seating arrangements, and other variables relevant to the instructional setting and delivery.

E. *Instructional Procedures:* List and describe how the skill will be taught to the student. Include instructional goals and objectives, a task analysis of the targeted skill, teaching strategies that will be employed, prompt hierarchy, and error correction procedures.

F. *Evaluation Procedures:* Describe how baseline assessment of student performance on the behavior will be conducted and evaluated. Include any data collection forms that will be used, define how learner progress will be assessed and measured throughout the instructional phase, and determine if performance data will be graphed.

G. *Generalization:* Indicate how generalization will be addressed within the instructional phase and assessed following instruction. This could include any number of generalization strategies, such as introducing natural contingencies (cues and consequences) found within the natural environment. This strategy is usually an effective approach for promoting generalization in that it seeks to use contextual variables specific to the environments where we hope the behavior will occur. These variables could consist of the typical daily schedule found within the classroom and building in cues and consequences designed to prompt and maintain the replacement behavior.

In summary, to use a program of systematic instruction within the classroom or other learning environment as a means for teaching replacement behavior, Browder (2001) recommended the following four steps be followed:

1. Define the skills to be taught and develop a data sheet to assess the skill and develop an instructional objective related to mastery.
2. Define the specific methods used to teach the skill, such as systems for instructional prompts and instructional feedback, and develop a systematic instructional plan.
3. Implement the instructional plan by determining when, where, how, and why the skill will be taught until performance criterion is reached.
4. Evaluate and review student performance on a daily, weekly, or biweekly basis; chart progress; and modify the program based on the performance data.

In conclusion, it is important to remember the considerations that should be taken into account when developing a plan for teaching replacement behaviors. As Berg (1992) indicated, the goal of the intervention plan should be to reduce the rate of challenging behavior and increase the replacement behavior. The steps in this process include understanding the function of the target behavior, the selection of an appropriate replacement behavior, the efficiency of the replacement behavior in terms of effort required from the student, the social validity or acceptability of the replacement behavior, and the long-term implications of the intervention.

## SUMMARY

This chapter provided a conceptual and applied overview in developing an instructional plan designed to teach replacement behaviors. It was organized around three major themes. The first theme addressed the issue of understanding skill deficits. As we learned, often children and youth within classroom environments who experience challenging behaviors exhibit skill deficits in major areas, such as academic and social skills. The presence of challenging behaviors in these youngsters can often be attributed to the absence of socially appropriate alternative skills coupled with academic and other learning and lifestyle challenges that they may be confronting. The combination of these life events and the frustration encountered from academic failure can result in challenging behavior.

In an effort to address these skill deficits, it is important to understand the role replacement behaviors have in reducing problem behavior. As described in the chapter, the second theme addressed the importance of selecting and teaching replacement behaviors. Replacement behaviors represent behaviors that are socially acceptable and designed to serve the same function as the challenging behavior (i.e., escape, attention, tangibles, or sensory). By selecting behaviors that serve the same function, it is hoped that these skills can be developed to efficiently meet the needs of the learner in academic and social contexts. Important to this concept is the development of an intervention plan, the third major theme in this chapter.

When developing an intervention plan, care must be given to design and engineer learning environments that promote the success of our intervention efforts with youngsters. Central to this is the use of schoolwide PBS that are designed to improve school climate and buy in on the part of all stakeholders, thus creating an optimal backdrop for the prevention of challenging behavior and the success of individual interventions.

Of course, any intervention plan must be accompanied by goals and objectives, and the chapter discussed the relationship between these two important instructional components. Last, the chapter examined how to assemble an instructional plan for teaching replacement behaviors, with attention given to the rationale of selecting behaviors to teach and the various elements of instruction and evaluation needed in the design of a systemic instruction plan.

## ACTIVITIES TO EXTEND YOUR LEARNING

1. Select and review samples of instructional plans designed for teaching replacement behaviors from Web-based and text sources. Examine the their characteristics, and compare and contrast each of these sources for continuity in the components recommended for instructional plans.
2. Develop a resource file of readings and handouts for later use on the design of instructional plans.
3. Evaluate the format and contents of instructional plans for teaching replacement behaviors within the context of practicum placements to ensuring your knowledge and understanding of the process.
4. Use a case study approach to develop an instructional plan for teaching replacement behaviors.
5. Within your practicum settings, identify replacement behaviors for some of your students who may be experiencing challenging forms of behavior in need of intervention.
6. Develop a sample instructional program for teaching a replacement behavior from an applied example within your practicum and discuss it with your instructor.

## FURTHER READING AND EXPLORATION

1. Compile a list of articles from journals such as *Teaching Exceptional Children, Young Exceptional Children,* and *Intervention in School and Clinic* on the use of various instructional methods for teaching academic and social behaviors. Contrast how these resources illustrate instructional goals and objectives and teaching methodologies.
2. Conduct a systematic review from behavior journals and compile resources on teaching replacement behaviors.
3. Develop an annotated bibliography of resources on methods for teaching potential replacement skills.

## REFERENCES

Agran, M. (1997). *Student directed learning: Teaching self-determination skills.* Pacific Grove, CA: Brooks/Cole.

Albin, R. W., Lucyshyn, J. M., Horner, R. H., & Flannery, K. B. (1996). Contextual fit for behavior support plans: A model for "goodness of fit" In L. K. Koegel, R. L. Koegel, & G. Dunlap (Eds.), *Positive behavioral support: Including people with difficult behavior in the community* (pp. 81–98). Baltimore: Paul H. Brookes.

Baer, D. M., Wolf, M. M., & Risley, T. R. (1968). Some current dimensions of applied behavior analysis. *Journal of Applied Behavior Analysis, 1,* 91–97.

Bambara, L. M., & Knoster, T. (1998). Designing positive behavior support plans. In *Innovations* (Vol. 13). Washington, DC: American Association on Mental Retardation.

Berg, W. K. (1992). Factors to consider in developing a treatment plan. *Iowa News, 92,* 1–2.

Browder, D. M. (2001). *Curriculum and assessment for students with moderate and severe disabilities.* New York: Guilford.

Carr, E. G., & Durand, V. M. (1985). Reducing behavior problems through functional communication training. *Journal of Applied Behavior Analysis, 18,* 111–126.

Carr, E. G., Horner, R. H., Turnbull, A. P., Marquis, J. G., McLaughlin, D. M., McAtee, M. L., et al. (1999). *Positive behavior support for people with developmental disabilities: A research synthesis.* Washington, DC: American Association on Mental Retardation.

DiGangi, S. A., & Maag, J. W. (1992). A component of self-management training with behaviorally disordered youth. *Behavioral Disorders, 17,* 281–290.

Dunlap, G., Clarke, S., Jackson, M., Wright, S., Ramos, E., & Brinson, S. (1995). Self-monitoring of classroom behaviors with students exhibiting emotional and behavioral challenges. *School Psychology Quarterly, 10,* 165–177.

Dunlap, L. K., Dunlap, G., Koegal, L. K., & Koegal, R. (1991). Using self-monitoring to increase independence. *Teaching Exceptional Children, 23,* 17–22.

Durand, V. M. (1990). *Severe behavior problems: A functional communication training approach.* New York: Guilford.

Guskey, T. R. (2000). *Evaluating professional development.* Thousand Oaks, CA: Corwin.

Jolivette, K., Scott, T. M., & Nelson, C. M. (2000). *The link between functional behavioral assessments and behavioral intervention plans.* Arlington, VA: The ERIC Clearinghouse on Disabilities and Gifted Education. (ERIC EC Digest No. E592)

Kanfer, F. H. (1975). Self-management methods. In F. H. Kanfer & A. P. Goldstein (Eds.), *Helping people change: A textbook method* (pp. 309–355). New York: Pergamon.

Kanfer, F. H., & Karoly, P. (1972). Self-control: A behavioristic excursion into the lion's den. *Behavior Therapy, 3,* 398–416.

Luria, A. (1961). *The role of speech in the regulation of normal and abnormal behaviour.* Oxford: Pergamon.

Mager, R. E. (1997). *Preparing instructional objectives* (3rd ed.). Atlanta, GA: The Center for Effective Performance.

Mahoney, M. J. (1974). *Cognition and behavior modification.* Cambridge, MA: Ballinger.

Martin, G., & Pear, J. (1999). *Behavior modification: What it is and how to do it* (6th ed.). Upper Saddle River, NJ: Merrill/Prentice Hall.

Massey, N. G., & Wheeler, J. J. (2000). Acquisition and generalization of activity schedules and their effects on task engagement in a young child with autism in an inclusive preschool classroom. *Education and Training in Mental Retardation, 35,* 326–335.

Meichenbaum, D. H. (1974). *Cognitive behavior modification.* Morriston, NJ: General Learning.

Meichenbaum, D., & Goodman, J. (1971). Training impulsive children to talk to themselves: A means of developing self-control. *Journal of Abnormal Psychology, 77,* 115–126.

Mesibov, G. B., Browder, D. M., & Kirkland, C. (2002). Using individualized schedules as a component of positive behavioral support for students with developmental disabilities. *Journal of Positive Behavior Interventions, 4,* 73–79.

Miller, M., Miller, S. R., Wheeler, J. J., & Selinger, J. (1989). Can a single-classroom treatment approach change academic performance and behavioral characteristics in severely behaviorally disordered adolescents? An experimental inquiry. *Behavior Disorders, 14,* 215–225.

Miltenberger, R. G. (2001). *Behavior modification: Principles and procedures* (2nd ed.). Belmont, CA: Wadsworth.

Reichle, J., McEvoy, M., Davis, C., Rogers, E., Feeley, K., Johnston, S., et al. (1996). Coordinating preservice and in-service training of early interventionists to serve preschoolers who engage in challenging behavior. In L. K. Koegal, R. L. Koegal, & G. Dunlap (Eds.), *Positive behavioral support: Including people with difficult behavior in the community* (pp. 227–264). Baltimore: Paul H. Brookes.

Sailor, W. (1996). New structures and systems change for comprehensive positive behavioral support. In L. K. Koegal, R. L. Koegal, & G. Dunlap (Eds.), *Positive behavioral support: Including people with difficult behavior in the community* (pp. 163–206). Baltimore: Paul H. Brookes.

Scott, T. M., & Nelson, C. M. (1999). Using functional behavioral assessment to develop effective intervention plans: Practical classroom applications. *Journal of Positive Behavioral Interventions, 1,* 242–251.

Sugai, G., Horner, R. H., Dunlap, G., Hieneman, M., Leis, T. J., Nelson, C. M., et al. (2000). Applying positive behavioral support and functional behavioral assessment in schools. *Journal of Positive Behavior Interventions, 2,* 131–143.

Sulzer-Azaroff, B., & Mayer, G. R. (1991). *Behavior analysis for lasting change.* Fort Worth, TX: Harcourt Brace College Publishers.

Utley, C. A., & Sailor, W. (2002). Positive behavior support and urban school improvement [Special section]. *Journal of Positive Behavior Interventions, 4,* 195.

Weatherby, A. M., & Prizant, B. M. (2000). *Autism spectrum disorders.* Baltimore: Paul H. Brookes.

Webber, J., Scheuermann, B., McCall, C., & Coleman, M. (1993). Research on self-monitoring as a behavior management technique in special education classrooms: A descriptive review. *Remedial and Special Education, 14*(2), 38–56.

Wheeler, J. J., Bates, P., Marshall, K. J., & Miller, S. R (1988). Teaching appropriate behavior to a young man with moderate mental retardation in a supported competitive employment setting. *Education and Training in Mental Retardation and Developmental Disabilities, 23,* 105–116.

Zirpoli, T. J., & Melloy, K. J. (2001). *Behavior management: Applications for teachers* (3rd ed.). Upper Saddle River, NJ: Merrill/Prentice Hall.

# Chapter 10

# Reducing Challenging Behavior

## CONCEPTS TO UNDERSTAND

*After reading this chapter, you should be able to:*

- List and describe the factors that influence challenging behavior

- Discuss alternatives for the prevention of challenging behaviors, such as the concept of capacity building within learning environments and the development of alternative skills that provide students with increased academic and social success

- Identify and describe the range of possible interventions for reducing challenging behavior, and the accompanying costs and benefits related to their impact on the lives of individual learners

- List and describe the methods most commonly used to reduce challenging behavior, such as differential reinforcement, extinction, response-cost procedures, time-out, and the use of punishment

## KEY TERMS

Continuum of intervention alternatives

Differential reinforcement

Extinction

Noninvasive treatment

Response cost

Reducing and eliminating challenging behavior within the classroom is one of the most frequently cited concerns continuously expressed by teachers and school administrators (National Education Goals Report, 1995). Such behavior only serves to disrupt the classroom for all parties concerned, including the child affected, students within the class, and teachers alike. Not surprisingly, the lifestyle outcomes for students who experience chronic behavior challenges are often bleak and plagued with problems that frequently include academic and social difficulties in school, school failure, suspensions, expulsions, increased difficulty in social and interpersonal relationships, and brushes with the criminal justice system.

Traditionally, public schools have responded to these forms of behavior through the use of rapid suppression approaches (Durand, 1990) aimed at quickly eliminating these responses. These methods have included a variety of punitive consequences, such as loss of privileges, time-out, in-school suspension, corporal punishment, and expulsion. These methods have also failed repeatedly over time to promote lasting behavior changes, are reactive by design, and fail to teach alternative replacement behaviors that have a more enduring effect. Crone and Horner (2003) have indicated that the inherent difficulty in addressing challenging behaviors within school settings is in how to effectively design individualized interventions and embed them within the context of classrooms and school environments. Changing how problem behavior is viewed and responded to within a school is the greatest challenge to an interventionist. These issues will be the focus of this chapter. How can we design not only individual interventions but also systems (i.e., schools) to better respond to challenging behaviors that interfere with learning and the educational success for children and youth?

## HOW CHALLENGING BEHAVIOR IS PERCEIVED

One of the most important insights gleaned from the research findings in the area of positive behavior supports (PBS) has been that challenging behaviors need not always be considered for behavior reduction. Such thinking seems almost contradictory to the practices employed within learning environments that have traditionally focused on the rapid elimination of these behaviors. Sulzer-Azaroff and Mayer (1991) identified a three-step intervention model aimed at promoting positive replacement behaviors as a constructive approach to reducing challenging behavior. The model consists of the following elements:

1. Assess the function of the problem, and if feasible, alter conditions to allow the individual access to the same or added reinforcing contingencies by means of a more acceptable action.
2. If that solution proves unworkable, before proceeding, consult laws and policies.
3. Select the least-restrictive method supported by research to promote optimal results. (p. 396)

This model addresses excessive behaviors from a constructive approach aimed at supporting the learner through skills building and the engineering of relevant environments, including classrooms, school, home, and community. These approaches have been expanded through the work of PBS and have served to enlighten professionals on the many alternatives for addressing excessive behaviors. For purposes of clarity, excessive behavior has been defined as a behavior that occurs at a high rate or intensity that is costly to a child or others in the long run (Hawkins, 1986). Excessive behavior infringes on the potential of youth to fully participate and achieve success within school and other settings. PBS has bridged the gap to some extent in facilitating an acceptance of behavior procedures in schools among teachers and school personnel. PBS has also reinforced the basic premises that problem behavior serves a function for an individual, that it is often associated with environmental events and circumstances, and that it most often stems from insufficient skills on the part of the student.

Sadly, the case can be made that educators and parents alike often look at the behavior excesses displayed by children rather than at the need for appropriate skills, and too often these perceptions result in the deployment of punitive consequences and an absence of any skills training. In short, it often becomes a habit to address excessive behavior that occurs at high rates from a reactive after-the-fact response that is directed toward its rapid elimination rather than to consider other options. Couple this with a lack of knowledge and skills about acceptable alternatives aimed at behavior reduction, active teaching of replacement behaviors, and the efficient use of these procedures within school or home settings, and the problem is only strengthened over time.

### Consider This

It is important to remember that replacement behaviors should be efficient. This also applies to training teachers and other professionals to rely on PBS rather than reactive procedures. Supports are needed in the form of training and reinforcement over time directed toward school personnel to encourage their professional development in this area.

Rapid suppression of behavior or elimination approaches have frequently been the intervention of choice within schools (Morris & Hawkins, 1999). In contrast, constructional approaches (Sulzer-Azaroff & Mayer, 1991) have advocated that behavior repertoires not be eliminated but be built and constructed to provide enriched environments that are designed to promote the development of appropriate skills. Constructional approaches foster interventions that are designed to enable children to obtain reinforcing consequences within their environments through expanded skill repertoires that are inclusive of those skills that are desired within their environment and that also serve a functional purpose for the student.

Jackson and Panyan (2002) offered some interesting perspectives toward furthering our understanding of the response from public education toward challenging behavior. Namely, the focus on behavior change as a primary outcome of public education results in a fix-it mentality among professionals, thus lending itself to the use of rapid suppression approaches as a means of fixing the problem behavior by squelching their occurrence. Second, as a result of children being labeled with problem behavior, specialists trained exclusively to address such problems are given the charge of fixing the problem, thus removing responsibility or ownership of this process from general education teachers and abridging the quality of the educational experiences for children labeled as behaviorally challenged. In addition, the authors also report that many children identified with behavior needs may be experiencing these behaviors as a response to the practices of teachers or schools that are insensitive to the individual needs of the child and to their familial and cultural factors.

Crone and Horner (2003) reinforced the basic assumptions that underlie PBS and the merits of this intervention philosophy within school settings. These are that (a) human behavior is functional, people behave the way they do for a reason, and even challenging behavior serves a function for the individual; (b) human behavior is predictable and directly related to the environments that children and youth are a part of; and (c) human behavior is changeable and through the practices associated with PBS, such as functional behavior assessment, challenging behavior can be reduced or eliminated.

Since the passage of the 1997 reauthorization of IDEA, schools have begun to address challenging behavior more proactively, thus meaningful strides have been realized as a result of these promising practices. One of the biggest remaining challenges is ensuring that all teachers are trained in these skills from both a philosophical and applied perspective and that schools are reinforced for their attempts at systemic change in reference to schoolwide behavior support initiatives.

## ALTERNATIVES FOR THE PREVENTION OF CHALLENGING BEHAVIOR

In understanding how to provide alternatives that are directed toward the prevention of challenging behaviors, it is necessary to view PBS from a systems level. Basically, within schools multiple behavior support systems (Horner, Sugai, Todd, & Lewis-Palmer, 1999–2000) are present. These include classroom systems, nonclassroom systems, and individual student support systems (Horner et al., 1999–2000). Figure 10–1 illustrates the relationship between schoolwide systems, non-classroom-specific systems, classroom systems, and individual student systems (Crone & Horner, 2003).

The model offered by Crone and Horner (2003) is a variation of the continuum of behavior supports model as developed by Sugai, Horner, and colleagues at the OSEP Center on Positive Behavioral Interventions and Supports in that it is presented from an ecological perspective that illustrates

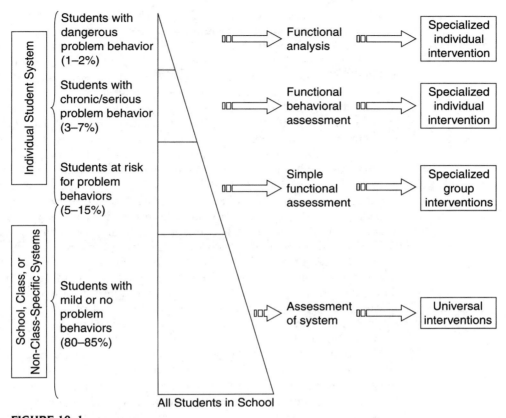

**FIGURE 10–1**
*Continuum of Effective Behavior Assessment and Support*
*Source:* Copyright 2003 by Deanne A. Crone and Robert H. Horner. Based on Walker et al. (1996).
Reproduced by permission of The Guilford Press.

the relationship of these systems through a series of concentric circles. The latter model describes the continuum of behavior supports within a school population and how these supports vary according to the needs exhibited by students.

At the base of the continuum of supports model (OSEP Center, 2000) are universal interventions, which consist of a schoolwide system that encompasses individual classrooms and is also directed at the primary prevention of problem behaviors among the majority of students within a school (80% to 90%). This population of students is composed of those who do not exhibit serious behavior problems and who require no specialized interventions targeted for behavior concerns. Secondary prevention is the next level on the continuum and targets students who are identified as at risk and who represent approximately 5% to 15% of the student population. The focus at this level is to prevent further problems for these students and to provide a model of support that is aimed at skills building and prevention. Last, the final level on the continuum is tertiary prevention. This level is designed for students with chronic and ongoing behavior challenges that require specialized interventions developed for individual students. It is estimated by Sugai and colleagues (OSEP, 2000) that students who display intense and chronic behavior challenges account for 1% to 7% of students within schools.

Sugai et al. (OSEP, 2000) conjectured that PBS consists of a systemic and proactive approach to promoting optimal behavior across multiple contexts, including community, families, schools, classrooms, playgrounds, and nonclassroom settings such as cafeterias, hallways, and playgrounds. The focal point of a systemswide PBS model such as those presented is prevention. It represents a proactive model aimed at understanding the problem and responding to the problems in a systematic manner. Walker et al. (1996) asserted that by incorporating the use of a continuum of behavior supports that new cases of problem behavior are prevented and reduced at the primary prevention stage, current cases of problem behavior are reduced at the secondary prevention stage, and the intensity and complexity of problem behaviors are reduced and controlled through PBS at the tertiary stage of prevention. Features of a systems-based model of behavior support are those that are built on a philosophy that is carried out effectively within the daily operations of a school.

In summary, the most important point to remember about developing comprehensive systems of support within school settings is that a school must first commit to change. This commitment is the first step in acknowledging that the current methods used to address challenging behaviors are not optimal and that improvement is needed to promote enhanced learning outcomes for all students. At the core of this philosophical change is the need for skill building in the area of PBS. Wheeler and Hoover (1997) identified some of the most relevant competencies required of school-based teams as they prepare for schoolwide implementation. These include the following:

### Philosophy of Practice

- Components of PBS
- Teaming and collaboration strategies
- Joint problem-solving methods

### Behavior Support Strategies

- Functional behavior assessment
- Analyzing functional assessment data
- Hypotheses development
- Development of behavior intervention plans
    a. Antecedent management approaches
    b. Development of replacement skills
    c. Reinforcement strategies

### Program Evaluation

- Evaluating performance data
- Social validity measures
- Student outcomes
- Team outcomes
- School outcomes

The next step in the process is the stepwise systematic implementation of a systemswide model of behavior support. Research findings have indicated that some unique performance indicators are associated with schoolwide PBS approaches. Sugai and Horner (2001) identified the following characteristics found within schools with schoolwide PBS. These characteristics include the following:

A. An agenda is aimed at primary prevention and is visible schoolwide.

B. Students and staff members within the school have been taught the expectations and have had regular intervals to practice and rehearse them and to be positively acknowledged by peers and supervisors alike for engaging in the practice of these skills.

C. A majority of students, staff, and families (in excess of 80%) can state the schoolwide positive behavior expectations and provide examples for each.

D. The majority of contacts between faculty, staff, and students are positive.

E. A full continuum of behavior supports exists at the school and district levels.

F. Personnel are well trained and competent in the use of PBS procedures.

G. A function-based approach serves as the foundation for addressing challenging behaviors.

H. All faculty, staff, and administrators participate in the delivery of schoolwide PBS practices.

I. A schoolwide behavior support team serves in the role as a designated leadership team committed to the use of research-based practices in behavior support.

J. Schoolwide data are reviewed at regular intervals and are instrumental in decision making and planning.

The final step in the process involves the evaluation of these procedures and their impact on schoolwide behavior outcomes. Sugai and Horner (2001) also concluded that the implementation of schoolwide PBS is feasible within a 1- to 2-year period; that office referrals typically decrease between 40% to 60%, with increases in academic performance measures occurring as more time is devoted to academic instruction when behavior improves; and that lasting impact can endure over a 5- to 7-year period when implementation includes systems change and the use of validated practices.

Finally, Sugai and Horner (2001) provided a series of brief suggestions on how to successfully implement schoolwide behavior supports. They include

- Concentrate on doing what is possible within your given resource structure, but be persistent over time in capacity building within the school.
- Invest in practices that work.
- Invest in outcomes that the school hopes to achieve.
- Be mindful of individual and cultural differences in the delivery of supports.
- Make data-based decisions as a means of promoting informed decision making.
- Work collaboratively as teams to attain desired outcomes.
- Work hard to develop the professional knowledge and skills among on-site personnel as a method for promoting buy in and lasting change.

The merits of schoolwide behavior support systems are numerous and beneficial in serving as a prevention tool for problem behavior. Through the implementation of such practices systemwide, schools are transformed as the cultures within these environments become more proactive in understanding the behavior support needs of the learners they serve. The outcomes to teachers, administrators, and staff members are also apparent as schools transform into a collective team-based unit committed to maintaining an environment of behavior support for all children.

## QUESTIONS TO CONSIDER WHEN CONTEMPLATING BEHAVIOR REDUCTION

It is very important to carefully consider the range of intervention options before embarking on a behavior reduction program. Many questions need to be answered about the social validity of such an intervention before its implementation. Questions concerning the nature and severity of the behavior also need to be examined. For example, does the behavior in question really pose such a challenge that it needs to be reduced? Are we being objective when looking at the behavior of an individual, or is it a subjective bias based on a conflict between personalities? Does the behavior of concern limit the options and freedoms of the learner?

Other considerations include whether there is consensus among staff or other team members that a student's behavior is in need of reduction. Does the behavior limit the personal freedoms or interfere with the student's learning or learning of others?

There are, however, instances in which behaviors are of such a magnitude that they are appropriate for behavior reduction programs. When behaviors cause a risk to the individual or others or cause damage to property and impede the quality of life for the individual or others, behavior reduction is warranted (Sulzer-Azaroff & Mayer, 1991). A range of examples of behaviors that could qualify for behavior reduction programs could include David, who is autistic and so fascinated by the rotation of the wheels of a car that he runs from his classroom and out onto the edge of the street to watch the cars so he can fixate on the spinning motion of the tires as they pass by; Julie, whose teeth grinding has become so chronic and persistent that she has caused permanent damage to her teeth; Jacob, who has been persistently pinching his classmates to the point that they choose to avoid him and are fearful of him; and Beth, whose chronic self-injury has nearly cost her the use of one eye from her repeated hitting in and about her eye. These behaviors serve as examples of those in need of a behavior reduction program. They qualify because they interfere with learning, they pose a threat to the learner or others, and they greatly inhibit the learner's quality of life by limiting their personal freedoms.

Before initiating a behavior reduction program, care and consideration should be given to conducting a thorough functional behavior assessment to ascertain the function of the problem behavior. In developing an intervention plan, policies and procedures should be consulted as well as the decision to use the least-intrusive intervention and most functional path as your first choice in the intervention process. Sulzer-Azaroff and Mayer (1991) recommended the following steps be considered before using a behavior reduction procedure:

1. Conduct a functional behavior assessment to identify the function of the target behavior and the specific antecedent and consequence events that are correlated with the occurrence of the behavior as well as interpersonal and physical or health issues that may be influencing high rates of the behavior.

2. If the functional assessment reveals antecedents that can be altered to prevent the occurrence of the behavior or indicates that alternative behaviors are needed to remediate the problem, then attention should be given to these areas. If this is not an option or attempts at intervention fail, then proceed to the next step.

3. Consider using a behavior reduction strategy after first consulting school policies and local, state, and federal laws to ensure the rights of the individual and compliance with all laws and policies.

4. Select the most plausible and least-restrictive intervention possible.

The right to **noninvasive treatment** continues to be an area of justified concern among professionals and advocates of persons in the areas of special education and services to persons with disabilities. The injustices suffered by persons with disabilities in the past led to the formation of human rights committees within state institutions serving persons with developmental disabilities and mental illness and have led to the development of nonaversive behavior interventions and the development of positive behavior supports. Substantial progress has been made over time in this area through a greater awareness among professionals, families, self-advocates, and policies that reinforce these beliefs and practices.

In terms of professionals in the field of psychology, for example, the American Psychological Association's (APA) Division 33 has formulated a resolution entitled *Guidelines on Effective Behavioral Treatment for Persons with Mental Retardation and Developmental Disabilities*. In this document, the use of restrictive procedures is addressed:

> Highly restrictive procedures (which may entail interventions referred to as aversive) shall not be instituted without the combined use of procedures that reinforce incompatible, alternate, or other behavior. Highly restrictive procedures shall not be employed until there has been sufficient determination that the use of less restrictive procedures was or would be ineffective or harm would come to the client because of gradual change in the client's problematic behavior.
>
> Highly restrictive procedures shall be discontinued when the individual's response to less restrictive procedures indicates that treatment benefits can be maintained through these less restrictive procedures. Evaluation of the individual's response to less restrictive procedures shall be ongoing and documented. (n.d., p. 2)

The positive behavior support movement has also contributed to understanding the limitations of restrictive procedures and their overall impact on the student. Care must be taken to ensure that least-restrictive procedures have been exhausted and documented to be ineffective before considering the use of restrictive procedures.

Within school settings for example, a common debate in some geographic areas is whether or not to permit the use of corporal punishment in schools. Corporal punishment has been defined as the intentional application of physical pain as a method of changing behavior (National Association of School Psychologists [NASP], 2003; Society for Adolescent Medicine, 2003). Corporal punishment does not include physical restraint by school officials to protect students from physically harming themselves or others (American Academy of Pediatrics, 2000). Currently 23 states in the United States still authorize the use of corporal punishment in schools. It is estimated that 1.5 million cases of physical punishment in schools are reported each year, and as a result of such punishment, 10,000 to 20,000 students receive medical care each year (Society for Adolescent Medicine, 2003). Conflicting data from the U.S. Department of Education estimates that approximately 400,000 students are hit in schools each year. Current data summarized by the Society for Adolescent Medicine indicates that physical punishment is more prevalent in Grades K through 8, in rural schools versus urban, in boys versus girls, and in disadvantaged children versus middle-class and upper-class Caucasians (Society for Adolescent Medicine, 2003). The form of corporal punishment most frequently used within the United States is the striking of a child with a wooden paddle (NASP, 2003).

There are many problems associated with the use of corporal punishment. Among these are the lack of this punishment procedure to produce lasting changes in behavior, not to mention the modeling of physical aggression against children to control their behavior; the reinforcement of escape and avoidance behaviors in children to avoid punishment; and the reinforcement to the user as a means of exerting control. In spite of decades of research and advocacy denouncing corporal punishment, it still remains a viable discipline alternative within almost half the states in the United States. The American Academy of Pediatrics (2000) and the Society for Adolescent Medicine (2003) have recommended that corporal punishment be abolished in all states by law and that alternative forms of behavior management be used. The evidence against corporal punishment serves to reinforce the lack of effectiveness of this method for promoting behavior change. The Society for Adolescent Medicine concurred from numerous research citations within their position paper on corporal punishment in the schools that these methods are not being used as "last resort" methods as well. Their findings reported that corporal punishment is an ineffective method of disciplining children and that it has serious and damaging effects on the physical and emotional health of those children who have it inflicted on them.

Furthermore, the use of corporal punishment does not contribute to the moral development of children, nor does it increase their respect of their teachers or authority figures, as many proponents of the practice believe. On the contrary, the use of corporal punishment promotes fear and distrust of authority figures and models aggression as a means of control. Serious psychological side effects can also be produced, such as school refusal behavior and other stress induced behaviors, which are collateral effects of corporal punishment in some children. Such evidence has led many organizations affiliated with medical and related professions to reject corporal punishment as a practice of addressing excessive behavior in the schools. Given the acceptable alternatives for treating behaviors through the use of applied behavior analysis and PBS, the practice of corporal punishment is unnecessary and unacceptable in our nation's schools.

The need for crisis intervention is a growing concern among school professionals and involves something completely different from suppressing behavior through the administration of corporal punishment. However, in the event of escalating behaviors that constitute a crisis, procedures need to be developed to address these circumstances. Crisis intervention procedures are essential as a component of a systems-wide behavior support model in the event that behaviors escalate to the point that they endanger the safety of the learner or others. These plans should identify the procedures to be used in addressing serious problem behaviors, the roles and responsibilities of personnel involved, and the plan of operation in the event a crisis occurs.

## CONTINUUM OF INTERVENTION ALTERNATIVES

The **continuum of intervention alternatives** that have been typically employed to reduce excessive behavior have included (a) differential reinforcement procedures, (b) extinction, (c) response-cost, (d) time-out procedures, and (e) punishment. The basic elements of each of these methods will be presented in terms of their strengths and limitations as methods used to reduce excessive behavior.

## Differential Reinforcement

**Differential reinforcement** is a method that uses reinforcement to eliminate or reduce challenging behavior. This form of intervention is called a *positive reduction procedure* (Cooper, Heron, & Heward, 1987) because reinforcement is used to decrease or eliminate problem behavior, rather than losing opportunities to earn reinforcers as a result of problem behavior.

There are four distinct types of differential reinforcement procedures that can be selected. These include (a) differential reinforcement of alternative behavior (DRA), (b) differential reinforcement of incompatible behavior (DRI), (c) differential reinforcement of other behavior (DRO), and (d) differential reinforcement of lower rates of behavior (DRL).

The first method, differential reinforcement of alternative behavior (DRA), reinforces a behavior that is a designated alternate behavior for the behavior targeted for reduction (Cooper et al., 1987). For example, if Josh continues working on his assignment rather than putting his head down on the desk and complaining, he is given praise and a token from his teacher, thus he is reinforced for his continued task engagement in the absence of the target behavior.

Differential reinforcement of incompatible behavior (DRI) is very similar to the previous method (DRA) that was described; however, with DRI the incompatible behavior is topographically incompatible with the target behavior. This is not the case with DRA. For example, in the case of an adolescent boy who engages in hitting classmates in his vocational class, keeping his hands busy with meaningful activity related to his metals class is the desired behavior, thus when he is not hitting but working on class projects, his teachers reinforce him verbally.

When using DRA or DRI procedures, the following guidelines are recommended (Cooper et al., 1987):

1. Select behaviors for intervention that are in the student's repertoire of responses that he regularly uses.

2. Select behaviors that are reasonable expectations, given the student's current skill level, to ensure rapid acquisition of the new skills.

3. Finally, select behaviors that will be supported within the student's natural environment on completion of training.

Differential reinforcement of other behavior (DRO) refers to when a behavior is not reinforced for a specific period of time. In other words, a child is reinforced for zero occurrences of a behavior for a specified period, such as if Jacob remains in his seat for the 20-minute period, he will earn points. If he leaves his seat only one time during that period, he will fail to earn his reinforcer. This method is very widely applicable within classroom settings and has been reported to reduce a broad range of behaviors, including aggression, spitting, hyperactivity, stereotypy, disruption, and so forth (Sulzer-Azaroff & Mayer, 1991). The benefits of DRO are numerous and include

- It is applicable across learning environments.
- Rapid behavior reduction is possible in a short time frame.
- DRO procedures have been demonstrated to maintain and generalize.

However, there are some negative attributes associated with this strategy. These include the fact that DRO does not teach an alternative behavior. It also attends to the negative behavior, and it can strengthen other negative behaviors in that only the targeted behavior cannot receive reinforcement when using a DRO procedure. You must be careful not to reinforce other problematic behaviors when using a DRO procedure.

The last form of differential reinforcement procedure is DRL (differential reinforcement of lower rates of behavior). DRL is an effective procedure to use when a behavior can be systematically reduced over time. Reinforcement would be provided for a gradual reduction of the target behavior over time, such as reducing caloric intake over a designated time period and then administering the desired reinforcer on meeting that goal.

To implement DRL procedures, it is recommended that reinforcement be provided in small incremental steps to facilitate sustained behavior change. If expectations for appropriate behavior exceed student capabilities and the time intervals reflect too significant a change, a regression in behavior change is apt to occur.

## Extinction

**Extinction** is the next intervention option on the continuum of treatments to consider for reducing behavior. Extinction occurs when a previously reinforced behavior is no longer reinforced. As an example of extinction, Louis continually interrupts his teacher during his interactions with other students. His teacher, Mr. Wilson, being new and concerned about the well-being of all his students, continually stopped what he was doing and gave his immediate attention to Louis. After reading about behavior redirection and extinction, Mr. Wilson no longer stopped what he was doing for Louis's interruptions, and they reduced. Coupled with direct instruction on how to obtain Mr. Wilson's attention, Louis developed appropriate skills for obtaining teacher attention as well.

If a behavior receives continuous or intermittent reinforcement, it will continue to occur (Miltenberger, 2001). One thing to consider when using extinction is that the phenomena known as extinction burst can occur when a previously reinforced behavior is no longer reinforced. An extinction burst occurs when the intensity or frequency of a behavior increases in an effort to obtain reinforcement. This increase may also result in the manifestation of novel behaviors that occur with the extinction burst, such as swearing or crying as emotional outbursts due to frustration (Miltenberger, 2001). An example of this occurred when Mac inserted the coins into his favorite vending machine and pushed the accompanying numbers for his favorite snack. As his favorite snack began to drop off its hook, it was snared and did not release. Mac pushed the button for a refund and nothing happened. As he became more frustrated, he kicked the machine as he feverishly pushed the coin return button. Finally, in his efforts to obtain his snack, he began rocking the machine back and forth, but to no avail. His snack was hooked, and he walked away exhausted and frustrated by his efforts.

Extinction will ultimately result in the reduction of the behavior and has been shown to be lasting in terms of its effects on challenging behaviors. As noted, however, the disadvantages associated with this procedure are

- Increased rates of behavior
- Development of novel behaviors
- Aggression resulting from frustration
- Time necessary to produce the desired effects

So when assessing the feasibility of extinction procedures in the behavior change process, carefully consider whether you have the willingness and patience to accommodate the slow and gradual reduction in behavior.

## Response-Cost Procedures

Response-cost programs have been used within school settings for a number of years as part of a classroom management system and have been largely prevalent within programs serving students with behavior disorders. **Response cost** is a behavior reduction procedure that attempts to reduce behavior through the removal or withdrawal of a quantity of reinforcement contingent on a response (Sulzer-Azaroff & Mayer, 1991). In other words, a loss of something of worth or value to the individual is a consequence for inappropriate behavior. One could think of this loss as a penalty or fine.

Perhaps one of the easiest examples is taken from the game of ice hockey. When a player commits a rule violation against another player, this is called a penalty; the player who has violated the rules of the game then receives a penalty of two minutes or more, depending upon the seriousness of the violation, and they must sit out the assigned penalty minutes in a penalty box until they can reenter the game. This is an example of a response-cost procedure.

Response-cost programs have also been frequently used by parents in managing children's behavior through the loss of privileges such as driving the family car, being grounded (i.e., unable to go out), or through loss of allowance following the occurrence of a problem behavior (i.e., a rules violation). Response cost has been a widely used procedure for students with behavior disorders. With this population of students, response cost has been used in conjunction with level systems that are tied to point systems that earn students points that can be redeemed for various forms of reinforcers that are made available to them within their classroom or school environments. These programs also remove points from students for problem behaviors through the deduction of points, tokens, or privileges as a penalty or fine. One of the major concerns with response-cost programs is that teachers frequently err in their design and implementation of these programs in that they remove points from students and provide no mechanism that allows them to re-earn points. Therefore, students with chronic behavior challenges are continually in debt or in a position of loss (see Vignette 10.1). This deficit creates an emotional burden for learners and results in a "what do I have to lose" mentality as a result of point deficits that have ensued because of the response-cost program. The creation of such a climate within a classroom increases problem behavior. It is therefore a better option to use reinforcement with response-cost programs as a method for developing desired responses.

## Vignette 10.1

### The Case of "How Not" to Use Response Cost

The teacher informed Alex that he should stop bothering his classmates and complete his work or lose 5 points for this infraction. Alex persisted and was warned a second time by his teacher, who also told him that she was subtracting 10 points from his total for not following her instructions. On receiving this reprimand, Alex, who was already more than 50 points in debt in terms of total point value, screamed at the teacher and threatened to do "a lot worse." At this point, the teacher deducted another 25 points as a consequence for issuing a verbal threat. Now that Alex has surpassed being 75 points in the hole, he feels he has nothing to lose and has escalated his behavior by shouting profanities at the teacher, thus earning him a detention and the loss of another 25 points.

We see from this illustration the perpetual cycle that can result from administering a procedure such as response cost in an inappropriate manner.

### Reflective Moment

What recommendations might you have in altering how this response-cost procedure was implemented? Identify how this situation could have been prevented. What are your thoughts on response-cost procedures and their application within the classroom?

Miltenberger (2001) identified some critical points to consider when using response-cost programs, which include: (a) Which reinforcer will be removed? (b) Will the loss of the reinforcer be immediate or delayed? (c) Is the loss of the reinforcer ethical (i.e., does it violate the rights of the learner)? and (d) Is the response-cost procedure practical and acceptable? In responding to these questions, it is important to note that the loss of a reinforcer should be considerable enough to reduce or eliminate the behavior. Second, the proximity of the loss of the reinforcer must be addressed. Is it better to suffer the loss immediate to the behavior so that it is more effective, or is the loss of reinforcement delayed, given the type of reinforcers used and the logistics within the classroom? It is also important to consider how such a program will be monitored and administered within the classroom to ensure fidelity or treatment integrity (i.e., that the intervention is carried out as intended).

Last is the loss of the reinforcer ethical and does it infringe on the child's rights? Consider the following example:

> The teaching assistant verbally reprimanded Jim for not engaging in his work and completing his assignment. Jim, who was diagnosed with autism, sat expressionless in his seat. The teaching assistant elevated her voice and said, "I told you to start working and because you did not, I am going to have your snack today." After that she proceeded to eat Jim's snack from his lunch box.

This example illustrates a very unethical practice that does indeed violate the rights of the child in this case. Frankly, one of the criticisms associated with the use of punishment procedures is that these procedures become reinforcing to the user. Too often, these programs belittle children and adolescents and are not implemented carefully nor monitored in terms of their treatment integrity. Some basic suggestions for controlling some of these issues are as follows:

**Guidelines to Consider When Using Response-Cost Programs**
- Identify and operationally define the desired behaviors.
- Determine the reinforcers that will be used and how they will be provided to students (e.g., points tallied, tokens earned).
- Clearly define the target behaviors that are not acceptable and the amounts that each infraction will be fined.
- Determine the immediacy of the reinforcers and fines (Will they be given immediately or delayed?).
- Implement the program and document student performance.
- Evaluate student progress and outcomes and refine the program to better address student needs based on the performance data.

## Time-Out

Time-out is a procedure commonly used to remove a child from access to reinforcement for a period of time following the occurrence of problem behavior. There are two forms of time-out. Exclusionary time-out refers to the student being taken out of the room or area where the behavior occurred and placed in another area. The second form of time-out procedure is called nonexclusionary time-out and involves the student remaining in the room or area where the behavior occurred, but being denied access to positive reinforcement (Miltenberger, 2001).

Time-out has been noted to be an effective procedure to use with behaviors that are maintained by social or tangible reinforcers because time-out denies access to these reinforcers by removing the individual from the environment in which the reinforcers are available (Miltenberger, 2001). Time-out procedures are relatively easy to use within classroom settings, they have been deemed to be generally acceptable by professionals, and the use of time-out procedures suppresses behavior rapidly and generalizes across time and settings (Cooper et al., 1987). Time-out should not be considered the first treatment of choice, and the use of time-out procedures requires strict adherence to policies within the school and the permission of families. As with any behavior reduction procedure, it should not be the first intervention of choice, and care should be taken in the development of guidelines to be adhered to in administering time-out procedures. The limitations of time-out are many, as pointed out by Sulzer-Azaroff and Mayer (1991). These include

- Time is lost from instruction. When in time-out, the learner loses valuable time from instruction.
- Time-out is not universally effective across all learners, yet is often deemed as such and is overly relied on for that reason.
- Time-out represents a negative contingency in that it removes the learner from reinforcing environments.
- The lack of procedural safeguards and legal liabilities associated with time-out are cause for concern in terms of its implementation with school-age children and youth.
- The potential for abuse exists because time-out is easy to use and therefore an overreliance by school personnel can result.
- The generalized suppression of other behaviors can occur, especially when the cues associated with the administration of the time-out procedure are not clear and consistent.

One point to consider when assessing the feasibility of using time-out procedures within your setting is to also assess how to make time in class more reinforcing (Sulzer-Azaroff & Mayer, 1991). Enriching learning environments through the design and delivery of exciting, stimulating, learner-centered activities represents a positive option when considering how to reduce or eliminate challenging behaviors of concern. After all attempts have been exhausted in terms of positive practices, consideration can be given to procedures such as time-out.

If time-out is selected as a behavior reduction procedure, all personnel must adhere to consistent implementation guidelines involved in the administration of the time-out procedures. Sulzer-Azaroff and Mayer (1991) recommended that staff should clearly communicate the conditions for time-out. The procedures must be consistent, staff must be trained and supervised in implementing the procedures, and the transition back to the classroom from the time-out must be planned to ensure that the student reenters the learning environment with appropriate behavior. The reason for this is that it is important to reinforce behaviors that are appropriate and desired within the learning environment before the student reenters the setting.

## Use of Aversives to Reduce Behavior–Punishment

Within this chapter we have presented alternatives for behavior reduction moving from least restrictive (reinforcement-based procedures) to more restrictive procedures such as punishment. Up to now we have explained and briefly presented some of the problems associated with the use of punishment to change behavior. Philosophically, the use of punishment defies what PBS is all about; however, given the importance and the responsibilities associated with behavior change, as a change agent, you the teacher need a fluent understanding of the continuum that has been traditionally used to address excessive behavior. Punishment, as we have previously mentioned, is still in use in many states within schools through the administration of corporal punishment. To examine punishment and understand why and how it has been used to treat excessive behavior, we must first understand the term.

*Punishment* is defined as the presentation of an aversive stimulus contingent on a behavior that results in the subsequent reduction of the behavior (Cooper et al., 1987). We, the authors, are philosophically opposed to the use of punishment procedures within learning environments, yet feel it our responsibility to address the topic for the benefit of our students and for those students who will read this text.

The limitations of punishment have been documented, such as the lack of long-term effectiveness of these procedures, the inconsistencies associated with the application of these procedures, the reinforcing effect that punishment has on the user, the aggressive models that it presents to students who witness or who are affected by it, the development of escape behaviors in persons subjected to it, and finally, the threat it presents to the well-being of an individual.

Historically, punishment has been used in the care and treatment of persons with disabilities and as a control for challenging behavior. An illustration is in the treatment of pica in persons with developmental disabilities. Pica is an eating disorder in which people ingest nonfood substances; this has been considered by some a form of self-injury (Burke & Lakey-Smith, 1999). Treatment for this behavior has often included the use of punishment in the form of mechanical restraints, misting of both water and lemon juice in the face of the individual, masks, and overcorrection (Burke & Lakey-Smith, 1999). Many such examples concerning the use of punishment exist in the annals of the research in the areas of mental retardation and developmental disabilities. Thankfully, the refinement of behavior intervention procedures through the years has resulted in the development of alternatives that are longer lasting and more effective than punishment in reducing problem behaviors.

Traditionally, the use of punishment procedures has incorporated the use of unconditioned aversive stimuli such as the administration of corporal punishment, restraint, or other procedures that are designed to cause physical pain and discomfort. An example of conditioned aversive stimuli is pairing a verbal threat or warning with the impending threat of a physical punisher such as a paddling. Overcorrection procedures are also within the category of punishers and consist of two components. These are restitutional overcorrection or positive practice (Alberto & Troutmam, 2003; Cooper et al., 1987). Restitutional overcorrection requires the individual to restore the classroom or situation above and beyond the state it was in before the infraction occurred. Consider Rodney, a young man with severe mental retardation who soiled his trousers one day at the day center. He was required to wash himself, wash his clothes, and mop and sanitize the bathroom and entire classroom as a form of punishment for his accident. Positive practice overcorrection, on the other hand, requires that the individual repeatedly practice the appropriate behavior over and over for a designated time period or for a specified number of responses. An illustration of positive practice would be having a student practice and repractice walking up and down the school hallway from her classroom to the cafeteria under the watchful eyes of her assistant principal as a consequence for running to lunch that day.

If there are any advantages to the use of aversive stimuli, they remain few. One could argue that they suppress the behavior, and they reinforce who is in control (i.e., teachers and not students). The disadvantages far outweigh the benefits of these procedures and do little to promote educational or behavior improvements that are of lasting duration.

## SUMMARY

The purpose of this chapter has been to explore the procedural alternatives used for reducing challenging behaviors. The chapter began with a discussion of how challenging behavior is perceived by professionals and caregivers and how these perceptions can result in our responses to behaviors that we often find annoying or overly problematic.

The importance of how behaviors are viewed by professionals and staff result in the responses that are selected to address these behavior challenges. Excessive behavior often occurs as a result of skill deficits paired with environments that are neither supportive nor instructive of skill deficiencies. This combination of personal and environmental skill deficits often results in high rates of problem behaviors that interfere with learning and the overall ease and functioning of the learning environment. The chapter also presented how within certain environments skill deficits that result in excessive behavior in students becomes the major focal point with no attention given to understanding the skills needed by the learner to eliminate the need for these responses. The need for a constructive approach (Sulzer-Azaroff & Mayer, 1991) in how we respond to challenging behavior was also presented. This viewpoint looked at adding skills to the behavior repertoires of individuals, rather than eliminating them.

One element that has emerged from the field of PBS has been the school-wide application of these principles within school systems as a means of preventing problem behaviors from occurring. This has been accomplished through the deployment of a continuum of supports within the school's behavioral support philosophy. The continuum of support (OSEP, 2000) identified three distinct levels within this continuum. At the base of the continuum is the primary prevention level. This level accounts for approximately 80% to 90% of the students within the school population. Interventions at this level are schoolwide and preventive in nature. The second level within the continuum is that of secondary prevention. This level on the continuum comprises approximately 5% to 15% of the school population, and interventions here focus on the unique needs of students who have been identified as at risk. The final level, tertiary prevention is directed toward individualized behavior support interventions for approximately 1% to 7% of the population.

The final portion of the chapter addressed specific behavior reduction methods, which were introduced on the continuum of least to most intrusive. These include the use of differential reinforcement as a method for promoting behavior reduction through the use of reinforcement designed to promote the development of alternative behaviors. Extinction was discussed along with the application of this procedure in the classroom as well as its limitations. More invasive procedures, such as response cost, time-out, and the presentation of aversives, concluded the chapter.

We hope that the material provided in this chapter offers a clearer picture of the methods that have been traditionally used to address excessive behavior and the merits of the alternatives provided through PBS. The reality is that children and youth will challenge the abilities of teachers and educational systems to proactively address their behavior and educational needs. It is imperative that educational personnel and systems be trained in the development of effective schoolwide systems designed to meet these challenges at every level for every student. We hope through prevention and the development of personal competencies and skills within caring and supportive environments that children and youth will learn positive alternatives to the behaviors that infringe on their potential.

## ACTIVITIES TO EXTEND YOUR LEARNING

1. Conduct a review of existing sources from the literature concerning the use of behavior reduction methods and critique these articles against the philosophy of practice offered by PBS.
2. Interview the parent of a child with a disability and have them offer their perspectives on the use of intrusive procedures to address behavior challenges in children with disabilities.
3. Visit a school and interview a principal, a general education teacher, a special education teacher, perhaps a counselor, and a group of students to determine whether a schoolwide behavior support model exists. Assess the availability of such models within area schools and determine whether these models provide a continuum of support as offered in the model by Sugai and colleagues.

4. Contact your local school system and ask them for information pertaining to their policies governing the use of behavior intervention approaches for the reduction of challenging behaviors.

## FURTHER READING AND EXPLORATION

1. Consult the following Web sites: http://www.pbis.org, http://www.nasponline.org, http://www.nasdse.org, and http://www.cec.sped.org for information pertaining to the use of positive interventions designed to address challenging behavior.
2. Assess the content of selected textbooks in the areas of PBS and applied behavior analysis and compare the content from these sources as they pertain to the use of behavior reduction strategies. How are these texts similar in their presentation of the topics and do they promote PBS as the method of choice in addressing challenging behavior? If not, what are the recommended practices offered by these resources?
3. Contact your local school system and ask them for information pertaining to their policies governing the use of behavior intervention approaches for the reduction of challenging behaviors.

## REFERENCES

Alberto, P. A., & Troutman, A. C. (2003). *Applied behavior analysis for teachers* (6th ed.). Upper Saddle River, NJ: Merrill/Prentice Hall.

American Academy of Pediatrics. (2000). Corporal punishment in schools (RE9574): Policy statement. *Pediatrics, 106,* 343.

American Psychological Association. (n.d.). *Guidelines on effective behavioral treatment for persons with mental retardation and developmental disabilities.* Retrieved June 26, 2003 from http://www.apa.org/divisions/div33/effectivetreatment.html

Burke, L., & Lakey-Smith, S. (1999). Treatment of pica: Considering least intrusive options when working with individuals who have a developmental handicap and live in a community setting. *Developmental Disabilities Bulletin, 27,* 1–16.

Cooper, J. O., Heron, T., & Heward, W. L. (1987). *Applied behavior analysis.* Upper Saddle River, NJ: Merrill/Prentice Hall.

Crone, D. A., & Horner, R. H. (2003). *Building positive behavior support systems in schools.* New York: Guilford.

Durand, V. M. (1990). *Severe behavior problems: A functional communication training approach.* New York: Guilford.

Hawkins, R. P. (1986). Selection of target behaviors. In R. O. Nelson & S. C. Hayes (Eds.), *Conceptual foundations of behavioral assessment* (pp. 331–385). New York: Guilford.

Horner, R. H., Sugai, G., Todd, A. W., & Lewis-Palmer, T. (1999–2000). Elements of behavior support plans: A technical brief. *Exceptionality, 8,* 205–216.

Jackson, L., & Panyan, M. V. (2002). *Positive behavioral support in the classroom*. Baltimore: Paul H. Brookes.

Miltenberger, R. G. (2001). *Behavior modification: Principles and procedures* (2nd ed.). Belmont, CA: Wadsworth/Thompson Learning.

Morris, T. L., & Hawkins, R. P. (1999). Behavior excesses and deficits in children. In J. R. Scotti & L. H. Meyer (Eds.), *Behavioral intervention: Principles, models, and practices* (pp. 129–147). Baltimore: Paul H. Brookes.

National Association of School Psychologists. (2003). Position statement on corporal punishment. *NASP Online*, http://www.nasponline.org

National Education Goals Report. (1995). http://inet.ed.gov/pubs/goals/

OSEP Center on PBIS. (2000). Applying positive behavior support and functional behavioral assessment in schools. *Journal of Positive Behavior Interventions, 2*, 131–143.

Society for Adolescent Medicine. (2003). Corporal punishment in schools: Position paper of the Society for Adolescent Medicine. *Journal of Adolescent Health, 32*, 385–393.

Sugai, G., & Horner, R. (2001). School climate and discipline: Going to scale. *A Framing Paper for the National Summit on the Shared Implementation of IDEA*, 1–8. Retrieved May 1, 2003 from http://www.pbis.org

Sulzer-Azaroff, B., & Mayer, G. R. (1991). *Behavior analysis for lasting change*. Fort Worth, TX: Harcourt Brace College Publishers.

Walker, H. M., Horner, R. H., Sugai, G., Bullis, M., Sprague, J. R., Bricker, D., & Kaufman, M. J. (1996). Integrated approaches to preventing antisocial behavior patterns among school-aged children and youth. *Journal of Emotional and Behavioral Disorders, 4*, 193–256.

Wheeler, J. J., & Hoover, J. H. (1997). A consultative model for the provision of behavioral supports to children with challenging behavior: Practical approaches for the development of school-based teams. *B. C. Journal of Special Education, 21*, 5–16.

# Developing
# Self-Determination
# Skills

## CONCEPTS TO UNDERSTAND

*After reading this chapter, you should be able to:*

- Define and describe self-determination
- Describe and discuss the relationship between positive behavior support and self-determination
- Discuss the relationships among quality of life, social validity, and self-determination of persons with disabilities
- Describe and discuss Bronfenbrenner's bioecological systems theory and its relationship to self-determination
- List and describe the four subsystems of the systems theory perspective and provide examples of self-determination in each
- List and describe the 12 teaching components of self-determination
- Discuss how self-determination is included in PBS for children and youth with challenging behavior at different ages, including infants and toddlers, early childhood, middle school years, and high school years

## KEY TERMS

Autonomy

Bioecological model

Feedback

Functional assessment

Inputs

Outcomes

Outputs

Personal appraisal

Person-centered planning

Processes

Psychological empowerment

Quality of life

Self-regulation

Self-determination

Self-management

Self-realization

Social validity

Systems theory perspective

The concept of self-determination has been briefly introduced in several of the previous chapters. It is most appropriate for self-determination to be at the end of the text because the overriding mission of positive behavior support (PBS) is to facilitate the self-determination of children and youth with challenging behaviors. Stated another way, everything that has been introduced to this point is intended to make it possible for persons with or at risk for behavior disabilities to be more self-determined, that is, to be more independent and in charge of their own lives.

Before getting into the specifics of self-determination as a construct and as an outcome that educators strive for in their work with all children and youth, and in particular those who have special needs, it is useful to briefly consider self-determination more broadly. Most people seek opportunities for and the ability to self-determine. Self-determination can be thought of as a lifelong pursuit for human beings. Individuals want to be "financially independent," to "do our own thing," to "not be under someone else's thumb," to "be our own person," to have opportunities and options, and to decide for ourselves what we will do to meet our needs and wants and how our behavior will be rewarded. Yet people are constantly faced with the reality that they are interdependent on others and that others have substantial influence on their behavior. The quality of our lives is not, of course, solely determined by the extent to which we are independent.

In his classic work *Beyond Freedom and Dignity*, the noted psychologist, Harvard professor, and father of modern behaviorism (leading to the experimental analysis of behavior, applied behavior analysis, and now, many suggest, positive behavior support) B. F. Skinner (1971) concluded his treatise on the necessity of a scientific view of human behavior by pointing out that human beings ("man") are controlled by the environment, but that environments are largely of their own making. Skinner said, "The evolution of a culture is a gigantic exercise in self-control" (p. 215). So rather than being a victim or passive observer of what happens to them, individuals can influence the environments, demands, expectations, and conditions that influence their behavior. Skinner further pointed out that the experimental analysis of behavior (now largely evolved to applied behavior analysis and PBS) changes the focus of human behavior as being grounded in their environments rather than being autonomous.

Viewed in this manner and related to self-determination, it may be logical to think of self-determination as being facilitated by the nature of the ecology—the environments in which we spend our time. For example, if one's work environment is monotonous, repetitive, highly controlled, constantly monitored, and requires no independent decision making, one might conclude that it is inconsistent with an individual's self-determination. One might conclude that a classroom teacher who must strictly adhere to the state-prescribed curriculum, has no say in which students are assigned to his class, has little planning time, and has hardly enough time to go to the restroom during the school day is not self-determined in his work environment. Both of the preceding examples are overly simplistic with regard to whether or not an individual is self-determining, as you will learn on further exploration of what is meant by self-determination.

In this chapter, the importance of self-determination is explained, and what educators might do to foster the acquisition and use of self-determination skills in the children and youth for whom they have responsibility is discussed. In particular, the emphasis is on individuals (with disabilities and/or challenging behavior) who have historically been deprived of, or at least frequently have insufficient attention provided for, opportunities for achieving self-determination.

## THE RELATIONSHIP BETWEEN POSITIVE BEHAVIOR SUPPORT (PBS) AND SELF-DETERMINATION

In Chapter 1, we introduced the various philosophical and theoretical perspectives that have been used to explain and to intervene with children and youth who demonstrate challenging behavior. Behaviorism and its application as represented by applied behavior analysis (ABA) is described as the approach that has produced the best outcomes in programs and services for children and youth with emotional and behavior disabilities. PBS is understood as having evolved from applied behavior analysis and as an extension of ABA. PBS relies on the use of person-centered interventions and employs meaningful consequences to enhance the quality of life of individuals with behavior issues.

Anderson and Freeman (2000) described PBS as having three prominent features. These features focus on (a) person-centered values (attention to individual needs, preferences, and socially valid goals), (b) recognition of individual needs and flexibility to accommodate them, and (c) meaningful outcomes that enhance the quality of life of individuals, including participation in inclusive educational and community settings. Although some argue that there is little if any difference between ABA and PBS, most experts in the discipline believe that PBS has brought greater focus to interventions that are socially valid, emphasize prevention and antecedent and environmental management, have wider relevance than exclusively special education populations, are positive and proactive, and are evaluated by the extent to which they improve the quality of life of individuals with challenging behavior. The quality of life for everyone, including those with challenging behavior, is in no small measure connected to the extent to which they are self-determined. Self-determination is inseparable from the planning, delivery, and evaluation of PBS.

It is useful to understand how self-determination, as it is represented and advanced as a part of PBS, is connected to more traditional and established behavior interventions and ABA. Alberto and Troutman (2003) detailed the desirability of and strategies for assisting students in managing their own behavior more capably. **Self-management** may be thought of as self-control or self-discipline and the ability to function to some extent independent of others in both determining aspects of the environment and in determining what the reinforcers are and how they are applied. Although this is only one way in which we might connect self-determination to prior descriptions of behavior interventions and ABA, it is very significant. For a number of years the guidance provided to educators through professional literature (textbooks and journal articles) on classroom management, ABA, and behavior interventions has emphasized the necessity of helping children and youth become more self-reliant and less dependent on external sources for antecedents (for example, environments, expectations, and consequences both rewarding and punitive).

Typically, the goal of helping students become more self-managed has been associated with their ability to apply the desired behaviors that they have learned to settings and circumstances in which there may be no adult supervision. Alberto and Troutman (2003) further emphasized that achieving self-control has long been a central aim of public education as posited by Dewey (1939), but that independence must be a focus of and taught as an important part of the school experience. It might be argued that although self-management and self-control have been much discussed in the special education discipline, they have all too often received insufficient attention compared to external controls. One area of criticism of special education is that it tends to make students with disabilities passive learners and overly dependent on adults for both direction and rewards. Although this criticism may be in part fair, it is certainly important to note that the nature and severity of particular disabilities has an impact for individuals on the extent to which they may be expected to become self-managed, self-reliant, and self-controlled.

## QUALITY OF LIFE AND PERSONS WITH DISABILITIES

In recent years, increased attention has been given in special education to enhancing the quality of life of persons with disabilities. Frequently included in the consideration of quality of life are issues and practices associated with socially valid outcomes, person-centered planning, development across the life span, roles and functions of the family, joy and happiness, personal well-being, and self-determination. In his review of how the concept of quality of life has developed, Schalock (2000) pointed out that in the field of mental retardation, quality of life was embraced in the 1980s and clarified in the 1990s. He suggests that in the decade of the 2000s, quality of life will be understood and applied more intensely by advocates, service providers, and those persons who evaluate quality outcomes. If this is in fact the reality, then professionals, whether in regular education, special education, or a related discipline, will be a part of planning, delivering, and evaluating educational services to children and youth with disabilities specific to the goal of self-determination and other quality-of-life dimensions.

Schalock (2000) defined **quality of life** as "a concept that reflects a person's desired conditions of living related to eight core dimensions of one's life: emotional well-being, interpersonal relationships, material well-being, personal development, physical well-being, self-determination, social inclusion and rights" (p. 121). In the 1990s, substantial changes were made with regard to moving the concept of quality of life more toward an outcome that may be assessed and measured (Schalock, 2000) through the use of both personal appraisal and functional assessment. Personal appraisal is largely qualitative in nature and refers to asking an individual how satisfied he or she is with aspects of their life. Functional assessment (see Chapter 6) refers to the application of various methods and instruments to observe and quantify how an individual functions in various environments. The combination of these two measures allows for a useful assessment of a person's quality of life, including on the dimension of self-determination.

Self-determination, as a dimension of quality of life for persons with disabilities, has been explored in professional literature. For example, Wehmeyer and Schwartz (1998), in a study of adults with mental retardation, found that people who were more self-determined reported a higher quality of life. Self-determination was advanced as an important goal in continued efforts to improve the quality of life for individuals with mental retardation and developmental disabilities. Wehmeyer and Schalock (2001) provided a perspective on the future roles of quality of life and self-determination in the planning and delivery of special education supports and services. They concluded that the emphasis on quality of life and self-determination could have the effect of fostering the further integration of special education and general education (see the discussion of unified systems reform in Chapter 2). That is, the emphasis on quality of life and self-determination is likely to become more important in the future in educational environments for all children and youth, and the systems of accountability will reflect more than just quantifiable, testing outcomes and more on personally valued outcomes. It is interesting to think of the focus of educators on the quality of life and self-determination of their students as a means of advancing the cause of integration and inclusion of children and youth with disabilities.

## SOCIAL VALIDITY

**Social validity** refers to the extent to which the objectives and outcomes of intervention are meaningful (valid) for the lives of the individuals for which they are intended. That is, does the education, special education, intervention result in behaviors, skills, and attitudes that are useable and functional in the context of a person's everyday life? Certainly the connection between social validity, quality of life, and self-determination is clear. Quality of life is enhanced when a person's repertoire of skills has utility and meaning in his or her life. Carpenter, Bloom, and Boat (1999) suggested that four criteria related to social validity and quality of life be kept in mind when providing special education services. They include a focus on increasing self-esteem of students, producing high levels of self-determination, increasing empowerment, and promoting joy in the lives of students. Just as was the case as noted earlier in the discussion of quality of life, the focus on socially valid outcomes has as much relevance for general education as for special education.

An important concern that arises when the matter of socially valid outcomes are examined more closely is determining whose point of view is represented in the judgments about the outcomes. To what extent are the outcomes agreed upon and determined by the person who is targeted for education and behavior change versus, for example, teachers, parents, other family members, or other stakeholders. Alberto and Troutman (2003) emphasized the role of persons involved in the student's education in determining the acceptability of outcomes. They further pointed out that social validity has relevance for not only outcomes, but also goals and procedures, and that social validity may be seen as the extent to which programs and procedures are acceptable to its consumers. There are many consumers, or stakeholders, and it is reasonable to assume that there will be times when there is disagreement between an individual's wishes (for self-determination) and the wishes of others. For example, in a study (Fox & Emerson, 2001) in which the researchers examined what different stakeholders viewed as socially valid outcomes for people with mental retardation and challenging behavior, clinicians and academics viewed direct efforts to reduce the challenging behaviors as more important and valid as outcomes than did the persons with developmental delays, their parents, or direct service providers. The point is that professionals must exercise caution in the conclusions they make about what constitutes social validity in intervention goals and outcomes.

## DEFINING AND DESCRIBING SELF-DETERMINATION

There are many ways to define the term **self-determination**. For purposes of this chapter, several definitions are useful. Turnbull and Turnbull (2001) defined self-determination as "living one's life consistent with one's own values, preferences, strengths, and needs" (p. 13). Turnbull and Turnbull equated the terms *self-determination* and *empowerment,* but pointed out that self-determination is more often associated with an individual who has a disability whereas empowerment is more often associated with a family. Other definitions have been provided as the concept of self-determination has taken form over the past decade. For example, Wehmeyer (1992, 1996) and Wehmeyer, Kelchner, and Richards (1996) suggested that self-determination refers to "acting as the primary causal agent in one's life and making choices and decisions regarding one's quality of life free from undue external influence or interference" (Wehmeyer, 1996 p. 22). A third definition offered by Schloss, Alper, and Jayne (1993) is that self-determination "refers to the ability to consider options and make appropriate choices in the home, at school, at work, and during leisure time" (p. 215). Taken together, these three definitions of self-determination address (a) the ability to make one's own decisions free from undue interference; (b) the consistency of options with one's own values, preferences, and needs; and (c) the application of self-determination across various environments (home, school, work, leisure). An organization of adults with disabilities, Self-Advocates Becoming Empowered (1996), defines self-determination as follows:

> . . . speaking up for our rights and responsibilities and empowering ourselves to stand up for what we believe in. This means being able to choose where we work, live, and our friends; to educate ourselves and others; to work as a team to obtain common goals; and to develop the skills that enable us to fight for our beliefs, to advocate for our needs, and to obtain the level of independence that we desire. (p. 3)

Finally, with regard to defining self-determination, a consensus definition has been provided (Field, Martin, Miller, Ward, & Wehmeyer, 1998) that appears to take into account all the elements and emphases of the others:

> Self-determination is a combination of skills, knowledge, and beliefs that enable a person to engage in goal-directed, self-regulated, autonomous behavior. An understanding of one's strengths and limitations together with a belief in oneself as capable and effective are essential to self-determination. When acting on the basis of these skills and attitudes, individuals have greater ability to take control of their lives and assume the role of successful adults. (p. 3)

Something to keep in mind in the understanding and application of definitions of self-determination is the effect that chronological and developmental ages have on the development of self-determination. Obviously, the younger a child is (with a disability or not), the less ability (and opportunity) he or she will have for self-determination, independence, and autonomy. Also, much of the literature describing self-determination is focused on adults with disabilities rather than children and youth in educational environments.

The elements and characteristics of self-determination have been described in various ways. As a part of the previous definition (Wehmeyer, 1996), four characteristics for determining the extent to which behaviors are self-determined are provided (Figure 11–1), including **autonomy**, **self-regulation**, **psychological empowerment**, and **self-realization** (Wehmeyer, 1999). These characteristics may be seen as developing because of particular skills and attributes that may be acquired and reinforced as part of a student's educational program and experience. Wehmeyer (1996) identified eleven components (skills and attributes) that accompany the four characteristics of self-determination, including (a) choice-making skills, (b) decision-making

**FIGURE 11–1**
*Four Characteristics for Determining the Extent to Which Behaviors Are Self-Determined*

---

### 1. Autonomous Functioning

- Acting according to one's preferences, free of undue external influence

### 2. Self-Regulation

- Engaging in self-management, goal setting and attainment, and problem solving

### 3. Psychological Empowerment

- Acting on the belief that one can exert control over areas important to him or her, that he or she possesses the skills necessary to exert control, and that exercising those skills will result in desired outcomes

### 4. Self-Realization

- Acting on an accurate knowledge of one's strengths and limitations

---

*Source:* From "A Functional Model of Self-Determination: Describing Development and Implementing Instruction," by M. L. Wehmeyer, 1999, *Focus on Autism and Other Developmental Disabilities, 14,* pp. 53–61.

skills, (c) problem-solving skills, (d) goal-setting and attainment skills, (e) self-management skills, (f) self-advocacy skills, (g) leadership skills, (h) internal locus of control, (i) positive attributions of efficacy and outcome expectancy, (j) self-awareness, and (k) self-knowledge.

Self-determination has been defined and described largely as it is associated with the skills and attributes of an individual who manifests the ability to self-determine. Various environments support or interfere with one's ability to self-determine, and those environments certainly include much more than educational settings. In their foundational book on self-determination, *Self-Determination Across the Life Span*, Sands and Wehmeyer (1996) provided perspectives on how this ability is important throughout one's entire life and in various settings, such as school, home, community, and place of work, and they suggest that the self-determination movement is a necessary part of other current social and educational movements, including school reform (unified systems) and inclusion. As noted earlier in the chapter, although self-determination might be a goal for which to strive, it is not synonymous with independence. Sands and Wehmeyer cautioned that misrepresenting self-determination as being the same as absolute individual control (independence) will interfere with educators' ability to address self-determination as an instructional goal, process, or outcome.

It is helpful in understanding self-determination to examine its relationship to the human ecology of children and youth. Self-determination, like other behaviors of children and youth, whether they do or do not have a disability, is built and maintained as a result of interactions across the various environments having relevance at various points in their lives. For example, with regard to choice-making skills, if a child has the opportunity to learn and maintain this skill in school, but the skill is ignored or even countered in other significant environments (for example, home, Sunday school, T-ball, Boy Scouts), then it may be only partially or unsuccessfully acquired as an element of the child's repertoire for self-determination.

## SELF-DETERMINATION AS AN ECOLOGICAL PERSPECTIVE

One prominent perspective on understanding the development of children and youth in the context of their environments is provided by Urie Bronfenbrenner as a part of his bioecological systems theory. You may recall that the ecological model was introduced in Chapter 1, which "views the child as developing within a complex system of relationships affected by multiple levels of the surrounding environment" (Berk, 2002, p. 27). Bronfenbrenner (1998) extended his perspective and characterized it as a **bioecological model**, taking more into account the interaction between heredity and environment in influencing development and behavior.

Bronfenbrenner's bioecological systems theory is represented as nested circles with the individual in the center surrounded by five concentric circles detailing the various contexts and systems within which the individual develops. The first is the microsystem, which is the bidirectional relationship and influence of the child and her immediate environment, such as family and school. If interactions in the microsystem occur often and over time, they tend to have a more significant and lasting effect (Collins, Maccoby, Steinberg, Heatherington, & Bornstein, 2000).

Adding to this ecological and developmental perspective the emphasis in Albert Bandura's social learning theory (1977) (see Chapter 1) on the importance of imitation of models for learning and the behavior principles specific to environmental arrangements and positive consequences, it is clear how experiences in the microsystem influence development and, in particular, the acquisition of specific skills associated with self-determination. One of the characteristics of self-determination is self-regulation. For example, children learn to self-regulate (self-manage) from the opportunities provided them by parents and teachers, by the fact that they are modeled by important persons in a child's immediate environment, and because the behaviors associated with self-regulation are valued and rewarding (either intrinsically or extrinsically).

The second level of Bronfenbrenner's bioecological systems theory is the mesosystem. Whereas the microsystem focuses on the relationship of the child to various near environments and influences (such as home and family members or school and teachers), the mesosystem is defined as the connections between microsystems (for example, the connection between home and school). Brotherson, Cook, Cunconan-Lahr, and Wehmeyer (1995) provided a model (see Table 11–1) for how three components (home, school, and community) might collaborate to build self-determination skills for children. The actions associated with home, school, and community, taken together, contribute substantially to a child's opportunities for gaining self-determination skills.

The third level of the bioecological model is the exosystem, which refers to settings such as the parent's workplace, that do not directly include children but that are likely to have a significant impact on their development and skill acquisition. Other examples of the exosystem are extended family, friends, and neighbors. Table 11–1 is actually a combination of occurrences associated with both the mesosystem and the exosystem. Brotherson and her colleagues pointed out that current federal policy associated with laws (such as the Americans with Disabilities Act and the Individuals with Disabilities Education Act) support and expect the use of PBS for persons with disabilities across collaborative environments.

The fourth level and outermost circle of the Bronfenbrenner model is the macrosystem, which is made up of laws, customs, cultural values, and resources. Certainly, there are connections between a child's acquisition of self-determination skills and the macrosystem. As stated earlier, current federal (as well as state and local) laws and associated policies support the need to prepare children and youth with disabilities to be more self-determined. At the same time, self-determination is not always a cultural value, or the extent to which it is valued varies considerably within and between cultures. For that matter, it varies considerably depending on other factors such as parenting styles, socioeconomic levels, and spiritual beliefs. These issues should be carefully considered and understood in the context of the family when assisting persons who are gaining self-determination skills.

The last element of the Bronfenbrenner model is the chronosystem, which is not a context for the development of children but rather a subsystem reflecting change over time. That is, life events change over time, and

**TABLE 11–1**
*Collaborative Efforts to Build Self-Determination Skills for Children Across Environments*

| Home | School | Community |
|---|---|---|
| • Give children a sense of control in their home environment | • Teach choice, decision-making, and self-advocacy skills | • Retrofit community to accommodate children with disabilities |
| • Expand daily activities to encourage independence and choice | • Structure school environment to ensure opportunities for choice | • Provide accessible stores, theaters, offices, community programs |
| • Balance the need for protections/safety with risk taking and decision making | • Serve as a resource for both home and community environments | • Educate community planners, architects, designers, and developers |
| • Offer suggestions to schools regarding accommodations to meet child's need | • Be advocates for community change and support parent advocacy | • Expand housing options in the community |
| • Expand accessible housing and supported living options in the community | • Support community in accommodating the needs of children | • Support landlords and builders to create supported living options in the community |
| • Provide families a greater voice in retrofitting communities | • Build partnerships with business and community leaders | • Work with schools and vocational rehabilitation to expand employment opportunities |
| • Support children with disabilities to voice their choices | | |

*Source:* Adapted from "Policy Supporting Self-Determination in the Environment of Children with Disabilities" by M. J. Brotherson, C. C. Cook, R. Cunconan-Lahr, & M. L. Wehmeyer, 1995, *Education and Training in Mental Retardation and Developmental Disabilities, 30,* p. 16. Copyright 1995 by CEC Division on Mental Retardation and Developmental Disabilities. Adapted by permission.

children experience developmental changes that impact their development in areas such as self-determination. It would be expected that as children get older and become more autonomous and (hopefully) more self-managed, they would more likely exhibit choice and influence their environments.

## SELF-DETERMINATION AS A SYSTEMS PERSPECTIVE

A system is "an integrated set of parts that function together for some end purpose or result" (Goldsmith, 2000, p. 32). Systems are made up of subsystems, or parts of the larger system. Urie Bronfenbrenner's ecological systems theory and bioecological model is intended to explain child development in the context of the five subsystems described. Many models and frameworks related to children and families have been used in education and other human service disciplines. Turnbull, Summers, and Brotherson (1984) provided a family systems framework to understand in particular what happens in families in which there is a member with a disability. From their systems perspective, the first subsystem is input, which refers to the characteristics of families. The second subsystem is process, which refers to the family's interactions. The third subsystem is output, which refers to how the family functions—what it does. One might use other terms to describe these three subsystems. Process in systems theory terms is sometimes referred to as throughput. These are the three basic elements of systems theory. Further systems theory assumes that when output is returned in some fashion to input, feedback has occurred.

Applying a **systems theory perspective** to educational environments and especially to the intent of helping children and youth gain skills in self-determination, one might use the following structure. Inputs may be considered the actions taken and information provided in relation to determining how an individual might be supported in gaining self-determination skills. Therefore, activities such as Individualized Family Service Plans (IFSPs), Individual Education Programs (IEPs), person-centered planning, functional assessment and other forms of assessment, and other means of establishing an individual's needs, strengths, and wishes related to self-determination are inputs. Processes (throughputs) might be thought of as the teaching, intervention, environmental arranging, and uses of particular methods, procedures, strategies, and curricula associated with self-determination. Outputs are the results of the processes. In educational terminology, outputs are most often referred to as outcomes. In fact, much of the literature on self-determination has focused on desired outcomes. However, the extent to which persons with disabilities at all developmental levels and ages have gained in self-determination as a result of special education intervention is somewhat undetermined empirically.

This systems approach with four subsystems, including **inputs** (assessment and planning), **processes** (teaching and intervening), **outputs** (outcomes and results), and **feedback**, has long been used in special education as a means of understanding how special education is designed to function most effectively.

To illustrate, it might be determined in the context of the evaluation and assessment process that a student needs to be more autonomous and self-managed—to have better self-determination skills (see Vignette 11.1). The student's IEP and person-centered plan, with the student's contribution, includes goals and activities specifically aimed at increasing self-determination. These are parts of the input subsystem.

## Vignette 11.1

### Self-Determination Process and Outcomes for Rhonda

Rhonda is a 17-year-old high school student who receives special education. She wishes to be more independent, to make some money on her own, and to spend less time around parents and teachers. She is placed in a part-time job in the community and then provided support and training, using the life coaching approach (Risley, 1996), in which emphasis is placed on learning on the job rather than in a prevocational setting. These are parts of the throughput (process) subsystem. Formative and summative judgments are made about how Rhonda is doing in her development of autonomy and self-management and the degree to which she is experiencing success and satisfaction in her job. These are parts of the output, or outcomes subsystem.

### Reflective Moment

Rhonda's placement is with a veterinary clinic where she works 3 hours each weekday afternoon doing a variety of jobs around the clinic, including routine care, feeding, and watering of the animals; clean-up and maintenance of the cages as well as the floors and exam and surgery rooms; some assistance in the office with clerical tasks; and occasionally serving as assistant to the veterinarian during routine exams or surgery. Given this placement and these responsibilities, can you think of some methods or strategies that Rhonda and others might employ to make judgments about her job satisfaction and her development of self-management and self-determination skills? What about ways to measure quality of life related to her job placement?

For the remainder of this chapter, a systems perspective will be used to examine the acquisition and maintenance of self-determination skills in children with and without disabilities and during the entire range of the developmental period from birth through age 21. Several fundamental assumptions are made. One is that becoming self-determined is a lifelong process for all people, whether they do or do not have disabilities. Another assumption is that self-determination is an important teaching and intervention goal and that it can be planned for and assessed; it can be systematically taught through methods, procedures, and curricula; and it is an outcome that can and should be measured and evaluated. Although the emphasis on PBS and its emphasis on quality of life and, in particular, self-determination is rather recent, behavior interventions and applied behavior analysis have long stressed the development of independence, self-control, self-reinforcement, generalization, and self-management (Alberto & Troutman, 2003).

## Assessing and Planning for Self-Determination (Input)

Numerous approaches have been used to assess children and youth to gain information useful in making plans for their education. There is an obvious close link between assessment and success in teaching. Generally, it has been held that the more program relevant the assessment procedures and instruments are (the extent to which they produce information that is directly applicable to intervention and teaching), the more useful and appropriate they are. **Functional assessments** (see Chapter 6), although not the only means of assessment for PBS, are the most prominent and applied. Functional assessment of challenging behavior makes four primary assumptions (Chandler & Dahlquist, 2002). Those assumptions are that behaviors are supported by the current environment, behavior serves a function, positive interventions will change challenging behavior, and functional assessment should be a team process.

Earlier in the chapter, self-determination was introduced as one important dimension of quality of life. The indicators of self-determination might include a person's level of autonomy, the extent to which they make choices and their own decisions, their personal control, their role in determining their personal goals and values, and the extent to which they are self-directed. How do we assess these indicators? One way, of course, is through functional assessment, or looking at the degree to which they are present or not present in real-life environments. Another way is through the use of **personal appraisal** (Wehmeyer & Schalock, 2001), or asking the person about how satisfied he is with various facets of his life. Although it may be somewhat oversimplified, it is useful to think of functional assessment as more of a quantifiable, measurable approach and personal appraisal as more of a qualitative and subjective approach.

The Council for Exceptional Children (CEC) and its Division on Career Development and Transition (DCDT), in response to the growing emphasis on self-determination in the field of special education, developed *A Practical Guide for Teaching Self-Determination* (Field et al., 1998). One section of the *Guide* is dedicated to the assessment of self-determination. As with other assessments, the primary purpose of assessment of self-determination is for instructional planning. The assessment of self-determination should be a team process, and most certainly the student should participate and be central to the process, along with professionals and the family. Measurement procedures might include interviews, behavior observations (for example, as a major component of functional assessment), psychometric tests, and curriculum-based assessment techniques, including portfolio assessment. Largely through the support of the U.S. Department of Education, Office of Special Education and Rehabilitative Services (OSERS), several assessment instruments on self-determination have been developed. Five instruments, including *The AIR Self-Determination Scale and User Guide* (Wolman, Campeau, DuBois, Mathaug, & Stolarski, 1994), *The ARC Self-Determination Scale* (Wehmeyer, 1995), *ChoiceMaker Self-Determination Assessment* (Martin & Marshall, 1996a), the *Self-Determination Assessment Battery* (Hoffman, Field, & Sawilowsky, 1996) and *The Self-Determination Profile: An Assessment Package* (Curtis, 1996), are summarized in Table 11–2.

Various planning processes and products result from the use of assessment information. For children with disabilities, planning will be manifest in the Individualized Family Service Plan (IFSP) for infants and toddlers from birth to 3 years of age and their families. For school-age children with disabilities, assessment data is found in the Individual Education Program (IEP) plan. Preschoolers with disabilities (ages 3 to 5), depending on the state and local education agency (LEA), will have either an IFSP or an IEP. Specific behavior support plans might also be used, in particular for children and youth with challenging behavior. **Person-centered planning** (PCP) has been defined (Turnbull & Turnbull, 2001) as "a process that was created to listen to the great expectations of individuals with disabilities and their families and to tailor lifestyle support to actualize those great expectations" (p. 296). Holburn (2001) has discussed the compatibility of person-centered planning with applied behavior analysis. He points out that PCP and ABA, rather than being at odds with each other, share many features with regard to improving the lives of persons with disabilities in natural environments and through enhancing skills in autonomy and self-management. However, Holburn suggests that PCP at present, subjected to the rigors of APA, would frequently fail to specify what is responsible for outcomes associated with the implementation of PCP.

The *McGill Action Planning System* (MAPS) is one primary example of person-centered planning (Forest & Lusthaus, 1990). The MAPS process provides the opportunity for a student with a disability, his or her friends, and teachers, parents, and siblings to get together and develop a vision as well as creating an action plan for the student to achieve the vision. All of these planning formats—the IFSP, IEP, behavior support, and person-centered planning—are opportunities to address quality of life and skills, support, and actions needed to facilitate self-determination.

## Teaching Self-Determination Skills (Process/Throughput)

As noted previously, the teaching and learning of self-determination skills for children and youth of all ages, whether or not they have a disability, is a worthwhile part of the mission of the educational enterprise in various environments. In fact, self-determination may be seen as an overriding ability that students need to benefit from much of their educational experience. Field et al. (1998) have described self-determination as being both a focal point of teaching and an umbrella for making curricular decisions. The Division on Career Development and Transition of the Council for Exceptional Children (Field et al., 1998) said, "Self-determination instruction during the elementary, middle, and secondary transition years prepares *all students* for a more satisfying and fulfilling adult life" (p. 118). In understanding this in the context of teaching strategies, procedures, and curricula, it is helpful to think of self-determination as being defined by 12 teaching components (Browder, Wood, Test, Karvonen, & Algozzine, 2001), listed in Figure 11–2.

**TABLE 11–2**
*Key Features of Five Instruments for Assessing Self-Determination*

| Instrument | Features |
|---|---|
| **The AIR Self-Determination Scale and User Guide** | • Purpose to assess and develop teaching strategies<br>• K–12 use<br>• Measures *capacity* and *opportunity* (home and school) related to thinking, doing, and adjusting<br>• 5-point Likert-type scale<br>• Three forms: educator, parent, and student |
| **The ARC Self-Determination Scale** | • Purposeful student self-report of self-determination<br>• Use with adolescents with disabilities, especially mild cognitive and learning disabilities<br>• 4-point Likert-type scale<br>• Measures four domains: autonomy, self-regulation, psychological empowerment, and self-realization<br>• Story (middle) completion format<br>• Up to 15 students at one time |
| **ChoiceMaker Self-Determination Assessment** | • Curriculum-based<br>• Use with middle to high school<br>• Emotional/behavior disabilities and mild-moderate learning disabilities<br>• Measures three areas: choosing goals, expressing goals, and taking action<br>• 0–4 rating scale profile and assessment |
| **Self-Determination Assessment Battery** | • Purpose to measure cognitive, affective, and behavior factors associated with self-determination<br>• Student, teacher, and parent perspective<br>• Battery of five instruments<br>• Instruments include: multiple choice, true/false, behavior checklist, classroom observation, self-report, teacher and parent questionnaire |
| **The Self-Determination Profile: An Assessment Package** | • Purpose to help youth and adults determine preferences, activities, relationships, and routines<br>• Card deck illustrates life now and in the future<br>• Part of "New Hats" curriculum |

*Sources: AIR Self-Determination Scale and User Guide,* by J. M. Wolman, P. L. Campeau, P. A. DuBois, D. E. Mithaug, and V. S. Solarski, 1994, Palo Alto, CA: American Institutes for Research; *The ARC's Self-Determination Scale,* by M. L. Wehmeyer, 1995, Arlington, TX: The ARC of the United States; *ChoiceMaker Self-Determination Assessment,* by J. E. Martin and L. Marshall, 1996a, Colorado Springs: University of Colorado; *Self-Determination Assessment Battery User's Guide,* by A. Hoffman, S. Field, and S. Sawilowsky, 1996, Detroit, MI: Wayne State University; and *Self-Determination Profile: An Assessment Package,* by E. Curtis, 1996, Salt Lake City, UT: New Hats.

### Consider This

- Because it is desirable and possible to teach self-determination skills in the classroom, what are some ways in which the 12 components (Figure 11–2) might be included directly and indirectly in pre-K–12 instruction?
- How might the instruction be the same or varied, depending on whether or not the student has a disability and if so, the nature and severity of the disability?

Remember, PBS has relevance for all students; it is not used exclusively as an intervention approach for children with challenging behavior or other special needs. Further, PBS is described as having at its center the mission of improving quality of life. One important component of quality of life (for all people) is the ability and opportunities to develop self-determination. Like most other abilities and skills, self-determination may be taught, learned, and maintained by the extent to which it is rewarding and rewarded. It is, of course, necessary to ask the question, Under what circumstances and in what environments is self-determination valued and rewarded? At the risk of an extreme oversimplification, educators are sometimes criticized for attending too much to compliance of students and too little to teaching in ways consistent with students' development of autonomy, independence, and personal responsibility. And special educators are sometimes criticized for attending too much to management and control of behavior and too little to addressing self-management, self-control, self-rewards, and control of students' own lives (Martin & Marshall, 1996b).

The guide developed by the Council for Exceptional Children and introduced earlier (Field et al., 1998) describes instructional practices that promote self-determination. The rationale for teaching self-determination is

**FIGURE 11–2**
*Teachable*
*Components of*
*Self-Determination*

- Decision making
- Choice making
- Problem solving
- Independent living (risk taking and safety skills)
- Goal setting and attainment
- Self-observation, evaluation, and reinforcement
- Self-instruction
- Self-understanding
- Self-advocacy and leadership
- Positive self-efficacy and outcome expectancy
- Internal locus of control
- Self-awareness

*Source: Teaching Self-Determination to Students with Disabilities,* by M. L. Wehmeyer, M. Agran, and C. A. Hughes, 1998, Baltimore, MD: Paul H. Brookes.

related to criticisms of public education in the United States and the need to prepare students to be successful in adult life. Specific to special education, the point is made (Agran, 1997) that there is a movement toward more participation of students with disabilities in decisions about the delivery of instruction itself. A point stressed in the guide is the role of the family and the necessity of a partnership between school professionals and families. Field (1998) and others summarize this point in the following statement:

> If the outcome that all children with disabilities leave school as self-determined young adults is achieved, educators must begin by providing instructional activities and environments that promote the development of component elements of self-determination while children are in early childhood and elementary school programs. This will require attention not only to school activities and structure, but also to the establishment of partnerships with students' families. (p. 63)

The emphasis on self-determination as an important component of curriculum and teaching strategies in special education is relatively recent. Certainly the Individuals with Disabilities Education Act of 1997 (PL 105–17) and its focus on the importance of engagement of students in learning, active student involvement, inclusion, and family partnerships have contributed to the development of curricula and strategies. There were, of course, a number of efforts prior to the legislation, primarily dating from the 1990s. Leaders in research and practice related to self-determination (Wehmeyer, Agran, & Hughes, 2000) conclude that the rationale for teaching self-determination is well established, and that it is time to focus on providing educators with methods, materials, and instructional strategies. They emphasize that this need for strategies and resources applies to all students, including those who have severe disabilities. Empirical evidence of the effects of specific strategies and curricula designed to address self-determination are just beginning to be published in the literature. For example, in a study (Agran, Blanchard, & Wehmeyer, 2000) designed to test the effects of the "Self-Determined Learning Model of Teaching" (Mithaug, Wehmeyer, Agran, Martin, & Palmer, 1998)—a model intended to enable teachers to teach goal setting, related actions, and associated adjustments to students with disabilities—the researchers found that 17 of 19 high school students made dramatic gains in their self-determination abilities. Although limited in scope, this study adds to the empirical evidence of the effectiveness of teaching self-determination for students with special needs. Other recent studies have produced similar results, but additional evidence is needed on the impact of self-determination teaching strategies for students in K–12, both with and without disabilities, and students with disabilities in inclusive settings.

Educators recognize that the teaching of self-determination in the classroom is important (Agran, Snow, & Swaner, 1999) and that it should be a high priority; however, self-determination skills are not or are infrequently found in Individual Education Programs (Wehmeyer & Shwartz, 1998; Wehmeyer et al., 2000). One possible reason for this is that educators are unaware of the curricular and other resources available to help them incorporate self-determination into classroom instruction (Test, Karvonen, Wood, Browder, & Algozzine, 2000). In fact, a recent review of resources on self-determination (Browder et al., 2001) found 51 data-based interventions, 61 curricula, and more than 675 other resources, such as books, chapters, and conceptual articles. So resources for understanding self-determination and applying established procedures and curricula are available, but many teachers are unaware of their availability or of how to apply them. You might consider the extent to which self-determination and its component parts are included as a part of your preparation to be an educator, whether at the early childhood, middle school, or high school level.

Browder and others (2001) suggested that teachers need a map for locating sources on teaching self-determination. One path of the map addresses the conceptual literature and helps teachers understand the concept, its specific components, and the rationale for its inclusion in instruction both as an overriding principle and as specific teaching content. The authors caution that there are potential pitfalls in teachers' conceptual understanding of self-determination. They include (a) failing to account for and respect a person's freedom of choice, (b) ignoring cultural values, (c) neglecting collaboration with families, (d) requiring prerequisites for self-determination, and (e) ignoring the social environment of the student (learning to be self-determined means little if the student's environments do not allow and support it). A second path suggested by Browder and her colleagues is the identification of curricular and other resources for teaching. Questions teachers might ask as they pursue this path are (a) Is the resource supported in research? (b) Can the resource be used in IEP development? (c) Are teaching strategies described? (d) How can I create an environment that promotes self-determination? and (e) Does this resource make me a more self-determined teacher?

## Outcomes of Teaching Self-Determination (Outputs, Results)

The third subsystem used to understand the systems approach to self-determination is the output or outcomes subsystem. The intent is that the assessment of the self-determination status of a child, youth, or adult (using, for example, personal appraisal and functional assessment and/or the instruments available) leads to a plan (IFSP, IEP, behavior support plan, transition plan, person-centered plan) associated with operationally defined and measurable objectives. The plan leads to the selection and implementation of useful, practical, and measurable methods, procedures, teaching, intervention, and curricula. The process (teaching/intervention) leads to outcomes that lend themselves to measurement in relation to self-determination skills and, more broadly, quality of life. The **outcomes** may be used to sum up (summative evaluation) the extent to which self-determination has been acquired, used, and maintained and to formulate (formative evaluation) new plans, goals, objectives, and activities aimed at improving self-determination skills. When feedback is provided from the evaluation for the purpose of revising plans and actions, the loop of the system is closed.

As noted previously, a criticism of the work that has been done related to enhancing the quality of life of children and youth with disabilities through the teaching of self-determination skills is that insufficient attention is paid to documentation and objective measurement of efforts (Baker, Horner, Sappington, & Ard, 2000). An example of this concern is found in a study that focused on examining the extent to which PCP processes and outcomes are quantified (Holburn, Jacobson, Vietze, Schwartz, & Sersen, 2000). Person-centered planning is, of course, used here as planning for self-determination. These researchers found that although this planning approach is growing in use and popularity, outcomes of PCP have been subjected to very little systematic assessment.

In an examination of the compatibility between PCP and ABA, Holburn (2001) suggested that they are compatible in the applied, behavior, and conceptual dimensions, but not with regard to the analytic or technological requirements. In other words, PCP and ABA "use procedures based on established principles to provide meaningful outcomes that can be measured; however, an evaluator who subjects PCP to the rigors of applied behavior analysis will not know with certainty what is responsible for outcomes" (p. 279). In a sense, this statement represents the concerns that some behaviorists have about PBS, quality of life, and self-determination. The outcomes frequently do not lend themselves to adequate measurement. However, leading proponents of PBS (Wehmeyer & Schalock, 2001) point out PBS applies the basic laws of behavior analysis to optimize environments for children and youth with challenging and problematic behaviors.

## POSITIVE BEHAVIOR SUPPORT, SELF-DETERMINATION, AND CHALLENGING BEHAVIORS

PBS is applied to impact behavior change for students with problematic and challenging behavior. PBS focuses on assessment of environments and environmental modifications (Horner, 2000) so that students "with problem behaviors experience reductions in their problem behaviors and increased social, personal, and professional quality of their lives" (p. 181). Once again, the connection has been made between PBS and quality of life. Self-determination is one fundamental component of quality of life. Therefore, supporting children and youth with challenging behavior through applications of PBS requires attending to self-determination and to the means by which it is assessed and planned for (input), acquired and maintained (process), and evaluated (outcomes). As has been noted, much of the literature and attention given to self-determination has focused on youth in transition or adults with mental retardation or other substantial developmental disabilities. However, the concept and its application are certainly applicable to children and youth from infancy through adolescence and across the life span (Doll, Sands, Wehmeyer, & Palmer, 1996), without regard for whether or not they have a disability or what the nature or severity of the disability might be. Following are brief examples of how self-determination might be included in interventions for children at various ages and their families.

### Infants and Toddlers

Early intervention services for infants and toddlers from birth to 3 years of age who meet states' definitions for eligibility are provided by federal legislation (Individuals with Disabilities Education Act, Part C) and through a family-centered approach. Services are based on what is specified in the IFSP. The IFSP is intended to include outcomes and associated action steps that are both family focused and child focused; however, the child is always viewed in the context of her family. Turnbull (2001) has advocated a new paradigm in which the early years of a child with disabilities are the launching pad to family quality of life. In other words, the supports, accommodations, and services are provided in accordance with the families' priorities related to the quality of life of all family members. This certainly has implications for what is stated in the IFSP and how outcomes and action steps are addressed (see Vignette 11.2).

## Vignette 11.2

### Bekah

Bekah is a 2½-year-old girl with spina bifida. Bekah is enrolled in a half-day, private, church-based toddler nursery school five mornings per week. The room is a natural environment for a toddler; there are nine other toddlers who are typically developing in the program. Bekah receives early intervention in the context of this environment. Both the early interventionist and physical therapist serve Bekah and her family by consulting with the teacher and doing periodic observations and functional assessments. Bekah's IFSP includes the following outcome statement: Bekah will share materials and toys with others and maintain her engagement during independent play. Action steps include things that could be done in the nursery school room as well as at home and in other environments. One action step is to provide Bekah with developmentally appropriate toys and materials and to encourage her choosing among them (choice-making skills and decision-making skills). This might be done as turn taking with another child to whom she would be close while playing. Another action is to provide toys and materials that require Bekah to find hidden objects or complete steps in a sequence (problem-solving skills). Some of this activity might be done as a shared activity with another child, for example, alternating putting shapes in a shape ball. Bekah might also have an action step that encourages her outcome to state what toys or materials she wants and have the adult confirm by saying, "This is what you asked for" (self-advocacy skills).

### Reflective Moment

How are this outcome and the associated action steps for Bekah relevant for the development of self-determination skills? Consider the four characteristics (autonomous functioning, self-regulation, psychological empowerment, and self-realization) introduced earlier in the chapter.

## Early Childhood

Brown and Cohen (1996) pointed out that although self-determination is established as an important goal or outcome for children, youth, and adults with disabilities, little attention has been given to self-determination and young children. We suggest that activity-based intervention, or ABI (Bricker,

Pretti-Frontczak, & McComas, 1998), is a good approach because it includes the elements of self-determination. ABI emphasizes natural environments, logically occurring antecedents and consequences, child-directedness, child-initiations, and active engagement (see Vignette 11.3).

## Vignette 11.3

### Theron

Theron is a 5-year-old boy who has a label of pervasive developmental disorder and has associated challenging behaviors. Theron is in an inclusive public preschool for children ages 3 through 5. He will soon be transitioning to a developmental kindergarten. Theron's IEP includes an objective to decrease his hitting other children when he is frustrated or upset. Theron's PBS plan is activity based, that is, addressing this objective will be undertaken in the context of the typical activities and routines of the classroom.

### Reflective Moment

How might he be more self-determined related to this objective? One way would be to provide Theron a concrete and simple means of keeping track of periods of time or units of activity when he has not hit another child (self-management) and associate the desired behaviors with a reward of his choosing (self-rewarding). With regard to activity-based intervention, this intervention is largely child directed, and Theron is actively engaged in a natural setting. Can you think of other ways that Theron might be self-determined?

Many useful examples and practical ideas for addressing challenging behaviors of young children can be found in a monograph published by the Division for Early Childhood of the Council for Exceptional Children (Sandall & Ostrosky, 1999). The DEC monograph incorporates ABA and PBS perspectives and illustrates how aspects of self-determination (for example, self-management) might be applied. Inclusion of young children with severe disabilities is very difficult to achieve unless there are sufficient support procedures in place (see Vignette 11.4). Koegel, Harrower, and Koegel (1999) described how over an academic-year–long period two children in kindergarten with severe disabilities (language, cognitive, and associated challenging behaviors) were successfully included through the application of a self-management approach. Increased levels of schoolwork and decreased disruptive behaviors were achieved with the assistance (gradually faded over time) of a support person in the classroom.

## Middle School Years

Students in the middle school years find themselves at a challenging point in their development. These years bring with them the desire for students to assert themselves and define their capabilities. Skill development at this stage is critical, especially in the development of social and emotional skills. These skills are vital for promoting self-determination, as evidenced in Vignette 11.4.

## Vignette 11.4

### Jason

Jason is a 10-year-old student attending Preston Middle School. He is a fifth grader, and changing classes each period is new for him this year. Jason was recently diagnosed and certified to receive special education under the classification of emotionally disturbed. He is also certified as intellectually gifted. Preston Middle School has a well-established and successful schoolwide behavior support system, and Jason requires support and intervention at the most intensive level of the support system. That is, he needs an individualized, systematic, data-based, and quantifiable intervention. He is included in all classes and does fine in his academic work. Each morning, Jason starts the day by visiting the school counselor's office for a few minutes.

Jason's IEP team includes Jason; his mom, dad, and older sister; his homeroom teacher (math); the special education consulting teacher; and the school counselor. Jason's IEP includes an objective focusing on increasing his interactions with peers. He tends to isolate himself and disconnect from children his age, and he has no friends. To develop the IEP, a functional assessment was conducted along with a personal appraisal approach. The personal appraisal and IEP participation contribute to Jason's self-determination (choice-making and decision-making skills, goal-setting skills, and self-advocacy as well as leadership skills). Jason, recognizes although it is not particularly pleasant for him, that he needs to be more sociable with others his age. One of the interventions used is a systematic analysis of decisions and cost/benefit approach (Doll et al., 1996), in which Jason writes down issues (for example, he doesn't enjoy the usual chatter that goes on across the table in the lunchroom) at the top of a page and then lists possible choices and related benefits and costs of each choice. This approach contributes to the characteristics of self-determination related to internal locus of control, positive attributions of efficacy and outcome expectancy, and self-management. Jason has a student partner in each class who helps by looking at his analysis pages and making comments, with support from the consulting teacher. Jason also shares his papers with the school counselor in the mornings and sometimes at the end of the day. Input and comments from other children and adults help Jason with self-realization, self-awareness, and self-knowledge.

### Reflective Moment

This approach to supporting Jason in establishing and maintaining peer relationships is especially designed to fit Jason's needs. It is rather unique and creative compared to typical intervention strategies. What are the elements that might make it work for Jason? What are the possible pitfalls?

## High School Years

Students at the secondary-age level typically are able to apply similar abilities for systematic decision making that are comparable to adults, which is important in planning and implementing self-determination for them. Doll (1996) and others state that "because most of the precursors to self-determination are intact in the typical adolescent, the primary emphasis of adult support for students at this level is the provision of frequent and varied opportunities to practice self-determination behaviors" (p. 85). Even though the focus of Vignette 11.5 is Annie, who has Down syndrome resulting in mild to moderate cognitive delays, this reality for typical adolescents also applies to her needs.

### Vignette 11.5

#### Annie

Annie is 19 years old and is a student in the vocational classes at her high school. She has the benefit of both a transition plan and a person-centered plan that are consistent and complimentary. One of the things that brings Annie the greatest sense of joy and fulfillment are children's books and music. She enjoys all types of music, and she sings proudly in her church choir. Annie's plan is that she will soon have a job in the community where she will earn a salary. She wants to live in an apartment with a friend or friends. A great deal of work has been done previously with Annie in her school experience and at home, as well as in her mesosystem—the connections between environments and people important in Annie's life. She is at a point where she is prepared to acquire more advanced self-determination skills.

The plan for Annie is that she will have a supported employment placement at the local bookstore/coffee shop. She will learn on the job, but experiences at school will reinforce the skills she needs at the bookstore. The positive behavior plan for Annie is that she will be supported and provided practice and skill refinement on the job, at school, and at home.

#### Reflective Moment

Given this brief description of the plan for Annie, how might her experience contribute to her autonomy? Self-regulation? Empowerment? Self-realization? How is the plan for Annie potentially connected to the enhancement of her quality of life?

## SUMMARY

PBS has as a central mission the improvement of the quality of life for children and youth with special needs as well those who do not have disabilities. One component of quality of life is self-determination. Although self-determination has been defined in various ways, a consensus definition has emerged (Field et al., 1998), which states that knowledge, skills, and beliefs combine to support persons in being goal directed, self-regulated, and autonomous. Self-determination requires that persons understand their strengths and limitations, along with a belief in their capability. Behaving in self-determined ways allows persons to take control of their lives and to be successful adults. Four characteristics (autonomy, self-regulation, psychological empowerment, and self-realization) and eleven components (Wehmeyer, 1996) have been provided to describe the concept of self-determination.

Self-determination may be further understood from a bioecological model and systems perspective. That is, the acquisition and maintenance of the ability to be self-directed develops in the context of a child's near and far environments over time, as described by Bronfenbrenner's bioecological systems theory. A system is "an integrated set of parts that function together for some end purpose or result" (Goldsmith, 2000 p. 32). For our purposes here, self-determination is the desired outcome or result. The subsystems that operate to contribute to that outcome are the inputs (assessment and planning), processes or throughputs (procedures, strategies, teaching methods, curricula), outputs (outcomes, evaluations of impact), and feedback. Various methods have been applied to assess self-determination in children, youth, and adults, including most commonly, personal appraisal and functional assessment. Assessment information is used to develop plans, such as the IFSP, the IEP, behavior support plans, or PCP. Self-determination is frequently not included in planning for students with special needs through the IEP. Teachers and other educational personnel often understand the place of self-determination as an important component of instruction but do not know about the resources available to support teaching with established curriculum and procedures as well as assessment tools. Browder and others (2001), in a review of resources for teachers in self-determination, found that there are 51 data-based interventions described in the literature, 61 curricula, and 675 other resources (such as books, chapters, or conceptual articles).

Self-determination as a skill, attitude, and belief has relevance for all children and youth, not just students who have disabilities. PBS and its components, such as self-determination, are seen as initiatives that will facilitate the movement toward inclusion and unified systems reform in education. Much of the self-determination literature and related assessment and methods literature are focused on children and youth with disabilities. Historically, there has not been sufficient attention given to addressing the needs of these students for self-management, autonomy, and self-directedness. It might be argued that the relationship between children and youth with challenging behavior and, therefore, the need for more intensive and direct intervention approaches and the teaching of self-determination is even less established. Much of the focus in addressing challenging behavior of students labeled behavior disordered or emotionally disturbed has been targeted at changing behavior by limiting choices and autonomy, controlling consequences, and imposing structure, rather than by providing opportunities for self-direction related to environments, learning content, behaviors, and rewards. Some examples of how self-direction might be included in the educational programming for children and youth at various age levels, and as a component of the provision of PBS with challenging behavior, are provided.

With the current status of reforms in education, including unified systems reform and inclusion, it may be expected that in the future self-determination will receive increasing attention as both a specific component of curricula and classroom instruction at all grade levels as well as a broader mission. Field (1998) and others have described self-determination as being not only a focal point of teaching but also an umbrella for making curricular decisions. A major criticism that continues to be related to self-determination is that there is insufficient evidence and documentation that the teaching of self-determination leads to an improved quality of life for persons with disabilities and their families. Hopefully in the future the associations among the inputs (assessment and planning), processes (throughputs, teaching, curricula, procedures, and methods), outcomes (results, output, and evaluation), and feedback (data for change) will be more clearly established by quantifiable, valid, and reliable measures.

In this chapter, we have used a number of descriptors to help define and describe self-determination as a part of quality of life and therefore an important component of positive behavior supports. Some of those descriptors are self-reliance, self-management, self-control, social validity, empowerment, primary causal agent, choice making, self-regulated, goal-directed, autonomous, self-realization, self-advocacy, self-awareness, self-knowledge, and self-rewarding. All of these descriptors are part of an understanding of what composes self-determination. These behaviors, beliefs, and attitudes are acquired over the life span as a result of experiences. They may be systematically planned and assessed, taught, and evaluated.

## ACTIVITIES TO EXTEND YOUR LEARNING

1. Find additional definitions of self-determination in the literature, compare them to the five definitions provided in the chapter, and develop your own composite definition.
2. In small groups of three to five participants in class, develop an outline of what you would consider a curriculum for teaching self-determination at the preschool level, early childhood years, middle school, and high school.
3. Go back to the chapter on ethics and attempt to determine the extent to which self-determination, as described by the four characteristics and eleven components, is represented in the various ethical codes and standards from the organizations.
4. Invite a group of college students with disabilities on your campus to come to class and share their perspectives on self-determination. Be sure to prepare them by letting them know about the chapter content, in particular, the definition from the Self-Advocates Becoming Empowered organization. You can make this contact through the office for students with disabilities on your campus. You will probably want to meet with them prior to their coming to class to share your goals and what they might expect, as well as how they think you might enhance the activity.

5. Depending on your interest with regard to age and grade level, divide into small groups. Using the book *Self-Determination Across the Life Span: Independence and Choice for People with Disabilities* (Sands & Wehmeyer, 1996, pp. 79–85), have each group select an age grouping. Review the material for that group, including the teaching ideas provided. Share with the class as a whole what your group found regarding strategies that you like to facilitate self-determination.

## FURTHER READING AND EXPLORATION

1. A federally funded effort, the Self-Determination Synthesis Project (SDSP) has the mission of synthesizing and disseminating information about best practices and the knowledge base related to self-determination. Visit the SDSP Web site at http://www.uncc.edu/sdsp and see what you can find.
2. Obtain the Test, Karvonen, Wood, Browder, and Algozzine article, "Choosing a Self-Determination Curriculum," from *Teaching Exceptional Children* (November/December, 2000). Use the sample of curriculum and components and the materials review checklist to help you understand what some of the primary curricular packages are and what criteria might be used to review them.
3. Go to the sources provided for the assessment tools introduced in the chapter and determine to what extent each is curriculum based, what age levels are covered, and for what children and/or youth they are intended.
4. Find journal articles on current movements for school restructuring and reform and accountability; see if you find self-determination discussed as an important part of the process. Try, for example, *Phi Delta Kappan* or *Educational Leadership*.
5. For an early childhood and early childhood special education perspective on challenging behavior, PBS, and self-determination, read the monograph, *Young Exceptional Children Monograph Series No. 1:* "Practical Ideas for Addressing Challenging Behaviors," from the Division for Early Childhood (DEC) of the Council for Exceptional Children (CEC) (Sandall & Ostrosky, 1999). In particular, look for guidance and examples of strategies that in your view reflect self-determination.

## REFERENCES

Agran, M. (1997). *Student-directed learning: A handbook on self-management.* Pacific Grove, CA: Brooks/Cole.

Agran, M., Blanchard, C., & Wehmeyer, M. L. (2000). Promoting transition goals and self-determination through student self-directed learning: The self-determined learning model of instruction. *Education and Training in Mental Retardation and Developmental Disabilities, 35,* 351–364.

Agran, M., Snow, K., & Swaner, J. (1999). Teacher perceptions of self-determination: Benefits, characteristics, strategies. *Education and Training in Mental Retardation and Developmental Disabilities, 34,* 293–301.

Alberto, P. A., & Troutman, A. C. (2003). *Applied behavior analysis for teachers* (6th ed.). Upper Saddle River, NJ: Merrill/Prentice Hall.

Anderson, C. M., & Freeman, K. A. (2000). Positive behavior support: Expanding the application of applied behavior analysis. *The Behavior Analyst, 23,* 85–94.

Baker, D. J., Horner, R. H., Sappington, G., & Ard, W. R., Jr. (2000). A response to Wehmeyer (1999) and a challenge to the field regarding self-determination. *Focus on Autism and Other Developmental Disabilities, 15,* 154–156.

Bandura, A. (1977). *Social learning theory.* Upper Saddle River, NJ: Prentice Hall.

Berk, L. E. (2002). *Infants, children and adolescents* (4th ed.). Boston: Allyn & Bacon.

Bricker, D., Pretti-Frontczak, K., & McComas, N. (1998). *An activity-based approach to early intervention* (2nd ed.). Baltimore: Paul H. Brookes.

Bronfenbrenner, U. (1998). The ecology of developmental processes. In R. M. Lerner (Ed.), *Handbook of child psychology: Vol 1. Theoretical models of human development* (5th ed., pp. 993–1028). New York: Wiley.

Brotherson, M. J., Cook, C. C., Cunconan-Lahr, R., & Wehmeyer, M. L. (1995). Policy supporting self-determination in the environments of children with disabilities. *Education and Training in Mental Retardation and Developmental Disabilities, 30,* 3–14.

Browder, D. M., Wood, W. M., Test, D. W., Karvonen, M., & Algozzine, B. (2001). Reviewing resources on self-determination: A map for teachers. *Remedial and Special Education, 22,* 233–244.

Brown, F., & Cohen, S. (1996). Self-determination and young children. *The Journal of the Association for Persons with Severe Handicaps, 21,* 22–30.

Carpenter, C. D., Bloom, L. A., & Boat, M. B. (1999). Guidelines for special educators: Achieving socially valid outcomes. *Intervention in School and Clinic, 34,* 143–149.

Chandler, L. K., & Dahlquist, C. M. (2002). *Functional assessment: Strategies to prevent and remediate challenging behavior in school settings.* Upper Saddle River, NJ: Merrill/Prentice Hall.

Collins, W. A., Maccoby, E. E., Steinberg, L., Hetherington, E. M., & Bornstein, M. H. (2000). Contemporary research on parenting: The case for nature and nurture. *American Psychologist, 52,* 218–232.

Curtis, E. (1996). *Self-determination profile: An assessment package.* Salt Lake City, UT: New Hats.

Dewey, J. (1939). *Experience and education.* New York: Macmillan.

Doll, B., Sands, D. J., Wehmeyer, M. L., & Palmer, S. (1996). Promoting the development and acquisition of self-determined behavior. In D. J. Sands & M. L. Wehmeyer (Eds.), *Self-determination across the life span: Independence and choice for people with disabilities* (pp. 65–90). Baltimore: Paul H. Brookes.

Field, S., Martin, J. E., Miller, R., Ward, M., & Wehmeyer, M. L. (1998). *A practical guide to teaching self-determination.* Reston, VA: Council for Exceptional Children.

Forst, M., & Lusthaus, E. (1990). Everyone belongs with the MAPS action planning system. *Teaching Exceptional Children, 22*(2), 32–35.

Fox, P., & Emerson, E. (2001). Socially valid outcomes of intervention for people with MR and challenging behavior: Views of different stakeholders. *Journal of Positive Behavior Interventions, 3,* 183–189.

Goldsmith, E. B. (2000). *Resource management for individuals and families* (2nd ed.). Belmont, CA: Wadsworth/Thomson Learning.

Hoffman, A., Field, S., & Sawilowsky, S. (1996). *Self-determination assessment battery user's guide.* Detroit, MI: Wayne State University.

Holburn, S. (2001). Compatibility of person-centered planning and applied behavior analysis. *The Behavior Analyst, 24,* 271–281.

Holburn, S., Jacobson, J. W., Vietze, P. M., Schwartz, A. A., & Sersen, E. (2000). Quantifying the process and outcomes of person-centered planning. *American Journal on Mental Retardation, 105,* 402–416.

Horner, R. H. (2000). Positive behavior supports. In M. Wehmeyer & J. R. Patton (Eds.), *Mental retardation in the 21st century* (pp. 181–196). Austin, TX: PRO-ED.

Individuals with Disabilities Education Act Amendments of 1997, Pub. L. No. 105–17, 20 U.S.C. § 1400 *et seq.*

Koegel, L. K., Harrower, J. K., & Koegel, R. L. (1999). Support for children with developmental disabilities in full inclusion classrooms through self-management. *Journal of Positive Behavior Interventions, 1,* 26–34.

Martin, J. E., & Marshall, L. (1996a). *ChoiceMaker self-determination assessment.* Colorado Springs: University of Colorado.

Martin, J. E., & Marshall, L. (1996b). Choice making: Description of a model project. In M. Agran (Ed.), *Student-directed learning: Teaching self-determination skills* (pp. 224–248). Pacific Grove, CA: Brooks/Cole.

Mithaug, D. E., Wehmeyer, M. L., Agran, M., Martin, J., & Palmer, S. (1998). The self-determined learning model of teaching: Engaging students to solve their learning problems. In M. L. Wehmeyer & D. J. Sands (Eds.), *Making it happen: Student involvement in educational planning, decision-making and instruction* (pp. 299–328). Baltimore: Paul H. Brookes.

Risley, T. (1996). Positive behavioral intervention for challenging behavior through life arrangement and life coaching. In L. K. Koegel, R. L. Koegel, & G. Dunlap (Eds.), *Positive behavioral support: Including people with difficult behavior in the community* (pp. 425–437). Baltimore: Paul H. Brookes.

Sandall, S., & Ostrosky, M. (Eds.). (1999). Practical ideas for addressing challenging behaviors. *Young Exceptional Children Monograph Series No. 1,* Division for Early Childhood of the Council for Exceptional Children. Longmont, CO: Sopris West.

Sands, D. J., & Wehmeyer, M. L. (Eds.). (1996). *Self-determination across the life span: Independence and choice for people with disabilities.* Baltimore: Paul H. Brookes.

Schalock, R. I. (2000). Three decades of quality of life. *Focus on Autism and Other Developmental Disabilities, 15,* 116–127.

Schloss, P. J., Alper, S., & Jayne, D. (1993). Self-determination for persons with disabilities: Choice, risk and dignity. *Exceptional Children, 60,* 215–225.

Self-Advocates Becoming Empowered. (1996). *The national self advocacy organization definition of self-determination* [Online]. Retrieved from http://cdrc.ohsu.edu/selfdetermination/leadership/alliance/documents/ Self_Advocates_Becoming_Empowered.pdf

Skinner, B. F. (1971). *Beyond freedom and dignity*. New York: Alfred A. Knopf.

Test, D. W., Karvonen, M., Wood, W. M., Browder, D., & Algozzine, B. (2000). Choosing a self-determination curriculum: Plan for the future. *Teaching Exceptional Children, 33,* 48–54.

Turnbull, A. P. (2001, December). *The early years: The launching pad to family quality of life*. Paper presented at the annual meeting of the Division for Early Childhood of the Council for Exceptional Children, Boston, MA.

Turnbull, A. P., Summers, J. A., & Brotherson, M. J. (1984). *Working with families with disabled members: A family systems approach*. Lawrence: University of Kansas, Kansas University Affiliated Facility.

Turnbull, A. P., & Turnbull, R. (2001). *Families, professionals, and exceptionality: Collaborating for empowerment* (4th ed.). Upper Saddle River, NJ: Merrill/Prentice Hall.

Wehmeyer, M. L. (1992). Self-determination and the education of students with mental retardation. *Education and Training in Mental Retardation, 27,* 302–314.

Wehmeyer, M. L. (1995). *The ARC's Self-Determination Scale*. Arlington, TX: The ARC of the United States.

Wehmeyer, M. L. (1996). Self-determination as an educational outcome: Why is it important to children, youth and adults with disabilities? In D. J. Sands & M. L. Wehmeyer (Eds.), *Self-determination across the life span: Independence and choice for people with disabilities* (pp. 17–36). Baltimore: Paul H. Brookes.

Wehmeyer, M. L. (1999). A functional model of self-determination: Describing development and implementing instruction. *Focus on Autism and Other Developmental Disabilities, 14,* 53–61.

Wehmeyer, M. L., Agran, M., & Hughes, C. A. (1998). *Teaching self-determination to students with disabilities*. Baltimore: Paul H. Brookes.

Wehmeyer, M. L., Agran, M., & Hughes, C. A. (2000). A national survey of teachers' promotion of self-determination and student-directed learning. *Journal of Special Education, 34,* 58–68.

Wehmeyer, M. L., Kelchner, K., & Richards, S. (1996). Essential characteristics of self-determined behaviors of adults with mental retardation and developmental disabilities. *American Journal on Mental Retardation, 100,* 632–642.

Wehmeyer, M. L., & Schalock, R. L. (2001, April). Self-determination and quality of life: Implications for special education services and supports. *Focus on Exceptional Children,* 1–16.

Wehmeyer, M. L., & Schwartz M. (1998). The relationship between self-determination and quality of life for adults with mental retardation. *Education and Training in Mental Retardation and Developmental Disabilities, 33,* 3–12.

Wolman, J. M., Campeau, P. L., DuBois, P. A., Mithaug, D. E., & Stolarski, V. S. (1994). *AIR Self-Determination Scale and User Guide*. Palo Alto, CA: American Institutes for Research.

# Chapter 12

# Reviewing Chapters and Considering Future Applications of Positive Behavior Supports

## CONCEPTS TO UNDERSTAND

*After reading this chapter, you should be able to:*

- Summarize each of the previous 11 chapters of the text
- Discuss the relationships among the chapters
- List and briefly describe six issues that impact the future planning, implementation, and evaluation of positive behavior support

## KEY TERMS

Antecedents

Behavior reduction strategies

Behavior support plans

Educational reform–unified systems reform

Ethical standards and conduct

Family-centered philosophy

Family partnerships

Functional assessment

Outcomes measurement

Positive replacement behaviors

Reinforcement

Self-determination

Single-subject designs

Transitions

Understanding behavior and behavior theory

Unifying disciplines

This final chapter is intended to briefly review what has been presented in the prior 11 chapters, to restate how the major themes of the textbook are interconnected, and to overview selected issues that will likely impact the future planning, implementing, and evaluating of positive behavior supports (PBS) in various educational environments. You no doubt noted from the previous chapter that there remain questions and needs associated with the continued development and refinement of the field of PBS. Positive behavior support as a distinct approach to addressing the behavior of children and youth is a rather recent development. Whether currently a practicing professional in education or a related discipline or a professional to be, you will probably have many opportunities to resolve issues associated with PBS and its planning and implementation.

Suppose, for example, that a kindergarten teacher, along with the special education consulting teacher–behavior specialist, are given the task by their principal of establishing a positive behavior support team and planning for the kindergarten unit of the school. There are three kindergarten rooms. One of the kindergarten teachers has the fundamental belief that children who exhibit chronic misbehavior should always be excluded from class, dealt with by special education, and allowed to return to class if and when their behavior is "fixed." A second teacher has the belief that for the most part the problem behavior of his students is a direct result of inadequate parenting or possibly a neurological or medical condition. A third kindergarten teacher depends very heavily on direct instruction or teacher-directed activities, a rigid schedule, and tangible rewards associated with a point system for all the children in the class.

Although this scenario may seem simplistic and negative, these points of view regarding the challenging behavior of young children are certainly not uncommon in educational settings. The teacher and her special education colleague have a significant challenge as they attempt to lead the formulation and implementation of a positive behavior support team and plan for the kindergarten unit.

Work toward a shared vision for the future of this plan will require addressing some of the issues that arise from the beliefs and styles of their fellow teachers as well as other emerging issues related to the successful application of PBIS. How will they get started? What can they do to begin to achieve a sense of being a team and having a common mission and shared vision? What are the concerns and misgivings of the other kindergarten teachers, and how will they be addressed? How will parents or family members, upper-grade-level teachers, and others in the school be included? How will the plan fit with the existing inclusion initiatives in the school? How is the **behavior support plan** integral to the emphasis on achievement accountability and testing? What expertise and other resources can be drawn on, and how will the plan be connected to research and established effective practice in early childhood education and early childhood special education? How will the impacts of the plan on everyone be measured, including students, teachers, and families? How does the plan fit with the overall school and system reform and restructuring that is under way?

These are a few of the questions and issues that might be encountered on the way to developing and applying a positive behavior support plan and associated interventions. Despite the fact that PBS appears to be a sensible, practical, and comprehensive approach to addressing the challenging behaviors of children and youth in educational environments, it will continue to be often difficult to actualize. PBS is a promising approach for the future, and resolution of the issues raised in this chapter is important for its future success.

# REVIEWING AND CONNECTING CHAPTERS 1 THROUGH 11

Before getting into the future directions of PBS, it will be useful to overview in general terms the first 11 chapters and review how they are linked. This will set the stage for consideration of issues that have relevance across more than one chapter. In Chapter 1, we introduced the common theories and associated practices used to understand and influence behavior in children and youth.

## Understanding Behavior

Obviously, primary attention was given to **understanding behavior and behavior theory** and intervention and its evolution over the past four decades. PBS was presented as a recent outgrowth of applied behavior analysis and as a meaningful and practical way to influence the behavior of all children and youth (whether they have a disability or not) across a variety of learning environments. In particular, positive behavior support was a central theme of and required in the 1997 reauthorization of the Individuals with Disability Education Act. The principles of PBS (Richey & Wheeler, 2000) are: behavior reflects a need, adult responses should be nonpunitive, developmental appropriateness is important, environments should be designed to prevent challenging behavior, and interventions should be positive and directed toward the active teaching and nurturing of positive forms of alternative behaviors.

## Partnering with Families

To understand and influence behavior, educators must be able to plan for and respond to behavior in the context in which it occurs. That requires attention to home, family, and the lives of the person with challenging behavior and his family members. Chapter 2 was somewhat of a departure from previous approaches to describing the place of family when students present troubling behavior. Rather than on families, many times the focus has been exclusively on parents (often the mother), and parents have been viewed as simply one of many stakeholders, rather than as partners and central to planning, implementing, and evaluating behavior interventions. Further, rather than a partnership between professionals and families, the notion of parent involvement has translated into an expectation by professionals that parents should be compliant in carrying out prescribed elements of the intervention in the interest of generalization. The text suggested a shift in this paradigm toward a more **family-centered approach** in which families are encouraged and supported to become partners, shared decision makers, and full participants in all aspects of intervention, as they wish and as is developmentally appropriate for them. It is often very difficult and "messy" to establish and maintain **family partnerships**. And yes, in some instances, families and family members (just as sometimes teachers!) are a primary source of causation. But that does not change the professionals' obligation to work toward partnerships with families. If we as educators cannot help, value, and enable parents and families, then we should strive to at least to do no harm. In Chapter 3, nine organizing themes were presented for understanding ethical behavior and PBS. Two of the themes are specific to the family—families should have active participation in all aspects of PBS, and family diversity should be respected and taken into account in the planning and implementing of PBS.

## Professional Ethics and PBS

Ethics are defined (Chapter 3) as the principles of conduct governing individual professionals as well as the principles governing a particular group or discipline. As we have discussed, PBS has relevance for all children and youth across various learning environments, without consideration for whether or not they have a disability and without consideration for the nature and severity of a disability. A separate code of ethics does not exist for PBS. Therefore, it is necessary to examine the different codes of **ethical standards and conduct** associated with several organizations and associations, as was done in Chapter 3. Looking across these various ethical positions and statements, it is possible to identify some common points and areas of agreement. For example, there is general agreement about recognizing and valuing the uniqueness of individual children without regard for their ability level, maintaining safe and healthy learning environments, emphasizing positive learning experiences associated with developing competence and enhancing life skills, and respecting family diversity. However, some ethical statements suggest differences or clearly reflect disagreements among the organizations. One of these is the ethical position taken related to the uses of punitive means, including corporal punishment, to influence behavior of students. Ethical considerations in the delivery of PBS govern all of our practices as educators and must be included as we discuss issues and future directions.

## Antecedents

**Antecedents** serve as triggers for behavior. Antecedents include people, environments, activities, and materials that precede a behavior. Setting events, which precede antecedents, are also important. For example, if a child comes to class in the morning and has just been the victim of a bully on the school bus (setting event), she might respond differently to the teacher and the learning activity (antecedents) than she would typically. Janney and Snell (2000) stated that, as a part of the process of developing individual behavior support plans, information about specific antecedents should be gathered. They suggested that antecedent information might be organized into who (people or groups related to the behavior), what (tasks and activities required of children), when (schedules and times), and where (environments and spaces). Examining these antecedents will help in better understanding the triggers for the challenging behavior or absence of a desired behavior. We have discussed in the text that positive behavior interventions and supports (PBIS) place a very strong emphasis on antecedent management, both as a means of preventing undesirable behavior and as an intervention strategy rather than, or in addition to, a focus on the consequences of behavior. Of course, most experienced and successful teachers understand that paying attention to the antecedent conditions in their classroom will go a long way toward preventing, minimizing, or eliminating challenging behavior.

## Reinforcement

"All that you are doing is bribing children." "You never pay attention to the student's good behavior and reward him for it." In truth, one of the long-standing sources of misunderstanding between special educators and general educators is how **reinforcement** (consequences) is viewed and applied in school settings. At the extreme (overstated here to make the point), the general educator might argue that students should behave because they are expected to, and they will get a sense of personal well-being and satisfaction for achievement, compliance, and productivity. The special educator might be inclined to systematically use herself as the source of reinforcement through the use of extraneous rewards (for example, stickers), awarding privileges (extra play time), or verbal praise ("Good job!"). These extreme points of view leave little room for common ground about how to influence the behavior of children and youth. In Chapter 5, we defined and described reinforcement and provided examples of its application as an essential element of positive behavior support.

Reinforcement has been described (Alberto & Troutman, 2003) as "a relationship between two environmental events, behavior (response) and an event or consequence that follows the response" (p. 282). Reinforcement requires that the behavior be increased or maintained as a result of the consequence. Reinforcement may be positive or negative. Positive reinforcement is the contingent presentation of consequence that increases behavior. For example, when the consequence of a student raising his hand is to be called on by the teacher, the child might be more inclined to raise his hand in the future. Negative reinforcement (Alberto & Troutman, 2003) "is the contingent removal of an aversive stimulus immediately following a response that increases the future rate and/or probability of the response" (p. 264). For example, when the professor assigns an outside reading, the students complain that it is too much work and too difficult. The professor then removes the required assignment, thereby negatively reinforcing the complaining and increasing the likelihood that it will be repeated the next time an outside reading assignment is made.

In addition to reinforcement being positive or negative, it can be understood as primary or secondary, intrinsic or extrinsic, delivered through different schedules, as naturally occurring, and as offered to students through options for menus of reinforcement. All these aspects of reinforcement were explained in Chapter 5. A central point to be made here is that the understanding and systematic application of reinforcement is not diminished as a result of the extension of applied behavior analysis to positive behavior supports and interventions. Rather, emphasis is given to the place of reinforcement for all children, and additional attention is given to planning environments that will foster intrinsic and naturally occurring reinforcers. Because PBS (one of its elements being reinforcement) is seen as a part of **unified systems reform** in education, the principles and practices of reinforcement should be understood and have meaningful application for all educators and all children and youth in various learning environments. The place of reinforcement in issues and future directions is described later in this chapter.

## Functional Assessment

There are, of course, various forms of assessment and evaluation of children. Assessment in general is intended to collect information that has relevance for planning educational activities, periodically checking to determine how children are progressing, and summing up how much gain has been made over a period of time related to goals and objectives. **Functional assessment** is the primary approach advocated as a part of PBS to understand the relationship between a child's (challenging) behavior and the environment. Functional assessment generally involves examining setting events, antecedents (for example, the environment or the curriculum), the target behavior, and the consequences of the behavior. Functional assessment may employ strategies such as observation and data collection in natural environments; interviews with children, teachers, or family members; and instruments such as checklists and profiles. The goal of functional behavior assessment is to provide a systematic analysis of behavior to design an intervention. Chandler and Dahlquist (2002) identified four assumptions regarding functional assessment: the current environment supports challenging behavior, behavior serves a function, positive interventions can change challenging behavior, and a team-based process is necessary for functional assessment. Issues and future directions have less to do with whether or not functional assessment is a good idea as an element of PBIS and more to do with the practical questions of how it will be implemented and by whom.

## Behavior Support Plans

The provision of positive behavior support through systematic planning and implementation may be thought of as occurring on three levels (Turnbull & Turnbull, 2001). Level 1 support is schoolwide, targets all students, and emphasizes clear expectations and positive feedback. Scott (2001) described how in an elementary school (K–5) the use of a schoolwide behavior support plan resulted in a decrease in the number of students requiring actions associated with their exclusion as a result of problem behaviors. Fox and Little (2001) identified three elements for the successful development of a schoolwide behavior support plan in a community preschool setting—active involvement of the school director, use of a team and attending to the overall school environment as well as the partnership with families, and the provision of individual intensive support systems when needed by a child.

Level 2 support is individualized for some students in classrooms and in the school environment and is of moderate intensity. Functional assessment undertaken by the individual education program (IEP) team of a student who has been identified as having special needs might be completed and limited to school settings. Although the strategies employed as a part of level 2 (such as modifying the environment, using schedules, curricular adaptations, attending more to positive reinforcement, and teaching replacement skills) are individualized, they are not as intensive as level 3 positive behavior support plans.

Level 3 support is comprehensive. That is, it cuts across home, school, and community. Functional assessment across the multiple settings is required, and the interventions required are intensive, pervasive, and comprehensive. Typically, children and youth requiring level 3 support have chronic challenging behaviors that serve as substantial barriers to their education and quality of life. Whatever level the positive behavior support and associated planning, there are some common features. It is important that positive behavior support planning be a collaborative team process. The plan should emphasize positive means of addressing challenging behavior. The plan should be based on the collection of relevant and useable data. The **outcomes** of the implementation of the plan should be **measurable** and judged against stated goals and objectives. Carr et al. (1999) have indicated that the outcomes of PBS should be supportive settings and skill enhancement allowing students to reach their potential. Obviously, the future of positive behavior support plans, as we have described them, is tied to the trends that are followed with regard to special education, general education, and unified systems reform in education.

## Single-Subject Designs

Is the teacher a researcher? If he or she understands the basic concepts of **single-subject design** and is involved in planning and carrying these designs to meet the individual needs of students with special needs, then the answer is yes. Richards, Taylor, Ramasamy, and Richards (1999) pointed out that the passage and subsequent reauthorization of the Individuals with Disabilities Education Act (IDEA), in which the mandate is to meet the individual needs of students with disabilities, makes the use of single-subject research designs especially relevant and needed. As stated in Chapter 8, single-subject research is rooted in the early work of behaviorists in the 1950s and 1960s and as intervention efforts were reported beginning in 1968 with the initiation of the *Journal of Applied Behavior Analysis (JABA)*. Single-subject research designs are and have always been highly applied in nature. That is, there is no difficulty in translating the research to practical applications, because it is always designed to answer applied questions about the effects of specific interventions, treatments, and instructional procedures.

In their foundational work and research (Baer, Wolf & Risley, 1968), three of the pioneers of the applied behavior analysis (ABA) field described what is intended by the terms *applied, behavioral,* and *analytic*. Applied suggests that the research has social relevance and validity and is meaningful to the individual and society. Behavioral refers to the focus on quantifiable behaviors that may be systematically observed. Analytic refers to events under the control of the researcher that account for the presence or absence of a behavior. Single-subject research designs as they have evolved over the past 30 years or more must meet the standards of the fundamental intent of applied behavior analysis. Perhaps the central issue for the future related to single-subject design and PBIS is how the different perspectives of traditional applied behavior analysts and those embracing the broader view of positive behavior support will be resolved. In general, there appears to be agreement between the two with regard to the importance of applied, substantial agreement with regard to the focus on targeting specific, measurable behavior, but much less common ground with regard to the third part of ABA analysis. Stated another way, it is the concern about measurable outcomes.

## Positive Replacement Behaviors

Chapter 9 was intended to present strategies for substituting negative, undesirable behaviors of children and youth with positive, adaptive, acceptable behaviors. Simply stated, if we intervene to eliminate a behavior, such as hitting other children, then we should include as a part of the intervention the replacement of the negative behavior (hitting) with a positive behavior (for example, verbal expression). As stated at various points in the text, behavior always serves a purpose, meets a need, and has a function. Maybe the function of hitting another student is to express anger. Related to **positive replacement behaviors**, the intent is not to replace the function (to express anger), but rather to replace the form of the behavior (hitting). The child has a need to express anger. Our goal is to help him use a positive behavior to do so, in place of the negative, problematic behavior. It is also described in Chapter 9 as a functionally equivalent response. That is, the response of verbal expression of anger serves the same function for the child as hitting. One of the primary ways of getting at the teaching of positive replacement behaviors is functional communication training. Helping children and youth become more skilled at expressing their needs and how they feel in genuine, positive ways is a primary approach to adding to their repertoire of positive replacement behaviors. Certainly current issues and future directions related to the roles of schools and school reform will need to address positive replacement behaviors as an alternative to punishment and rapid suppression techniques.

## Behavior Reduction Strategies

Specific strategies are applied for the purpose of reducing challenging behaviors. Several strategies are described in Chapter 10, including, for example, ignoring to extinguish a behavior, antecedent management and environmental arrangement, differential reinforcement, and the use of contracts and token economies. Positive behavior support understood in total has the purpose of promoting desired behavior by systematically arranging antecedents and consequences, increasing frequency and intensity of desired behaviors, and reducing the occurrence of challenging behaviors. This is the area (**behavior reduction strategies**) that tends to receive the most attention, of course, because it is the most problematic for educators. Reducing and eliminating behaviors that interfere with the role of the teacher and the learning of the student exhibiting the behavior, as well as that of the other students in the class, is of primary importance. How will we in the future apply more effective ways of general and special educators collaborating through the use of agreed-upon strategies for the reduction of challenging behavior? What kinds of new, innovative strategies might we discover and empirically establish over the next 5, 10, or 15 years that will be consistent with the tenets of PBIS in reducing undesirable behaviors?

## Self-Determination

Underlying the mission of PBS is the belief that all that is done on behalf of children and youth with challenging behaviors (and, in fact, all children and youth in educational environments) is that professionals are obligated to enhance (or at least not damage) their quality of life. For everyone, including the readers of this text and the authors, a central part of everyday life is the improvement of the quality of life. One component of quality of life is **self-determination**. A consensus definition of self-determination has emerged (Field, Martin, Miller, Ward, & Wehmeyer, 1998):

> Self-determination is a combination of skills, knowledge, and beliefs that enable a person to engage in goal-directed, self-regulated, autonomous behavior. An understanding of one's strengths and limitations together with a belief in oneself as capable and effective are essential to self-determination. When acting on the basis of these skills and attitudes, individuals have greater ability to take control of their lives and assume the role of successful adults. (p. 2)

What are the current issues that will impact what is done in the future related to the enhancement of self-determination skills, knowledge, and beliefs of children and youth in educational environments? Certainly economic, political, and educational trends have direct implications for how public and private educational environments will develop and evolve in the future. What, for example, might be the impact of the testing and accountability movement on self-determination? How will the inclusion movement influence self-determination as a part of implementing positive behavior supports and interventions? Early childhood education for children from birth through age 8 has described developmentally appropriate practice as having a substantial dependence on play-based and child-initiated activities, which may be equated with self-determination. Early childhood special educators are more likely to emphasize teacher-directed, direct instruction strategies targeting individual children. If inclusion and natural environment approaches are to be employed, how might these different emphases be merged and differences resolved related to positive behavior supports and interventions as contributors to self-determination?

## CONNECTIONS AMONG CHAPTERS 1 THROUGH 11

The 11 chapters have been briefly reviewed for a very specific purpose. The chapters are connected and related as the reader considers some of the current issues in PBS and how those issues will possibly impact future directions. It is important for educators to have a basic understanding of behavior. The behavior perspective as represented by applied behavior analysis and PBS is a useful and meaningful way of doing so (Chapter 1). For educators to understand and influence behavior, they must be able to plan for and respond to behavior in context. That requires a special attention to and partnership with parents, families, and the home environment, beyond simply treating the parents as one of many stakeholders (Chapter 2). Professionals should be guided by ethics—the principles of conduct governing them and their disciplines. In order to understand the ethics associated with PBIS, one must examine the standards provided by various organizations and professional associations (Chapter 3). In the application of PBIS significant attention is given to the antecedents, or circumstances, of behavior, as a means of preventing challenging behavior, increasing the occurrence of positive behavior, and reducing the occurrence of challenging behavior (Chapter 4). When the consequence of a behavior maintains or increases the behavior, it is reinforced. Sometimes the antecedents (environment, curriculum, toys, people) serve as reinforcement.

Often it is important to understand and manipulate the external reinforcers (primary or secondary) to influence behavior (Chapter 5). The starting point of PBIS is typically conducting a functional assessment (Chapter 6), which allows the systematic understanding of setting events, antecedents, and consequences (reinforcement) associated with challenging behavior. Functional assessments provide the information needed to develop level 2 and level 3 behavior support plans (Chapter 7). Behavior support plans frequently require that the team responsible for their design and implementation make use of single-subject designs (Chapter 8), direct teaching of positive replacement behaviors (Chapter 9), and behavior reduction strategies (Chapter 10). Finally, just as ethics are an overriding consideration in positive behavior support, the valuing and teaching of self-determination, as a component of addressing the quality of life of children and youth with challenging behavior, is of tantamount importance. Schalock (2000), in a review of three decades of quality-of-life studies, suggested that for the first decade of the 21st century, quality of life will be studied from three perspectives, including the pursuit by individuals of quality of life, providers producing quality products, and evaluators analyzing quality outcomes.

## SIX ISSUES AND RELATED FUTURE DIRECTIONS IN PBS

No doubt as you progressed through this text, you identified content that is controversial and subject to different interpretations. The material was purposefully presented to acknowledge and identify areas in which consensus is not found and in which future directions are not altogether clear. Positive behavior support is, after all, a relatively new area of study. It draws largely from applied behavior analysis as has been described, but it also includes a focus on related but distinct areas of special education such as mental retardation and developmental disabilities. Also positive behavior support has been advocated by many as a part of unified systems reform, therefore of relevance to general educators as well as special educators.

Although there certainly are others, a focus on six topics for the understanding of issues and future directions is provided. Each is briefly discussed in the following text and is connected to prior content of the text. The six issues, introduced in the following order, are the educational reform movement, the evolution of ethical codes of conduct related to PBS, the emergence of a unified disciplinary perspective on PBS, the family-centered philosophy and PBS, the place of outcome measures in PBS, and the uses of PBS in transitions of children from early intervention and preschool to school-age programs and transitions from school to the adult world of work and independent living.

### Educational Reform

What will schools look like in the next 5, 10, or 15 years? How will they be different from what they are at present? Yes, most will agree that there will be more technology and that it will be much more sophisticated, while being user friendly and accessible. But what about how schools are organized, led, and managed? What will be the curricular and extracurricular emphases, and how will economic and political factors influence schooling? Current debates are occurring (evidenced in newspapers and related editorials) over, for example, the pros and cons of school uniforms; the return to basic academics; the elimination of costly and presumably unnecessary programs such as music, art, and physical education; the disagreements with inclusion of children with disabilities; and suggestions that maybe the number of students in the classroom does not make that much difference. These issues regarding school reform are, of course, also to be found in the current professional literature in education, but the connection between the two is seemingly minimal.

What impact will the advocates of voucher systems and private school options have on educational reforms in the United States? Much has been written about the rapidly expanding population of non-English-speaking students and culturally, religiously, and ethnically diverse school populations. Although the reality of this change for the future is undeniable, how it is being planned and how it will change the look of schooling is undetermined. In some instances, there are only partial answers for the questions posed with regard to school reform. Each will have implications for the future design, implementation, and evaluation of positive behavior support.

One issue of school reform is the focus on unified systems reform as compared to reform in general education or special education (Turnbull & Turnbull, 2001). Over the past three decades or so, educational reform has been evidenced in special education, with the impetus of the IDEA legislation initially passed in 1975 and the publication of *A Nation at Risk: The Imperative for Educational Reform* (National Commission on Excellence in Education, 1983) and subsequent reports advocating significant changes. Current federal policy is reflected in the statement, "Leave no child behind" and by the effective schools process advocated by the National Alliance for Effective Schools (Taylor, 2002). However, the changes in special education and general education were seen as only peripherally related and largely separate. More recently and with the 1997 reauthorization of the Individuals with Education Act, the reform movements have to some extent merged to constitute a "unified systems" reform movement. Most researchers and practitioners who write about, describe, and advocate for PBIS do so in the context of its schoolwide application and relevance at different levels for all students, including those who have challenging behaviors, those who have other disabilities, and those who do not have disabilities. Scott (2001), for example, described the effective implementation of a schoolwide system of positive behavior support in which a K–5 elementary school, through the creation of schoolwide teams, significantly decreased the number of students excluded from classrooms for problem behaviors. Fox and Little (2001) provided an example of how the elements of a schoolwide behavior support plan can be developed and implemented at the preschool level. Turnbull, Wilcox, Turnbull, Sailor, and Wickham (2001) described the value of PBS to all schools for dealing with behavior issues and made a connection between PBS and the realization of safe schools.

Therefore, a significant current issue is the extent to which positive behavior support will catch on as a schoolwide approach to not only intervene in the case of challenging behavior, but also to be the central approach for generalized planning and actions for establishing a positive school environment for all students and for preventing problematic behavior. But in fact, it remains to be seen if PBS will become the prominent approach to addressing the challenging behavior of children and youth with disabilities, despite the fact that it is clearly called for in the 1997 reauthorization of the Individuals with Disabilities Education Act. Additionally, many special educators are resistant to the movement away from more traditional behavior management and strict applied behavior analytic approaches. The future of PBS as a part of school reform, whether it is unified systems, special education, or general education, is unclear. A question to further assess this issue is, when it has the opportunity in various educational environments (such as preschools, elementary schools, middle schools, junior high schools, or high schools), does the school have a schoolwide behavior support plan? What does it look like? Does it include the elements of PBS described in the textbook? Does it address behavior on a continuum from prevention to intensive interventions? Is there a shared vision by the teaching faculty? That is, is the plan owned by all the teachers or a particular subgroup, such as the special education teachers or the behavior specialist?

## Ethical Codes of Conduct

The second issue is specific to the question of what ethical codes and standards will guide educators in the future with regard to the use of positive behavior intervention and support. Paul, French, and Cranston-Gingras (2001) point out that, surprisingly, the field of special education has devoted little attention to the study and development of applied ethics. In Chapter 3 a variety of professional education associations and organizations were introduced, each of which has established, formalized, written codes and standards for ethical practice in their discipline. Many of the codes are complimentary and say much the same thing in different ways. However, there are clear differences as one examines the codes specific to behavior. For example, there are different points of view with regard to the appropriateness of the use of punishment strategies, specifically physical punishment (such as paddling). One might point out that the ethical codes and standards introduced in Chapter 3 were confusing and confounding, and that it would have been more helpful to identify ethics specifically related to PBIS. That is true, of course. The difficulty is that those standards do not exist at present. Further, if we return to the consideration of the previous issue of unified systems reform, presumably if there is a schoolwide positive behavior support plan, then all the teachers might want to look at the same ethical standards, rather than exclusively the ones associated with their discipline and professional organization.

Getting professional organizations and associations, whether at the local, state, national, or international level, to work together is frequently quite challenging. Each has reason to develop, maintain, and support their particular constituency and to advocate for their part of the educational enterprise.

Two notable exceptions described in Chapter 3 (and there are others) are the substantial collaboration efforts achieved by the National Association for the Education of Young Children (NAEYC) and the Division for Early Childhood (DEC) of the Council for Exceptional Children (CEC). Also, the Learning First Alliance, a partnership of 12 leading educational associations, serves as a prime example of a collaborative effort, including addressing standards related to the behavior of students in elementary and secondary school settings.

## Unifying Disciplines

The third issue is the question of how various disciplinary and within discipline perspectives will become more unified or possibly more divergent. Many perspectives on the philosophy and practices of PBS are found in the literature. It is reasonable to state that the more **unified** the **disciplines** associated with the education of children and youth are, the more benefit will be derived from the application of PBS in the future. Although there are many others, five perspectives are briefly considered here. It is not intended to suggest in this discussion that these perspectives are mutually exclusive.

Professionals (researchers, professors, program developers and practitioners, behavior analysts, teachers, school psychologists, and others) who maintain a strict adherence to an applied behavior analysis approach to challenging behavior have maintained that PBS is not substantially different from what has been done for decades, and that its weakness is that outcomes (see later in this chapter) of PBIS are frequently impossible or difficult to quantify and measure. A second perspective comes from the professionals and other advocates who have been concerned primarily with the quality of life of persons (including adults) with mental retardation, developmental delay, and comprehensive disabilities. They have emphasized the process of providing PBS to enhance the quality of life for these individuals by focusing, for example, on community programs and supports, person-centered planning, happiness and joyful living, self-determination, and collaboration and partnerships with parents. A third perspective is provided by professionals who focus on early childhood special education and early intervention. For these individuals, PBS is frequently seen as applicable in the context of family-centered practices (families as developing partners, rather than one of many stakeholders), natural environments, and inclusion. This requires that PBS translates into principles and practices that communicate with and are useful to early childhood educators, caregivers, and family members.

A fourth perspective comes from professionals who are predominately in the general education category. Articles describing PBS are beginning to be published in the mainstream journals associated with elementary schools, middle schools, secondary education, reading, and other areas. Keep in mind that the origin of PBS, although it is viewed as having relevance for all students, is special education, and the 1997 reauthorization of the Individuals with Disabilities Education Act includes specific coverage of

PBIS. A central issue is the extent to which general K–12 educators will accept and incorporate PBS in schoolwide behavior support planning. A fifth and final perspective is provided by the professionals who have taken the lead in the articulation of PBS as a distinct field of behavior intervention. In the premiere issue of the *Journal of Positive Behavior Interventions* (*JPBI*), the editors (Dunlap & Koegel, 1999) emphasized the collaborative and interdisciplinary nature of PBS, its focus on quality of life, its focus on positive and nonaversive interventions, and its place as the embodiment of a changing and expanding field of behavior intervention. Once again, these are not presented as mutually exclusive perspectives on PBS. However, they do represent different points of view and emphases. The manner in which these perspectives are brought together and unified will affect your participation in future applications of PBS in the educational environments in which you will be involved.

## Family-Centered Philosophy

The fourth issue is specific to the way families will be viewed in the future in PBS. Special educators have experienced an interesting history in which parents' roles have changed (Turnbull & Turnbull, 2001) over the past century from the source of their children's disabilities, to organization members, to service developers, to recipients of professional decisions, to parent as teacher, to parent as political advocate. Family involvement has been established as essential related to the education of children with disabilities. *The Twenty-First Annual Report to Congress on the Implementation of the IDEA* underscores the importance of family involvement in learning and school performance (U.S. Department of Education, 1999).

Related to challenging behavior, behavior disorders, and emotional disturbance, parents have been viewed as trainees for behavior interventions, stakeholders, and monitors of the generalization effects of interventions. What does the future hold for you regarding your responsibilities with families and PBS?

It is arguable that there is a movement away from the notion of involvement of parents and toward partnerships with families. These may be seen as distinctly differing approaches. Parent involvement might focus on mother and/or father and their contributions to the school's educational goals for their children. Partnerships with families might focus on the child as a part of the family unit and extended family and on their central role as decision makers. A partnership with families approach does not assume that families are but one of many stakeholders for a child with challenging behavior. One important manifestation of the partnerships viewpoint is the family-centered values, supports, and services advocated in early intervention. The fundamental idea behind family centeredness (Richey & Wheeler, 2000) is that services not be delivered in a way that fails to consider the child as a part of the family unit, and it is essential that the families' participation is used in ways that take into account their strengths, needs, and wishes. The extent to which this family-centered philosophy and associated values, principles, and practices are incorporated into PBS remains to be seen. Finally, it is important to note (Singer, 2000) that the connections between professional–family partnerships and PBS need much more thought and research. Singer stated, "Because there are many overshadowing contextual variables, we will need to either create PBS service systems that can deliver a variety of services, or we need to team up with more comprehensive service agencies" (p. 124).

## Outcomes

PBS may be understood as including inputs (planning, such as a functional assessment, the Individual Education Program, or a person-centered plan), process (the delivery and implementation of supports and interventions, curriculum, strategies to increase or decrease behavior, services), and outputs (the outcomes of the provision of PBIS). At issue is not whether PBS results in positive outcomes for persons with challenging behavior, but rather the extent to which those outcomes are quantifiable, measurable, and related to the intents. As noted in this textbook, specific requirements in the conducting of PBS require careful attention to outcome measures. However, important components of PBS are more difficult to measure, such as quality of life, self-determination, happiness, and systems (such as schoolwide) change. In particular, the proponents of a more systematic applied behavior analytic approach have suggested that the future effectiveness of PBIS is somewhat dependent on its ability to produce measurable outcomes. On the other hand, one of the sources of contention historically between special education and general education is the focus in special education on counting, measuring, and quantifying outcomes (individual objectives), possibly to the detriment of the process in the context of regular classrooms and group settings.

## Transitions

The sixth and last issue impacting future directions in PBS is **transitions**. Transitions are major changes across learning environments. Special education has tended to describe them as "sending" and "receiving" programs and services. Some examples of major transitions for children with special needs are from hospital (Neonatal Intensive Care Unit, for example) to home, from home to infant–toddler settings, from infant–toddler to preschool programs, from preschool to kindergarten, from kindergarten to grade-level classrooms, from early elementary to middle school, from middle school to junior high or high school, and from high school to employment, community living, or further formal education. Important transitions also occur within these settings, for example, transitions from regular classrooms to resource rooms and transitions among activities and subject areas. All the major transitions typically require systematic advanced planning for their successful implementation. How are behavior support plans and interventions impacted by transitions? In some instances there is a natural and smooth process and a good fit between the sending and receiving environments regarding PBS. But there are also frequent difficulties associated with transitions between environments and the successful use of PBS. It is probable that coping with discrepancies between settings is more difficult for children and youth with challenging behavior than it is for others.

## SUMMARY

The text provided an introduction to PBS in the context of its origins, being primarily behavior theory and the principles and practices of applied behavior analysis. PBS, although a practical and comprehensive approach to addressing the challenging behaviors (and preventing problematic behaviors) of children and youth in various educational environments, continues to be somewhat difficult to actualize. Six issues and related future directions were introduced and briefly discussed. (a) How will PBS evolve in the context of unified systems reform in education as a comprehensive approach to facilitating the desired behavior of all children and youth in educational environments? Will it be "a special education thing," or will it be understood more broadly as a means of PBS for the entire school, with levels of intensity depending on needs of children? (b) What will be the ethical code standards and codes of conduct that guide educators in the uses of PBS? Will ethical codes and standards apply to all professionals, or will they be used only by particular disciplines and subdisciplines? (c) Perspectives on PBS differ from various disciplines and constituencies, for example, general education, applied behavior analysis, early childhood, and comprehensive disabilities/mental retardation. How might these differing perspectives be unified to fit together under the banner of PBS? (d) Will the movement toward family centered philosophy, values, and principles, as espoused by early intervention, be applied as a part of PBS? If so, how will it fit with the more traditional view of parent involvement and parents as trainees and extensions of professionals, especially related to behavior interventions for challenging behavior? (e) There is substantial concern from applied behavior analysts and others as to how the field of PBS will be more effective in establishing measurable outcomes. This criticism may be seen not only in the context of traditional behavior interventions, but also from the point of view of the accountability movement in public education. (f) Last, major educational transitions present challenges as well as opportunities for planning, implementing, and evaluating PBS. The growing and expanding field of positive behavior supports and interventions shows great promise for enriching educational environments for all children and youth, teaching and maintaining desired, successful behavior and independence, and providing a proactive and positive continuum for planning in schools. Specifically, PBS has great promise for advancing the tenets of applied behavior analysis and related interventions for children with challenging behavior and needs for more intensive intervention.

## ACTIVITIES TO EXTEND YOUR LEARNING

1. Divide the class into small groups of four to six members each. Assign to each group the topic of PBIS issues and future directions in either the general education literature as represented by the *Phi Delta Kappan* journal, the early childhood special education literature as represented by the *Journal of Early Intervention*, the comprehensive and severe disabilities area as represented by *The Journal of the Association for Persons with Severe Handicaps*, the applied behavior analysis perspective as represented by the *Journal of Applied Behavior Analysis*, or the PBIS perspective in the *Journal of Positive Behavior Interventions*. Have each group review the recent (last five years) journals related to issues and future directions. Small groups report their findings to the class as a whole and engage in a discussion and consideration of commonalities and differences among these perspectives.

2. Prepare an outline of the text by chapters and develop a list of 5 to 10 issues that you might associate with each chapter topic from your perspective as the professional responsible for implementation of PBIS.

3. Present a panel discussion in which you invite representatives from a school in which a schoolwide PBS plan is in place. Be sure that you have representation for general education, special education, administration, and related services personnel. Learn from the panel how their plan was developed, how it is working, and what challenges and issues exist for continuation.

## FURTHER READING AND EXPLORATION

1. Go to the Web site of the Center for Positive Behavioral Interventions and Supports (http://www.pbis.org) and look for information about issues and future directions in PBIS. Individually or as a small-group activity, e-mail the center and request their perspective on current and future issues.

2. To gain a more in-depth understanding of the issue of PBIS as it is related to the parent–professional partnership and family-centered supports and services, read the special section of *The Journal of the Association for Persons with Severe Handicaps (JASH)*, 22 (4), 1997, pages 185–223. This provides a thorough and thought-provoking description of the issues and future directions of PBIS related to parents and families as they were articulated in the beginning of the development of the field of positive behavior interventions and supports. After studying this material, ask a panel of family representatives to come to class to discuss issues gleaned from the reading.

## REFERENCES

Alberto, P. A. & Troutman, A. C. (2003). *Applied behavior analysis for teachers* (6th ed.). Upper Saddle River, NJ: Merrill/Prentice Hall.

Baer, D. M., Wolf, M. W., & Risley, T. R. (1968). Some current dimensions of applied behavior analysis. *Journal of Applied Behavior Analysis, 1,* 91–97.

Carr, E. G., Horner, R. H., Turnbull, A. P., Marquis, J. G., Magito-McLaughlin, D., McAtee, M. L., Smith, C. E., et al. (1999). *Positive behavior support as an approach for dealing with problem behavior of people with developmental disabilities: A research synthesis.* Washington, DC: American Association on Mental Retardation Monograph Series.

Chandler, L. K., & Dahlquist, C. M. (2002). *Functional assessment: Strategies to prevent and remediate challenging behavior in school settings.* Upper Saddle River, NJ: Merrill/Prentice Hall.

Dunlap, G., & Koegel, R. L. (1999). Welcoming editorial. *Journal of Positive Behavior Interventions, 1*(1), 2–3.

Field, S., Martin, J. E., Miller, R., Ward, M., & Wehmeyer, M. L. (1998). *A practical guide to teaching self-determination.* Reston, VA: Council for Exceptional Children.

Fox, L., & Little, N. (2001). Starting early: Developing school-wide behavior support in a community preschool. *Journal of Positive Behavior Interventions, 3*(4), 251–254.

Janney, R., & Snell, M. E. (2000). *Behavioral support: Teachers' guides to inclusive practices.* Baltimore: Paul H. Brookes.

National Commission on Excellence in Education. (1983). *A nation at risk: The imperative for educational reform.* Washington, DC: U.S. Government Printing Office.

Paul, J., French, P., & Cranston-Gingras, A. (2001). Ethics and special education. *Focus on Exceptional Children, 34*(1), 1–16.

Richards, S. B., Taylor, R. L., Ramasamy, R., & Richards, R. Y. (1999). *Single subject research: Applications in educational and clinical settings.* San Diego, CA: Singular Publishing Group.

Richey, D. D., & Wheeler, J. J. (2000). *Inclusive early childhood education: Merging positive behavioral supports, activity-based intervention, and developmentally appropriate practice.* Albany, NY: Delmar/Thomson Learning.

Schalock, R. I. (2000). Three decades of quality of life. *Focus on Autism and Other Developmental Disabilities, 15*(2), 116–127.

Scott, T. M. (2001). A schoolwide example of positive behavioral support. *Journal of Positive Behavior Interventions, 3*(2), 88–94.

Singer, G. H. S. (2000). Ecological validity. *Journal of Positive Behavior Interventions, 2*(2), 122–124.

Taylor, B. O. (2002). The effective schools process: Alive and well. *Phi Delta Kappan, 83*(5), 375–378.

Turnbull, A., & Turnbull, H. R. (2001). *Families, professionals, and exceptionality: Collaborating for empowerment* (4th ed.). Upper Saddle River, NJ: Merrill/Prentice Hall.

Turnbull, H. R., Wilcox, B., Turnbull, A., Sailor, W., & Wickham, D. (2001). IDEA, positive behavioral supports, and school safety. *Journal of Law and Education, 3*(3), 445–504.

U.S. Department of Education, Office of Special Education Programs. (1999). Parent involvement in educating children with disabilities: Theory and practice. In the *Twenty-First Annual Report to Congress on the Implementation of the IDEA.* Washington, DC: Author.

# Name Index

# Subject Index